D1548456

BLACK BISHOP

Studies in Anglican History

Series Editor

Peter W. Williams, Miami University

*Sponsored by the Historical Society
of the Episcopal Church*

A list of books in the series appears at the end of this book.

BLACK BISHOP

Edward T. Demby and the Struggle
for Racial Equality in the
Episcopal Church

Michael J. Beary

University of Illinois Press

Urbana and Chicago

For my parents

Library of Congress Cataloging-in-Publication Data
Beary, Michael J. (Michael Jay), 1956–
Black bishop : Edward T. Demby and the struggle for racial equality
in the Episcopal Church / Michael J. Beary.
p.   cm. — (Studies in Anglican history)
Includes bibliographical references and index.
ISBN 0-252-02618-7 (alk. paper)
1. Demby, Edward T. (Edward Thomas), 1869–1957. 2. Episcopal
Church—Bishops—Biography. 3. Episcopal Church. Diocese of
Arkansas—Biography. 4. Afro-American clergy—Biography. 5. Race
relations—Religious aspects—Episcopal Church—History—20th
century. 6. Southwestern States—Race relations—History—20th
century. I. Title. II. Series.
BX5995.D46B43   2001
283'.092—dc21   00-009541

C 5 4 3 2 1

In journeyings often, in perils of waters, in perils of robbers, in perils by mine own countrymen, in perils by the heathen, in perils in the city, in perils in the wilderness, in perils in the sea, in perils among false brethren; in weariness and painfulness, in watchings often, in hunger and thirst, in fastings often, in cold and nakedness. Beside those things that are without, that which cometh upon me daily, the care of all the churches.

—2 Corinthians 11:26–28

SERIES EDITOR'S PREFACE

Peter W. Williams

Studies in Anglican History is a series of scholarly monographs sponsored by the Historical Society of the Episcopal Church and published by the University of Illinois Press. It is intended to bring the best of contemporary international scholarship on the history of the entire Anglican Communion, including the Church of England and the Episcopal Church in the United States, to a broader readership.

In this volume Michael Beary, an independent scholar who lives in Arkansas, tells the story of the struggle for racial justice within the Episcopal Church through a biography of Edward T. Demby, the first African American to be elected a bishop in that church. In telling Demby's story, Beary evokes the divided but intersecting worlds of black and white Episcopalians in the American South prior to the civil rights era. It is a story of sometimes bizarre ecclesiastical politics as well as behavior and belief about race now difficult to imagine. It is also a tribute to Demby and other African American pioneers who tried to balance patience and assertiveness in overcoming the color line.

CONTENTS

PREFACE

Do all biographers dream about their subject? In the eight years it took to construct this monograph, I have had three dreams about Bishop Edward T. Demby. Whatever their intrinsic value may be, they all had one quality: they made Demby more real to me. I hope this book has the same quality for the people who read it.

I hope this is good church history. My experience with church history is that most of it is written to praise, which necessarily makes it suspect—like the family album which carefully omits that picture of cousin Bob at the family reunion and "that . . . that new wife of his who would not shut up until everyone finally gave up and went home. Nevermind that she threw a wet blanket on the festivities and that Bob was planned out of several gatherings because of her and that he was so offended he finally moved to California, which is the reason for that whole new branch of the family scattered up and down the West Coast—the ones we never see." Opening up the photo album, we behold none of this. The reunion would appear to be overrun with children, potato salad, fried chicken, and harmony. "Cousin Bob? I think he wasn't there. He moved to California. Isn't that right, Honey?" This is not to say that these "Who's Whos" of church history have no value. On the contrary, they are invaluable research tools, being loaded with dates, places, names, and events. But that is all. Generally speaking, they do not reflect the warp and woof of church life that makes it so edifying, intriguing, and woefully frustrating. That is why no one actually reads them except people who attend the church in question—and historians. How can history enlighten and instruct when it is only a half-truth to begin with? The very thing that makes the Scriptures so instructive is that they are so candid. There are no unblemished heroes, save one, and there are a good many events and personalities that would have to be omitted from your standard church history. Of course, there is the other danger. One may also include information that is controversial or downright unpleasant, all to no good end; in other words, gossip. Please know that, despite the bonanza of controversial material between the covers of this volume, there is another volume of discarded information in the wastepaper basket. I hope I am not a gossip. In the course of my research, I have worried one or two archivists with the sensitive nature of Demby's ministry and I have been turned away on at least one occasion—with the suggestion that the wisest course of action is always to suppress controversy. Many years ago, I was wholeheartedly in agreement with that maxim. In fact, when Professor Walter L. Brown of the University of Arkansas first suggested the Arkansas Episcopal election of 1932 as a thesis topic I rejected it out of hand, refusing to participate in what I perceived to be the habitual erosion of Christian credibility in academic circles. Three years later, I dropped in at the Archives of the Episcopal Diocese of Arkansas in a different frame of mind. To my astonishment, I discovered the collected papers of the Reverend William P. Witsell at the diocesan archives and began an article, which ultimately led to this book. Tertullian tells us that "Truth makes no appeal on her own behalf, because she does not wonder at her present condition." I take this to mean that Jesus can take care of himself if one will just tell the truth.

Demby's ministry was controversy from beginning to end, most of it revolving about the volatile issue of race. I found that many white people were afraid that I would be too critical of the past and many black people were afraid I would not be critical enough. Thus, I have agonized over objectivity again and again and I am pleased with the final result. If people of both races are equally pleased—or equally displeased—I will probably have hit dead center on the truth. That was Demby's experience.

This preface would not be complete without a word or two on the more technical aspects of writing church history. There is a saying that a United States Marine will salute a fencepost just to be sure that everyone in authority has been acknowledged. However true that may be, it is undoubtedly true that Episcopalians capitalize practically everything in order to either make a point or avoid offense. Bishop Demby and his contemporaries were not exceptions to this "denominational disability." I have striven to decapitalize my text, just as I have striven to de-Episcopalize my language. I hope that a Baptist layperson will not need to hunt up a glossary to read this book. Demby's ministry has some universal applications that should not be hindered by Episcopalese. Furthermore, please note that I have had to reconstruct some events according to that which I know to be true and that which normally occurs. For instance, in chapter 5, "The Newport Incident," I describe the procession as it entered St. Paul's Church, Newport. However, I was not able to find anyone with a knowledge of where the black clergy marched in the opening procession of the diocesan conventions of Demby's day. But these things I do know. The black clergy were not members of the convention but were nonetheless sheep in the flock of the diocesan bishop. Therefore, they probably marched after the white clergy and directly in front of the white diocesan bishop, who, as always, must bring up the rear, driving his flock before him. Demby, of course, would be at the rear of the line of colored clergy, wedged in between the black priests and the diocesan bishop. He, too, had a flock. My description of the "doorway interlude" is based on this scenario. Wherever such an assumption or a hypothesis is made, I believe I have duly noted it either in the text or in the notes.

Before thanking those who have helped me in this study, I would like to correct a popular myth pertaining to black Episcopal history. The error is a bit of benign misinformation innocently and inadvertently propagated by Sarah and Elizabeth Delany, the daughters of Bishop Henry Beard Delany. Those who have read their recollections in *Having Our Say: The Delany Sisters' First One Hundred Years* will note that their father is described as "the first elected Negro bishop of the Episcopal Church, U. S. A." This is incorrect. Bishop Edward T. Demby was the first black bishop in the United States. Demby was elected first and consecrated first. The confusion arises from the circumstances surrounding their elections. Demby and Delany represent the two halves of the suffragan bishop plan. Demby served the Southwest and Delany served the Southeast; two separate attempts at a single experiment in segregated church government. They were elected within months of each other and consecrated within weeks of each other. Nevertheless, "firsts" are a very important event to a race that has traditionally been compelled to overachieve in order to gain recognition and I would be remiss not to correct the error. I would also note that the Dembys have remained true to the tradition of their illustrious forebear and withheld public comment, trusting, I guess, that the author, or God, or both, will set the record straight.

At the top of the list of those to be thanked for bringing this book to a successful completion are my many benefactors. They are: Mary S. Donovan, president of the Historical Society of the Episcopal Church; Herbert S. Donovan Jr., former bishop of Arkansas and present bishop of New Jersey; Larry E. Maze, bishop of Arkansas; Harold T. Lewis, rector of Calvary Church, Pittsburgh, who generously aided my research in his capacity as staff officer for black ministries; Lynn Collins, the present staff officer for black ministries; Mark Duffy of the Archives of the Episcopal Church; James R. McLean and the good people of St. Paul's Church, Batesville, Arkansas; William E. Smalley, bishop of Kansas; Hays H. Rockwell, bishop of Missouri; Claude E. Payne, bishop of

Texas; James M. Coleman, bishop of West Tennessee; John C. Buchanan, bishop of West Missouri; and Robert G. Tharp, bishop of East Tennessee.

My gratitude goes out to the young Episcopal women of the decades between 1920 and 1940. They played a decisive role in my research. Although they have enjoyed a longer life span than their Episcopal brethren, they were largely excluded from church government in Demby's day, which necessarily limits the amount of information they could contribute to a study of this kind. Yet I am happy to say that Mildred W. Page and Lady Elizabeth Luker of Newport, Arkansas; Josephine Jones of Batesville, Arkansas; Carolyn Rainey Harris of Fayetteville, Arkansas; Dora Strong Dennis of Forrest City, Arkansas; Roberta Church of Memphis, Tennessee; Margaret Weston of St. Louis, Missouri; and Marguerite Gamble of Little Rock, Arkansas, took a keen interest in the affairs of church—notwithstanding their distance from the action—and have provided marvelous contextual information for this book, and not a few specifics about some difficult moments in Episcopal church history. Like Sarah and Elizabeth Delany, they have "had their say."

Other people who have contributed letters, personal research, and interviews are: Herbert Donovan; Beth Matthews, secretary to Bishops Donovan and Maze; the late Joseph B. Tucker, former historiographer of the Diocese of Arkansas; Michael McNeely, historiographer of the Diocese of Arkansas; Harold T. Lewis; Philip L. Shutt and Betty Leinicke, the former and present historiographers of the Diocese of Springfield; Peter H. Beckwith, bishop of Springfield; John M. Allin, presiding bishop of the Episcopal church (retired); Mary J. Adams, historiographer of the Diocese of West Texas; Thomas S. Logan Sr., historiographer of black Episcopalians; Franklin Wright, historiographer of the Diocese of West Tennessee; Ron Carden of South Plains College, the world's greatest authority on Bishop William M. Brown; Stan Upchurch, archivist of the Diocese of Oklahoma; William T. Holt II; Clark Wood, son of Tom Wood; J. Carleton Hayden of Howard University; Orris J. Walker, bishop of Long Island; Ethel Broadnax Driver; Beverly (Granny) Fennell; Kirtley Yearwood, Bishop Demby's other biographer; Charlene Neal; Joyce Howard, historian of the Bishop Tuttle School for Social Work; Emery Washington; Thomas E. Harris; Jim Jones; Wooley Whitley; Al Nimocks; Lemuel Parks; George K. Cracraft; Richard Allin of the *Arkansas Democrat Gazette;* Cotesworth P. Lewis; Lewis A. Powell; Dennis C. Dickerson, historiographer of the African Methodist Episcopal Church; Charles White; Rosemary White, daughter of Rev. George G. Walker; Charlie Hull; Minnie Warren; James R. McLean II; Clarence M. Lancaster; Joe Thompson; James Temple; R. K. Young; Allen Beck, historiographer of the Diocese of Colorado; Dorothy Demby and Betty Payne, nieces of Bishop Demby; Edward T. Payne, great nephew of Bishop Demby; the late Dennis Wilson; Willard B. Gatewood of the University of Arkansas; Daniel D. McKee, historian of St. Paul's Parish, Newport, Arkansas; Ron Johnson; and Phoebe Arrington.

Research institutions that lent me special assistance in this endeavor were: the Special Collections Division of Mullins Library, University of Arkansas, Fayetteville, Arkansas; Mark Duffy, T. Matthew De Waelsche, Jennifer Peters, Christina Southwell, and Stephanie Walker of the Archives of the Episcopal Church, Austin, Texas; Randall K. Burkett of the W. E. B. DuBois Institute, who simply knows where everything is; Dean Covington and the incomparable Camille A. Beary of the Mabee-Simpson Library, Lyon College, Batesville, Arkansas; Patricia Willis and the staff of the Beinecke Rare Book and Manuscript Library, Yale University; Matthew Grande and the staff of St. Mark's Library, General Theological Seminary, New York City; Clifton H. Johnson and the staff of the Amistad Research Center, Tulane University, New Orleans; the staff of the Dupont Library, University of the South, Sewanee, Tennessee; and the staff of the Enoch Pratt Public Library, Baltimore, who were so helpful with the *Church Advocate*. A special thanks goes out to Charles Witsell, who allowed me the liberal use of his grandfather's papers, and to Thomas Logan Sr. for the use of Rev. Harry Rahming's very illuminating letter.

I would be remiss not to mention the logistical assistance of parties who helped solicit interviews for me and direct me to sources. They are: Harold Lewis; Wilma Colmes and the Northern Ohio Chapter of the Union of Black Episcopalians; Betsy Jacoway of Newport, Arkansas; Kenyon C. Burke; Walter D. Dennis, bishop of the Diocese of New York; Edward Norman of Christ Church, Forrest City, Arkansas; and some friends affiliated with Lyon College, Batesville, Arkansas. Dr. Jacoway was an invaluable help in soliciting interviews in Newport, and Lyon College was a godsend on the exhilarating and exhausting last leg of the journey. Thanks especially to Terrell Tebbetts and Karen Austin in this regard.

Then there are the readers who have scrutinized this project from a proposed article to its present published form. Let me thank, especially, Willard B. Gatewood of the University of Arkansas for his supervision and encouragement at the thesis stage, as well as his colleagues, Daniel E. Sutherland and Thomas C. Kennedy, who contributed some scrutiny of their own. Thanks also to Terrell Tebbetts and George K. Lankford of Lyon College for all of their red ink and to the effervescent Twyla Wright, who knows all about writing, controversy, Christianity, and African American history from hard personal experience. Lastly, I wish to thank the late Daniel J. Fagg, without whose encouragement and criticism this one-time "note in a bottle" might have sunk beneath the waves.

I have one major regret, namely that I was not able to include the fascinating and well-documented events regarding the civil rights era as it bore upon Episcopal Arkansas. My apologies to Beverly (Granny) Fennell, founder of St. Francis House, Little Rock; Edward Norman, warden of Christ Church Mission, Forrest City; Emery Washington of All Saint's, St. Louis; Charles and Rosemary White of Trinity Cathedral, Little Rock; and the late Joseph B. Tucker, former historiographer of the Diocese of Arkansas. Your story needs telling, but it is truly a different experience from that of Demby and his colleagues. I still intend to tell it.

Thank you, Robert Husband of the University of Illinois at Urbana-Champaign for your encouragement and God only knows what else.

Historians, like forensic scientists, pour their energies into the study of dead people. However, those of us who are professing Christians should consider that we are also writing about the living. That being the case, I would hope that the "living" (provided they had the freedom to do so) have kept me close to the facts and that they, too, are pleased with the final result. We shall all find out eventually.

Thank God.

BLACK BISHOP

INTRODUCTION
An Old Problem Revisited

But when Cephas came to Antioch, I opposed him to his face, because he stood self-condemned; for until certain people came from James, he used to eat with the Gentiles. But after they came, he drew back and kept himself separate for fear of the circumcision faction.

—Galatians 2:11–12, NRSV

Sitting at the back of the church, the Right Reverend Edward T. Demby, the only black Episcopal bishop with jurisdiction in the United States, looked up to see the Right Reverend Edwin Saphore, the acting bishop of Arkansas, extend the communion plate in the direction of the black clergy. Simultaneously, the Reverend William T. Holt, rector of the host church, stood to one side of Saphore and gesticulated with all the dignified urgency he could muster, a silent yet unmistakable "Would the colored clergy please come forward for communion!" Heads turned. The organist struck up another stanza of the communion hymn, prolonging the invitation and suppressing whispers. The situation Demby had tried desperately to avoid was upon him. He had been told that the black clergy were not welcome at this service. Yet the proposed alternative, a separate service for the black priests in the basement of the church, was out of the question. Resigned to sit out the festivities on the back pew, Demby looked up in amazement as those responsible for this humiliation exhibited a change of heart. The two white clergymen beckoned the erstwhile outcasts to come forward and receive the Body and Blood of Christ, after all. Demby sat stoically while his long-established habit of accommodation made war with the clear moral imperative rising up within him. He must not, at all costs, allow himself to be forced across that vacillating frontier separating discretion and Uncle Tom. According to Lily Billingsley, wife of the senior warden, or chief layman, of St. Paul's, Demby turned to the four black priests beside him and whispered, "If they ask you to come, refuse."[1]

Racial integration means trouble. That is, whenever an organization incorporates a racial pariah into its membership, with all the rights and privileges pursuant thereto, conflict is a foregone conclusion. The Christian church, despite its prophetic and otherworldly aspirations, fits the pattern. Indeed, as the opening citation indicates, the church has fit the pattern ever since its inception. Hardly had the church at Antioch been underway, we are told, when the "Gentile question" reared its ugly head. What to do with the Gentiles? According to the Book of Acts, the Apostle Peter received more than one revelation to the effect that "God is no respecter of persons," and he successfully carried that message to the Jewish Christians in Jerusalem. The church, they acknowledged, was truly all-inclusive, or, to use a term from the Nicene Creed, catholic. Nothing, however, was said regarding the implications of being a truly catholic church. Evidently, the Gentile believers were definitely "in," but retained a sort of second-class status in the eyes of Jewish Christians. Perhaps Peter and James, the brother of Jesus and head of the church in Jerusalem, hesitated to create a more catholic institution in the hope that God would also reveal something in the way of practical applications of this new truth. To Peter's dismay, however, practical applications arrived by way of a public rebuke from the Apostle Paul: "You are a Jew, yet you live like a Gentile and not like a Jew. How is it, then, that you force Gentiles to follow Jewish customs!" Spurred by the Antioch incident, the apostles converged on Jerusalem to decide the "Gentile question" once and for all. They decided, after some earnest and thorough deliberations inundated with prayer, to incorporate the Gentiles fully into the church, asking only that the newcomers obey a few general rules of right conduct: abstain from sexual immorality, etc. The keynote address to the Jerusalem Council was Peter's injunction, being essentially a gentler recapitulation of the lambasting he received from Paul at Antioch. This left James, the leader of the Jewish hard-liners, very much alone—if, indeed, he was still a hard-liner at this point. James acknowledged the truth of Peter, Paul, and company and joined them. Moreover, he led them in promulgating the letter.[2]

One may ask what bearing the events at Antioch and Jerusalem have on the subject of this book: the struggles of Edward T. Demby. To begin with, there is the obvious corollary with regard to the opening thesis, "Racial integration means trouble," or, to put it another way, Christians are respecters of race. The many branches of Christendom have experienced this problem and resolved it, to varying degrees, as the church has spread. For the Protestant Episcopal Church in the United States of America, the vortex of the struggle over race was the period from 1883 to 1953, when the church succumbed to the anti–African American spirit of the country and institutionalized segregation in the name of Christianity, which is to say, order. Bishop Demby's ministry was the embodiment of this experience. He represented the many black Episcopalians of his era who believed that the keys to assimilation into the life of the church, and the country, for that matter, were education and moral rectitude. They maintained that a pious and learned soul is a currency that all men honor, even as the color line circumscribed their lives again and again.

In this era of disillusionment and compromise, Demby lost respect and he won respect. Unlike many of his black Episcopal brethren, Demby never quite made the transition to collective action. For the most part, he practiced accommodation in the face of racist behavior, working within the system to achieve his ends rather than challenging it directly. He was not a prophetic spirit in the traditional sense of the word but preferred to lead by example; an example of African American character and achievement in the heyday of Jim Crow; an example of sound churchmanship and generosity of spirit in the face of racial indignities and the oftentimes crippling naiveté of white authorities; and, most especially, an example of perseverance in ministry. Demby knew full well that the credibility of all black bishops rested, in large measure, on his shoulders and that, try as he might, a good many white people would never acknowledge his abilities and achievements because of his color. Although he was sometimes painfully aware of being scrutinized, he felt it was his destiny to trailblaze in the Episcopal Church in order to render it more equitable for African Americans. But these were secondary considerations, for he was at heart a creature of calling, a man going about the business of being a Christian. Looking at it from his perspective, he aspired to orthodoxy, which, given his office, necessitated innumerable affirmations of certain biblical truths regarding the equality of men before God. He was being obedient. Eventually, however, doggedness and orthodoxy created an opportunity. In one of the keynote speeches in Episcopal history, Demby heralded the demise of the segregated church, converting the church's leading experiment in segregation into an iconoclast of segregation. Demby's ministry represents the zenith and the demise of Jim Crow in the Episcopal Church. Therefore, to understand America's first black bishop, we must first understand the encroachment of segregation as he and his colleagues experienced it.

Perhaps there is nothing so descriptive of ecclesiastical segregation as the language that was used—or, for that matter, not used—to justify it. Segregation, said its advocates, means order, which spells peace and harmony, which, in turn, means church growth. An integrated church, on the other hand, means racial conflict, ultimately leading to ugly confrontations, empty pulpits, empty pews, and empty coffers. In this sense, segregation became "good" and integration "bad" in the eyes of the predominantly white Episcopal Church at about the time of *Plessy* v. *Ferguson*.

The language of segregation, however, would hardly allow for anything so blatant as a statement calling segregation "good," and when one looks for the theological pretext behind the segregation movement, one discovers a veritable explosion of pragmatic theology on both sides of the color line—the black clergy, in this case, acting in self-defense. Black Episcopalians reasoned that they must either segregate voluntarily on their own terms or be "read out" of the government of the church by the white majority. The rhetoric of segregation was in some ways similar to its contemporary, the Social Gospel, and the liberation theology of the civil rights movement sixty years later, a tradition of biblical allusion to the American social dilemma. Just as civil rights leaders utilized Moses and Exodus metaphorically, so early twentieth-century black Episcopalians utilized the division of Canaan between Lot and Abraham. There was, for instance, the Very Reverend George A. McGuire, archdeacon for "Colored Work" in the Diocese of Arkansas (1905–8), who, like Demby, embodied the aspirations of the church's black contingent. In answer to the objection that the election of black bishops over black churches alongside white bishops over white churches would create problems of jurisdiction, McGuire queried: "Is it forgotten that in Apostolic times, St. Peter was sent to the Circumcision and St. Paul to the Uncircumcision by the Mother Church, in Jerusalem, each to minister to the same wide field, and each given jurisdiction, not over so many square miles, but over people differing racially, socially, and otherwise?"[3]

As a corollary, leading ecclesiastics of both races found it necessary to adjust the language of catholicity to the pressures of the day; that is, to remove it to the realm of a "great spiritual ideal." Said McGuire, "We are grappling at present, not with ideal theories of church oneness and equality, but with the actual conditions confronting us."[4] Ultimately, they rendered the all-inclusive church (a) true, but unattainable in this life, which perhaps the white majority preferred, or (b) nonthreatening, but nonetheless true, which encapsulates the black perspective. Generally speaking, however, the fundamental theological issue, that is, the inherent goodness or evil of segregation, was deliberately underemphasized for the sake of "peace, success, and the full development of all parties."[5] The vast majority of the interracial dialogue was devoted to "how" segregation was to be implemented rather than its theological justification. Or, to put it another way, the theology of segregation would have been impossible but for the words "practical," "expedient," and "necessary." Demby recalls from his memoirs: "In a conversation on the question of a better and more mutual understanding . . . between Caucasians and Negroes, with several [white] persons, they frankly told me, with blood in their eyes, 'What you say may be the ideal, but you should remember that we were white people before we were Christians.'"[6] Everyone, it seems, felt compelled to expound the virtues of segregation—the absence of racial conflict, the opportunities for black leadership that could not be had in an integrated church, and the possibilities for growth inherent to all-black churches unshackled from the daunting enigma of white oversight. Thus, by a heavy application of pragmatic theology, the advocates of segregation came to represent the best interests of African Americans, conveying to some Episcopalians an implicit "goodness" to segregation—albeit almost no one ventured to call it that.

And why didn't they? It seems that in spite of the reams of material written and expounded on behalf of segregation by such leading lights as McGuire's superior, Arkansas bishop William M. Brown (1897–1912), the church's white majority either did not believe in the inherent goodness of segregation or they were not prepared for the black reaction which would surely follow such a blatant endorsement of white supremacy. Indeed, it was Brown who tried hardest to make segregation "good," proclaiming his "God-implanted race prejudice," before the House of Bishops.[7] By virtue of his dogmatic insistence that the Episcopal Church should be able to delineate all of its actions as either good or evil, including segregation, Brown repeatedly and uncomfortably broached the most incendiary social issue of his day. Certainly some bishops, particularly in the South, were in agreement with Brown, as this excerpt from Bishop Demby's memoirs would indicate:

> A bishop asked me, "What do the Negroes think of me?" I said, "They are very fond of you." He then asked me, "Do they think I am a member of the K. K. K.?" My reply was [that] I had never heard any so express themselves. He then asked me, "What do you think?" I said, "My dear Bishop, if I were a Caucasian, and, especially, of the South, by birth, education, contacts, and training, and environment, I would, no doubt, belong to the K. K. K., because, as an organization, it is against Jews, and members of the Roman Communion, and, especially, Negroes." He dropped his head and said, "The truth is, I did belong to the organization, but came out of it about two years ago."[8]

However, most of Brown's fellow bishops considered him a crackpot and, judging by their actions, preferred to deal with the race issue individually, discretely, and without delving into moral absolutes. Their job, as they saw it, was to cope with the "color line," rather than justify it or challenge it.

Black Episcopalians had an entirely different meaning for expediency when it came to segregation. Theirs was the difference between approval, as the white majority would have it, and tolerance, as the African American majority understood it. Yet tolerance is too passive a word here, for the black Episcopal leadership of this era, represented by the Conference of Church Workers among the Colored People and personified by their foremost spokesman, the Reverend George F. Bragg Jr., pursued a form of segregation that would allow the church's black contingent some vestige of power and equality. Someday, they believed, wiser, cooler, and less racist heads would prevail, the instruments of ecclesiastical segregation would be dispensed with, and the church's black membership would be duly recognized for its contribution to the life of the church. But until that time, said Bragg and his colleagues, it behooved African Americans to remain faithful to the church and capitalize on the most equitable representation available to them, and, above all, to elect black bishops. In a church manifestly committed to the principle of government by bishops, said Bragg, some of the bishops must necessarily be black if the church seriously intends to extend itself among African Americans. With this in mind, the conference and its white allies fell wholeheartedly behind the missionary district plan, an amendment to church law designed to allow the creation of black missionary districts in the United States. Had the plan passed into law, it would have resulted in two or three black missionary districts overlapping several white dioceses, primarily in the South. Represented by black delegates to the church's triennial General Convention, and supervised by fully vested black bishops, the racial districts would have been political equals to all non–African American missionary districts. To quote Harold Lewis, arguably the preeminent historian of the black Episcopal experience, the conference took a "calculated [risk] . . . believing that it was easier, as it were, to achieve access to the first class carriage of the train from the second class compartment than to attempt a leap from the side of the tracks."[9] And the risks were great. Looking at it from another angle, the missionary district plan signified, in the words of David Reimers, a "strategic retreat" for the nation's black Episcopal leadership, which had repulsed an earlier attempt to segregate the church.[10]

In 1883, black leaders first organized themselves into the Conference of Church Workers in order to defeat the Sewanee Canon, an amendment to church law with the potential to disenfranchise all African American Episcopalians. The proposed legislation embodied eighteen years of frustration on the part of the southern bishops. After emancipation, the majority of black Episcopalians in the South left the Episcopal Church to join all-black Christian denominations or white denominations with a tradition of cultivating black leadership, such as the Methodist Episcopal Church. This severely depleted the numbers of black Episcopalians in the South, where their numbers had been substantial before the war. Ante-bellum South Carolina, for instance, had listed approximately three thousand African American communicants, or one-third of the communicant strength of the entire diocese. The national church tried to counter the trend by way of the Protestant Episcopal Freedmen's Commission. Organized by the General Convention of 1865, the commission endeavored to ease the freedmen's transition into free society and help them to establish churches and schools in the South. However, as the agency tried to carry out its mission, it became increasingly clear that most black Episcopalians preferred to leave the church of their masters unless black teachers ran the schools and black clergy ran the churches—a change opposed by the white Episcopal leadership in the South. White Episcopalians, especially laity, habitually resisted measures necessary to the growth and establishment of black churches in the South. They were more alarmed by the prospect of black clergy and black churches seeking representation in their diocesan conventions than by the prospect of a continuing black exodus from the Episcopal Church.

Daunted by the intransigence of the white membership, the bishops of the South, along with their clerical and lay representatives, convened at Sewanee, Tennessee, in July 1883 and drew up a piece of legislation that could have established a precedent for the wholesale segregation of the Episcopal Church. They called for a separate and subordinate organization of black churches in every diocese that deemed such a separation necessary; a revolutionary development in a church that had, heretofore, given no official sanction to segregation.

The nation's black clergy, led by the Reverend Alexander Crummell, realized the implications of the amendment, lobbied against it, and won. At the 1883 General Convention, the House of Bishops approved the plan, but the clergy and laity assembled in the convention's other deliberative body, the House of Deputies, voted it down.

National rejection did not prohibit local enactment, however, and the "spirit"[11] of the Sewanee Canon soon began to manifest itself in the conventions and canons of the southern dioceses, most notably in South Carolina and Virginia. The Conference of Church Workers responded with a memorial to the 1889 General Convention, calling on that body to "define the status of Colored Churchmen," an explicit challenge to segregation and an implicit challenge to racism proper.[12] This time, the conference enjoyed a valuable ally in the Reverend Phillips Brooks, a white priest who may have been the best Episcopal preacher of his day. Brooks's minority report on the status of Colored Churchmen "met the issue completely," writes Bragg, but lost to the majority report, which "diplomatically evaded the point at issue."[13]

Over the next fourteen years, the General Convention continued to "evade the point," while the Conference of Church Workers, alarmed by the national recalcitrance and the seemingly relentless tide of ecclesiastical segregation, resolved to fix the status of black churchmen before it was fixed for them. In 1903, they rallied to the missionary district plan.

The plan had its pros and cons. On the one hand, it promised autonomy with the equal representation demanded by Bragg and others, as well as political empowerment that could serve as a precedent for universal black participation in the church at a later date, a means for blacks to experience, in full, the substance of Episcopal government, not to mention being a proof text for those whites in doubt as to African Americans' "capacity" for such government. On the other hand, it presented the spectacle of black Episcopalians campaigning for segregation, which could only make the old challenge to "define the status of Colored Churchmen" somewhat less compelling. Segregation became "good" in that African Americans found it acceptable on their own terms. It came to represent order.

And order is key. Harold Lewis contends, along with John Kater, another historian of black Episcopalians, that order is the preeminent consideration of the Episcopal Church and that the church can only be prompted to change in the name of order. Conversely, when the status quo begins to jeopardize order, the Episcopal Church tends to realign itself with the forces of change. Such, says Lewis, was the case when the church "gradually began to adopt an integrationist policy" in the wake of *Brown* v. *Board of Education*.[14]

Thus, the white bishops of the early twentieth century were prepared to haggle interminably on the virtues of various plans for segregation. After all, the blacks themselves were persuaded to segregate voluntarily. It only remained to find the right kind of segregation. Said Bishop Brown, who insisted on the establishment of a separate black Episcopal denomination, "They will take what they can get."[15] It was this very confusion of aims that produced the loud and public schism between Brown and Archdeacon McGuire. "Expedient," to paraphrase McGuire, meant merely expedient, and certainly not "good." Brown felt differently.

Ironically, the missionary district plan was thwarted, repeatedly, by an unlikely convergence of the church's hard-core catholic, or all-inclusive, element, which deemed all divisions along racial lines to be unchristian, and the church's reactionary racist element, which considered a fully vested black bishop—even under the terms of the missionary district plan—a dangerous precedent. The conference's campaign for the missionary district plan lasted from 1904, when the conference first endorsed it before the General Convention, until 1940, when it met its final demise before the same body.

By another ironic turn of events, the principal detractor of the missionary plan in 1940 was Edward T. Demby, the nation's only black bishop. Demby was one of two black suffragan bishops elected in 1917–18 in an experiment that was widely—and correctly—regarded as a placebo for the missionary district plan, the suffragan bishop plan. The suffragan plan, involving the reinstatement of a long-repealed office by the 1907 and 1910 General Conventions, was passed into law precisely because it was less threatening than the missionary plan. First and foremost, the suffragan bishop legislation did not write racial segregation into the laws of the national church. The suffragan bishop, being an assistant bishop to a diocesan bishop, was a generic office. A diocese might elect a black suffragan to promote the black ministries of a diocese or region, but that remained a diocesan prerogative to be spelled out by diocesan law. Furthermore, suffragans had no vote in the House of Bishops—although they did enjoy the privileges of the floor—and no right of succession to the office of diocesan. The legislation was ratified in 1910, but there was no rush to elect black suffragans. Only after another seven years of rankling about the value of black suffragans and another exasperating effort by the Conference of Church Workers to enact the missionary district plan was the first suffragan elected. In 1917, the Diocese of Arkansas elected Demby "Suffragan Bishop for Colored Work in Arkansas and the Province of the Southwest," an area encompassing Arkansas, Texas, Kansas, Oklahoma, Missouri, and New Mexico. The Diocese of North Carolina followed suit and elected a second black suffragan, the Right Reverend Henry Beard Delany, to supervise all the black churches in the Carolinas.

In 1918, Demby embarked on the southwestern experiment in hopes of transforming his well-meant, but ill-conceived, office into something more substantial and becoming the nation's first black missionary bishop. That dream, however, went unrealized due to the restrictions placed upon him by his office, the Great Depression, and overwhelming white apathy. By 1940, when the missionary district plan came before the House of Bishops for the last time, Demby had suffered a change of heart. Speaking to his peers, Demby declared, in so many words, that it was folly for black Episcopalians to endorse the missionary district plan or ecclesiastical legislation in any form. This, he implied, did nothing but establish that segregation was indeed "good" in the eyes of white Episcopalians, transforming social necessity into something like genuine virtue—because it promoted order.[16]

The most well known, if not the quintessential, indictment of the ecclesiastical predilection for order in the face of racism is the Reverend Martin Luther King Jr.'s "Letter from a Birmingham Jail." King wrote in response to a collective remonstrance, in the form of an open letter, issued by several leading white clergymen of Alabama. The white clergymen, including an Episcopal bishop, C. C. Carpenter of Alabama, argued that the King-led Birmingham protests were ill-timed, overly demonstrative, and certain to bring down the wrath of Birmingham's duly constituted authorities. How then, they queried, could the protests be construed as "Christian"? While gently reprimanding the white clergymen for their lack of compassion and, especially, discernment, King urged them to reconsider. He lamented his continuing "disappointment" with the "white church and its leadership," so typified by their letter. Furthermore, King implied that their letter represented the voice of the "white moderate," in whom "I have been gravely disappointed." He continued:

> I have almost reached the regrettable conclusion that the Negro's great stumbling block in the stride towards freedom is not the White Citizens Councilor, or the Ku Klux Klanner, but the white moderate who is more devoted to "order" than to justice; who prefers a negative peace which is the absence of tension to a positive peace which is the presence of justice; who constantly says, "I agree with you in the goal you seek, but I can't agree with your methods of direct action"; who paternalistically feels that he can set the timetable for another man's freedom; who lives by the myth of time and constantly advises the Negro to wait until a "more convenient season." Shallow understanding by people of good will is more frustrating than absolute misunderstanding by people of ill will. Lukewarm acceptance is much more bewildering than outright rejection.[17]

The Episcopal Church, it would seem, personifies the maxim that the Christian church follows society and not vice versa. Change must ultimately come from within and be done in the name of order, but the stimulus for change usually comes from without. Take, for example, the church in France. While it is true that the Gallican church fell victim to the revolution of 1789, it is also true that the French clergy, in large measure, joined the revolution. It was defections from the clergy to the Third Estate that broke the impasse in the Estates General, leading to the establishment of the National Assembly. Returning to things Episcopal, there would probably be no Anglican Communion—and no Episcopal Church, had not the English clergy substantially followed the lead of Henry VIII. And when the Episcopal Church, the church home of a multitude of slaveowners, imparted its own moral legitimacy to the institution of slavery, the pattern held true. The gradual imposition of Jim Crow in the late nineteenth and early twentieth centuries had, as its natural corollary, the ecclesiastical segregation of mainline Protestantism. Baptists,

Methodists, Congregationalists, and Presbyterians segregated their meetings and, in some cases, their government. The Episcopal Church, with its approximately twenty thousand black communicants at the time of Demby's consecration, was in the vanguard of the movement and nowhere was the trend more evident than in the Diocese of Arkansas.

By virtue of its primary determination to keep the races separate, its secondary concern for church growth and self-reliance among African Americans, and its peculiar succession of bishops, Episcopal Arkansas became a proving ground for segregation. Two experiments, envisioned as national prototypes, resulted in three parallel and subordinate black Episcopal governments. Their nomenclature and dates represent the spirit of the times.

Afro-American Convocation (1903–20)
Colored Convocation (1920–39)
Negro Convocation (1939–47)

Yet they were not merely white schemes perpetrated on unwilling black communicants. The black leaders of the Arkansas experiment in segregation tried valiantly, albeit unsuccessfully, to demonstrate the efficacy of separating the races. Archdeacon McGuire breathed credibility into Bishop Brown's Afro-American Convocation, or "Arkansas Plan," for a two and a half years, until Brown drove him away. After limping along for a decade, Arkansas's black churches, newly designated the "Colored Convocation," revived under Demby, reaching the pinnacle of their development in the early 1930s, when they went into decline again, borne down by the Great Depression and Demby's adversarial relationship with the Diocese of Arkansas. The black leadership simply could not make it work. The black suffragan plan, like the Arkansas Plan before it, was a prototype turned into a liability. Indeed, if Demby's experience did nothing else for the Episcopal Church, it invalidated ecclesiastical segregation.

In 1938, the Diocese of Arkansas presaged the direction of the nation and the church at large by quietly, yet dramatically, reversing itself. At the insistence of its new bishop, the Right Reverend William B. Mitchell, the Episcopalians of Arkansas resolved to put an end to the experiment. How was this so? Certainly thirty-seven years of ecclesiastical Jim Crow had demonstrated the detrimental effects of a separate church for African Americans. The anticipated numerical growth and self-sufficient black churches had, by and large, failed to materialize. The congregations were few and small, the buildings in poor condition, the salaries of black clergy and teachers in some cases an embarrassment. "Separate is better" could more accurately be stated "Out of sight, out of mind." Yet there was one factor that mitigated against the continued existence of the Colored Convocation but that is not borne out by statistical evidence. The Episcopal government of Arkansas had virtually self-destructed in the 1930s by reason of a struggle between the state's two largest churches; the culmination of a long-standing rivalry dating back to Reconstruction. Twice this rivalry had exceeded the bounds of propriety and entered into schism and public debate. On both occasions, the political status of Arkansas's black Episcopalians was the escalating factor. When Arkansas elected a bishop in 1897, the argument over African American suffrage played havoc with preexisting theological, political, and personal conflicts. Rancor over the election boiled over into the national church press and secular newspapers, but eventually subsided. In 1932, it happened again—with disastrous results. By 1938, the race question had so exacerbated partisanship in the Diocese of Arkansas that partisanship itself became anathema. The people had had enough. Thus, when bishop-elect Mitchell insisted that he be bishop of all the Episcopalians in Arkansas or none of them, he found a willing flock. Over the next nine years, the Diocese of Arkansas slowly, but obediently, disposed of its version of the American social anomaly, removing the last vestiges of segregation in 1947. Order is key.

This is the story of Edward T. Demby, agent of order and change. It is also the story of the many dioceses he served. It is the story of the Arkansas experiments, how they came about, how they progressed and failed, and their significance for the church at large. It is the story of a ministry embodied in a national experience and how that ministry came to influence the Episcopal Church. It begins in 1869 with the birth of one Episcopal bishop and the election of another. Both were born and raised in the North. Both were extremely high Anglo-Catholics converted to the Episcopal Church as adults. Both served extensively in the South prior to becoming bishops. Both served in Arkansas and neighboring states after becoming bishops. Both were missionaries by temperament and jurisdiction. Both were stalwart, universally minded "catholics" when it came to racial divisions in the church. The senior of the two was the Right Reverend Henry N. Pierce, fourth missionary bishop to Arkansas and first diocesan bishop (1870–99), who set Arkansas on a very unusual path with regard to African American participation in the church. The junior of the two was Demby, who spent a very long time preparing to be a bishop.

NOTES

1. Lily G. Billingsley to Edward T. Demby, 15 Aug. 1932, Collected Papers of the Reverend William P. Witsell, Archives of the Episcopal Diocese of Arkansas, Little Rock, Ark.

2. Acts 10, 12; Gal. 2, NRSV (New Revised Standard Version). All citations refer to text, notes, and commentary.

3. George A. McGuire, "Missionary Report," *Journal of the Thirty-Fourth Council of the Protestant Episcopal Diocese of Arkansas* (1906): 81, hereafter cited as *Arkansas Journal*.

4. George A. McGuire, "Second Missionary Report," *Arkansas Journal* (1907): 87.

5. Ibid.

6. Edward T. Demby, "Off of the Record since 1939——," MS, James Weldon Johnson Collection, Yale Collection of American Literature, Beinecke Rare Book and Manuscript Library, Yale University, New Haven, Conn., 66, hereafter cited as "Off of the Record."

7. William M. Brown, *The Catholic Church and the Color Line,* quoted in Gavin White, "Patriarch McGuire and the Episcopal Church," *Historical Magazine of the Episcopal Church* 38 (June 1969): 113.

8. Demby, "Off of the Record," 66.

9. Harold T. Lewis, *Yet with a Steady Beat: The African-American Struggle for Recognition in the Episcopal Church* (Valley Forge, Pa.: Trinity Press International, 1996), 73.

10. David M. Reimers, "Negro Bishops and Diocesan Segregation in the Protestant Episcopal Church: 1870–1954," *Historical Magazine of the Protestant Episcopal Church* 31 (Sept. 1962): 234.

11. Ibid., 233.

12. *Journal of the General Convention of the Protestant Episcopal Church* (1889): 266.

13. George F. Bragg Jr., *History of the Afro-American Group of the Protestant Episcopal Church* (Baltimore: Church Advocate Press, 1922), 153. Brooks was later elected bishop of Massachusetts.

14. H. Lewis, *Yet with a Steady Beat,* 147–48. See John Kater, "Experiment in Freedom: The Episcopal Church and the Black Power Movement," *Historical Magazine of the Protestant Episcopal Church* (Mar. 1979): 68.

15. William M. Brown, *Crucial Race Question* (Little Rock, Ark.: Arkansas Churchman's Publishing Co., 1907), 254.

16. Demby, "Off of the Record," 160–63, 433–36; Reimers, "Negro Bishops," 240.

17. James M. Washington, ed., *A Testament of Hope: The Essential Writings and Speeches of Martin Luther King, Jr.* (San Francisco: Harper, 1986), 295.

1

A Time of Preparation

The church sexton of St. George's Methodist Church, Philadelphia, demanded that the African Americans stop praying and move to their newly designated seats. Although they had paid for the refurbishing of the section where they knelt, Absalom Jones, an ex-slave and a leading figure in the group, asked only that they might finish praying, then move. But the sexton would brook no delay. Suddenly Jones felt the pressure of a hand placed under his arm and found himself being lifted off of his knees and onto his feet. It was time to go. This was not the first racial indignity the blacks had experienced at St. George's, but they resolved that it would be their last. They left St. George's physically and permanently in order to establish the Free African Society, a nondenominational Christian organization for mutual aid and reform. Although Richard Allen, another leader in the society, would eventually found the African Methodist Episcopal Church, Jones went a more traditional route. Representing that portion of the group whose religious convictions were similar to his own, he consulted with the Right Reverend William White, the Episcopal bishop of Pennsylvania, about organizing a church for people of color. Subsequently, Jones and company launched St. Thomas's Episcopal Church, Philadelphia. Organized in 1794, St. Thomas's was the first truly independent black church of any denomination in the United States. In 1802, Jones, having pastored St. Thomas's from its inception, became the first black priest in the Episcopal Church. The ecclesiastical trailblazing of Jones and St. Thomas's stopped there, however, as St. Thomas's was denied a seat and a vote in the Pennsylvania Episcopal convention until 1863, the year of universal emancipation.[1]

The St. George's incident is as much a watershed for all African American Christians as the Newport incident, described in the introduction of this book, is a watershed in the life and ministry of Edward T. Demby. Both incidents figure heavily in the history of black Episcopalians. But the commonalities between Jones and Demby do not end there. Both were natives of Delaware. Converted a century after Jones and company founded St. Thomas's, Demby also left Methodism for the Episcopal Church, with the expectation of becoming an Episcopal clergyman. In the Episcopal Church they both found a denomination whose theology so appealed to them that they were willing to endure a less than equal status as the price of membership. Furthermore, in choosing to submit to a predominantly white and occasionally hostile church government, they risked the stigma of being "Uncle Toms" in the eyes of other African Americans. They were, as most black Episcopalians are, thoroughgoing Episcopalians. Perhaps it is serendipitous that Demby's birthday, February 13, falls on the same day as the Feast of Absalom Jones.

Edward T. Demby's pilgrimage to the Episcopal Church consumed the first twenty-six years of his life, followed by another twenty-three years, as he preferred to think of it, in preparation for the episcopate. Indeed, he looked upon all of life as a preparation for the remainder, which best explains the paucity of biographical information he left behind. Demby was an optimist, engrossed in current developments and their implications for the future rather than in his own past. His surviving records indicate, if anything, a humble man, not prone to boast of his achievements, but one who discovered, at a very late date, that his lineage and upbringing were unique and had profoundly influenced his equally unique life and ministry. This personal revelation inspired a cascade of material, bound in seven loose leaf notebooks and deposited in the James Weldon Johnson collection at Yale University in 1953. Titled "Off of the Record since 1939," Demby's memoirs are primarily reflections on those topics that most interested him, peppered with recollections of personal experiences that serve to drive home his point. Ultimately, Demby tells us a great deal about himself in "Off of the Record," but it is the Demby Family Papers, deposited posthumously at the Schomburg Center for Research in Black Culture, that reveal most about his early life.[2]

The first son and oldest child of Edward Thomas Demby IV and Mary F. Anderson Tippet Demby was born in a wagon en route to Baltimore from Wilmington.[3] Christened Edward Thomas Demby V, he tells us that he learned his lineage from his mother and his maternal uncle, but, unfortunately, he omitted a few details in his memoirs. He indicates that he had West Indian ancestors, but does not indicate whether one or both of his parents were West Indian. Nor does he specify a location in the West Indies. Evidently both of his parents were freeborn in the United States. Mary came from "Protestant" stock. She and her brother, Professor Eddy Anderson, traced the Anderson lineage to the "Modalto tribe" of Abyssinia, members of the "Caucasic family [of] Africa." "My great grandparents," writes Demby, "arrived in this country about 1800." Edward Demby Sr. was the progeny of a Roman Catholic family that relocated from Maryland's eastern shore to Darby, a suburb of Philadelphia. Family tradition held that the Dembys issued from the "Galla Tribe," a "Hamitic" people of Africa.[4]

Demby is effusive in praise of his parents. He once said that his father, a minister, had inspired him to enter the ministry from the age of seven.[5] However, on closer inspection, it appears that Demby Sr. was not an ordained minister; rather he was a lay minister of some kind, who supported his family as a brick mason and an "inside house decorator." He enjoyed boxing, running, and wrestling, besides being "an excellent and good husband and a most loving father."[6] Demby said of him, "Father never failed to give [of] his line of work (brick mason), especially to churches and societies for the sick and otherwise afflicted persons. It was said by all who knew him that I am very much like him. He was a most likeable person—he had many friends, and at his passing the people of the community, the Caucasian and the Negro race alike, lamented; [they] pathetically bewailed [his death]."[7] To the chagrin of his siblings, Demby Jr. insisted that he loved his father more than they—an opinion he maintained his entire life.

Demby was equally fervent in praise of his mother, the better-educated of his parents and a highly prized domestic worker in Wilmington. "Mother failed not in doing all within her power for the advancement and security of each one of the children—we owe everything to her, and during the years after reaching manhood and womanhood we never failed to supply her every need. She was a most generous person, too much so we thought. [Out] of her meager income she would give . . . something, though small[,] to every call for Christian and social uplift, so much so [that] she was denominated 'Charitable Mary.'"[8]

Mary and Edward cultivated self-reliance and a reverence for education in their eleven children. Mary trained all of them to be "efficient in the household arts" and Edward saw that each boy learned a trade, Edward Jr. being schooled in "the art of making matches and bricks, starting from the ground up." Demby's remembrance of household duties has an almost ethereal quality: "There was a daily schedule as to the household duties and obligations, indeed as to the keeping of the back yard and the front in supreme condition [in] which we failed not, so much so, [that] many of the community would come and see how and with what spirit of unity we went about our daily tasks, out of which we got much happiness, each one trying to outdo the other. [In return] some three or four times a year our parents would give each of us a needed gift."[9]

One of the most telling lessons that the Dembys imparted to their children was the value of sacrifice. It was certainly not lost on their oldest child, who boasted that his parents "made every sacrifice to [educate their children]. Each week they would put aside a certain amount of their small weekly wage for that purpose. They also saw to it that the children were so conditioned to get the best religious and cultural training." The children, he says, responded in kind. "We would save our pennies and put them together and purchase for them at Christmas and Easter a worthwhile gift and sometimes it was so touching. They would cry and we would join in with them." Demby remembers a model family who reached out to those around them out of their abundance of spirit. They had the admiration of their neighbors.[10]

Implicit to all of the Dembys' endeavors to raise up their children was the idea of leading by example, a personal creed and a trademark of their neighborhood. The Dembys were part of a small but aspiring black middle class in Wilmington, located in a sort of buffer zone between the black slums and the white community. Although the Dembys were poor, Wilmington's black middle class did not define itself strictly by income. One's trade or profession, education, values, church affiliation, and lineage also contributed to one's place in society. According to Gina Pressley,

> Successful blacks . . . lived in the center of town in a mixed neighborhood around Tenth and French Streets. There they were joined by an occasional black who succeeded, through hard work or education, in escaping from the ghetto to the high ground. Gradually, a colony of educated prosperous mulattoes developed in the neighborhood, a group whose way of life was as differentiated from the ghetto blacks as it was from the life of the white upper class. Successful blacks fought hard to maintain the value of their property and the standards of their lives. They sent their children to Sunday school, high school, and out-of-state colleges. They owned their homes and kept them painted and repaired. The rigid caste system enforced by the white majority barred all Negroes, no matter how successful or prominent, from meaningful participation in local society or government, and so successful blacks assumed the leadership of the colored community. They built churches, community centers, homes for the aged, and institutions for delinquents.[11]

Demby reveled in the accomplishments of his peers born and raised "over Third Street Bridge." "[We] were said to be socially at our best," he recollects, "when fishing, catching frogs, wading in the marsh . . . along old Market Street road, trapping muskrats and fighting mosquitoes and the like." Out of the marsh, so to speak, emerged such notables as Jefferson S. Coage and William J. Winchester, who rose to prominence in politics, the Reverends Solomon and Lewis Banton, who were renowned pastors, and Seth Lowe, John Thompson, and John E. Johnson, Episcopalians who acquired reputations as Christian and civic leaders in the Wilmington's black community.[12]

The greatest boon to Demby's youth, other than his parents, was Eddy Anderson, who tutored his nephew for perhaps a decade. Anderson operated a private high school at the rear of Ezion Methodist Episcopal (Northern Methodist) Church, located at the corner of Ninth and French Streets. Demby recalls: "As a child I was very sickly, so much so, it was said that my earthly continuance would be of short duration. . . . [Therefore] most of my education, grade and high school, was private under the direction of my uncle, Professor Eddy Anderson who was one of the very few Negro Americans of his day who was highly educated in the arts, sciences, general literature and languages, especially in Latin, Greek, French, and Spanish."[13]

Evidently, Edward Jr. was raised a Methodist at Ezion. Along with the Union Church of Africans, Ezion figured prominently in the life of Wilmington's east side. Both churches were a hub of activity during the annual revival and festival called the "Big Quarterly." Originally, the Big Quarterly was a slave holiday celebrated in the fall, after the harvest. Masters would release their slaves on their own recognizance for one day in order that they might participate in a sort of marathon camp meeting that enveloped the black community up and down French Street. Slaves and free people of color converged on Wilmington from Virginia, Delaware, southeastern Pennsylvania, and Maryland's Eastern Shore to reunite with old friends and family, worship, and play. By reason of the one-day limitation the festivities would extend far into the night, keeping a vigil in the knowledge that the morning would mean a return to slavery. After emancipation, the Big Quarterly not only remained in place but grew in importance.[14]

There are, however, a couple of oddities in Demby's recollections of his close-knit family life. While he left numerous photographs of Mrs. Demby's family to posterity, he left behind no photographs of his own family, save one small, poor quality photograph of his younger brother, William Tatnall Demby. Likewise, he failed to mention the names of any of his siblings in his retrospective writings, save for his sister, Alice. "Alice," he wrote, "became an outstanding Christian leader—she was excellent in music, instrumental and vocal, and in addition was a very good public speaker."[15] Dorothy Demby, niece of Bishop Demby, has suggested that this omission can best be explained by the stress characteristic of a household with so many children and so little money. There was an omnipresent need to get the children trained and educated and out on their own.[16] Be that as it may, Demby relished the emotional sustenance of his early years, which, no doubt, inspired the optimism, self-reliance, gentleness, and willingness to sacrifice that were the trademarks of his ministry. One can see in this "greatly admired" family of Wilmington's east side a powerful precedent for someone whose lifelong ambition was to set an example for others.[17]

Demby graduated from Eddy Anderson's school and somehow managed to attend the Institute for Colored Youth in Philadelphia, a high school for freeborn blacks and arguably the nation's preeminent black preparatory school. In Demby's day, it was "a strong academic institution" with a collegiate level curriculum of "classics, sciences, and higher mathematics." Willard Gatewood, author of *Aristocrats of Color: The Black Elite, 1880–1920*, tells us that "a majority of the Institute's graduates became teachers, and many occupied some of the choicest faculty positions in the best black schools in both the North and the South."[18]

From the Institute for Colored Youth, Demby made the grand tour, so to speak, of elite black colleges in the North and East. First, he attended Lincoln University in Pennsylvania, a school with Presbyterian roots that came to have an unusually high number of black Episcopal priests to its credit. Next, Demby moved to Baltimore in order to attend Centenary Biblical Institute, a Methodist Episcopal institution that changed its name to Morgan College in 1890. Demby stipulates that he finished the "normal course" at Centenary, meaning that he was qualified to teach school at the conclusion of his studies and perhaps an indication of the growing trend toward industrial education at black colleges and universities. From Centenary, Demby matriculated to Howard University, Washington, D.C., which many blacks and whites regarded as the best education any black university had to offer. In 1892–93 he completed the junior and senior years at Howard Divinity School.[19]

Demby may have encountered Antoinette Martina Ricks, his future bride, at Howard. She was attending the Lucy Webb Hayes Deaconess School at about the same time. Heralded as "Little Nettie, the Most Beautiful Girl of Cleveland," at her coming-out party, she was debutante, social worker, missionary, and crowd favorite. Demby recalls that Frederick Douglass and other prominent black figures around Washington "were constructively interested in her" while she attended the Lucy Hayes School. Presumably, this means that they helped support her through school, or tried to lend her assistance by their influence.[20]

Nettie, as she preferred to be called, was the only child of Benjamin Hockaday Ricks and Sarah Virginia Ricks of Cleveland. Like her future husband, she had endured a chronically ill childhood only to bloom in her late teens. Her father was coachman to a leading merchant family of Cleveland and may have been an Episcopalian. Her mother, educated in a Roman Catholic convent in

Toronto, was a member of Mt. Zion Congregational Church and also "assisted" Cleveland's first families. The Rickses impressed refinement, good character, and a good reputation upon their daughter. They taught her that the culmination of education is service to one's fellow human beings.[21]

The Rickses exemplified how one could live in a city in which the color line was comparatively relaxed and blacks enjoyed an unusual measure of upward mobility. As persons of mixed ancestry affiliated with predominantly white denominations and champions of charitable causes in the city, the Rickses not only identified with Cleveland's notoriously exclusive light-skinned black society but lived on the fringe of white society as well. Thomas and Sarah married at Christ Episcopal Church, Oberlin, Ohio. Their daughter graduated from the preparatory school at Oberlin College, where many of the nation's black elite sent their children. Oberlin College was an unusually integrated institution where black students could study comfortably as part of a predominantly white student body and profit from the high academic standards. Nettie became a "staunch Presbyterian" at an early age, which enabled her to participate in a citywide Sunday school program. By virtue of her fluent German, she was appointed teacher over a class of German immigrant children in an area called the "Bad Land." Thus, she enjoyed a certain liberty when it came to racial norms. She believed that Christian character and education were the keys to assimilation.[22]

It appears that Demby supported his education during his Lincoln-Centenary-Howard days by teaching. We know that he conducted private "academies" in Denver and Wilmington during the course of his studies. The Wilmington "academy" suggests that perhaps he taught at the Eddy Anderson High School. In light of his parent's financial situation, it seems safe to assume that he taught in some capacity wherever he furthered his education. He is credited with having operated a school in sacred languages via the mails, purportedly the first African American correspondence school in the United States.[23]

Having attended three colleges, but having as yet no degree, Demby decided on a Bachelor of Divinity from Payne Theological Seminary, Wilberforce University, another elite black institution. By this time he was a proven academic and the seminary appointed him to an assistant teaching job, thereby easing his financial burden. Demby taught New Testament Greek, Hebrew, sacred oratory, and some general church history. He obtained his B.D. in 1893 and presumably entered the ministry of the African Methodist Episcopal Church upon graduation. However, he preferred an academic environment to the pastoral ministry, and moved to Chicago, where he obtained an S.T.D. from National University (the University of Chicago) in 1894. From 1894 to 1896, he was

Dean of Paul Quinn College, Waco, Texas, an A.M.E. institution. He taught
theology at Paul Quinn and published a book under the aegis of the college, *A
Bird's Eye View of Exegetical Studies: The Writings of St. Paul and St. James.*[24]
During this interlude, he was not totally inactive as a clergyman. The Reverend George F. Bragg, the chief historian of black Episcopalians in Demby's era,
describes him as a "traveling preacher" during his A.M.E. hiatus, which is what
it proved to be.[25]

At this point things become confused. In 1895, midway through his tenure
at Paul Quinn, Bishop John Spalding of Colorado confirmed Demby in the
Episcopal Church. While Demby does not speak of his pilgrimage to the Episcopal Church, we know that he was by nature a very high churchman in matters of worship and laid great emphasis upon historical tradition as a valida-
tion of a denomination's orthodoxy. The deciding factor was probably the
doctrine of apostolic succession and the mood of the church at the time. In the
late nineteenth century, the Oxford and Cambridge movements of the Anglican Church rippled through the Episcopal Church in the form of the "Anglo-
Catholic revival," an attempt to reestablish, or reemphasize, pre-Reformation
claims to orthodoxy. One would think that the Anglo-Catholic revival might
have pointed Demby toward the Roman Catholic Church, but as he examined
the church of his father he found it wanting "in view of the fact [that] the
Church of Rome withdrew from the Church of England" and that the "Church
of Rome" was a foreign entity. More importantly, he condemned the doctrine
of papal infallibility as a pernicious heresy, robbing the established canon of
sacred writings of their authority by adding to them. Many years later, when
Pope Pius II invoked papal infallibility in promulgating the doctrine of the
Assumption of the Virgin Mary, Demby would respond: "The proclamation
of the new teaching gives strength to Unitarianism, humanitarianism, New
Thought, Christian Science, theosophy, Bahai'sm, and the like; it belittles the
Glories of the Mother of Jesus and to Him all praise, who is God and man
(Theanthropos) and other basic teachings of Christianity."[26] "Infallibility,"
wrote Demby, "resides only with the universal church." Thus, he perceived a
church with a strong historical claim on orthodoxy, much like that of the Episcopal Church, but clearly moving away from it.

At the same time he saw that the Episcopal Church was moving in the opposite direction. He felt that there were only two churches worthy of serious consideration: the Anglican and the Eastern Orthodox. At the time of Demby's
conversion, a good many Episcopalians had drawn the same conclusion. The
Lambeth Conferences, the worldwide meetings of all the bishops of the Anglican Communion, seemed very near to unifying with the Eastern Orthodox

Church. Even though the process was deadlocked on the wording of the Nicene Creed, many Episcopal leaders still hoped that it could be resolved. Given the opportunity to design a church many years later, Demby would choose a Byzantine style. The Anglo-Catholic revival also reemphasized the role of ritual in worship, prompting liturgical and aesthetic changes. Demby, being a passionate ritualist and wholeheartedly in agreement with the theological shift, felt very much at home. And there was, of course, the matter of race. Of consummate importance to a revitalized apostolic succession, the Anglo-Catholic revival laid new emphasis on being a truly catholic church, wherein racial, class, and ethnic differences were no impediment to membership and participation. Although the racial aspect of the revival had, to say the least, questionable appeal among the white laity of the Episcopal Church, the fact remained that leaders on both sides of the color line had at least raised the issue of racial equality and some were even contending for it. All of these developments could only have pleased Demby, whose memoirs, sermons, and reports are inundated with the Nicene phrase "one, holy, catholic, and apostolic church." On the other hand, the African Methodist Episcopal Church, having been established in 1816 instead of A.D. 33 and predicated on racial homogeneity, was no longer acceptable.[27] Like many of his Episcopal contemporaries, Demby referred to all Protestant churches as "denominational churches."[28]

We do not know how Demby decided upon Colorado. We do know that the Diocese of Colorado operated an integrated seminary, St. Matthew's Hall, and that at least one other former A.M.E. clergyman, the Reverend Daniel E. Johnson Sr., was there at about the same time. According to Bragg, Johnson spent eight years as an A.M.E. "traveling preacher," before coming to St. Matthew's.[29] He arrived in Denver in 1893, became a deacon, and was elevated to the priesthood upon graduation from St. Matthew's Hall in 1895. While attending St. Matthew's, he was the first pastor of Holy Redeemer Church, Denver. Holy Redeemer was a new church, composed predominantly of Anglo-Catholics, mixed by complexion and southern in origin. Many of its members, Johnson included, came from Memphis, Tennessee. It quickly acquired a well-deserved reputation for being the church home of Denver's black society. In light of their similar A.M.E. backgrounds, their preference for things Anglo-Catholic, and Demby's subsequent move to Tennessee, it appears that the relationship between Demby and Johnson may have predated and inspired Demby's move to Colorado. Once again, Demby supported himself by teaching. He operated an integrated private school in Denver. He was also catechist to Holy Redeemer after Johnson's departure and graduated from St. Matthew's in 1896.[30]

The choice of St. Matthew's Hall, in lieu of the church's designated route for black seminarians, Bishop Payne Divinity School, Petersburg, Virginia, is worth discussing. It may have been a matter of convenience or race, or both. The outlook in Petersburg was not encouraging to a prospective seminarian. In 1889, the Diocese of Virginia excluded black delegates from the Virginia convention and, as a result, the number of students at Bishop Payne plummeted.[31] It is also possible that Demby anticipated racial duplicity at Bishop Payne. Black Episcopalians of this era had a reputation for being "bluevein"; that is, they were said to practice discrimination based on the lightness of one's skin. Blueveinism, a reference to skin so light that one might see the blueness of one's veins, was a also a trait frequently attributed to the nation's black elite, which numbered a disproportionate number of persons of mixed ancestry—and Episcopalians. "The denomination that perhaps included more aristocrats of color than any other," writes Willard Gatewood, "was the Protestant Episcopal Church." Certain black Episcopal churches, like St. Mark's, Charleston, were notoriously bluevein, and those that were not suffered a sort of guilt by association.[32] As for Demby, he was about five and a half feet tall, very dark, with very African features. Speaking in the third person, he recalls the question of color and its influence upon his decision to join the Episcopal ministry: "I know a young man who desired to enter the ministry. He [was highly qualified], but because of his color he was informed that it would be best for him to give up the idea. However, the young man matriculated in a Western diocesan seminary and in time was ordained."[33]

In 1896, Demby came to Tennessee, by way of an agreement between Bishop Spalding and Bishop Thomas F. Gailor of Tennessee, with the understanding that there would be a trial period prior to ordination. Thus, Demby assumed charge of St. Paul's Church, Mason, Tennessee, in the capacity of a lay reader. St. Paul's was one of eleven black missions in the Diocese of Tennessee and one of the more rural ones. Located northeast of Memphis, it was, with the exception of Emmanuel Church, Memphis, the largest black mission in Tennessee. It was the church home of about fifty communicants, many of them third-generation Episcopalians. It was also one of six black missions operating a day school in 1897, a phenomenon characteristic of black Episcopal Churches in the South. Black Episcopalians, as a rule, were willing to sacrifice in order that their children might benefit from a parochial education. Those churches that could manage a day school usually did so, and the clergy were expected to teach the children. Congregations also looked upon their schools as a means of reaching the community with the gospel. It was often their one avenue of evangelism, an opportunity made possible by the poor condition of black public schools. Many southern blacks found the Episcopal service too stiff, bookish, and ritualized, and felt nothing but disdain for a black church with white oversight, but they were willing, nonetheless, to pay for the privilege of sending their children to Episcopal parochial schools. As an illustration, the six churches operating day schools in Tennessee averaged forty communicants, while the number of students averaged forty-four. Or, to better illustrate, St. Paul's, Nashville, had four communicants and a student body of fifty, and St. Cyprian's, Gallatin, had six communicants and a student body of forty. This truth would be a cornerstone of Demby's ministry over the next forty years.[34]

Demby took up his first charge with unbridled enthusiasm, adding eighteen communicants the first year. He was the sole teacher to a day school of seventy students, utilizing a single church building and a budget of $200, which included his salary. According to the *Church Advocate,* he won the "love and hearty cooperation of the people, both black and white."[35] On Gailor's first visit, he was delighted with "the intelligent interest of . . . this colored congregation." The import from Colorado was clearly in his element.[36] One year later, Gailor ordained Demby to the diaconate before a packed St. Paul's, "a considerable number of white people" being in attendance.[37] On 8 May 1899, Gailor advanced him to the priesthood with even greater fanfare. Demby capitalized on his examination for the priesthood to drive home a point about the supposed intellectual inferiority of black people and created a local sensation. When scrutinizing black candidates for the priesthood, it had been the practice of the examiners to forego certain academic qualifications that the white candidates were required to pass. Demby insisted that he not be exempted from any test, his reason being "that should I ever be elected as a bishop in the church, it could not be said that I did not take a complete examination." Therefore, he was examined for three days "against the will of the examiners" and by Gailor's orders. When Demby scored in the 90 percentile in all areas, the examiners were flabbergasted, going so far as to admit that there were parts of the examinations which "no one" could have done better. He was ordained at Emmanuel Church, Memphis, before a capacity crowd including "all of the leading ministers of the leading Christian communions [in the city]."[38]

Thereafter, Gailor broadened the field for Demby by appointing him vice-principal to Hoffman Hall, Nashville, in addition to his regular duties at St. Paul's, Mason. Hoffman Hall was a small African American seminary belonging to the Diocese of Tennessee and Demby's brief tenure there is hardly worth recording, except that he made his first acquaintance of a lifelong friend. In 1899, the Reverend James R. Winchester, the white rector of Christ Church, Nashville, engaged him in a long interview on the "Negro problem, especially in the South." Although Winchester was eager to talk, he warily broached the "delicate subject," keeping in mind Demby's northern roots. He recalls: "I was greatly impressed and surprised at your attitudes and answers to my questions on your part without sacrificing any of the principles of manhood, and within the teachings of our Lord Christ. . . . I went over our conversation with Bishop Gailor, and he was delighted. I said to myself, if the time ever came when we would have Negro bishops in the church with jurisdiction in the United States, I would like to see you among them."[39] They were kindred spirits from the beginning.

Sometime in 1899, Demby assumed responsibility for a third flock, tiny St. Stephen's Church in Burlison, Tennessee. St. Stephen's, like Hoffman Hall, was not a significant landmark in his professional career, except that it, too, had a long-range significance for his aspirations to be a bishop. According to Demby, the congregation, consisting of two families and thirteen communicants in 1899, once numbered in excess of a thousand communicants. The original St. Stephen's Mission, being the postwar renaissance of a huge slave congregation, had erected a "beautiful" house of worship in the 1880s. However, most of the members had "connected themselves with the different negro denominations" after the building burned in October 1888. A "poor building" sufficed for the remnant. Demby attributed the demise of St. Stephen's to a lack of clerical oversight—the kind of oversight that a black bishop could have provided. Moreover, it convinced him that the situation would continue to deteriorate for black Episcopalians in the South unless the church began to elect black bishops.[40]

Other events connected with St. Stephen's were of a more personal—and more tragic—nature. It appears that Demby met and married his first wife, Polly Alston-Sherrill, while he was serving at Burlison. Presumably Polly was related to the Reverend Ossian P. Alston, the man whom Demby had replaced. The elder Alston was, according to Demby, "the first colored clergyman in Tennessee."[41] He was an ex-slave from nearby Ravenscroft, a man of "deep piety and zeal," who, despite a physical handicap, had ministered to black Episcopalians in west Tennessee for two decades.[42] Thus Demby, with his ministry well established and a new bride from one of Tennessee's first black Episcopal families, prepared to settle down and raise a family in west Tennessee. Unfortunately, Polly died in November, bringing what was otherwise a very promising ministry to a close. In March 1900, Demby transferred to St. Augustine's Church, Kansas City, Missouri.

Demby's new post was very much to his liking. His salary was about double what it had been at St. Paul's, Mason, and he felt free to indulge his high liturgical tastes in the more urban and cosmopolitan setting of St. Augustine's.

A church with all the earmarks of a black Episcopal Church at the turn of the century, St. Augustine's was located in an upscale black neighborhood on Kansas City's east side and its pews were occupied by a disproportionate number of Kansas City's professionals, intellectuals, and businessmen. One of the high points of Demby's tenure was a requiem mass for the repose of the soul of the Reverend Thomas W. Cain, a pioneer in black ministries in Texas and the first black Episcopalian with the distinction of having been a delegate to two General Conventions. So moving was the service that the *Church Advocate* praised St. Augustine's new priest for his singing and his remarks celebrating Cain's ministry. Demby established, as always, a reputation as a civic leader and as an ambassador to the white community. He had a short but successful tenure in Kansas City and he left behind many friends.[43]

Demby either met Nettie Ricks at this time or met her anew. She was prospering and had, without a doubt, found her calling. Although she had fallen ill and dropped out of the Lucy Webb Hayes Deaconess School, she returned to Washington, changed her field of study, and graduated with the first nursing class of Freedmen's Hospital, Howard University, in 1896. Since that time, she had served as a nurse in the Spanish American War, as head nurse of Douglass Hospital, Cleveland, where she had the distinction of being the first African American registered nurse in that city, and as head nurse of Freedman's Hospital, Kansas City, Kansas. She also studied at Tuskegee Institute, where she may have been an instructor as well. As her an unpublished manuscript titled "A Pocket Manual for the Nurse, the Doctor, the Church, and the Community Social Worker in Action" makes abundantly clear, she considered nursing to be her Christian vocation.[44]

Although she had accomplished a great deal before marrying Edward Demby and would be a substantial partner in his ministry in years to come, most of what we know about Nettie Ricks, we know because her husband-to-be wrote it down in his memoirs. In this way she epitomizes the changing Episcopal, not to mention Presbyterian, ideal of Christian womanhood at the turn of the century. In her we see an emerging professionalism alongside the traditional subservient and self-effacing role of the Christian woman; a strong sense of vocation and united action in social work joined to anonymity.[45] Apparently Nettie and Edward met, or met again, while she was employed at Freedman's Hospital. He was busy on "her" side of the Missouri River with the organization of the Church of the Ascension and pastoral duties connected with the black mission at Leavenworth, Kansas.

They married in 1902. During the third week in September, the bride-to-be was baptized by the rector of St. Andrew's, Cleveland's black Episcopal church, and confirmed an Episcopalian by the bishop of Ohio. A few days later, she and Edward were married, but elected to have the ceremony at her parents' home instead of St. Andrew's. It was, like Nettie's coming-out party, a much celebrated affair.[46]

That year was not without its hardships, however. According to Isaac and Ruth DeLoach James, parishioners of St. Augustine's, Demby's ministry was a success in spite of "great trials" that he endured along the way. Perhaps his greatest trial was the loss of his father, who died while Demby was bedridden with sickness in Kansas City. Shocked and depressed at being unable to be at his father's bedside or his graveside, Demby grieved over this experience for a long time. His greatest consolation was that Edward T. Demby IV had followed the example of his namesake and died an Episcopalian.[47]

In January 1903, the Dembys moved their ministry to Cairo, Illinois. Cairo was a bustling river town, heavily populated with black emigrants from the South. Having crossed the Ohio River, many of them chose to remain in Cairo. Consequently the black community, bursting at the seams and—if we are to believe the publications of the Diocese of Springfield—sometimes took on the aura of a mining camp.

St. Michael's was Cairo's black Episcopal mission and a serious challenge for the Dembys. The mission boasted a parochial school of sixty-eight children in 1902. In this report taken from the *Diocese of Springfield* newspaper we see the disparity between the mission's program and its environment. The student body included

> the best and most intelligent colored children of the city, who are being carefully trained in the teachings of the church, English studies, and industrial occupations as well. [The Reverend B. W. Paxton] is assisted by his wife, a cultivated and competent teacher, who instructs the girls in sewing and household duties, and by Mr. Spring, who, in addition to the regular school instruction, teaches carpentry to the boys. . . . Rev. Mr. Paxton is devoted and faithful in his labors and is battling against a strong opposition of ignorance and sectarianism in a town with a shifting population and much immorality among the class of people he is endeavoring to benefit.[48]

Physically speaking, St. Michael's was a rather large church in comparison with most of Demby's other charges. Formerly the Church of the Redeemer, it was Cairo's old white Episcopal church. When the white congregation moved to a new location, they converted the old building into a black mission. The Right Reverend George F. Seymour, bishop of Springfield, erected a "large schoolhouse, well located and admirably arranged" nearby. However, by 1902, the school was greatly in need of repair and equipment. School, rectory, and mission were valued at $15,000–$20,000.

Although the previous administration had offered vocational training at St. Michael's, the Dembys' arrival signaled the true advent of industrial education at the school. The school, renamed St. Michael's Parochial and Industrial School, was primarily Mrs. Demby's responsibility. As principal to an average of about sixty-five children and two teachers, she quickly discovered that her Tuskegee education opened doors in the white community, "Tuskegee" and "Booker T. Washington" being catchwords for black progress. In 1903, the *Diocese of Springfield*, excited at this new development, exhorted its readers to support the school in the name of moral and spiritual uplift in the black community: "We have Africa [St. Michael's] as a mission field right in our midst. Can we, dare we, neglect it?"[49] One year later, however, the *Diocese* explained and celebrated the changes in curriculum but made only a passing reference to "the spiritual side of teaching." This would appear to be a small affirmation of Harold Lewis's contention that the joining of industrial education to black Episcopal institutions of higher learning in the South resulted in a decline in the religious orientation of those institutions. Predicated on training black people in the practical aspects of a better life in this world, schools became progressively less interested in preparing them for the next. Of course, Lewis speaks specifically of the secularization associated with the American Church Institute for Negroes, but a perusal of the 1904 report on St. Michael's school would lead one to believe that the price of pecuniary assistance was to deemphasize the catechism and broadcast the virtues of industrial education.[50] This is not to imply that the Dembys imparted anything less than a rigorous catechism at St. Michael's; rather, they learned to capitalize on the system. School and mission prospered at their hands, earning them a commendation from Cairo's Board of Education. Demby boasts that ultimately "there were more than 150 children connected with the school," many of whom came from Cairo's public schools.[51] Considering that St. Michael's Church had only thirty-two communicants, the size and composition of the student body was but another affirmation of Demby's belief in the evangelical value of parochial schools.[52]

In early 1904, the Dembys moved again, this time to Florida. The Right Reverend William C. Gray, bishop of South Florida, had a problem similar to that of the bishop of Springfield. St. Peter's, Key West, was in need of a priest capable of administering a parochial school and pastoring a church in a community inundated with black transients. A good many West Indian immi-

grants, many of them Anglican, lived in Key West. Looking about for someone to minister to this swelling congregation in flux, Gray landed on Demby.

St. Peter's may have been the most trying and, at the same time, the most
rewarding charge of Demby's career. It was certainly different from his previous experiences. A church composed primarily of West Indian Anglicans, it
had never known mission status, having been organized as a parish at its inception in 1875. There was a white parish on Key West at the time, but the
newcomers, being perhaps a thousand souls and unwilling to be Jim Crowed
in any fashion, determined to establish a church of their own. They also determined, in consultation with Bishop John F. Young of Florida, the liturgical
direction of St. Peter's. The services, said Young, "were to be chorally conducted
throughout, and with as high a ritual, as in my judgement, should be compat-
ible with sound Anglican theology."[53]

It would appear that Bishop Gray recruited the Dembys with the intention
of launching a black parochial school at St. Alban's Mission in Key West, a
satellite of St. Peter's. The school first appears in the "Abstract of Parochial and
Missionary Reports" for 1904, numbering seventy students and three teachers, a good indication that the Dembys established the school immediately
upon their arrival in Key West. They were joined by a newly ordained deacon,
Montraville E. Spatches, who was assigned to St. Alban's.

Spatches was a product of Key West and, presumably, St. Peter's, but his relationship to Demby may have predated his return to the home island. He
graduated from Fisk University in 1898, a year before Demby became vice-
principal of Hoffman Hall. While we cannot be certain if Spatches had an
academic relationship to Hoffman, we do know that Fisk students, generally
speaking, looked upon Tennessee's black Episcopal seminary with condescen-
sion and disdain; the elite black college versus the theological extension of
Tennessee's white Episcopal hegemony. Likewise, we note a shift in Demby's
own educational philosophy while serving alongside Spatches in Key West. The
intense debate between the advocates of industrial education, personified by
Booker T. Washington, and the advocates of liberal education, represented by
W. E. B. Du Bois, was at its zenith. Heretofore, Demby had always been heavily biased toward liberal education, but had gradually and grudgingly acknowledged that there was a certain wisdom to Washington's philosophy. However,
by the end of his Florida tenure, Demby was adamantly and publicly opposed
to the encroachment of industrial education upon liberal arts, and decried the
overall poor academic standards so typical of black education in the South.
The school at Key West, we gather, was the antithesis of St. Michael's, Cairo;
more of a liberal arts school with higher academic standards and a strong re-

ligious program. By the end of 1906 it had doubled in size, boasting four teachers and 150 students. Mrs. Demby may have been the school's headmistress and it would be safe to assume that she taught there. The plant at St. Alban's expanded in proportion to its student body, being valued at $1,800 in 1902 and $6,400 in 1906.[54]

St. Peter's flourished under Demby's leadership. A church of 436 communicants in 1902, it grew to 582 communicants by the end of 1906, an increase of one-third over three years. Likewise, the number of baptized members increased from 1,000 to 1,112 over the same period. Demby's pride and joy was "the church Sunday School which was properly graded in the line of the public schools—there was a high school department—we had commencements on the same level as the city public schools without any friction whatever."[55] The number of Sunday school students increased from 250 in 1903 to 388 in 1906. At this time, St. Peter's was the second largest black parish in the United States, St. Philip's, Harlem, being the largest.

The growth of Demby's church parallels that of his personal enlightenment. At home with a large congregation whose liturgical and theological inclinations were much to his liking, he published with regularity. In addition to his contributions to *Catholic Opinion,* the parish newsletter of St. Peter's, he published two pamphlets on theology and liturgy: *My Companion: A Booklet on the Sacrament of Prayer and Penance* and *The Devotions of the Cross.* However, the pamphlet that he is most often remembered for—and the one that, in a sense, came back to haunt him—was *The United States and the Negro,* an Emancipation Day speech delivered at the San Carlos Theatre, 1 January 1907. It was a condemnation of Jim Crow as it encroached upon the liberties of black people, and as such it sums up Demby's ideology on the race issue thus far.

United States was predicated on "the brotherhood of man and the fatherhood of God" in Adam. Demby opposed contemporary anthropological studies suggesting that the human race originated in more than one place. Likewise, he opposed those works propagating a belief in the separate origins of the races, citing one in particular. "Some years ago, a man (?) by the name of Carroll, wrote a book entitled, *The Negro: A Beast.* Each page of the book displays more ignorance to the square inch than in darkest India to the square mile."[56] Racism, he said, is a denial of this obvious truth and there is only one way to attack it:

the one effort of the educated and self-respect[ing] Afro-American is to break down the walls of prejudice between the races: he has long since acknowledged that the only remedy for racial troubles is honest education and true Christian training; he calls for the united support of all black and white teachers and clergymen and men and women of every other honorable calling to be true to their profession [as an example to those] who are largely responsible for the present unhealthy racial conditions: to cultivate each the friendship of the other and thus establish good will which will go a long way in the solution of the race problem in America.[57]

Then, with an eye to that most dangerous impediment to improved race relations, Demby introduced a caveat. He denied that the "brotherhood of man" implies "racial amalgamation"; rather, that the races will ultimately retain their "distinctiveness" and continue to progress in that distinctiveness, which, he said, is good. He was not advocating miscegenation.

Having identified the problem, affirmed the solution, and belayed the objection, Demby moved on to specific complaints, such as the Brownsville affair of August 1906. After the killing of a white man in a shooting spree in Brownsville, Texas, the white citizens of that town blamed the black soldiers encamped nearby, saying that the soldiers attacked the town by night in retaliation for racial indignities. Pursuant to a furtive and racially jaundiced investigation, 167 black soldiers, some of whom had earned the Medal of Honor in Cuba and the Philippines, were issued less than honorable discharges from the United States Army. President Theodore Roosevelt affirmed the tribunal's judgment, and when the nation's black leadership cried out for him to reconsider, he refused to listen. Demby lamented that "Our President had the audacity to recently humiliate us by putting out of the army Afro-American soldiers whose brothers rescued him and caused him to be the President of this great nation."[58]

"Jim Crowism," said Demby, is the unjust punishment for a race whose labor is part and parcel of the making of America. "All we ask for is human treatment—we don't want social equality in any sense: what we want is to be treated as people and not like brutes. Surely, this is not asking too much, is it?" Demby devoted much of his text to the evils of disfranchisement, saying essentially that to disfranchise one group on a racial pretext only invites disfranchisement of other groups on other pretexts, ultimately leading to oligarchy and a violent reaction from the politically dispossessed. The disfranchisement of blacks, he continued, is a particularly gross injustice in light of the thousands of white immigrants who, by virtue of their color and in spite of their ignorance of things American, are allowed to vote. In summary, the Republican Party had abandoned African Americans and should to be taught a lesson in the 1906 election: "The Republican party is each day oppressing the Negroes and the poor ignorant whites and the laboring class who are the back-bone and strength of the commercial and financial institutions of this country; hear me! the Afro-Americans and the laboring classes of whatever color or race, will sweep the Republican Party off of the face of American soil. . . . The only salvation for the Republican Party, as far as we are concerned, is in that champion of human rights and justice[, the] Hon. J. B. Foraker, whom we believe, will be the next President of the United States."[59]

Regarding education, Demby followed the formula "common school education for all, industrial education for the many, and classical education for the few." Moreover, he said, academic standards, salaries, and facilities should be equal, regardless of race. However, he saved his opinion of Booker T. Washington and Tuskegee for the end. After relating statistical evidence to substantiate the educational and material progress of African Americans, he asked the question "Who made Prof. Washington the leader of the race? The same individuals who behind closed doors dictated the speech he recently delivered before the Negro Business League in Atlanta, Ga.?" He lambasted Washington for creating a nationwide monolithic educational structure "which develops the muscles but reduces the brain power." He continued:

> This false system of training the race has worked and is working hardships against our higher institutions of learning; so much so that they have been forced to add industrial adjuncts to retain their few benefactors. . . . [They] must do away with adjuncts of industrialism. . . . Prof. Washington is the Industrial Agent, and the arch-money beggar of the century—at the sacrifice of the manhood, womanhood, dignity, and the miserable humiliation of the race, that is destined to play a more important part in the true development of the Christian civilization of this country. . . . No! Washington is not the leader of the race, he is one of the proficient leaders of the race in his line of life-work of which the race is proud. I admire him as a man, a leader, and one that is doing at least, some good, like the rest in his chosen profession; but when he sits behind closed doors and dictates the educational, political, social, and religious program of the race, I say he is a dangerous man, a proof of which had been too often exhibited.[60]

Demby's protest regarding the declining status of blacks in the United States and the role of Booker T. Washington in that decline encapsulates the racial atmosphere of 1907, a watershed in black Episcopal history. Although Demby does not mention it before his ecumenical audience, 1907 was the year that the missionary district plan, the black Episcopal version of the Atlanta Compromise, did not quite pass in the General Convention; the year that the suffragan bishop plan, a placebo from the predominantly white church, did; the year that W. E. B. Du Bois, a fourth-generation Episcopalian, demanded of the white authorities: "Do not entice [black Episcopalians] to ask for a separation which your unchristian conduct forces them to prefer; do not pretend that the distinctions which you make toward them are distinctions which are made for the larger good of men, but simply confess in humility and self-abasement that you are not able to live up to your Christian vows; that you cannot treat these men as brothers and therefore you are going to set them aside and let them go their half-tended way."[61] Although Demby was a "Du Bois man" not affiliated with the Conference of Church Workers, he was, nevertheless, an enthusiastic proponent of the missionary district plan. In the year preceding the 1907 General Convention, he used *Catholic Opinion* to mobilize his parish behind the plan while he contended for it in the major church weeklies. He published two letters to the editor in the Milwaukee *Living Church* and one in the *Church Standard:* "I am the rector of one . . . of the largest [black parishes] south of New York City, with a communicant list of nearly six hundred, every one of whom is praying for [the passage of the missionary district plan]."[62]

On a more personal note, *United States and the Negro* symbolized a new phase of Demby's ministry. In Tennessee, he won his spurs, so to speak; in Kansas City, he mastered an urban black Episcopal church; in Illinois, he and Mrs. Demby mastered educational enterprise; in Florida, they combined all of their previous experience in a church and school that particularly suited them. There was, in the Demby of Key West, a sense of having arrived, vocationally speaking. Rarely given to outright defiance, Demby tweaked the nose of the most powerful black personage in the land. Heretofore, he had aspired to be a good priest. At St. Peter's he realized that he had become one.

The Dembys also proved their mettle in Key West in ways not readily discernible from diocesan abstracts. In the fall of 1904, they suffered the death of their first and only child, Thomas Benjamin Demby, who perished at two weeks of age. As they recuperated from this tragedy, news came that Mother Ricks, Demby's mother-in-law, had died. Mrs. Demby, being particularly devoted to her mother, grieved deeply over the loss. Meanwhile, storms wrecked the church—twice. And twice they rebuilt. In 1907, Demby became chronically ill and transferred back to Tennessee for health reasons.[63]

Demby's call to Emmanuel Church, Memphis, was serendipitous. Emmanuel was a church ready to be led and Demby was ready to lead it. It was a church doggedly keeping on, waiting on some clerical direction. No fewer than ten part-time or short-term clergy had supervised Emmanuel between 1885 and 1906. According to Roberta Church, granddaughter of Robert R. Church Sr., the Reverend William T. Manning, a future bishop of New York, was curate to Emmanuel during the very early days of his ministry.[64] The old building was far off and bad off. Organized in 1875, Emmanuel was in its second location, a former Lutheran church in downtown Memphis. Unfortunately, many of its parishioners lived far to the south and east, necessitating a long commute. As for the building itself, it was, to quote the official history, "dilapidated and fast becoming uninhabitable." And, to add insult to injury, "the Italian populace residing nearby caused some unrest."[65] Demby was not impressed with the old church of his ordination. It was here that Winchester met him anew. "While I was rector of Calvary Church, Memphis [1905–11], I learned that the missionary at Emmanuel Church was ill. I called and found him and his devoted wife in a bleak little room adjoining the church. Exposed to the cold wind, the Negro missionary was suffering from pneumonia and had no nurse except his wife."[66]

On the other hand, Emmanuel was a church with tremendous potential. It was church home to many of Memphis's aristocrats of color, most notably the Robert R. Churches and the Josiah T. Settles. Church was a banker and businessman, a mainstay of Memphis's black and tan Republican Party who exercised considerable influence in obtaining government appointments for Memphis's black citizens. He was reputedly worth $500,000 and generally regarded as the wealthiest "colored" man in the South. His father was steamboat entrepreneur Captain Charles B. Church, who took him to work on the river as a teenager. Captain Church taught his son to be a gentleman and defend himself against against racial indignities by fighting, if need be. Technically, Church was born into slavery, but always contested the fact by reason of his upbringing. He was not a religious man, to speak of, for most of his life. His creed was primarily one of rugged individualism.[67] His family, however, was overwhelmingly Episcopalian. His mother, Emmeline, a seamstress and a slave of Malaysian descent who "never did any menial work in her life," was reputedly "the first colored person confirmed in the State of Arkansas."[68] His second wife, Anna Wright, as well as her mother, Jane, and aunt, Eliza, were founding members of Emmanuel Church. Anna was the church's organist and choir director.[69] Josiah Settle was a wealthy lawyer, an Episcopalian, and another leader of Memphis's "black and tan" Republicans, the African American contingent of the local party. Drs. E. Irving and O. B. Braithwaite also attended Emmanuel, along with several other notable families of Memphis.[70] Altogether, the church had held on remarkably well over the previous twenty-one years. Its members were determined to remain in business and despite their reputation as a congregation of light-skinned African Americans, they were not dissuaded by the complexion of their new priest. In his memoirs, Demby notes that he was priest to two reputedly bluevein churches before he became a bishop. Undoubtedly Emmanuel was one of them. In both cases, however, the stereotype failed; he was warmly received and enjoyed the love and respect of all of his congregations.[71]

Demby's first objective was to build a new church in a better location, a move which energized Bishop Gailor and practically all of Episcopal Memphis. Settle and Winchester also figured prominently in the move. Gailor sold the old church for $12,000. The money went toward the purchase of two lots on Memphis's southeast side: one for the church itself and one with an existing house. The Diocese of Tennessee helped in part, as did the American Church Building Fund Commission, an agency of the Episcopal Church empowered to loan money for the construction of churches. The new church was Demby's design. It had a Byzantine quality, a cruciform brick structure with a cupola over the intersection of the transept and the nave and icons decorating the interior. Part of the building was set aside as a parish hall and, much to the Dembys' relief, the attractive and comfortable house next door became the rectory. Gailor consecrated the new Emmanuel in March of 1910.

Emmanuel responded enthusiastically to Demby and the move. Thanks to the sacrificial giving of the congregation, the church was well appointed within and even possessed a confessional—a gift from the church's young people and one more evidence of Demby's Anglo-Catholic influence. Membership increased and the services became a sort of musical event. The choir, said Demby, was "the best choir in the city," and the organist, Julia Hooks, was reputedly one of the best in Tennessee. Overflow crowds on Christmas, Palm Sunday, and Easter became commonplace.[72]

Demby seemed to hit his evangelical stride with the move to South Memphis, the most celebrated evidence being the baptism and confirmation of Robert R. Church Sr. In the latter part of 1909, Church underwent instruction in the catechism with the intention of being baptized and confirmed in the Episcopal Church. Although he was widely regarded as a generous and honorable man, not to mention a loving father, Church had somehow escaped the net until his seventieth year. We do not know for sure what inspired him to make the change, but we do know that his mother-in-law, the indomitable Jane Wright, died the same year. In March 1910, immediately following Emmanuel's move to Cynthia Street, Church bent the knee, publicly acknowledged his faith in God, and was baptized by Demby along with fifteen others. Six weeks later, he was confirmed at the hands of Bishop Gailor and made his first communion, thereby completing what might be described as a real-life episode of *Life with Father*. When Church died two years later, Demby conducted his memorial and graveside services. In his eulogy, Demby celebrated Church's baptism and confirmation, and especially his auricular confession and absolution from his sins. He cited Church's two years of pious living as evidence of the depth of his conversion. Then he turned his attention to those present and pointed out, in a very diplomatic way, that Memphis's most important person of color had accumulated a good many critics in his lifetime, as well as friends, and it was time for them to forgive and forget: "It is not my purpose to make you believe or even to think that our dead brother was anything less or more than a man: if he had any imperfections; if he ever gave evidences of ethical weakness; if he ever lived and did, as many of us think, he should not have lived and done . . . he like the rest of us was but human."[73] Demby published his newfound zeal for evangelism in a pamphlet and created a society by the same name, "The Guild of One More Soul." In his spare time he started missions at other locations in Memphis's black community and rode circuit on the missions in nearby Burlison and Covington.[74]

Demby himself became a drawing card. He seemed to be everywhere in Memphis's fraternal societies and charitable enterprises, the embodiment of W. E. B. Du Bois's maxim that "the work of the educated Negro was 'largely the work of leadership.'"[75] He was a charter member of Delta Boulé, the Memphis chapter of Sigma Pi Phi, or Boulé as it is usually called. Established in 1904, Boulé was an attempt to gather together the nation's black elite into one secret fraternal society. In the words of Willard Gatewood: "Boulé's members adhered to a code of unimpeachable personal conduct and in fact constituted a model of the genteel society. The organization shunned publicity, and therefore accounts of its activities rarely appeared in the black press. But contemporaries knowledgeable about the Negro community and social structure were fully aware that Boulé represented, in the words of one member, 'the flower of the race.'"[76] Irving, Braithwaite, and Settle were also members of Delta Boulé. Likewise, Demby was a leading figure with the Elks and the Prince Hall Freemasons, "the oldest and most respected secret fraternity among the blacks of his day."[77] He was also involved in church and secular organizations whose activities crossed racial lines, such as the Southern Conference for Human Welfare, the American Academy of Political and Social Science, and the NAACP. During his years in Tennessee, he established and presided over Associated Charities of Memphis (1913–15) and organized the Sociological Congress of Memphis (1914–18). He remained decidedly assimilationist and integrationist, looking for avenues to benefit the community and improve race relations at the same time.[78]

Like most black clergymen in the South, Demby regarded himself as an ambassador to the white community. Occasionally, this entailed calling the behavior of white authorities into question, which was, to say the least, a very delicate business—even for a man of the cloth. In his memoirs we find him playing the racial intermediary on at least two occasions. To illustrate the criminal absurdities of Jim Crow, Demby describes being shifted, along with the rest of the black passengers, forward and backward in a streetcar by a conductor. When he questioned the shifting, as opposed to the usual practice of making blacks sit in the rear, the conductor explained that there had been several accidents in this "hilly" town. Some of the cars, he said, had "got away" from the motormen, plunging downhill and crashing. After some fatalities, said the conductor, "'an order was issued that in going down such streets the niggers are to sit in the front and up hilly streets the niggers are to sit in the rear.'"[79] Eliciting an explanation, however, did not imply a corresponding ability to intervene, and Demby usually found himself helpless to stop injustice and sometimes agonizingly so. He records one particularly tragic encounter:

> In a Southern town in which I lived, I appeared at the corner of a certain street when two policemen were beating, unmercifully two Negro Boys overgrown for their years, with their clubs. The police knew me. I asked the officers, what was the trouble, and the reply was, "You don't know how much we hate to do this sort of a thing, but if we do not take such characters in hand, respectable people, white and niggers, would not be able to walk our streets." I got busy to learn something definite about the trouble, and it was this: two men, Caucasians, called the boys for some purpose which I did not learn, and because the boys did not take off their hats and say, "Yes sirs," and "No, sirs," they were slapped and a fight was the result and the officers were told of [the] conduct of the boys. [The officers] said to the [boys], hitting them with their clubs at the same time, "Don't you niggers know how to address white people? If not, let this be a lesson to you and such other damn niggers!" The officers took the boys, covered with blood, several blocks from the street where the trouble began, and let them go saying, "If we hear anything about this, it will be too bad for you, so make away or we will shoot both of you!"[80]

An ambulance, says Demby, picked the boys up off the street in the morning. "Such treatment of Negroes is common at most anytime in most of the Southern cities and towns on the slightest provocation."[81]

Pleased with Demby's rapid progress with Emmanuel, Bishop Gailor once again broadened his field. In 1912, Demby became archdeacon for "colored work" in the Diocese of Tennessee and principal of Hoffman-St. Mary's Industrial Institute, Mason, Tennessee—in addition to his duties as priest to Emmanuel Church. For three years he endured this grueling schedule until the appointment of a new priest at Emmanuel relieved him of that obligation. The two other posts, archdeacon and principal, overlapped, but for reasons of clarity should be addressed separately.

Demby arrived in Memphis just as the Diocese of Tennessee was segregating itself. The impetus behind this movement was the campaign for black bishops and the desire on the part of Tennessee's white Episcopalians to remove black representatives from the Tennessee convention. As mentioned in the introduction, the Conference of Church Workers first lobbied on behalf of the missionary district plan prior to the 1904 General Convention. That attempt having failed, they resolved to double their efforts and win the church to the plan before the 1907 convention. Although their intent was to win black representation at the national level as the price of segregation, the resulting debate over the missionary district plan served to crystallize white opposition to black representation in the various conventions of the Southern dioceses. Those opposed to black representation in their diocesan conventions saw in the conference's request a concession to diocesan segregation. In today's terms, this could be compared to a couple debating the various aspects of an impending divorce, such as child support, alimony, property, and so on—the moral issue of divorce, per se, being superseded by the battle over the Chevy. Both sides having acknowledged the inevitability of separation, it only remained for the stronger party to set the terms.

Sometimes the terms of segregation were governed by the widely accepted rationale for segregation, namely, the virtues of black autonomy, lack of strife, and evangelism; sometimes they were dictated by a more racist pretext, that is, the actual source of the "strife." The argument went something like this: (a) African Americans are incompetent for ecclesiastical administration, (b) they are socially inferior, and (c) since they are politically inept and socially inferior, it follows that they should not be part of legislative bodies. This rationale permeates what may be called the convocation movement, the gradual and local enactment of the Sewanee Canon of 1883.

The logjam at the General Convention regarding the desirability of the missionary district plan was no impediment to the segregation of each diocese according to its own plan. By 1920, black Episcopalians in the South were largely disfranchised or organized into separate "convocations" having little or no representation at the diocesan level. The convocations paralleled the white dioceses in geographic jurisdiction but convened separately. They were subordinate to the white bishops and conventions of the white dioceses. Each white diocese regarded its black convocation as its mission to the blacks of the diocese, much like an overseas missionary endeavor; such a separation reinforced the idea of blacks as objects rather than as brethren. In 1931, the General Convention appointed a special commission to investigate the desirability of the missionary district plan in light of the disfranchisement of African Americans in some southern dioceses. The commission recommended to the 1934 General Convention "that the church pass no legislation [the missionary district plan] and allow the individual dioceses to solve this problem."[82] This, in effect, translated into policy what had always been practice.

The convocation movement was grounded in the laity but also had its representatives in the bishopric. True, some southern bishops opposed it and many others were basically only acquiescent, but some wholeheartedly embraced it. Bishops Alfred M. Randolph of Southern Virginia, William M. Brown of Arkansas, and Thomas F. Gailor of Tennessee fall into the last category. According to Randolph, "The question, with reference to the Negro as a legislator in the Episcopal Church, is not a question of race, a question of color, but it is a question of faculty, of ability. It is a question of a capacity of character."[83] As for Brown, he segregated Arkansas out of acquiescence and for all those "higher" reasons named above. Then, he gradually imbibed racism until he ultimately set the standard. He preferred that the blacks should leave the Episcopal Church and establish a separate denomination, also in affiliation with the Anglican Communion. As a corollary, he also championed the expulsion of the "black and tan" element from Arkansas's Republican Party.[84] Gailor was very similar to Brown, but with this variation: rather than exclude African Americans altogether, he believed it in everyone's best interests to keep them in the church, separate and subordinate to the white bishop and convention. Like Brown, he believed that blacks should be politically disfranchised in the secular arena. While he conceded that there were intelligent, property-owning blacks worthy of suffrage, the great mass of black people, said Gailor, were "illiterate, unmoral, and thriftless inferiors." Furthermore, he believed that the racial antagonism aroused by their political presence mitigated against them, just as it mitigated against them in diocesan conventions across the South. "Almost any Republican and Northern school teacher in this part of the country will admit that the elevation of the Negro is well-nigh hopeless so long as he has the right to vote and is consequently the instrument of designing politicians."[85]

Yet Demby did not find Gailor oppressive. Gailor ameliorated his deep-rooted benevolent paternalism with a keen personal interest in all of the Tennessee clergy, whatever their color. He vigorously supported the initiatives of his black priests, as evidenced by the relocation of Emmanuel Church and the reestablishment of Hoffman-St. Mary's Industrial Institute. Furthermore, Gailor's outrage over lynchings in Tennessee boiled over onto the pages of the Memphis *Commercial Appeal* and into his public speaking engagements. We cannot be absolutely sure that it was Gailor, but Demby tells us that he knew a certain bishop who was an outspoken opponent of lynching and "was censured for his attitude by thousands of his people who were Christians."[86] When asked to speak on racially motivated violence and the oppression of blacks in general, Gailor constructed a long speech ending with a page from Demby's book, "The one hope of the world is the belief in Christ's proclamation of the fatherhood of God and the universal brotherhood of man."[87] Gailor's paternalism was the type so often utilized by apologists for Jim Crow; namely, northerners will not do anything to blacks, but neither will they do anything for them.

On some topics Gailor and Demby agreed. For example, they both considered the black "denominational" religious experience to be, generally speaking, long on emotion and short on substance. Moreover, there was something quite genuine in Gailor's concern for black ministries, which Demby acknowledged. In 1935, the Dembys would travel all night to attend his funeral. In 1907, however, the bishop of Tennessee delivered his version of Brown's "God implanted race prejudice" to an equally paternalistic Tennessee convention:

> And yet the [Negro] work languishes, and why? Well, I believe that it is largely due to our system. We would not welcome the day when the church communicants among the Negroes were numbered by the thousands and their representatives would have the right to fill the seats in this convention. We shrink from the thought that people of another race should rule over us in ecclesiastical affairs. We respect our own race; and that is not an earthborn prejudice, but a God-given instinct. A white man who is not jealous for the purity of his blood and [the] supremacy of his race is a degenerate.[88]

Gailor followed with two major pronouncements regarding "Negro work." First, he announced that he wanted to establish a convocation of black churchmen in Tennessee, "which shall meet annually, with the bishop presiding, and discuss the progress and methods of Negro work. This convocation shall have no right to legislate and it shall have only a limited and, in fact, a nominal representation in the diocesan convention. It will hold out to the Negro the right to talk, but no right to do anything. Such a convocation we have already organized, and I ask you to make canonical provision for it at this convention."[89] Second, he announced that he planned to vote for the missionary district plan at the 1907 General Convention, the bottom line being that there would still be enough white oversight, even over a black missionary bishop, to make it feasible. The lesser alternative, called the suffragan bishop plan, would allow the election of black assistant bishops without title or jurisdiction. They would be accountable to one diocesan bishop and officiate in several dioceses at the direction of the bishop of each diocese. In Gailor's opinion, the suffragan plan did not offer enough authority to develop black executive ability.

Gailor's initiatives got mixed reviews. The convention took no immediate action to establish a black convocation in Tennessee, but it did enthusiastically endorse the idea. The Committee on Colored Work, however, had a great many objections regarding Gailor's endorsement of the missionary district plan. They objected on the grounds that the two largest African American convocations in the South, South Carolina and Southern Virginia, were strongly opposed to the plan, and that the plan's loudest proponents were "eastern Negro priests who would . . . not be in the jurisdiction" of such a bishop. The argument that carried the most weight with the committee centered on the allegedly notorious amoral behavior of existing independent black religious organizations in the South. The committee feared the same result for black Episcopal churches constituted under the missionary district plan. "We think that a gradual declension in moral tone is more to be feared than the danger of schism, which has led some to oppose this proposal." The committee endorsed the suffragan bishop plan in light of the fact that it would not write segregation into church law, since the black suffragan bishop would be merely a local application of a generic office. Furthermore, the black suffragan plan would allow for much more in the way of white oversight.[90]

The following year, with Demby present, Gailor reported that he had had a change of heart about the missionary district plan for several reasons: opposition to the plan among African Americans, the absence of qualified black candidates for bishop, the sufficiency of the suffragan bishop plan, and the schismatic nature of the missionary district plan. Having read Bishop Brown's *The Crucial Race Question*, Gailor was "convinced" that the missionary plan would lead to the emergence of a black Episcopal Church. With that, the Diocese of Tennessee laid aside the debate over the plans, ratifying the suffragan plan in 1910.[91]

In 1909, the Diocese of Tennessee passed the Colored Convocation of the Diocese of Tennessee into law, consolidating nine missions and six clergy into an organization paralleling the Tennessee convention. The Reverend A. M. Hildebrand was the first black archdeacon of the convocation and presided over its first meeting, held at the Emmanuel Church the following year, just two weeks before consecration of the new building. Demby was secretary for the first two years, succeeding Hildebrand as archdeacon in 1912. Demby also held the title "Dean of the Colored Convocation."

As archdeacon, Demby exercised intermediate oversight of about six hundred black communicants, as well as representing the bishop and convention before the convocation and the convocation before the bishop and convention. He had the responsibility of organizing and moderating the convocation's annual meetings, delivering annual reports to both the convocation and the convention, keeping an agenda for the future of the convocation, representing the convocation before church and civic groups, and supervising parochial schools.

Demby's 1915 report to the convocation, published as a pamphlet with his photograph emblazoned inside the cover, is typical of his conservative high churchmanship and his oratory. He was far more the sacramentalist than the revivalist; far more the exhorter than the critic. He challenged Tennessee's black clergy to promote religious education in their schools and churches, in stark and wholesome contrast, he said, to the excessive emotion and lack of sound instruction that seemed to plague the black religious experience as a whole. He offered a reading list for their perusal, which included all the leading church newspapers except the *Church Advocate,* the unofficial organ of the Conference of Church Workers. Presumably he found it too radical. He rejoiced at the efforts of Baptists, Congregationalists, Presbyterians, and Methodists to unify their respective denominations. Denominational unification, he said, heralded the "organic unity" of the church. "We may not live to see it," he proclaimed, "but ere long it shall come to pass, the return of modern sectarian and Protestant churches to the Church of the Ages," leading ultimately to convergence in the "one, holy, catholic, and apostolic church." Organic unity, added Demby, would cure a multitude of sins, "racial arrogancy" among them. Moving to the practicalities of establishing unity, he implicitly endorsed the suffragan plan: "[Regarding] the healing of Protestantism among colored Americans . . . I believe . . . that the bestowal of the episcopacy in some historic and catholic form upon a few of our own clergy . . . will mean much in creating true interest in the organic unity of of American Christianity among our people."[92] On a less optimistic and somewhat contradictory note, he called for a renewed enthusiasm for the sacraments of the church in light of the spiritual lethargy in the church and the country at large.

Then Demby set aside his exhortation for a moment in order to register a specific complaint against the Episcopal Church. In a tone reminiscent of *The United States and the Negro,* he lamented the small numbers of black Episcopalians in Tennessee versus "the rise of [much larger] organized colored religious denominations . . . under the religious excitement of uneducated, untrained, and inexperienced leaders playing upon the sympathies and prejudices of their people." Demby laid the blame for their success upon the Episcopal Church and its recalcitrant attitude toward black ministries since the Civil War: "Had the American Church exercised the same wisdom in dealing with her colored members in the Southland as she did with the white, I believe three-fourths of our people in these parts would be today communicants of the American Church. . . . The Church in her general and diocesan efforts to Christianize and educate our people has had in view the few instead of the many, the classes instead of the masses, and that, too, with as little money as possible."[93] A virtual paraphrase of W. E. B. Du Bois's well-known remark that no "aggregate of Christians" had done less for black people than the Episcopal Church,[94] the statement shows that the Demby of Key West was not totally subdued by the paternalism of Tennessee. He would grow less outspoken in the years to come.

Before closing, he returned to form, rejoicing at the opportunities before the convocation and calling for no fewer than four new rectories, two new high schools, two new elementary schools, three new chapels, and repairs to the churches at Mason and Burlison, which he called "a disgrace to the American church."

Being archdeacon helped prepare Demby for the episcopate. As the bishop's representative, he became liaison between Gailor and Tennessee's black Episcopalians, influencing the distribution of missionary funds and the placement and recruiting of black clergy. Since a bishop is primarily a pastor to priests, the new appointment gave Demby the opportunity to grow in that direction.

His chief claim to fame, however, was the reestablishment of the diocese's primary educational enterprise for African Americans, Hoffman-St. Mary's Industrial Institute, Mason, Tennessee. The new school was the reconstruction of two defunct experiments in education: Hoffman Hall and St. Mary's Training School for Colored Girls, both in Nashville. Demby, of course, was a former vice-principal of Hoffman Hall. In the years since he left Nashville, Hoffman had gone into decline. It had eventually been dissolved, being replaced by St. Mary's on the same property.

Hoffman was the brainchild of Gailor's predecessor, the Right Reverend Charles T. Quintard, bishop of Tennessee. Quintard needed black clergy, as did most southern bishops of the late nineteenth century. Their main problem was an overall lack of commitment to the evangelization of blacks on the part of white Southerners. According to Harold Lewis, there was no shortage of black candidates for ministry, but they strove against an unwillingness on the part of white Southerners to bring into the church those very people who, in many cases, were once their slaves.[95] White people preoccupied with trying to repair their devastated homeland preferred to look upon the freedmen as a remote missionary project, like Chinese or African missions—and prioritized their giving accordingly. Married to this apathy was the fear of black representation in diocesan conventions and the social intermingling that might result. With

the exception of the Sewanee Canon, the southern bishops dealt with this issue individually, each according to his own wisdom. Quintard, Gailor tells us,
despaired "of getting Negro ministers who would become satisfactory leaders for our Southern Negroes, secured a gift of money from the Rev. Dr. Charles
F. Hoffman of New York, and opened a theological school for Negro students
in . . . Nashville, and a white clergyman, the Rev. C. S. Bassett, was placed in
charge."[96]

Hoffman Hall was short-lived, a casualty of the vision that brought it into
being and of geography. The main problem, it seems, was its proximity to Fisk
University. At the time when Demby was vice-principal, Hoffman's eighteen
students were completing much of their course work at nearby Fisk, an elite
black college affiliated with the Congregational Church. Fisk boasted high
academic standards comparable to those of most white colleges and universities and a faculty representing the cream of southern black intelligentsia. Apparently this arrangement worked for a few years. The Reverend C. A. Caswall,
Tennessee's archdeacon for "colored work," reported in 1898: "[The students
of Hoffman Hall] make good progress in their studies at Fisk University, and
received high encomiums from the professors and teachers."[97] However, seminary and university had a falling out of some kind, resulting in the closure of
the seminary and, eventually, the sale of the property. Bishop Gailor explains,
"Unfortunately, the young men who applied for admission [to Hoffman] had
not the academic preparation to fit them for theological studies and the attitude of the nearby [Fisk] University was not favorable to the enterprise."[98]

Consequently, the diocese closed down the seminary and, "in response to many
appeals," opened an industrial school for black girls on the same property—St.
Mary's Training School for Colored Girls, "where girls of approved character and
intelligence might be given an industrial education." "This school," says Gailor,
"was even more displeasing to the students of Fisk." It limped along until the
Reverend A. M. Hildebrand became archdeacon in charge of "colored work" in
Tennessee. Then Gailor sold the property and he, Hildebrand, and Demby relocated the school to Mason, Tennessee, in 1912. Mason was chosen because of
the "generous cooperation" of Edward Tarry of nearby Keeling, who offered to
sell 110 acres of land at a very reasonable price. In addition, Mason enjoyed a
"large Negro population of very respectable farmers," and, of course, St. Paul's
Church, the site of Demby's ordination to the diaconate. While Gailor and Hildebrand chose the site and completed the sale, Demby was the one most responsible for the actual reestablishment of the school.[99]

We are told that Hoffman-St. Mary's Industrial Institute, so named by Bishop Gailor, was truly "born in a barn," that being the only building available at

the outset. The curriculum included sewing, cooking, housekeeping, and farm-ing in addition to reading, writing, arithmetic, and religious education. And the school strove to support itself. Students worked the farm and operated a cannery. At its inception, Hoffman-St. Mary's boasted the only high school in Tipton County. The people of the county, black and white, fell behind the school enthusiastically. For example, when Bishop Gailor contemplated erec-tion of new buildings to replace the original structures in the early years of the Great Depression, Tipton county farmers "pledged five thousand dollars in labor and gifts towards the erection of the new buildings." In its heyday, it had a student body of about 250 students.

During his tenure at Hoffman-St. Mary's, Demby experienced a change of heart with regard to Booker T. Washington and industrial education, symbol-ized by the affiliation of Hoffman-St. Mary's with the American Church In-stitute for Negroes. Being essentially a third reconstruction of the old Protes-tant Episcopal Freedmen's Commission, the ACIN was an autonomous body affiliated with the Board of Missions. It gradually consolidated all of the black Episcopal colleges in the South into one organization for their mutual benefit, and, as previously mentioned, promoted the systematic implementation of industrial education at those same schools, resulting in a more secular outlook. We have no record of Demby's opinion of the institute at the time of its estab-lishment in 1906, but we can guess that it had his tacit approval, at best. Be that as it may, the founding father of Hoffman-St. Mary's concluded that Booker T. Washington had chosen wisely, given the handicaps of African Americans in the South. Industrial education—with the appropriate modifications—was about the best that could be done in many cases. Hoffman-St. Mary's was a hybrid of the Episcopal catechism, liberal education, and industrial educa-tion—in that order. Demby writes: "We are determined to make this institu-tion a great blessing to all young people by giving them [an education, but] not at the sacrifice of what is commonly called higher education. Any educa-tion that is an every-day working education and makes the recipient exhibit the qualities of Christian manhood and womanhood, industry, thriftiness, decency, respectability, and citizenship . . . is the higher education that is need-ed by every people."[100] This is not to say that he was wholeheartedly in favor of industrial education. Evidence suggests that it always rankled him, because it implied a second-class education for a lesser people, but he left Tennessee more of a believer than when he arrived.

Demby always left his charges when they were in bloom, because success, being what it is, creates opportunities. So it was with Tennessee. In the spring of 1917, his old friend and colleague, James R. Winchester, visited Mason in his new capacity as bishop of Arkansas. Winchester brought along two other bishops and an offer.[101]

NOTES

1. George F. Bragg Jr., *History of the Afro-American Group of the Protestant Episcopal Church* (Baltimore: Church Advocate Press, 1922), 47–48, 64–68; see also Harold T. Lewis, *Yet with a Steady Beat: The African-American Struggle for Recognition in the Episcopal Church* (Valley Forge, Pa.: Trinity Press International, 1996), 27–31.

2. Demby's urgency to recall the past and pass on the wisdom of his eighty-four years of experience is evident in the rambling topical style in which he speaks his mind. As a young priest realizing his potential as a man of letters, he wrote to instruct in the liturgy, the sacraments, the devotional life, and evangelism. The manual was his forte and his style was lucid and succinct. In his early years as bishop, however, his writing style began to deteriorate noticeably as he turned from his first love in order to concentrate on reports and exhortations. He became less inclined to objectify the spiritual life on paper as his ministry made progressively greater demands upon him. In the aftermath of the Newport incident, described in chapter 5, his style took another noticeable turn for the worse, and by the time of his speech to the House of Bishops in 1940, discussed in chapter 7, he was overwhelmingly the exhorter. Despite a voracious reading habit, writing was simply not the priority that it had once been. When he wrote to inspire, which was his usual intent, he habitually rambled and made grammatical errors. The trend continued through the 1940s, culminating in "Off of the Record." Only volume 7, the biography of his wife, Antoinette Martina Ricks Demby, follows a clear chronological format, relating the high points of a life no less unique than his own.

3. J. W. Yancy, *Meet the Most Illustrious Dean of Paul Quinn College* (Waco, Tex.: n.p., n.d.), Bishop Edward Thomas Demby Biographical File, Archives of the Episcopal Church, Austin, Tex., 5.

4. Edward T. Demby to Paul Anderson, 17 June 1953, Demby Family Papers, Manuscripts, Archives, and Rare Books Division, Schomburg Center for Research in Black Culture, New York Public Library Astor, Lenox, and Tilden Foundations, New York, box 1, folder 6, hereafter cited as the Demby Family Papers.

5. Addison W. Sommerville to E. T. Demby, 25 June 1950, including an excerpt from Addison W. Sommerville and F. C. Sumner, "The Persistence of Vocational Preference in Successful Individuals," *Journal of Psychology* 30 (1950), box 1, folder 6, Demby Family Papers.

6. Edward T. Demby, black notebook, box 2, Demby Family Papers, 16–17, hereafter cited as black notebook.

7. Ibid., 25.

8. Ibid., 24.

9. Ibid., 16.

10. Ibid., 17–18.

11. Gina Pressley, "The Black History of Delaware," MS, [1976], Typescript File, Historical Society of Delaware, Wilmington, Del. At the time of Demby's birth, Delaware could best be described as an unreconstructed southern state in its treatment of its black citizens. Delaware's solidly Democratic legislature "emphatically rejected the Thirteenth, Fourteenth, and Fifteenth amendments" and openly declared, as did its governor, its intention to keep the black populace in a servile condition. Although this attitude gradually became more understated and was mollified by the actions of educational philanthropists such as Pierre S. Du Pont, it did not change appreciably until the advent of the civil rights movement. Thus, Demby's upbringing, and especially his education, were unique for a state which had only two black high schools as late as 1921. See also Milford Gilchrist, "The Black Man in Delaware during the Reconstruction Period," MS, [1970], Typescript File, Historical Society of Delaware, Wilmington, Del.

12. E. T. Demby, "A Purview Reminiscent Felicitation of a Friend of Many Years; The Number Let Him Tell," letter or address by proxy celebrating the accomplishments of an unidentified friend at an unidentified gathering in Wilmington, Del., 1947, box 1, folder 1, Demby Family Papers, 9.

13. Demby, black notebook, 15.

14. For some residents of black Wilmington, the Big Quarterly also represented class conflict. In 1932, Alice Dunbar Nelson, one of Wilmington's more famous aristocrats of color, scolded her peers for their snobbish attitude toward the Quarterly: "No amount of disgust and frowning upon the quaint custom by the high-brows of the race can change the mental attitude of the hoi-polloi" (Alice Dunbar Nelson, "Big Quarterly in Wilmington," excerpted from *Every Evening,* 27 Aug. 1932, Historical Society of Delaware, Wilmington, Del.).

15. Demby, black notebook, 24.

16. Dorothy Demby and Elizabeth Demby Payne, interview by author, 14 Oct. 1995, New York, transcript.

17. Demby, black notebook, 17.

18. Willard B. Gatewood Jr., *Aristocrats of Color: The Black Elite, 1880–1920* (Bloomington: Indiana University Press, 1990), 253.

19. Demby, black notebook, 19; Gatewood, *Aristocrats of Color,* 265–66; Rev. Canon Thomas S. Logan Sr., interview by author, 19 Oct. 1995, Yeadon, Pa., transcript; Yancy, *Meet the Dean,* 5–10.

20. E. T. Demby, "A Biographical Epitome of Antoinette Martina Ricks Demby," MS, James Weldon Johnson Collection, Yale Collection of American Literature, Beinecke Rare Book and Manuscript Library, Yale University, New Haven, Conn., 15, 21–25, hereafter cited as "Epitome."

21. Ibid., 1–8; Demby, black notebook, 81–82.

22. Demby, black notebook, 81–82.

23. Yancy, *Meet the Dean,* 1–5.

24. Demby, black notebook, 20.

25. *Church Advocate,* Jan. 1918, 2.

26. Northern Ohio Chapter of the Union of Black Episcopalians, *He Is as He Ever Was,* a compilation of documents commemorating the dedication of Bishop Demby's gravestone, (Cleveland, Ohio: Northern Ohio Chapter of the Union of Black Episcopalians, 1992), 5, hereafter cited as *He Is.*

27. Ibid., 5, 7, 9.

28. Edward T. Demby, "Off of the Record since 1939," MS, James Weldon Johnson Collection, Yale Collection of American Literature, Beinecke Rare Book and Manuscript Library, Yale University, New Haven, Conn., 74–77, hereafter cited as "Off of the Record."

29. *Church Advocate,* Jan. 1918, 2.

30. Anna M. Skillern to Edward T. Demby, 17 Dec. 1918, Edward T. Demby Collection, St. Matthew's Episcopal Church, Wilmington, Del., hereafter cited as St. Matthew's Papers; Allen D. Breck, *The Episcopal Church in Colorado, 1860–1963* (Denver: Big Mountain Press, 1963), 124.

31. Bragg, *History,* 183, 220; H. Lewis, *Yet with a Steady Beat,* 200.

32. Gatewood, *Aristocrats of Color,* 275.

33. Demby, "Off of the Record," 112.

34. "Statistics of Colored Work," *Journal of the Proceedings of the Annual Council of the Protestant Episcopal Diocese of Tennessee* (1898): 95, hereafter cited as *Tennessee Journal.*

35. *Church Advocate,* Jan. 1918, 1.

36. Thomas F. Gailor, "Official Acts," *Tennessee Journal* (1898): 67.

37. *Church Advocate,* Jan. 1918, 1.

38. Demby, black notebook, 69–70.

39. James R. Winchester to Edward T. Demby, 24 May 1931, *He Is,* 3.

40. *Church Standard,* 22 Dec. 1906, 258. In reminiscing about St. Stephen's, Demby does not actually name the church. He speaks of a church that he was put in charge of "seven years ago" and then goes on to describe it. Given the date of the article and the "Abstract of Parochial Reports" from the 1899 *Tennessee Journal,* the church in question would be St. Stephen's.

41. E. T. Demby, "Report of the Suffragan Bishop for Negro Work," *Journal of the Annual Convention of the Protestant Episcopal Diocese of Arkansas* (1927): 74.

42. Robert C. Caswall, "Report of the Archdeacon for Colored Work," *Tennessee Journal* (1898): 42.

43. *Church Advocate,* Jan. 1918, 2; Isaac and Ruth DeLoach James to Edward T. Demby, 9 Feb. 1918, St. Matthew's Papers; Harry E. Rahming to Thomas S. Logan Sr., 10 May 1978, Private Correspondence of the Reverend Thomas S. Logan Sr., Yeadon, Pa.

44. Demby, "Epitome," 63–86; Antoinette Ricks Demby Professional Papers, box 3, folders 4 and 5, Demby Family Papers.

45. See Mary S. Donovan, *A Separate Call: Women's Ministries in the Episcopal Church, 1850–1920* (Wilton, Conn.: Morehouse-Barlow, 1986), 1–6.

46. Demby, "Epitome," 26–32.

47. Demby, black notebook, 16–17, 25.

48. *Diocese of Springfield,* Feb. 1902, 30.

49. Ibid., Mar. 1903, 37.

50. Ibid., Jan. 1904, 4–6; see H. Lewis, *Yet with a Steady Beat,* 125–36.

51. Demby, black notebook, 21.

52. *Journal of the 27th Annual Synod of the Holy Catholic Church in the Diocese of Springfield and Two Special Synods* (1904), abstract for 1903.

53. *Church Advocate,* Apr. 1915, 2.

54. The Dembys' relationship to St. Alban's School is deduced from abstracts of the Diocese of South Florida, the timing of their arrival, the nature of their ministry, Bishop Demby's all-too-brief recollections of Cairo and Key West from his memoirs, and the fact that St. Alban's was an outreach project of St. Peter's. While he boasted that Mrs. Demby was headmistress at St. Michael's, Cairo, Demby does not mention their relationship to St. Alban's School, or even that it existed. On the other hand, he notes that St. Michael's student body numbered 150 students during Mrs. Demby's tenure, which, taken in light of the South Florida abstracts, leads one to believe that he may have confused St. Michael's with St. Alban's, and that she may have been principal to both schools. Although the author was unable to verify the 150 student figure in connection with St. Michael's, the South Florida abstract for 1906 indicates that 150 students enrolled at St. Alban's that year. A Sister Myrtle Catherine, affiliated with the Convent of the Transfiguration, Glendale, Ohio, attended St. Peter's during Demby's tenure and mentions attending the St. Peter's parochial school, which, according to the abstracts, must necessarily have been St. Alban's. *Journal of the Annual Council of the Protestant Episcopal Diocese of South Florida* (1907), abstract for 1906; ibid. (1906), abstract for 1905; ibid. (1905), abstract for 1904; ibid. (1904), abstract for 1903; E. T. Demby to Sister Myrtle Catherine, 9 Nov. 1945, box 1, folder 5, Demby Family Papers; Demby, black notebook, 21–22.

55. Demby, black notebook, 21–22.

56. Edward T. Demby, *The United States and the Negro,* 4. *United States* is located in the black notebook.

57. Ibid., 5–6.

58. Ibid., 10. See Nathan Miller, *Theodore Roosevelt: A Life* (New York: Morrow, 1992), 465–69.

59. Demby, *United States,* 14.

60. Ibid., 19–21.

61. Booker T. Washington and W. E. B. Du Bois, *The Negro in the South: His Economic Progress in Relation to His Moral and Religious Development,* in *Writings by W. E. B. Du Bois in Non-Periodical Literature Edited by Others,* ed. Herbert Aptheker (Millwood, N.Y.: Kraus-Thomson, 1982), 94.

62. E. T. Demby, "The Question of Negro Bishops," *Church Standard,* 22 Dec. 1906, 258.

63. Demby, "Epitome," 33, 37; Demby, black notebook, 22.

64. Roberta Church, interview by author, 17 Aug. 1994, Memphis, Tenn., transcript.

65. Emmanuel Episcopal Church, *Centennial Celebration: Emmanuel Episcopal Church, November 21–23, 1975* (Memphis, Tenn.: Emmanuel Episcopal Church, 1975), 10.

66. James R. Winchester, "A Pastoral Experience, No. 11: God's Faithful Servant," Bishop Edward T. Demby File, box 13, RG 282, Bishop James R. Winchester Papers, Archives of the Episcopal Church, U.S.A., Austin, Tex.

67. Gatewood, *Aristocrats of Color,* 19

68. Annette E. Church and Roberta Church, *The Robert R. Churches of Memphis: A Father and Son Who Achieved in Spite of Race* (Ann Arbor, Mich.: Edwards Brothers for Annette E. Church and Roberta Church, 1974), 4, 29–30

69. Roberta Church and Ronald Walter, *Nineteenth Century Memphis Families of Color,* ed. Charles W. Crawford (Memphis, Tenn.: Murdock Printing for Roberta Church and Ronald Walter, 1987), 114–16.

70. T. O. Fuller, *History of the Church Life among Negroes in Memphis* (n.p., n.d.), excerpt, located in Demby, "Off of the Record," 397; Demby, black notebook, 23.

71. Demby, "Off of the Record," 112.

72. Demby, black notebook, 22–24. Said Demby, "I never saw church people give of their small means as did the communicants of Emmanuel Church."

73. E. T. Demby, The Order of Service for the Late Col. Robert Reed Church, Sr., 1 Sept. 1912, box 1, folder 7, Demby Family Papers.

74. Ibid.; A. M. Hildebrand, "Report of the Archdeacon for Colored Work," *Tennessee Journal* (1910): 36; E. T. Demby, *Address by the Reverend Venerable E. Thomas Demby to the Ninth Convocation of Colored Churchmen in the Diocese of Tennessee, April 1915,* Bishop Thomas F. Gailor Papers, University of the South Archives, Dupont Library, University of the South, Sewanee, Tenn., 14, hereafter cited as Gailor Papers; Demby, black notebook, 23.

75. W. E. B. Du Bois, *The College-Bred Negro American* (Atlanta: Atlanta University Press, 1910), 73, quoted in Gatewood, *Aristocrats of Color,* 247.

76. Gatewood, *Aristocrats of Color,* 234.

77. Ibid., 212.

78. Fuller, *Church Life,* excerpt, located in Demby, "Off of the Record," 397.

79. Demby, "Off of the Record," 68.

80. Ibid., 69.

81. Ibid.

82. *Journal of the General Convention of the Protestant Episcopal Church* (1934), quoted in David M. Reimers, "Negro Bishops and Diocesan Segregation in the Protestant Episcopal Church: 1870–1954," *Historical Magazine of the Protestant Episcopal Church* 31 (Sept. 1962): 239.

83. Alfred M. Randolph, address to the Virginia convention (1899), quoted in Odell Greenleaf Harris, *A History of the Seminary to Prepare Black Men for the Ministry of the Protestant Episcopal Church* (Alexandria: Virginia Theological Seminary, 1980), 46; and H. Lewis, *Yet with a Steady Beat,* 69.

84. David E. Finch, "Little Rock's Red Bishop Brown and His Separate Black Church," *Pulaski County Historical Review* 20 (Sept. 1972): 29.

85. Thomas F. Gailor to the *New York Journal,* n.d., Gailor Papers.

86. Demby, "Off of the Record," 70. Outraged by a particularly gruesome lynching, which was even more unjust than most, Gailor established himself as an anti-lynching activist with a speech titled "The Lynching in Fayette County." See T. F. Gailor, "The Lynching in Fayette County," Gailor Papers.

87. T. F. Gailor, "The Law and the Negro," Gailor Papers.

88. T. F. Gailor, "Bishop's Address," *Tennessee Journal* (1907): 40.

89. Ibid.

90. "Report of the Committee on Colored Work," *Tennessee Journal* (1907): 54–56.

91. T. F. Gailor, "Bishop's Address," *Tennessee Journal* (1908): 48–49.

92. E. T. Demby, *Address to the Ninth Convocation,* 7, Gailor Papers.

93. Ibid., 10, 11.

94. W. E. B. Du Bois, *The Negro Church* (Atlanta: Atlanta University Press, 1903), 139.

95. H. Lewis, *Yet with a Steady Beat,* 51.

96. T. F. Gailor, "The Church and the Negro," Gailor Papers, 5.

97. Robert C. Caswall, "Report of the Archdeacon for Colored Work," *Tennessee Journal* (1898): 43.

98. Gailor, "Church and the Negro," 5.

99. Ibid., 5–6.

100. Demby, *Address to the Ninth Convocation,* 14.

101. Demby's influence with Hoffman-St. Mary's continued long after his departure. The Reverend George A. Stams, whom Demby called "my son in the faith and the ministry," was the principal of Hoffman-St. Mary's from 1926 to 1938.

2

Arkansas Prologue

One of the recurring themes of this study is that outward circumstances have defined the inner life of the Episcopal Church, especially when it comes to race relations; the church's predilection for order makes this so. This necessarily makes the context of Bishop Demby's ministry extremely important, for his was a ministry largely defined by the circumstances in which he found it. This chapter is devoted to describing the lay of the social, political, and ecclesiastical land that he inherited. Before proceeding to the episcopal election of the Right Reverend Edward T. Demby, let us look at his election in light of the diocese that elected him; let us place the suffragan experiment in its historical context.

By 1917, Arkansas had become a pioneer in segregated Episcopal government. However, those privy to the establishment of the Diocese of Arkansas know that this pioneering spirit, as it were, was in fact a reaction, a swinging of the pendulum away from a far more egalitarian venture that preceded it. This is the story of Bishop Henry Niles Pierce and his successor, Bishop William M. Brown; a story of Civil War and Reconstruction; a story of the Solid South and the advent of Jim Crow; a story of Democratic ascendancy and Republican demise; a story of high church versus low; a story of the preeminence of order.

Had Demby met Pierce, Arkansas's fourth missionary bishop and first diocesan bishop, he would have liked him immediately. Pierce could be described as high church with spurs. A native of Rhode Island and an instructor of mathematics at Brown University, he converted to the Episcopal Church as an adult, being persuaded that the Episcopal Church was in every respect the hub of orthodoxy, the "one, holy, catholic, and apostolic" church to which practically every denomination in the United States owed its existence. Pierce personified the Anglo-Catholic Revival. He relished the ecclesiastical, architectural, and liturgical changes attendant to the Oxford Movement. He loved vestments, choral services, chanting, and Gothic Revival architecture. He valued the sacraments more than the pulpit. He despised pew rentals and strongly disapproved of congregational government, which operated, ex officio, throughout the church. Conversely, he rejoiced to see bishops build cathedrals and centralize church government. He excelled in the jot and tittle of church law, avoiding irregularities like an ominous rattle beside the water hole. He revered offices and downplayed personalities. Pierce so cherished the idea of the church unification that he took a leading role at the early Lambeth Conferences and, despite the demands of establishing a frontier diocese, only ceased attending Lambeth when he realized that the Eastern and Anglican churches could not resolve their differences over the wording of the Nicene Creed.[1]

Pierce was imposing. Mated to his high churchmanship was an irrepressible missionary spirit. A robust man with a powerful voice, he would gladly "talk church" with captive audiences on every boat, barge, carriage, coach, and railroad car that carried him. His Episcopal critics complained, with some justification, that he was autocratic and overly manipulative in his exercise of episcopal authority, and his most virulent opponents went so far as to condemn him as a scheming politician in episcopal robes. Documentation, however, does not entirely bear out Pierce's conspiratorial image, which was the product of fears real and imagined. He certainly had an agenda for Episcopal Arkansas and he pressed it home with every canonical prerogative at his disposal. Yet he could be both painstakingly circumspect and forthright on controversial issues. However manipulative he may have been, it is equally obvious that the opposition, which was just as passionate about its own agenda, was somewhat intimidated by him personally and, being intimidated, habitually "saw through" him.

Pierce served in Texas, Louisiana, New Jersey, Alabama, and Illinois before coming to Arkansas. His achievements were most noteworthy in the South. In the late 1840s, he was being tutored in preparation for the ministry but had to leave Rhode Island for Texas because of health reasons. Ordained by the Right Reverend George Washington Freeman, missionary bishop of Arkansas and the Indian Territory "south of 36½ degrees and to exercise supervision over the missions of this Church in the Republic of Texas," Pierce was the first Episcopal clergyman ordained in the Republic of Texas. Freeman appointed him general missionary to Texas and Pierce organized at least two churches and pastored a third during his tenure. However, he truly defined his pastoral ministry in the summer of 1858, when he and a Roman Catholic priest were the only ministers to remain in Mobile, Alabama, through the yellow fever epidemic that swept through the city.[2] To top it all off, and complicate everything else, Pierce was unabashedly "catholic" in the sense that Demby used it. "Good old Bishop Pierce," as the Reverend George F. Bragg liked to call him, believed that all people, blacks included, were equals before God and especially in the church.[3]

This is not to say that Pierce acted without caution on matters of race. Consecrated by six southern bishops and one northern bishop, he was no stranger to the mores governing race relations in Arkansas. He was resolute but understated, preferring to act on racial issues rather than engage in public debate, which, no doubt, contributed to his autocratic image. On the other hand, he was prepared to practice ecclesiastical equality, though not at the price of social intermingling, which, he said, "would be for both [races] alike unpleasant."[4] He hoped to achieve the one without involving the other.

Initially, it seemed that Pierce and the Diocese of Arkansas were determined to set a new standard for black ministries in the South. In 1871, the General Convention of the Episcopal Church, alarmed at the postwar exodus of southern black Episcopalians to all-black denominations, exhorted Episcopalians everywhere to lend "hearty, united, and systematic support" to missionary work among the freedmen. The Primary Convention of the Diocese of Arkansas, meeting just two months before the General Convention, anticipated the concern of the national body and acted in kind. They resolved that "it is the duty of the Diocese to organize a plan by which the claims of the Protestant Episcopal Church may be brought before the colored people of this state, with a view towards educating worthy and promising young men of African descent for the ministry."[5] Based on the experiences of the Protestant Episcopal Freedmen's Commission, the church's principal agency to aid the freed slaves, this was the primary consideration of the moment. The exodus, said the commission, would continue until black clergy ran the churches and black teachers ran the schools.[6]

Running contrary to the wisdom of ordaining black clergy, however, was the resistance of white southerners to include black churches and clergy in their conventions. In 1869, for example, the Diocese of Virginia voted down the incorporation of St. Stephen's, Petersburg, a black parish, despite several "radical speeches upon the floor of the convention for the full and free admission of colored delegates."[7] Likewise, the Reverend George F. Bragg, a young parishioner of St. Stephen's in 1869, tells us that Bishop Thomas Atkinson of North Carolina organized black parishes and had them admitted to the North Carolina convention "in the face of a hard, bitter, and unrelenting prejudice." He continues: "And when the Standing Committee refused to pass the papers of a colored candidate for holy orders, [he] invited two 'Yankee' Negro priests to come into his diocese, and admitted them into full privileges in his convention. Other Southern bishops labored earnestly to do the same thing, but could not."[8]

By comparison the Diocese of Arkansas seemed totally uninhibited by racial norms. When a South Carolina clergyman inquired as to whether the Diocese of Arkansas would unqualifiedly accept black clergy and churches into the Arkansas convention, the secretary of the diocese replied that he believed that it would. At its next assembly, the Arkansas convention made the secretary's theory a fact, the Reverend Caleb A. Bruce presenting a successful resolution "that the [convention] cordially approved the answer sent by the secretary and hereby express in our official capacity our desire to welcome such congregation and clergy to all the rights and privileges of this [convention]."[9] Bruce was an outspoken "Scot Anglican" in the mold of his friend Bishop Pierce, who had recruited him out of Illinois.[10]

For the moment, however, there were no black churches or clergy to welcome, a situation brought about by demographics and the Civil War. Before the war, most, if not all, of Arkansas's black Episcopalians were slaves. Arkansas's earliest Episcopal churches were established by Bishop, later Confederate general, Leonidas K. Polk. Polk was a Tennessee slaveowner and one of those Episcopalians most concerned with holding masters accountable for the religious lives of their slaves. The establishment of slave chapels was a trademark of his ministry. Rt. Rev. Henry C. Lay, Arkansas's bishop during the Civil War, was like-minded, confirming slaves here and there and holding services for them in the afternoons. On Easter Sunday, 1861, for instance, he baptized forty-nine slaves at St. John's Church, Helena.[11] Yet however effective Arkansas's white Episcopalians may have been in evangelizing blacks prior to secession, their actions were all but negated by war and Reconstruction. No longer constrained by the slave/master relationship, Arkansas's Episcopal freedmen joined the postwar exodus into all-black churches. "The history of the church among the Negroes of Arkansas," says Demby, "is very meager; in fact there is nothing really reliable . . . outside of certain families who were members before the Civil War, during which the old relations were broken up, due to the horrors of war and the new conditions."[12] Despite the fact that Lay was one of two southern bishops consulted on the establishment of the Protestant Episcopal Freedman's Commission, and that he invited the commission to work in Arkansas, it would appear that very little came of his efforts.

That is not to say that Arkansas's white Episcopalians ignored the plight of the freedmen. According to Randy Finley, historian of Reconstruction Arkansas, they "led the way in favor of schools for blacks. Fort Smith Episcopalians purchased books from New York for neighboring black schools, which prompted the [Federal Freedmen's] bureau agent Pinkney Lugenbeel to vow, 'The Episcopalians are the only persons here who are interesting themselves in the education of colored children.'"[13] Lay wanted to start a school for "colored" girls in conjunction with Christ Church, Little Rock, but was handicapped by a war-ravaged jurisdiction preoccupied with economic recovery and a populace indifferent—if not opposed—to the development of black ministries. Indeed, a quotation from his 1866 report to the Board of Missions suggests that his enthusiasm for "Negro work" may have been qualified by other developments: "At Fort Smith during the month of March, rations were issued by the Government to 3,107 white persons. Poor creatures! The road was full of them. A woman walking forty miles sometimes with a child in her arms to draw some bread and bacon, which she must carry on her shoulders to the children at home. Not a tithe of the misery can be reached. The Freedmen are well-to-do."[14]

Lay was also stymied by demographics. The key to the establishment and growth of black Episcopal churches has always been an independent and viable black leadership. Thus, it is no surprise that the slave chapels that proliferated in the antebellum South did not survive the war. The field hands who comprised the vast majority of their membership joined black Methodist and Baptist churches, for the most part. Only the independent and semi-independent black Episcopal churches located along the South's Atlantic seaboard remained. Their congregations consisted almost entirely of people who were freemen before the war and former house slaves; a coterie of the better-educated, more skilled, property-owning members of the black community who could not only read the *Book of Common Prayer* but remained convinced of the orthodoxy of the Episcopal Church, racism notwithstanding.[15] In 1866, Arkansas had no history of independent or semi-independent black churches and no nucleus of freemen and former house slaves willing to organize one.

Bishop Pierce tried to establish black churches on several occasions. Aided by Arkansas's white Episcopalians and even the Reverend A. D. Drummon of Tennessee, he gathered together promising groups of African Americans and preached to them on confirmation. He conducted services at places such as Osceola, Pine Bluff, Brownstown, Fayetteville, and his Little Rock home with the intention of establishing black churches. Some gatherings were large and enthusiastic, but the prospective converts never organized themselves into congregations. Pierce included a separate but equal seating arrangement in the plans for his proposed cathedral, but he was not reconciled to this as an answer to the problem. He was determined that given the proper leadership a black congregation would constitute itself.

Despite his failures, Pierce retained his catholic outlook when the southern bishops convened at Sewanee, Tennessee, in July 1883. The bishops met with the intention of drawing up a plan for segregating the church, diocese by diocese, in the name of the evangelization of African Americans. With the exception of Arkansas, all of the dioceses of the former slave states and the three border states of West Virginia, Missouri, and Kentucky sent a delegation of some kind. Pierce did not attend and he sent no one in his stead. Judging by the fact that he never addressed the Arkansas convention regarding the Sewanee Canon, it seems plain that the bishop of Arkansas not only opposed ecclesiastical segregation, he thought it unwise to raise the subject at all. These actions would coincide with another aspect of Pierce's catholicism, namely, his dogmatic belief in the sanctity of a bishop's jurisdiction. He may have considered the pretext for the meeting and its canonical outcome as meddling in the affairs of bishops who should be handling these matters individually and without fanfare. Had the Sewanee Canon passed into law, it could, by its very existence, have put pressure on all southern bishops to implement it.[16]

While Pierce's absence was probably an act of dissent, one southern bishop expressed outright opposition to the canon. Incredibly, the only dissenting opinion at Sewanee came from the only bishop elected and consecrated by the Protestant Episcopal Church in the Confederate States of America, Bishop Richard Wilmer of Alabama. Wilmer called it "class legislation." Three other unidentified Sewanee delegates could be said to have followed Pierce in spirit. They registered their dissent by declining to vote. Ultimately, of course, the canon was defeated at the 1883 General Convention. Having passed in the House of Bishops, it failed in the House of Deputies.[17]

Judging by his actions, if Bishop Pierce drew anything from the defeat of the Sewanee Canon, one would have to say that it inspired him to hold fast to the previous resolutions of the Arkansas convention regarding the training and ordination of black clergy and the incorporation of black churches into the Arkansas convention. Two years after Sewanee, St. Philip's, Little Rock, Arkansas's first black Episcopal church, came into being on the initiative of Trinity Cathedral. The key was Mrs. Pierce.

In 1885, the former Nannie Haywood Sheppard of Matagorda, Texas, rented a second-floor room over a store on West Ninth St. in Little Rock, the main artery of Little Rock's black community. Every Sunday afternoon, she and her daughter, Elizabeth, welcomed the curious from off the street. Elizabeth played the organ and Mrs. Pierce led the singing. Once the hymns and chants became familiar to the people of the mission, Mrs. Pierce familiarized them with the Episcopal service. The bishop assigned a priest to the mission and purchased a lot near Trinity Cathedral with the intention of building a church. In 1887, another of the bishop's daughters and her husband, Mr. and Mrs. William C. Stevens, took it upon themselves to build St. Philip's. They also trained and robed the mission's boys' choir. By the spring of 1889, St. Philip's was eligible for admission to the Annual Convention of the Diocese of Arkansas as a parish.

The timing could hardly have been worse. Political developments in the state at large were not conducive to the inclusion of black delegates in any white legislative body. This was the time, says George F. Bragg, when "a movement was obtaining through the Southern states [resulting in] the 'disfranchisement' of the great body of colored voters in that section of the country. It so happened that many Southern laymen who were prominent in state affairs were likewise prominent in the affairs of the Kingdom of God."[18] The late 1880s and early 1890s were the years of Republican demise in Arkansas, as signified by the assassinations of the Reverend G. E. Trower and John M. Clayton in 1887 and 1889, respectively. Trower, a black minister, was a Republican state representative. Clayton was brother to former Republican governor Powell Clayton. Both men represented the aspirations of "African-Americans, white Republicans, and poor white farmers mobilized by the state's native-born populist movement, the Agrarian Wheel."[19] Their unsolved murders were part of a successful campaign to wrest control of Conway County away from the numerically superior Republicans. The Democrats settled the issue "through electoral fraud, racial violence, and political murder."[20] By 1893, blacks and poor whites were largely disfranchised in Arkansas. As stated in the introduction to this book, the sacred and secular tend to operate in tandem on the issue of race, the preeminent theme being the establishment of order. By presenting St. Philip's for admission, Pierce was manifestly swimming against the current. Nevertheless, the diocese made good on its promise and the three lay delegates from St. Philip's took their seats at the 1889 convention without incident.

The peace, however, was short-lived. The lay representatives of Christ Church, Little Rock, boycotted the 1890 convention in protest of the presence of St. Philip's delegates and continued to do so for the next five years. Likewise, Christ Church, the wealthiest, most populous, and most influential of Arkansas's churches, withheld its support for the diocese. At the 1890 convention, the Reverend Wallace Carnahan, rector of Christ Church, presented a letter explaining the boycott, signed by himself, the vestry, and wardens of Christ Church. They contended that

> the admission of Negroes . . . inevitably injures the cause of Negro evangelization by antagonizing the white race.
>
> But we confess that our chief reason for opposing retention of Negro delegates . . . is their conspicuous incapacity for the difficult task of ecclesiastical legislation and their susceptibility to manipulation.[21]

The rest of the letter was devoted to their allegation that African Americans were "brought into the [convention] for the purpose of defeating reform." In short, Christ Church and its allies had an agenda for the diocese which Pierce opposed. The bishop, they said, was violating widely accepted racial norms in order to pack the convention, an irreconcilable escalation of a conflict dating back to Reconstruction.[22]

Organized by Bishop Polk in 1839, Christ Church had been the "mother church" of Episcopal Arkansas since its inception. It had also acquired a reputation as the church home of many wealthy and influential Arkansans. During Reconstruction, these old families came to represent traditional southern values, and, especially, an antipathy to things northern. Their nemesis, so to speak, was a growing contingent of northern and eastern emigrants who joined Christ Church in the years immediately after the war—particularly the families of United States military personnel and officials of the Republican government. Mary Fletcher, a southerner with ambivalent feelings about the "Yankees," described the situation this way: "Many carpet baggers and their families joined: in fact they soon got control of the church offices. They established the most operatic choir in town. The leading soprano was a beautiful woman whose voice was lovely as a lark's. It was the social center of town. . . . A prominent doctor started to Christ Church there and after a few weeks he left. They asked him why he stopped coming and he said: 'All I get out of that church is a d—— blue streak of Yankee soldiers going up and down the aisle.'"[23]

The Brooks-Baxter War of 1873 almost, but not quite, divided the factions into two churches. Brooks-Baxter was a military coup/political donnybrook that heralded the return of southern Democrats to power and the end of Reconstruction in Arkansas. The Democrat-friendly Regular Republicans won the gubernatorial election of 1872, but the hard-line Liberal Republicans called foul play. Both parties laid claim to the governor's office. The Liberal Republicans filed suit, hoping the state Supreme Court would resolve the issue in their favor. Meanwhile, Elisha Baxter, the Regular Republican governor of Arkansas, weakened his position in the party as a whole by being too generous with the Democrats in the distribution of appointments. Republican hard-liners from both factions united against him, prompting Baxter to call out the state militia in the spring of 1873. Thus, at the time of the annual Arkansas Episcopal convention, it looked as if armed conflict might break out at any moment. The leadership of all parties was heavily represented in the pews of Christ Church. The "Liberal Republican Episcopalians," if we may call them that, chose this moment to capitalize on Bishop Pierce's plan to build a cathedral in Little Rock; they volunteered to leave Christ Church and form the nucleus of Pierce's most beloved vision. Led by state district attorney William H. Whipple, they petitioned the convention for the right to establish a second church in Little Rock on the grounds that Christ Church was filled to capacity, or, to put it in the vernacular: "There ain't room in here for the both of us."[24] However, they were dissuaded from moving by two things: first, Christ Church was hit by lightning and burned to the ground, leaving all of the belligerents in need of a house of worship; second, the war ran its relatively bloodless course, removing the fear of impending violence. Both sides reconciled to worship together for the next ten years, from 1874 to 1884, while their respective buildings were under construction.

When Pierce had gathered enough money to begin building a cathedral, he asked the people of Christ Church, since they had plans to build again anyway, if they would not like to be the cathedral. They declined. The Christ Church congregation did not acknowledge the need for a cathedral, per se, being content with the more congregational form of government that had been the mainstay of Episcopal Arkansas since its inception. The "old mother church" preferred her present condition.

Completion of the new buildings gave renewed vigor to old quarrels. Trinity Cathedral and Christ Church opened for worship in 1884 and 1886, respectively. Both were monuments to Gothic Revival architecture, Christ Church being decidedly more imposing than Trinity. However, it is the intervening year that truly marks the escalation of the conflict. In 1885, the year of the establishment of St. Philip's, the Reverend Wallace Carnahan became rector of Christ Church.

Carnahan may have done more to fill the empty pews of Trinity Cathedral than all the efforts of Bishop Pierce. He was a Virginian of strong opinions and many of them were inflammatory to the situation. The "carpetbaggers," as he saw it, needed some encouragement to leave Christ Church. Again, Mary Fletcher lends us a synopsis: "All went well until the pulpit was occupied by a rampant Irishman [Carnahan] who did not like that kind of religion [Christ Church's social life]. He began looking up the past of some of the most prominent members. Then he told all he knew from the pulpit, and soon another church [Trinity Cathedral] was formed by the Northern element."[25]

The most notorious (or celebrated) episode of Carnahan's "purge" is that of the Roots family. The Roots brothers, P. K. and Logan H., came to Arkansas during the Civil War with the Union army of occupation, Logan being affiliated with the federal commissary in Little Rock. The two brothers moved their living south after the war and engaged in some highly profitable land speculation and farming. Logan served the Republican government as congressman and United States marshal. He figured prominently in the Militia War of 1868, an attempt by the Ku Klux Klan to subvert Arkansas's Reconstruction government. The Roots brothers became the quintessential "carpetbaggers" of the Christ Church congregation. Oral tradition holds that one Sunday morning during the period of the Christ Church boycott, Carnahan physically barred the Logan Roots family from entering Christ Church. As they ascended the steps, he stood spread-eagled in the doorway and exclaimed, "We don't worship with Yankees and carpetbaggers!" or words to that effect. Roots removed his family to Trinity Cathedral.[26] The structures, themselves, bear witness to the episode. The altar of the new Christ Church sanctuary and the window behind it were donated by P. K. and Logan, respectively. Nine years later, the family of Logan H. Roots paid off the remaining debt on Trinity Cathedral.

The difference between crosstown rivals went well beyond political affiliation. Christ Church was as low church as Trinity Cathedral was high. The genuflecting, the generous use of candles, the chanting, the incense, and the weekly communion services at Trinity Cathedral contrasted sharply with practices at Christ Church, where the sermon was clearly the worship emphasis and the pews were rented. Moreover, the people of Christ Church rallied to their new rector, who considered the cathedral to be a social club with a religious pretext. One admiring parishioner wrote:

> How different the outcome of these three years of the "new regime" has been from what was predicted by some people who did not know that the Episcopal Church taught religion. What a storm was raised when the new Rector did away with the fantastic show business in the choir, put a stop to suppers, lotteries, and fandangos as a means of raising money for the church, and preached the necessity of piety in church members. Many people predicted that "if the rector went on with these novelties he would soon be preaching to empty pews, and have no salary." Thank God the horrid nightmare of irreligion in Christ Church is past. No one now speaks of this parish as a "social club for Sunday amusement."[27]

Carnahan publicized his complaints via the parish newspaper of Christ Church, the *Arkansas Churchman*. They were, for the most part, not very subtle criticisms of his bishop. In an article concurrent with the incorporation of St. Philip's into the Arkansas convention, Carnahan contrasted the two schools of thought separating the two largest churches in Arkansas. "Conservative Low Churchmen," said Carnahan, lay greater emphasis upon the necessity of conversion and one's personal relationship to God. "Ultra High Churchmen," like high churchmen in general, lay greater emphasis upon the "sacraments as a means of grace" and the "Apostolic ministry." However,

"Ultra High Churchmen," or "Ritualists," as he preferred to call them, are scarcely discernible from Roman Catholics in their views on confession, absolution, communion, prayers for the dead, requiem masses for the repose of souls, and even the authority of the Pope—less, of course, papal infallibility. "How any honest man, especially a clergyman, can hold [these views] and remain in the Protestant Episcopal Church, in peace of mind, is an ethical mystery."[28] All of this was directed at Pierce. Carnahan would later add that those clergymen who rely upon the weight of their office in order to get their point across, rather than their "personal power and moral worth," are likewise in the wrong.[29] Here again, we may safely presume, he is speaking of Pierce. In Carnahan's farewell sermon at Christ Church, he rejoiced that he was not leaving his flock to a "bastard Romanist."[30]

The explosive quality of St. Philip's can readily be understood in light of this prolonged diatribe, but the protest was not as schismatic as it might have been. Christ Church's lay representatives stayed away from the convention for six years and Carnahan renamed the *Arkansas Churchman* the *Anglo-Saxon Churchman*. The new title, said Carnahan, signaled the paper's transformation from a traditional church paper to an agent of ecclesiastical and political reform, a prophetic challenge to the destructive influence of carpetbaggers, ritualists, and "immoral" clergy controlling the Diocese of Arkansas. High on the list of proposed reforms was the exclusion of African Americans from the Arkansas Episcopal convention. According to Carnahan, whites who advocated equality for blacks were fanatics who were trying to ignore "the divine stamp of inferiority on the black man."

> What utter humbug is all this talk about the "Catholicity of the Church" demanding the admission of negroes to the ministry and to [church conventions], which winds up with a sheepish apology for excluding them from our places of worship. The simple truth is, that the advocates for the admission of negroes . . . *have not the courage of their convictions.* They *must* (unless they are utter hypocrites) *believe* in worshipping with the Negro. The influential white layman shakes his finger at the clerical advocate for race equality and says, "No, sir, you may sentimentalize as you please about the 'colored brother,' but you shall not bring him into my church to sit next to my wife and daughter." And the clerical advocate of race equality yields.[31]

Presumably, the leaders of Christ Church hoped for a groundswell of opinion to affirm their actions in the Arkansas convention and force Pierce to reconsider, but it did not happen. Pierce called for an investigation of the Christ Church protest at the 1890 convention. The convention found nothing amiss.

The real story, however, is the investigating committee itself. Pierce appointed the committee—at the direction of the convention. This was his diocese. Most of the churches in Arkansas were founded during the previous twenty years of his administration. Likewise, many of the clergy of those churches were brought into the ministry under his tutelage. Having organized a far-flung missionary enterprise into a diocese, he had constructed a cathedral with only a modicum of assistance from the diocese, and Mrs. Pierce had purchased the bishop's house out of her own pocket. For most of Arkansas's Episcopalians this was no time to desert their Right Reverend Father-in-God.[32]

The rancor over St. Philip's is typical of the struggle over black representation in diocesan conventions across the South. Already touched upon with regard to the dioceses of Tennessee and Southern Virginia in the previous chapter, and North Carolina and Virginia in this chapter, the clash between orthodoxy and social acceptability knew no greater conflict than that in South Carolina. Bishop William Howe of South Carolina, the original author of the Sewanee Canon, apparently had a change of heart after 1883. In 1887, he and the white clergy of his diocese stood as one man in favor of seating a black clergyman in the South Carolina convention. Opposing them were most of the lay delegates. Howe, who intimated that his resignation would be forthcoming if the issue were lost, was sustained. As a result, some of South Carolina's oldest churches withdrew from the convention. Howe lamented the loss but would not concede the issue: "As I review the question I do not see how we could have acted otherwise than we have done."[33] Ultimately, Howe found his position untenable and the Diocese of South Carolina segregated in 1889.

There were similar developments elsewhere. At the 1889 General Convention, the Conference of Church Workers challenged the segregation of South Carolina and called upon the national body to define the "status" of black Episcopalians.[34] The convention, says Bragg, sidestepped the moral issue underlying segregation in favor of a jurisdictional one; namely, the right of every diocese to determine its own policy.[35] Five years later, the Diocese of Texas experienced a miniature version of Bishop Howe's debacle in South Carolina. In 1889, Texas had been one of two southern dioceses to send the first black delegates to the General Convention. However, in 1894, Bishop George H. Kinsolving of Texas, a kindred spirit to Howe, felt compelled to draw his line in the sand. Kinsolving was no stranger to racial conflict. While he was priest to a church in Cincinnati, he and his vestry had deadlocked over the inclusion a black woman who had applied for a pew rental. When he threatened to tender his resignation, the vestry backed down and admitted her to the parish. Although he was a former Confederate officer, Kinsolving was singularly devoid of the sentimentality associated with the "lost cause." In 1900, he would tell the student body of Virginia Theological Seminary, "We trafficked in human flesh and blood and we suffered the consequences."[36] Thus, he was not cowed by the angry racial outburst associated with a service preliminary to the 1894 Texas convention. The trouble began when several white communicants walked out of the church in protest to the presence of a black clergyman, the Reverend J. N. N. Thompson, in the chancel. Kinsolving refused to yield the point and the protesters attacked him via the secular press. Ultimately, he stood his ground with his clergy at his side and the protest spent itself. Said Bragg, "This one instance, and there are so many others, constitutes a living and historic witness to the absolute sincerity of the Southern episcopate in attempting to do the right thing under difficulties sufficient to break the heart of hope."[37]

At about the same time as the Texas confrontation, Bishop Pierce, enfeebled by old age, began tying up loose ends in Arkansas. St. Philip's was one of them. In 1893, Arkansas's only black church was declared free from debt and Pierce ordained an African American, the Reverend Isaiah P. Daniels, to the diaconate. He placed Daniels in charge of St. Philip's and advanced him to the priesthood in 1894, the centennial year of St. Thomas's, Philadelphia. Likewise, at the 1895 Arkansas convention, Pierce announced that Trinity Cathedral was finally paid off and ready for consecration. He also confessed that he was worn out and in need of a coadjutor bishop to assume his missionary duties as soon as possible. The convention resolved to elect Pierce's successor at the next convention.

At the 1896 convention, the lay delegates of Christ Church rejoined the convention under new leadership. Carnahan's successor, the Reverend John M. Gass, had accomplished the near impossible for an incoming priest, having won the hearts of his flock while the memory of his much beloved predecessor had hardly had time to dissipate. We do not know where Gass stood on the St. Philip's issue, but he hailed from South Carolina and may have been more sympathetic toward Pierce in light of the struggles of Bishop Howe. Be that as it may, it appears that he used his newfound popularity to help persuade Christ Church to rejoin the convention and he was aided by a change in vestrymen. In order to ease the process of reconciliation, he asked the priest of Trinity Cathedral, Dean D. I. Hobbs, to motion that Christ Church's unpaid diocesan assessments from 1890 to 1895 be remitted. Hobbs complied and the convention, eager for a resolution of the conflict, passed the measure.[38]

Pierce was jubilant in welcoming Christ Church back into the fold, but it would appear that the "old mother church" rejoined the diocese out of mixed motives. Despite the unfeigned good will exhibited by all parties, subsequent events make it clear that the members of Christ Church, who said nothing about St. Philip's upon their return, were still pushing their agenda. With Pierce on the decline, they probably looked upon the upcoming episcopal election as their opportunity to put the diocese on what they regarded as the right track.[39]

As it turns out, there was no election in 1896, because there was not enough money to pay the salary of the bishop-elect. Pierce, by virtue of his having come to Arkansas as a missionary bishop, had been drawing his salary from the Board of Missions of the national church. His successor, however, would have to draw his salary directly from the Diocese of Arkansas. As of the 1896 convention, the Episcopal Endowment Fund of Arkansas was still insufficient for the task. Therefore the election was postponed for a year while a committee set out to rectify the problem.

However, at the 1897 convention, the Episcopal Endowment Committee reported that it had made no progress and confessed its unwillingness to col- lect money because of the depressed state of the economy. Pierce was outraged, but he had prepared for this contingency. He told the assembled delegates that they needed to elect a proven missionary (a) of such reputation that he could embellish the endowment by soliciting money from the church at large, or (b) with "large means" of his own, who would not need a salary, or (c) with little in the way of family obligations. Having laid out a course, he demanded that the convention act immediately in order to avoid a vacancy caused by his own demise. They complied and proceeded to the nominations.[40]

There was only one nominee: Archdeacon William M. Brown of Ohio, nom- inated by Dean Hobbs. Brown's missionary talents were superlative and he could fit into any of Pierce's three fiscal categories. He was credited with the establishment of seven churches and twenty-one mission chapels in Ohio. His colleagues, he said, complained that he "was making Episcopalians out of fence posts."[41] He had the enthusiastic endorsement of his bishop and was regard- ed far and wide as a champion of orthodoxy by reason of a book he had re- cently published, *The Church for Americans*. Brown's book, which came out the same year that Edward T. Demby was confirmed an Episcopalian, was a call for all Americans to join the Episcopal Church, the American branch of the "one, holy, and apostolic church." His defense of Anglican dogma prompt- ed accolades from clergy vexed with the repercussions of rationalism in gen- eral and Darwinism in particular. He was also modestly wealthy and married but childless. Hobbs, who distributed copies of *The Church for Americans* to all of the Arkansas clergy, and Brown had been classmates in seminary.[42]

Brown's popularity, however, glossed over his weaknesses. First of all, he was only a missionary. Having sort of leaped from project to project for many years, he had precious little experience in the grind of running a parish church, let alone a diocese. Second, there was a similar problem stemming from his seminary experience. Brown was a graduate of Bexley Hall, the popular name for the Theological Seminary of the Diocese of Ohio, renamed the Divinity School of Kenyon College in 1892.[43] His theological education consisted primarily of tutorials that indoctrinated him but did not challenge his personal convictions. It failed to reveal a certain lack of authenticity in Brown that he was not, as yet, even aware of—a superficiality in his faith that should have precluded him from being a bishop, or, perhaps, even a clergyman. At the time of his deposition from the ministry in 1925, Brown confessed that his early successes as a missionary were due to the fact that he was "naively orthodox," or "cocksure," as he put it.[44] His preaching, like the book that made him famous, was the regurgitation of his tutorials. He was a testimony, to paraphrase the Apostle Paul, that the Gospel can do its own work in spite of the speaker.[45] Thus, as the new bishop coadjutor of Arkansas, he embodied the error that Paul warned against in 1 Timothy—a young believer vested with authority inordinate to his maturity, a man in imminent danger of being "puffed up."[46] Of course, all of this is retrospective. In 1897, he looked pretty good.

The Arkansas election process called for the clergy to nominate candidates for bishop, vote on the nominees, and pass on the winner to the laity for confirmation. The laity could confirm or deny the clergy's choice, but had no power to nominate a candidate of their own. Brown won the clergy, but the laity, feeling very limited in their choices, balked. A special convention was slated for December.

At the special convention, there were three nominees: Brown, Gass, and the Reverend F. F. Reese, a future bishop of Georgia. Brown won a bare majority of the clergy on the first ballot, garnering nine out of sixteen votes. Gass came in second with six votes and Reese received one. The laity ratified the clergy's choice by the same margin, eight to seven. Brown won.[47]

Those lay delegates opposed to Brown's election greeted the announcement with astonishment, turning to spontaneous debate and, in some cases, rancorous indignation. While the legality of the vote cast by the lay delegate from St. James's, Eureka Springs, in favor of Brown would later come under official scrutiny, one immediate object of scorn was the lone lay delegate from St. Philip's, Little Rock—Samuel Speight. Speight, a detective with the Little Rock Police Department, was no stranger to internecine political quarrels based on race. He was a Republican and a leading combatant in the struggle to thwart lily-white Republicanism in Arkansas.[48] Thus, unless he had somehow missed the significance of the Christ Church protest of 1890–95, we may be sure that he voted for Brown, who was widely regarded as Pierce's "man." Electing Brown not only meant loyalty to Pierce, Hobbs, and the cathedral, it prevented the election of the rector of Christ Church. Had Speight voted otherwise, it would have been proof positive of his "conspicuous incapacity for the difficult task of ecclesiastical legislation." However, for those in sympathy with the rationale behind the Christ Church boycott, Speight's action was prophecy fulfilled, proof positive of African Americans' "susceptibility to manipulation." We may safely presume that Speight's rector, I. P. Daniels, also voted for Brown and for the same reasons. That being the case, we deduce one of the more bizarre electoral contests in Episcopal history: William M. Brown, soon to become the quintessential Jim Crow bishop, won the bishopric of Arkansas by the difference of one black vote in each order.

We read in Pierce's diary that William H. Whipple, previously mentioned in connection with the founding of Trinity Cathedral, "was almost insanely enraged by at the result and showed it by his anger at Sam Spight [sic], delegate from St. Philip's and at the Rev. G. W. Flowers."[49] Despite his membership at Trinity Cathedral, Whipple was a devotee of John Gass and may have found Speight's vote particularly galling because of his personal experiences in the political arena. Whipple was one of those responsible for the legal contrivance that turned the Brooks-Baxter War from "cold" to "hot" in 1874.[50] Despite the defeat of the Liberal Republicans, he remained a "staunch Republican" and forged ahead in Arkansas politics. After serving two terms as mayor of Little Rock, he lost the 1892 gubernatorial election, mainly by reason of the Republican Party's alliance with the Agrarian Wheel and its substantial African American contingent. The racial climate of the state turned his black support into a tremendous liability.

The day after Brown's election, Whipple joined some influential members of Christ Church in a public protest. Arkansas governor Dan W. Jones and former Arkansas governor T. J. Churchill, both of Christ Church, joined Whipple in condemning Brown's election from the pages of the *Arkansas Gazette*. They listed several alleged irregularities and portrayed Pierce as an unscrupulous manipulator. Their declared intent was to dissuade Brown from accepting the election. Pierce called a meeting at Christ Church in order to hear out the dissidents and make a defense. Brown accompanied him but tried to refrain from comment. Jones and Whipple acted as the plaintiffs in a stormy session that closed on a more cordial note, though without any substantial resolution of the conflict. Among their many complaints, they "accused" Brown of winning on the "colored" vote, but were apparently refuted by the argument that Brown's one-vote victory could be attributed to anyone who voted for him.[51] Subsequently, Whipple moved his membership to Christ Church, which Pierce privately described as a "decided gain."[52]

To the amazement of many onlookers, Brown accepted the election. Although Pierce and his standing committee encouraged Brown to disregard the "exaggerated" opposition, Brown investigated Whipple's allegations on his own and concluded that there was nothing irregular about the election, or, to be more specific, he could find nothing to justify nonacceptance. Brown noted that the dissenters had not found fault in him, personally, and that Gass had gone so far as to assure him of his loyalty, should he accept the election. Furthermore, Brown felt honor bound to Hobbs, who had campaigned for his election at two conventions, and Pierce, who insisted that the election was valid and should stand, protests notwithstanding.

An ecclesiastical climber by nature, Brown had been defending his candidacy, with the help of Hobbs and Pierce, since October. Between the two conventions of 1897, he had heard that he was being portrayed as an "inefficient, stammering, ignoramus" by Pierce's enemies in Arkansas.[53] In fear for his reputation and his future, the candidate from Ohio wrote a rebuttal to at least one Arkansas official. If Arkansas deemed him unfit, he reasoned, it might lead to other rejections in other dioceses. Brown justified his brazen ambition on the grounds of Scripture, citing the words of the Apostle Paul, "He that desireth the office of a bishop, desireth a good thing." His superior, Bishop William A. Leonard of Ohio, began to regret having recommended him for the episcopate.[54]

Brown was committed to rising as far and as fast as propriety would allow, an attitude inspired by the drudgery and misery of his earlier life. When his father died in the Civil War, he was "bound out" to a Dunker farmer at the age of six. Life was hard under the "German ogre," as he would later call him, and once, when the young farmhand was terribly ill, he promised God that he would enter the ministry if only he might be allowed to live. Brown never forgot the promise. When he was in his midteens, the authorities took mercy on Brown and liberated him from his taskmaster. After several years of hard work and education ad hoc, he found himself under the tutelage of Mrs. Mary Scranton Bradford, a matriarch of Cleveland society. He adored her. Bradford was a devout Episcopalian and when her young friend expressed an interest in the ministry of the Episcopal Church, she sponsored his less-than-thorough theological education. Brown was far more intent on establishing his credibility in the field than in the classroom. A young cleric with a zeal for evangelism and an ax to grind with regard to his humble beginnings, he quickly surpassed his better-educated fellows as a missionary and became a nationally renowned defender of the faith.[55]

When Brown accepted the Arkansas election, the laity of Christ Church mobilized to block his confirmation by the House of Bishops. They drew up a petition in protest of the election and circulated it around the Diocese of Arkansas. Christ Church and five other churches, totaling about 20 percent of Arkansas's 2,439 communicants, signed the petition, which was circulated among all the bishops and standing committees of the church. Alarmed at the scope of the protest, Pierce wrote Brown, "You cannot withdraw your acceptance without doing me an unalterable and unpardonable wrong."[56] He need not have worried. Brown had long satisfied himself as to the validity of his election and the small numerical size of his opposition. In fact, he and Pierce had been anticipating the protest since December. The bishop of Arkansas defended Brown's election in the *Church Standard* of February 5. The protesters, who had been promised a reply but had not, as yet, seen one, were caught off guard. With time running out, they issued a second protest circular in rebuttal to the *Church Standard* article. The second protest, which appeared the second week in February, included only four churches instead of the original six, but the number of petitioners increased to not quite one-third of Arkansas's communicants. Undaunted, Brown countered with a circular of his own in mid-February, bolstered by a circular from Dean Hobbs on February 28. Both Brown and Hobbs addressed the "Negro question" as it applied to the 1897 election. Hobbs recounted the Christ Church boycott of 1890–95, using it to portray Christ Church as a chronically disruptive influence in the diocese. Brown recapitulated his earlier defense against allegations that he had been elected on the "colored vote." Hobbs, Pierce, and Brown effectively rendered all of the objections to Brown's confirmation invalid, save Brown's ambition. The most telling argument against Brown's confirmation, in and out of Arkansas, was the bishop elect's willingness to accept the election in spite of the protest. Brown, however, softened that objection by conveying himself as someone honoring a promise to those who nominated him and representing the will of the majority of Arkansas's Episcopalians.[57]

At one point, Pierce, Brown, and Hobbs actually feared that the standing committees and bishops might deny Brown the necessary consents, and Pierce tallied his forces with the intent of electing Brown at the 1898 Arkansas convention. Brown, of course, received the necessary consents, but it is more than a little interesting that St. Philip's did not declare itself for Brown on the bishop's list. Perhaps Pierce though it wiser to omit St. Philip's; perhaps the diocese's only black church did not want to be the focal point of another schismatic election; perhaps both. Be that as it may, Brown and company won their case with the bishops and standing committees, and Brown was consecrated Bishop Coadjutor of Arkansas in June 1898. In 1899, Pierce died and Brown succeeded him.[58]

Bishop Brown exemplifies the North/South rapprochement on the race issue. By 1900, most northerners were reconciled to letting the South deal with the "Negro problem" according to its own lights. The Supreme Court had established a national precedent with *Plessy v. Ferguson;* Booker T. Washington seemed to concur; and northerners were tired of the whole business. It was no longer worth the fight. As for Brown, he came to Arkansas basically "tabula rasa." Bishop Leonard may have been a salient advocate of black ministries, but his former archdeacon was not. Brown, by reason of his lack of contact with black Episcopalians, was an untried catholic who formulated his strategy for black ministries out of other considerations. Despite his reputation for orthodoxy, he proved to be an extremely pragmatic missionary whose overriding concern was to eliminate all impediments to evangelism. When he perceived Arkansas's integrated church government to be a missionary hindrance, the die was cast. Brown, in a radical departure from Bishop Pierce's policy, determined that the races must be separated for the greater good of the church.

The Diocese of Arkansas segregated in 1903. This is how it came about. Brown inherited the exigencies of the Trinity Cathedral–Christ Church battle, which required, among other things, that he must choose whether to be a second champion of black representation in the Arkansas convention or to acquiesce to the "old mother church" and her allies. Thus, with the death of Bishop Pierce, Brown knew that if he did not formulate a strategy for "Negro work," it might be formulated for him. He also knew that he must not act in haste or arbitrarily. He was, after all, widely perceived as Pierce's chosen successor and the perception that he had won his office on the "black vote" mitigated against him in the minds of some Arkansans. Said Brown: "Before coming to Arkansas . . . I had never been South of Louisville, Kentucky. Accordingly, I thought it wise not to give expression to my Northern convictions on the vexed color question until I had made it the subject of a prolonged and careful study."[59]

Therefore, at the 1900 Arkansas convention he appointed an advisory committee on "Negro work" composed of two priests, two laymen, and two laywomen. After two years of consultation with the committee and an unsuccessful attempt to reinvigorate struggling St. Philip's, Brown concluded "that if the church is ever to do any extensive and satisfactory work among the colored people of Arkansas, we must have two [conventions], one for white churchmen and one for colored churchmen."[60] In other words, he was in partial agreement with the protest of 1890; the inclusion of African Americans was an evangelical blunder.

There is more than a hint that the Christ Church congregation courted rather than confronted Brown on this and all controversial matters—and that they found a sympathetic ear in nearly every case. In his first address to the Arkansas convention, Brown expressed it this way: "Human nature being what it is, this is more than I dared hope for. I really expected and dreaded a good deal of coldness and some opposition. But in this I have been most happily disappointed. . . . Not only have I escaped opposition from the quarters in which it was expected but some of my most efficient helpers have been from among those most strenuously opposed to my consecration."[61]

Insofar as Brown may be designated a Trinity Cathedral bishop or a Christ Church bishop, events would prove him to be overwhelmingly the latter. In fact, another item from his 1899 address touched upon the "Ultra-High Churchmanship" associated with Trinity Cathedral. He said: "Being profoundly convinced that ritualism is, speaking generally, harmful in the mission field, I shall do all that I can to discourage it."[62] In subsequent years, he lowered the worship at the cathedral, decentralized the work of church extension, and tried to reduce the cathedral to the status of a parish church. Although he is chiefly remembered for his experimental black church and his excommunication for Communism, his first brush with national controversy, apart from his election, sprang from his "deritualizing" the Diocese of Arkansas.[63]

From Brown's perspective, the convergence of his aims with those of Christ Church was coincidental to his own broad churchmanship, the segregation of the diocese being a prime example. Prior to 1904, Brown maintained church growth as the sole reason for segregation. Racial homogeneity, he maintained, means harmony and growth; racial integration means internal conflict, a bad press, and, consequently, minimal growth.

In 1902, the bishop broached his plan for "systematic work among the colored people" of Arkansas to the Arkansas convention. He proposed the adoption of Canon 54 A and B, the legal foundation for the establishment of a separate black church in the diocese. According to Canon 54, "any colored minister or ministers that may be in the diocese from this time on shall, with the lay representatives from the colored parishes and missions constitute a Convocation of Afro-American Episcopalians and submit its actions to the Annual Convention of the diocese for review." It stated unequivocally that said clergy and congregations would not have a seat or vote in the Arkansas convention.[64] Also at the 1902 convention, the bishop declared his intent to find another black minister for St. Philip's, which had been under the supervision of white clergy since the departure of Daniels in 1899. The new black rector, he said, would double as a missionary to blacks throughout the diocese. Two unidentified dissenters forestalled the passage of articles A and B by insisting that the parishioners of St. Philip's and Daniels, who still resided in the diocese, examine the plan and agree to it of their own accord.

The bishop lost no time in securing the agreement of St. Philip's and Daniels. Two weeks after the convention, Brown dispatched Archdeacon W. D. Williams to St. Philip's in company with Dean Percy J. Robottom of Trinity Cathedral, the interim rector of St. Philip's. Williams relayed Brown's suggested separation, citing the greater efficacy of an autonomous black church, or convocation, in Arkansas—a church predominantly supervised by blacks. The archdeacon recapitulated Brown's request in the manner prescribed: "[Bishop Brown desires] that St. Philip's Parish should not only seek membership in the proposed convocation, but should ask for the privilege of withdrawing from the diocesan [convention], in order to take the initial step in the formation of the convocation, and constitute the nucleus for this new organization."[65] Williams further stated that the state was to be divided into four convocations, three white and one black, in order to coordinate missionary work in Arkansas. All four would be supervised by the bishop and convention. These words, presumably designed to ameliorate the sting of segregation, were countered by a query from Samuel Speight. Speight said that he understood that St. Philip's had been reduced from a parish to a mission. Was this not so? Williams responded by saying that he understood that St. Philip's was still a parish, making it eligible to lead the Afro-American Convocation into existence. This conversation would hardly be worth recording, except for the fact that Speight was correct. St. Philip's had been reduced to a mission in 1900. Williams's oversight suggests that St. Philip's parish status was being reinstated, undeservedly, in order to enact Canon 54 A and B and expedite the end of African American representation in the Arkansas convention. Subsequent to the 1902 meeting, St. Philip's returned to parish status.

Returning to the meeting itself, another member of St. Philip's declared "that there has never been a 'color line' drawn in the Protestant Episcopal Church, and that he supposed a Church (which he named) had endeavored to create such a line. Archdeacon Williams assured the inquirer that so far as he knew, no church and no individual had approached the bishop upon any such question. The plan of the Bishop, he believed to be strictly and absolutely his own and entertained for the good of the colored race."[66]

Nevertheless, the meeting closed with Williams having substantially won his case, as evidenced by the petition signed by the wardens and vestrymen of St. Philip's on the following day. The wording of the petition was wholeheartedly in keeping with Brown's wishes. Moreover, it was an expression of loyalty and trust, being inundated with the bishop's own rhetoric. It concluded: "Hoping that our petition may be granted and praying that under the new convocational system, our beloved church may rapidly lengthen and strengthen her stakes until she securely shelters multitudes of the colored race, we are, dear Bishop . . . Your obedient children in Christ."[67]

St Philip's wholehearted acceptance of Canon 54 bespeaks the mission's theological roots and its hopes for the future. As a church conceived and championed by the former bishop of Arkansas and his family and a church supervised by the bishop's cathedral for most of its existence, St. Philip's looked upon Brown with innate fealty. They wanted to believe that he knew what he was doing, even if they doubted him, and that things would work out for the best. They were devoted high churchmen and he was their bishop. In other words, Brown reaped Pierce's harvest of obedience. Furthermore, Brown's scheme had genuine merit in the eyes of St. Philip's congregation. Arkansas's only black church was on the wane, as indicated by its newly acquired mission status. It had not had a black priest for four years. We do not know the specific reason for Daniels's resignation, but existing documents provide at least two possibilities. First of all, we know that his congregation did not pay him well. Second, we know that Daniels resigned the same year that Pierce died, suggesting that the ongoing pariah status of St. Philip's and the absence of his chief advocate in the Arkansas convention may have been crucial in his decision to leave. Said Brown of the situation when Daniels headed St. Philip's: "There has been, and is, only one colored minister in this diocese, and while he had a seat in the [convention], he cost the church so much in the way of dissension and alienation, that so long as the colored clergy and congregations were entitled to representation in the [convention], no other importation was likely to occur."[68]

St. Philip's also had an image problem. The bluevein reputation of the church, coupled with its convention troubles, made it both elitist and Uncle Tom in the eyes of some Little Rock blacks. While an observer in a 1901 article in the *Indianapolis Freeman* described St. Philip's communicants as the "blue veins," the "1905 Handy Map of Little Rock" made it quasi-official, geographically speaking, by following the name of St. Philip's with the designation "(Bluevein, col.)."[69] Perhaps the congregation hoped to destigmatize itself by way of Brown's metamorphosis. A black "cathedral," so to speak, at the head of a parallel black church probably stood a better chance of attracting a new black rector and new members than the St. Philip's of 1903.

Furthermore, St. Philip's parishioners wished to capitalize on Brown's plan for the physical improvement of the church. Despite having moved from the vicinity of Trinity Cathedral to a new location in Little Rock's black community and despite having made some repairs on the new building, St. Philip's was still substandard and relatively remote. The congregation aspired to a more central location and a building consonant with its higher calling. Judge Mifflin W. Gibbs, perhaps the best-known personage of black Little Rock and the "most influential black Republican" in Arkansas, apparently functioned as a consultant in the relocation movement.[70]

Bishop Brown presented St. Philip's petition to the 1903 convention, along with a similar communication from Daniels, who officially tendered his resignation from his seat in the Arkansas convention. Brown reaffirmed evangelism as the pretext for the plan, adding, as further justification, that dioceses were segregating across the South and that racial segregation was practiced in the North as well. Regardless of region, he said, Episcopal churches were either all-black or all-white and "the same arguments which will justify of separate Parishes for colored people will . . . justify the existence of separate convocations, if not separate dioceses for them." Brimming with confidence, the bishop expressed his hope that the newfound autonomy of Arkansas's black Episcopalians would lead to the establishment of twenty black congregations among the state's four hundred thousand African Americans, each church to be accompanied by a "house of industry for the practical uplift of the race."[71] The assembly passed Canon 54 into law without further ado.

The segregation of the diocese was not so well received outside of Arkansas. Brown's practice was to spend July through October every year in the North, living out of his summer home in Ohio. In 1903, he went north to raise money for missionary work in Arkansas. He preached black autonomy and the virtues of Arkansas's experiment in segregation. The controversial nature of his message prompted an interview by the *Cleveland Plain Dealer,* a black newspaper. The article focused on Brown's opinion on lynchings in the South and his philosophy with regard to "drawing the color line" in every area of life. Brown, a self-styled "Southernized Northerner" tried to capitalize on the lynching query by making a regional defense—to wit, northerners lynch blacks too.[72] The Associated Press condensed and disseminated the bishop's comments, making him a byword for bigotry overnight. The news, said Brown, "spread over the North like wildfire and issued so many condemnatory editorials and resolutions that for weeks afterward I hardly had the courage to look a Christian squarely in the face."[73]

He was reeling from this blow when he was attacked from another quarter.

The Conference of Church Workers, convened for the first time since passage of Brown's legislation, censured the Diocese of Arkansas for violation of the "inherent ecclesiastical rights" of its black Episcopalians. In a letter mailed to the bishops and church weeklies, the conference stated that it "unqualifiedly deplores and condemns" the actions of the Arkansas convention, and pledged to do everything in its power to obstruct the spread of similar legislation and to persuade Arkansas to rescind the measure.[74]

Many white clergy abandoned Brown, resulting in the removal of many erstwhile benefactors from the bishop's list. This was especially true of the Boston clergy, who canceled Brown's speaking engagements in their area. However, once Brown was able to compose himself, he decided that he ought to make a defense in Boston. Over the protests of many Massachusetts priests, the bishop of Massachusetts allowed Brown a single speaking engagement. In a lecture entitled "The American Negro Problem," Brown elaborated on and defended his previous remarks. He reasserted his paradigm of segregation, because, he claimed, the "Negro" "is inferior to the Anglo-Saxon American, [in] that speaking generally he is degenerating, especially is this true of the women of the race, that the colored people of the South must have the hand of the Southern white people in order to get out of the mire of degradation into which they have sunken since the Civil War; that this hand cannot and will not be extended until the color line has been drawn around the political, social, and ecclesiastical fields."[75] In defending his infamous remarks on lynching, Brown recapitulated: "they do unfortunately lynch [in] the South and they also lynch in the North; that the lynchings of the South are more excusable than those of the North [being done in the name of self-defense], and that, therefore, Northerners should not criticize the Southerners in this matter until they set a better example."[76]

Brown's defense initiated a second maelstrom of public outcry in an episode he dubbed the "Boston Incident." It forever stamped him as a crackpot to the Episcopal Northeast and cost him dearly in the way of support for Arkansas's missionary work.

Yet Boston is also a bellwether of Brown's personality. Criticism almost invariably stimulated him to greater argument. Ultimately, he would add layer upon layer of defense to his race philosophy and defend it at least twice before the House of Bishops. He summarized it in a pamphlet, *The Great American Race Problem,* and a book, *The Crucial Race Question.* For the moment, however, he was in need of some encouragement, which he got from a most unexpected source.

In 1904, the Conference of Church Workers addressed a gathering of southern bishops in Washington. Their object was to persuade the bishops to support the missionary district plan at the upcoming General Convention. Ironically, the Washington conference allowed Bishop Brown and the Conference
of Church Workers to strike an alliance. In a further irony, he was persuaded
to their cause, and they to his, through the agency of his erstwhile critic, the
Reverend George F. Bragg.

Bragg was the leading black advocate in the Episcopal Church, a priest whose
smallness of stature and high, thin voice belied his irrepressible spirit. First and
foremost, he was the venerable rector of the South's first independent black
church, St. James's, Baltimore. Through St. James's he was mentor to several
black priests who rose to prominence as church builders—most notably, the
Reverend Cassius M. C. Mason of All Saints', St. Louis, and the Reverend James
E. Thompson of St. Thomas's, Chicago. Bragg was also secretary of the Conference of Church Workers and had been practically every year since its inception. With the exceptions of James Weldon Johnson and W. E. B. Du Bois, he
was the leading black man of letters in the Episcopal Church, being the editor
of the conference's unofficial organ, the Baltimore *Church Advocate*. He was a
vociferous advocate of black issues before the General Convention and kept
up an ongoing critique, via the *Church Advocate*, of the various bishops of the
United States with regard to their treatment of black Episcopalians. It was Bragg
who signed the conference's 1903 letter censuring the bishop of Arkansas.

Brown, meeting with the Conference of Church Workers representatives face
to face and probably for the first time, did the wisest thing he could have done:
he asked for their help in finding an archdeacon to lead Arkansas's Afro-American Convocation. Bragg was delighted. Time and again, he and his colleagues
had called for black oversight in the appointment of black clergy, only to be
disappointed by the actions of white bishops. Perhaps he best expressed this
dilemma in connection with an incident in Florida some years later when,
judging by the context of the passage, a disreputable black priest had been
deposed from the ministry: "There is not a single colored clergyman we know,
and we know a number of them, of sufficient character to be a bishop, who
would not promptly put such characters outside of the ecclesiastical breast-
works. There have been a number of such men who have slipped into our
ministry, who could not have possible gotten in under any Negro priest qualified to be a bishop. And yet such scamps are charged up to us when we know
not whence they come. A perfectly blind Negro bishop, in the dark, could
hardly make such blunders."[77]

Evidence suggests that Brown had already tried to find an archdeacon on his own and had failed.[78] However, as he listened to the conference representatives state their case before the southern bishops assembled in Washington, he was so engrossed and inspired by the logic behind the missionary district plan that he asked to meet with them afterwards in order to discuss the Arkansas experiment. They adjourned to St. Luke's, the most prestigious of Washington's black Episcopal churches, where Brown and Bragg were mutually and pleasantly surprised by one another.[79] Bragg tells us that in spite of their differences, he and his colleagues were pleased with their erstwhile nemesis: "[Bishop Brown] met with us as men and brethren. He was frank and unreserved. He not only expressed himself as being in most hearty agreement with our wishes, but laid upon us the responsibility of securing the right man for the work in Arkansas. And when secured he promised to make him as much a 'bishop' as he could. . . . He desired to act upon our best judgement and he acted upon it."[80]

Bragg and Brown looked upon the Arkansas's Afro-American Convocation as an opportunity to demonstrate the value of black autonomy—an additional argument, thought Bragg, for the missionary district plan. "By Bishop Brown's plan there would at least be a chance of growth and, in the end, [it would] contribute toward undoing the very plan itself, and restoring actual corporate unity."[81] Brown was beginning to think in terms of a separate black denomination, but it is not clear whether he broached this to the members of the conference.

The bishop of Arkansas felt absolved, if not vindicated, by the whole episode and he began to write on the "Negro question" with newfound authority. Speaking to the 1904 Arkansas convention, Brown revealed his conviction that race prejudice is ordained by God, a further justification for what he would later call the "Arkansas Plan" for segregating the church. He outlined his strategy for its success. He reasoned as follows. Since the African American is "degenerating" and must necessarily be limited to that occupational state to which God has called him, he needs industrial and moral training if he is ever to raise himself out of his degradation—not a liberal education. His own religion is, by and large, "fetishism" and cannot be expected to remedy the situation. Ultimately, the federal government must shoulder the burden of industrial education and African Americans themselves must shoulder the burden of establishing a separate Episcopal denomination. Until such time as the federal government assumes its responsibility and African Americans establish their own denomination, it behooves the Episcopal Church to provide for their moral and industrial training. The Afro-American Convocation of Arkansas can provide an avenue for the moral and industrial training of Arkansas's four hundred thousand African Americans, provided it has the resources to "build combination Chapel and Industrial Halls in all the larger centers of population throughout the 'Black Belt' . . . at the rate of two a year." Eventually, the convocation would serve as a model for the whole church, leading toward the establishment of a separate black Episcopal denomination.[82]

Brown closed his remarks on a surprisingly contrite note by calling into question the demeaning language of the Arkansas Plan. On the solicited advice of several bishops, he announced "that we shall be obliged to change our Constitution and that we ought to change our Canons, so as to omit all reference to race distinctions." Specifically, he found Canon 54, the legal foundation for the convocation, objectionable. It was unnecessarily "irritating and discouraging" to African Americans, he said, and needed to be revised.[83] Accordingly, the Arkansas convention removed any references to color, making the exclusion of St. Philip's pursuant to a constitutional amendment specifying those churches with membership in the convention. St. Philip's would be absent from the list. Furthermore, black churches were effectively barred from entering the convention at a later date by a law requiring a two-thirds majority of the convention to approve the admittance of any new congregation. As for the Afro-American Convocation, it became the convocation embracing all those churches not assigned to a geographical convocation, namely, the black churches. Besides eliminating color distinctions in the diocesan constitution, Brown strove to give the Afro-American Convocation some semblance of catholicity by allowing the convocation the right to vote for members of the Standing Committee of the diocese, deputies to the General Convention, and bishops of Arkansas. But the convocation was to vote on these matters outside of the convention and submit its ballot to the convention for certification.[84]

For the next year and a half, the Arkansas Plan lay dormant while Brown relocated St. Philip's and the Conference of Church Workers made good on its commitment to find Brown an archdeacon. Bragg and company recruited the Reverend George A. McGuire of St. Thomas's, Philadelphia. McGuire was a rising star in black Episcopal circles. He was born in Antigua in 1866, the son of a Moravian mother and an Anglican father. His father owned an estate, "Magnola," and engaged in the sugar trade. Baptized an Anglican, he attended Lady Mico Teacher's College on his native island and proceeded to the theological seminary of the Moravians on St. Thomas. After seminary, he was pastor to a church on St. Croix. His matriculation into the Episcopal ministry coincides with Demby's experience in several details. McGuire arrived in the United States in 1894. He, too, had a brief sojourn in the ministry of the African Methodist

Episcopal Church. In 1895, the year of Demby's conversion, he was confirmed by the bishop of Delaware. The Reverend Henry L. Philips, pastor to the Church of the Crucifixion, Philadelphia, and mentor to numerous black Episcopal clergy, took McGuire under his wing. In 1896, when Demby was cutting his teeth as a lay minister to Holy Redeemer, Denver, McGuire was doing the same at St. Andrew's, Cincinnati. In 1896, he was ordained to the diaconate, followed by his ordination to the priesthood the following year. He left Cincinnati in 1899, and after a brief tenure in Richmond, Virginia, became the rector of St. Thomas's, Philadelphia (1901–5). Thus, in the space of six years, he moved from confirmation to filling the shoes of Absalom Jones.[85] St. Thomas's was one of the three or four most prestigious black Episcopal churches in the United States, the others being St. Luke's in Washington, St. James's in Baltimore, and St. Philip's in Harlem. In a church which denied black clergy the opportunity to become bishops, the rectorates of the "big four" were tantamount to bishoprics in the eyes of black Episcopalians.[86]

A born leader with a flair for organization, McGuire was bright, articulate, a good writer, and, in his own words, a "conservative churchman," disinclined to embark on experiments in segregation, be the authors black or white.[87] He was not in favor of the missionary district plan and when Bragg et alia first approached him about leading the Arkansas Plan into existence, he turned them down. True, the archdeaconship of Arkansas's Afro-American Convocation was, as Bragg said, "the highest position yet opened in this country to colored priests," but it was irregular, and untried, and patently racist. "We entreated him, as did other friends, to change his mind," says Bragg, but to no avail.[88]

Then, in May 1905, McGuire resigned the rectorship of St. Thomas's, took an hiatus of several months, and accepted Brown's offer. McGuire does not enlighten us with the particulars of his change of heart. Possibly this hiatus was an abortive attempt to establish himself in the medical field, in which he had had some training. At any rate, in the fall of 1905, he decided that his calling lay in Arkansas and that the conference representatives were right, after all; some black priest should capitalize on the Arkansas Plan and help pave the way for the election of black bishops. Indeed, if Bishop Brown had his way, the archdeacon of Arkansas's Afro-American Convocation might become the first black bishop in the United States.[89] Like Brown, McGuire was accustomed to a meteoric rise through the ranks.

McGuire's vision for his Arkansas ministry arrived by way of the train that brought him to Arkansas. On All Hallows Eve, 1905, McGuire rode from St. Louis to Little Rock in company with a car full of black clergymen belonging to another denomination. Homeward bound after a lengthy convention, they relaxed and began to speak freely as the night rolled by. He quotes one of them: "I had an all-day rally in my church a month ago. I had so-and-so to preach for me in the afternoon, and you believe me sir, that big yellow Negro didn't preach a single thing, and out of a big crowd of people I just took up $40.00. At night I just had to turn in and fill the pulpit myself. Before 15 minutes, I just had them Negroes shouting and hollering, and I wound up things with a $300.00 collection."[90] A long and energetic discussion on the pecuniary qualities of good preaching persuaded McGuire that the southern black religious experience was, by and large, long on emotion and lacking in moral substance. "I then and there resolved that very night that I would, with the commission of the church, publish among my people in Arkansas the glad tidings of redemption and release from sin, immorality, and vice of every kind."[91] On this one point, if no other, he and Bishop Brown were emphatically agreed.

With his archdeacon in hand, Brown was irrepressible. He had already relocated St. Philip's, Little Rock, to a very central location at Ninth and Gaines streets. Formerly Cook Memorial Hall, the new St. Philip's was an attractive brick structure, a building far more worthy of its quasi-cathedral status. He also purchased a new rectory. A firm believer in the proverb that "an empty hive draws a swarm of bees," Brown looked to McGuire for direction in building churches and purchasing property. When McGuire obliged, Brown spent faithfully and sometimes to the point of financial embarrassment.[92] Over the next eighteen months, Brown constructed St. Philip's House of Industry, adjacent to the church of the same name, St. James Mission in south Little Rock, and purchased a former boardinghouse for St. Mary's, Hot Springs. Elsewhere, he helped pay for rented facilities and, as of 1907, began taking donations toward the construction of a bona fide cathedral for the convocation. Stretched to the limit, Brown solicited aid in a pamphlet published by the national office, *Five Years of Missionary Work in Arkansas,* and from interested individuals. The $1,800 per annum allotted by the Domestic and Foreign Missionary Society for "Negro work" in Arkansas became progressively more inadequate, especially with the arrival of McGuire's colleagues.

The archdeacon's "aristocracy of righteousness," as he and Brown called it, had, at its core, ten individuals: McGuire, Mrs. McGuire, a woman social worker from Philadelphia, and seven lay readers aspiring to holy orders. McGuire was general missionary and pastor to all. The social worker, who, for some reason, remains anonymous, was charged with St. Philip's House of Industry.[93] Assisted by Mrs. McGuire, she also ran a kindergarten. The seven lay readers appear to have been recruited outside of Arkansas by the Conference of Church Workers. All of them attended Bishop Brown's Arkansas Theological Chautauqua School, a short course in Episcopal theology similar to the one Demby experienced at St. Matthew's Hall in Denver in 1895–96. Like St. Matthew's Hall, the Arkansas school was biracial in composition. The studies, however, were segregated in part, if not in whole. Brown tried to give his candidates for ministry the academic rudiments of a seminary education, utilizing an Arkansas priest to run the school and augmenting the curriculum with lectures by visiting bishops and other scholars. It is interesting to note that the Diocese of Arkansas elected to forego Greek and Latin requirements at the Arkansas school because of the advanced age of the trainees.[94] Nevertheless, when McGuire's lay readers scored fair to excellent on their Greek and Latin examinations, Bragg published their scores on the front page of the *Church Advocate*. We may deduce that McGuire insisted that his people qualify in Latin and Greek, exceptions notwithstanding. He had, like Demby, a point to drive home. Brown even conceded that the black students were "way ahead" of the white students with regard to Latin and Greek.[95] Four of the seven graduated from the school and five of them were ordained to the ministry.

To describe McGuire's protégés is to describe the pattern of black ordinations at the turn of the century. There was, as previously stated, a shortage of black clergy, particularly in the South, where black ordinations trickled through a grid imposed primarily by the white laity. And, to make matters worse, those few blacks who achieved ordination to the diaconate often found themselves unable to advance to the priesthood. One of the Arkansas recruits, John J. Pusey, whom McGuire called a "man of deep learning and sterling character," was a former Baptist minister from Virginia. Despite the fact that Pusey had joined the Episcopal Church in his home state many years before, he found it necessary to come to Arkansas as an aged missionary in order to be ordained. Said Bragg, "Alas, the good Southern bishop who by confirming him had taken away his living, left him stranded."[96] Brown's answer to this dilemma, like Bishop Frank Gailor's answer discussed in chapter 1, was to segregate his diocesan convention, thereby opening the door for the seven trainees. The Arkansas convention was willing to allow Brown all the black ordinations he desired—provided they convened separately and the Diocese of Arkansas did not have to pay for them.

The situation of the Arkansas trainees is reminiscent of the situation encountered by Demby and McGuire at the time of their ordination. Already possessed of considerable education and ministerial expertise, they, too, had to find a niche, a bishop willing to employ them as lay readers while they prepared for ordination. Three of the Arkansas lay readers came from ministries in other denominations—one Baptist, one Methodist, and one Moravian—and at least five of them had some seminary or college experience. Two had studied at King Hall, an Episcopal seminary for blacks in Washington, D.C., another at Howard University, a fourth had an M.A., and a fifth had graduated from Demby's old charge, Hoffman Hall in Nashville. Walter T. Cleghorn had attended McGuire's alma mater, Lady Mico's Teachers' College in Antigua, served as headmaster to two parochial schools in the British West Indies, and graduated from Oska College in 1907.

McGuire, Pusey, Cleghorn, Joseph M. Matthias, and Augustus C. Roker also represent a burgeoning West Indian ministry among black Episcopalians, an opportunity created by converging racist policies. The United States held a special attraction for West Indians aspiring to the priesthood, because the ministry of the Anglican Church in the West Indies remained solidly white in spite of the fact that the church as a whole was almost entirely black. The white clergy kept it that way. Therefore, ministerial candidates from the islands had basically two choices: missionary work in Africa or immigration to the United States where the aforementioned shortage of black clergy since the Civil War compelled American bishops to look abroad. To quote Harold Lewis, "scores of West Indian students came to the United States at the invitation of American bishops, studied for the priesthood, and were ordained to serve black parishes both in the South and the North."[97] On their heels came a general migration of West Indians, particularly in the years between 1900 and 1930, a migration which included a high proportion of West Indian Anglicans. The number of black Episcopalians increased from approximately fifteen thousand at the turn of the century to about forty thousand by 1930, primarily due to West Indian immigration.[98]

Arkansas's Afro-American Convocation blossomed under McGuire's hand, transforming St. Philip's from a questionable parish of fifty communicants into a hub of missionary activity in Little Rock's black community. St. Philip's grew by at least a third during McGuire's first eighteen months, and, just as important, assumed responsibility for all its current expenses, including the salary of lay reader William A. M. Tucker. It became, said the archdeacon, a "parish in deed as in name."[99] St. James's, Little Rock, was founded in the Braddock addition, an upscale black neighborhood in south Little Rock. After a "Baptist fight," as one member called it, the mission resolved to overcome its differences and began to grow. Several members of St. Philip's, most notably lay reader E. C. Knox, acted as lay missionaries in the establishment and reconciliation of St. James's, which boasted a large Sunday school and even a small day school.[100] St. Philip's House of Industry, however, was not an easy sell for the convocation. Some natives of Little Rock found the idea of developing Christian character adjunct to training in domestic work a little condescending. "We know how to work," they complained. "We don't want to be trained as servants." "How much are you going to pay us?"[101] Nevertheless, after a rocky start in 1906, St. Philip's House of Industry began to show progress, training and placing domestic workers under the guidance of the aforementioned "city missionary" from Philadelphia. Her salary was paid by a black church in Philadelphia.

McGuire was equally successful outside of Little Rock. St. Augustine's Fort Smith, which had gone into eclipse since its admission to the Arkansas convention in 1896, reemerged in 1906–7 with thirty-six confirmands, who, said the archdeacon, were of "the best Negro type."[102] McGuire placed St. Augustine's in Pusey's charge and predicted that it would soon be the largest black mission in Arkansas. St. Andrew's, Pine Bluff, got off to a fast start under the leadership of lay reader Matthias in December 1906 and numbered twenty-seven communicants one year later. The people of St. Andrew's, said McGuire "are of the same type as those in Fort Smith. Indeed they may be described as 'hustlers.'"[103] None were more representative of the congregation than Mr. and Mrs. George Black. George Black was a prominent businessman in Pine Bluff and treasurer of the Episcopate Endowment Fund intended to support Arkansas's black bishop-to-be. Mrs. Black organized and presided over the Ladies Guild, which raised a large initial contribution toward St. Andrew's building fund. The Blacks continued as pillars of St. Andrew's for the remainder of their lives and were particularly devoted to Bishop Demby. The fortunes of St. Mary's, Hot Springs, vacillated with the economic climate of the spa city and corresponding economic migrations. The nineteen original members came from Chicago, Louisville, and St. Louis. Cleghorn, the lay reader in charge, was hard pressed but persevered with the enthusiastic assistance of the rector and congregation of St. Luke's, Hot Springs's white Episcopal church. The building purchased by Bishop Brown was "in bad repair," but a concerted effort by all parties repaired and renovated the structure, turning the upstairs into a rectory. Brown purchased a lot for a new building in a good location and St. Mary's raised a substantial building fund, relative to its size and composition.[104] As of May 1907, its twenty-three communicants were defraying all of their expenses, save Cleghorn's salary. Roker, McGuire's "jewel in the rough," capitalized on the archdeacon's preaching missions to Newport, Arkansas, and established St. Luke's Mission in 1907.[105] Roker's determination and flair for visitation inspired the rapid organization of a small congregation and a day school. The school, which numbered about thirty-five children, was held in the local Colored Methodist Episcopal church, rented for the purpose at $5.00 a month. All of the missions noted material and clerical assistance from white Episcopal churches in their localities. Altogether, the convocation could report about $1,000 raised toward building and maintenance and several missions on their way to self-sufficiency. After a year and a half, the convocation had increased by five missions, one house of industry, and about 150 communicants.

Despite the numbers involved, this was no small matter. Since the Civil War, practically all of the black Episcopal churches in the South had been founded with monetary assistance from church agencies or the various dioceses—and the majority of them remained dependent. Unfortunately, most of the problem could be directly attributed to the stifling influence of their diocesan benefactors. Viable and independent black churches required black initiative in the person of black clergy, the same black clergy who were essentially banned from service for reasons already given. Thus, church after church endured long periods without clergy and found themselves excluded from the government of the larger body. Frequently, bishops and conventions tried to ameliorate the problem by placing the struggling black missions under the guidance of local white parishes or diocesan committees created especially for their supervision. The results were disastrous. Churches that should have established their independence long ago, or, in some cases, had already done so, languished as wards of the dioceses that created them. As a corollary, those same proscriptions that mitigated against their independence rendered them agents of religious servility in the eyes of other blacks. Shackled by this image, they had little success in extending the church to the black community. This, in turn, cut down on their numbers, curtailing their ability to support themselves. Therefore, McGuire, Brown, Bragg, the Conference of Church Workers, and a good many bishops scrutinized the progress of the Arkansas Plan, looking eagerly for signs of growing self-reliance. For good or ill, it became the national model Brown intended.[106]

The high profile of the Arkansas Plan made both McGuire and Brown national spokesmen in the battle over segregation. In 1907, the year Demby preached the evils of Jim Crow and Tuskegee from Key West and Du Bois looked on with contempt at all plans for segregation of the Episcopal Church, the Conference of Church Workers and its allies made an unprecedented effort on behalf of the missionary district plan at the 1907 General Convention. Brown was determined to stop them and to persuade the House of Bishops to legislate a much more radical plan. The missionary district plan, as he saw it, was undesirable in that it would mean the elevation of blacks to equality in the House of Bishops and promote social intermingling—a "nauseating" development, to use the bishop's adjective.[107] Brown made it known that the only satisfactory solution to the "Negro problem" in the Episcopal Church was the establishment of a separate black denomination. He also asked McGuire to expound his own views on the subject. McGuire had been an opponent of the missionary district plan prior to the 1904 General Convention, but had reappraised it in light of his Arkansas experience and found it much more to his liking. Nevertheless, he said the plan would never pass because it was too radical and should be dropped in favor of the suffragan bishop plan, which stood a much better chance of being enacted. The suffragan plan, which would allow the election of black bishops under a universal provision permitting the election of assistant bishops under diocesan bishops, made no breach with catholic orthodoxy, because it would not write Jim Crow into law at the national level. If passed, it would enable dioceses to elect black suffragans to supervise black ministries under the authority of white diocesan bishops. Brown, on the other hand, foretold that the black suffragan would be no more than a glorified archdeacon. Both men spoke their views before the 1906 Arkansas convention, whereupon Bishop Brown consolidated both speeches, along with other pertinent materials, into a book, *The Crucial Race Question,* and distributed the same at the 1907 General Convention. By that time the harmonious public relationship between Brown and McGuire was rapidly deteriorating.

Reading the archdeacon's report to the 1907 Arkansas convention, one would never have known there was trouble between the two men, or that McGuire was "radically at variance," as he later put it, with Brown.[108] Comparing blacks in general to white Episcopalians, McGuire maintained: "We are still a child race—only three centuries removed from barbarism, only half a century emancipated from a degrading condition of slavery, and we therefore feel grateful for the examples set us for imitation by the men and women of your race whose beautiful lives and characters give wings to our aspirations and stimulus to our pursuit after righteousness."[109] And he praised Brown with unstinting admiration: "I thank God that He has appointed me to serve under such a bishop, who . . . has not been unmindful of the fact that until the church provides us with bishops of our own race who are not restrained in any measure from meeting us and touching us in every point like as we are, he is the Bishop of all the people, white and black. To him, more than to any man, belongs the praise for what has been accomplished."[110] He published his praise of Brown, seconded by Bragg, on the front page of the *Church Advocate* of March 1908. Ironically, he also published an open letter on page 4, detailing his reasons for leaving Arkansas. Among other things, he stated, "I have been able to add to the church about two hundred communicants, not because, as has been stated, but in spite of the Arkansas Plan."[111] What happened?

The crux of the problem was Brown's ever-increasing racism. With a zeal typical of "Southerners by adoption," Brown became a veritable sponge for theories contrived in support of Jim Crow.[112] Worse still, he published his conclusions without due consideration for McGuire's ministry, to say nothing of the archdeacon himself. For instance, Brown espoused the view that mulattoes, being the progeny of degenerate white men, were themselves physically degenerating. Thus, he made a derogatory comment that could be applied to perhaps a majority of black Episcopalians in the United States, and probably to McGuire specifically. McGuire tried valiantly to maintain some sort of common ground with his superior in his reports to the Arkansas convention. In his 1907 report, he even tried to capitalize on the pathological fear of black sexual assault that seemed to permeate the white community. Due to the influence of the Anglican Church, said McGuire, "the 'usual' crime for which summary punishment is so often visited upon the head of the criminal, is practically unknown in the West Indies."[113]

However, it was his 1907 report that awakened McGuire to the extent of his plight. In 1906, he had addressed the Arkansas convention, convened at St. Paul's, Newport. This speech, given at Brown's behest, was the "unveiling," so to speak, of McGuire and the Arkansas Plan. The novelty of a black priest addressing the Arkansas convention so electrified the proceedings that the Arkansas Woman's Auxiliary "crashed" the convention in order to hear the archdeacon's address—an altogether appropriate gesture in light of the fact that white women had been the "most consistent" supporters of black missionary work since the Civil War.[114] With his usual erudition, McGuire acquitted himself well. In fact, Brown tells us that he so impressed those gathered at St. Paul's that many of them went so far as to abandon racial decorum and shake the archdeacon's hand. Brown and McGuire were pleased and amazed when the convention responded with a rousing endorsement of the Arkansas Plan. Sometime later, McGuire told Brown in jest that when he returned to his room, he stared into a mirror to see if he were not a white man. Thereafter, the archdeacon looked upon his annual address as an opportunity to dispel racial stereotypes, reaffirm the qualities of the people he represented, and secure the assistance of the parallel white church in Arkansas. But he never got the opportunity. Newport was his first and last address.

The 1907 convention was held at Christ Church, Little Rock, which probably had something to do with McGuire's exclusion from the proceedings. Just

as the archdeacon prepared to leave his residence and go across town to deliver his second annual address, the phone rang. The caller informed him that
he was not legally entitled to the floor of the convention and asked if he would
please submit his report to the secretary. McGuire was stunned, but he made
the delivery and pondered the significance of his exclusion on the way home:

> I was an "orphan" priest of the church, without rights, privileges, or courtesies,
> denied even the opportunity for which I had made special preparation, and which
> it was intimated would be afforded me to relate what had been accomplished in
> a missionary way among the people of my race. I am not willing to admit that I
> was chagrined because I wanted to be on social equality with white churchmen
> as my bishop would have contended, had I discussed the situation with him. God
> forbid! I am willing to admit, however, that I realized more than ever the futility
> of the feeble efforts which we are making to reach the educated Negroes of this
> section.[115]

After the 1907 convention, conflict began in earnest. McGuire and the Reverend William V. Tunnell, former director of King Hall, wrote letters to Brown,
taking him to task for his dogma on the degeneracy of African Americans.
Brown responded with a rebuttal, ignoring their statistical information in view
of traditional southern mores. This exchange also filled the pages of *The Crucial Race Question*. Brown closed his book with an observation that must have
grieved McGuire when he read it, a brief chapter describing the archdeacon's
triumph at the 1906 Arkansas convention and his jocularity before the "looking glass."[116] True, said Brown, McGuire exhibited fine literary and oratorical
skills, "But he is a Negro!" and only by virtue of segregation was he entitled to
the floor in the first place. He had no right to address the convention, but the
convention, put at ease by that very fact, could invite him to speak. McGuire,
he said, concurred in the wisdom of this exclusion.

One might say that the 1907 Arkansas convention moved McGuire to the exit
and the 1907 General Convention pushed him through. Having disseminated
The Crucial Race Question to the 1907 General Convention, Brown made a
dramatic plea for an autonomous Negro Episcopal Church, because, as he said,
the "Divine law of racial antipathy" precludes the election of black bishops in
a white church.[117] Brown's highly publicized exposition on the inherent evils
of integrated ecclesiastical government did not go unheeded by blacks in Arkansas, who, said McGuire, had already formed a negative opinion as to the
attitude of the Diocese of Arkansas. "The intelligent, progressive, and thought-
ful Negroes to whom this church should most appeal are holding aloof. . . . they
are content to visit our services without seeking membership in a church which

offers them salvation at the price of their manhood."[118] Ultimately, McGuire found that continued service to Brown made him look and feel the "Uncle Tom," and that his attempts to find common ground only served to amplify the problem.[119] The same could be said of the convocation as a whole.

The General Convention rejected Brown's Negro Episcopal Church out of hand. The missionary district plan also failed. However, the suffragan bishop plan passed—albeit in a less ambitious form than the one McGuire had originally endorsed. The new suffragan was entitled to a seat in the House of Bishops and enjoyed the right to the floor, but he had no voting rights. Brown quickly reconciled to this, resolving to elect a black suffragan as soon as the various dioceses ratified the legislation pursuant to the 1910 General Convention. We can safely assume that he planned to elect McGuire.

However, the bishop's mind, churning with racist dogma, had no time for the obvious. In early 1908, he sent McGuire east on a fund-raising tour for the Afro-American Convocation. McGuire returned, informed Brown that he had accepted a call to St. Bartholomew's, Cambridge, Massachusetts, and left Arkansas for good. Brown was thunderstruck and humiliated. He lamented openly before the Arkansas convention: "The unkindest cut of all was the losing of the archdeacon to Boston. That was almost more than I could bear; for Boston, you will remember, is the citadel of the opposition to the Arkansas Plan. Archdeacon McGuire had gone over soul and body to the enemies' camp!"[120]

The Arkansas Plan was at an end. Concurrent to the 1908 Arkansas convention, Brown ordained Cleghorn, Pusey, Roker, and Tucker to the diaconate, designating the latter as McGuire's successor. But these were hollow gestures. By 1910, the new deacons were scattered to the wind in search of their own "St. Bartholomews." Pusey transferred to South Carolina. Cleghorn transferred to Los Angeles, where he remained priest-in-charge of St. Philip the Evangelist Mission until his death in 1932. Tucker transferred to Kentucky. Roker founded St. Philip's Mission, Muskogee, Oklahoma, in 1910 and remained there for the next sixteen years.[121] All, save Pusey, became priests. Matthias was ordained by the bishop of Oklahoma in 1909 and advanced to the priesthood in 1912.

Brown did not last much longer than McGuire. He was decisively defeated in 1909–10 on two other measures. First, he lost a battle with the congregation of Trinity Cathedral when he unsuccessfully attempted to fire their dean. Second, the 1910 Arkansas convention rejected his ecumenical *Level Plan for Church Union*. This new plan, which called for an end to the doctrine of apostolic succession, was blatantly heretical to the Episcopal Church and as dear to Brown as the Arkansas Plan. The Reverend Henry M. Hyde, rector of Christ Church, Little Rock, led the opposition in passing a thundering resolution in condemnation of the Level Plan. For once, Trinity Cathedral and Christ Church were agreed upon something—Brown had to go. The effect of being defeated on this third major "bill" was to render Brown emotionally unable to continue in office. He had had enough. He complained of poor health and took a leave of absence, returning only long enough to supervise the election of his successor, the Reverend James R. Winchester, in 1911. He officially resigned in 1912.

In retirement, Brown became a heretic by degrees, attacking Christian supernaturalism and propagating a hybrid of Christian ethics and Communism. And he repeatedly challenged the House of Bishops by publishing his theories. In 1925, they finally took the dare and deposed him from the Episcopal ministry, but it only served to inspire his pen. He published rebuttal after rebuttal until his death in 1937, challenging the validity of their actions and maintaining that he was still a bishop in the "catholic" sense, by virtue of his consecration as a bishop in the "Old Catholic Church," a sect defined by its opposition to papal infallibility. Brown argued that his Old Catholic consecration, which took place on the eve of his deposition from the ministry, superseded his Episcopal consecration. These wranglings did little to reestablish his reputation in the Episcopal Church, which by and large came to regard him as a poor, misguided soul. However, it is a significant but little-known fact that Brown recanted his racist propaganda in his old age and acknowledged that he was wrong in his views about black people.[122]

Unfortunately for McGuire, the Diocese of Massachusetts proved more discreet in its racism than the Diocese of Arkansas, but just as close-minded, a situation encapsulated in Harold Lewis's words, "In the North we call it Jim Crow, Esquire."[123] When McGuire made his fund-raising tour of the Northeast in early 1908, he found the congregation of St. Bartholomew's struggling along in a defunct white church. Driven to self-determination by the white people of nearby St. Peter's—who had ostracized them out the door—they issued a call to McGuire, who came to their rescue, increasing the membership tenfold and rallying the congregation to self-sufficiency. The Diocese of Massachusetts, however, refused St. Bartholomew's its rightful parish status and its corresponding membership in the Massachusetts diocesan convention. McGuire, doubly outraged by the hypocrisy of this denial, left the parish ministry after two years for a post with the American Church Institute for Negroes, which he served as field secretary for two years. In 1913, he removed to Antigua and took up a pastorate on his home island.

McGuire's trials and triumphs over the next two decades epitomize and exceed the struggle of African American Episcopalians for recognition and independence and, ironically, demonstrate a degree of religious pragmatism at least equal to that of Bishop Brown. In 1919, he returned to the United States and joined the vanguard of Marcus Garvey's United Negro Improvement Association. He became chaplain general of the UNIA and, as such, gave its religious expression a very Episcopal flavor; so Episcopal, in fact, that some of its members complained that he was using the UNIA to proselyte. At about the same time, he established the Independent Episcopal Church, which might have been the fulfillment of Brown's Negro Episcopal Church, had it succeeded. McGuire's chief impediment in the establishment of the new denomination was the need for bishops. Roman Catholic and Episcopal authorities refused to consecrate him, but he continued to pursue consecration with other religious bodies until two bishops of the American Catholic Church, a subdivision of the Old Catholic Church, agreed to consecrate him. By that time, the new organization had been redesignated the African Orthodox Church in anticipation of an Eastern Orthodox consecration that failed to materialize. In 1921, McGuire became the founding father and the first bishop of the African Orthodox Church. The AOC, like the Arkansas Plan, was predicated on racial homogeneity and is often remembered for the image of the black Madonna and child. Primarily due to its substantial following in the New York, Philadelphia, Boston, Chicago, and Miami areas, the AOC is estimated to have had about twenty thousand adherents at its height, denuding America's black Episcopal churches of several thousand West Indian Anglicans during the 1920s and 1930s. McGuire was elevated to primate of the AOC before his death in 1934.[124]

The third epilogue to the Arkansas Plan was the election of suffragan bishop for "colored" work. In 1910, Arkansas ratified the suffragan plan, but failed to elect a black bishop by reason of Brown's declining ministry. Two years later, Winchester assumed Brown's jurisdiction. Less catholic than "good old Bishop Pierce" but more compassionate than Bishop Brown, he blew on the embers of the Arkansas Plan, hoping to raise up something black and Christian and manifestly good. Enter Edward T. Demby.

NOTES

1. Pierce was in favor of resolving the deadlock by accepting the Eastern church's interpretation, "from the Father through the Son," versus the Anglican, "from the Father and the Son." With the stalemate over the wording of the Creed, Pierce became disillusioned with Lambeth and even fearful that it might evolve into a worldwide Anglican Council capable of usurping the powers of the General Convention. Such was his fear of the church's extraordinary councils. He was, no doubt, wary of the Sewanee council of 1883 for similar reasons. Joseph B. Tucker, interview by author, 13 Nov. 1994,

Pine Bluff, Ark.; Margaret Sims McDonald, *White Already to Harvest: The Episcopal Church in Arkansas, 1838–1971* (Sewanee, Tenn.: University Press for the Episcopal Diocese of Arkansas, 1975), 144.

2. McDonald, *Harvest*, 81.

3. "Arkansas," *Church Advocate*, Feb. 1918, 4.

4. McDonald, *Harvest*, 116.

5. Ibid.

6. J. Carleton Hayden, "After the War: The Mission and Growth of the Episcopal Church among Blacks in the South, 1865–1877," *Historical Magazine of the Protestant Episcopal Church* 42 (Dec. 1973): 426.

7. George F. Bragg, *History of the Afro-American Group of the Protestant Episcopal Church* (Baltimore: Church Advocate Press, 1922), 183.

8. George F. Bragg, "The Episcopal Church and the Negro Race," *Historical Magazine of the Protestant Episcopal Church* 4 (Mar. 1935): 50, quoted in Harold T. Lewis, *Yet with a Steady Beat: The African-American Struggle for Recognition in the Episcopal Church* (Valley Forge, Pa.: Trinity Press International, 1996), 52.

9. McDonald, *Harvest*, 109–10, 117.

10. H. C. Carvill, "Episcopal Family Heritage," MS, Family History Files, Arkansas History Commission, Little Rock, Ark., 9.

11. George E. N. De Man, ed., *Helena, the River, the Ridge, the Romance* (Little Rock, Ark.: Phillips County Historical Society, 1978), 105.

12. Theodore Du Bose Bratton, *Wanted—Leaders! A Study of Negro Development* (New York: Presiding Bishop and Council, Department of Missions and Church Extension, 1922), 203.

13. Randy Finley, *From Slavery to Uncertain Freedom: The Freedmen's Bureau in Arkansas, 1865–1869* (Fayetteville: University of Arkansas Press, 1996), 126.

14. Henry C. Lay, Report to the Board of Missions, 1866, quoted in McDonald, *Harvest*, 71.

15. Hayden, "After the War," 426–27.

16. Although the "Official Acts" section of Pierce's 1884 address indicates that he was in Tennessee for the month of July, his diary for 1883 indicates that he was on a fundraising tour of the Northeast at the time of the Sewanee Conference. This concurs with the records of the conference, itself, which do not indicate that he was present. *New York Churchman*, 25 Aug. 1883, 205; Henry N. Pierce, Diaries (1883), Archives of the Diocese of Arkansas, hereafter cited as Pierce Diaries; Henry N. Pierce, "Bishop's Address," *Journal of the Proceedings of the Thirteenth Annual Council of the Protestant Episcopal Church in the Diocese of Arkansas* (1884), 24, hereafter cited as *Arkansas Journal*.

17. "An Account of a Conference Held at Sewanee, Tenn., July 25 to 28, 1883, on the Relation of the Church to the Coloured People," *Journal of the General Convention of the Protestant Episcopal Church* (1883): 595–600.

18. Bragg, *History*, 152.

19. Kenneth C. Barnes, "Who Killed John M. Clayton? Political Violence in Conway County, Arkansas, in the 1880s," *Arkansas Historical Quarterly* 52 (Winter 1993): 371.

20. Ibid.

21. William P. Witsell, *A History of Christ Episcopal Church, Little Rock, Arkansas, 1839–1947* (Little Rock, Ark.: Christ Church Vestry, n.d.), 72–73.

22. Ibid., 72. "In the afternoon of the second day . . . ," writes Witsell, "St. Philip's . . . was admitted into union with the diocese as a *parish,* and, therefore, entitled to . . . representation in the [convention] by lay delegates." Witsell seems to indicate, by way of italicizing the word "parish," that the protest was primarily a political one, with racial overtones. In other words, there might not have been a schism had St. Philip's been admitted as a nonvoting mission. This distinction could also be construed as an indication that the Christ Church laity believed that St. Philip's had been admitted as a parish undeservedly.

23. Mary P. Fletcher, "A Reminiscence of Little Rock Churches," *Arkansas Historical Quarterly* 13 (Autumn 1954): 261–62.

24. Cassius M. C. Barnes, a protégé of Republican Judge Liberty Bartlett, joined Whipple in organizing the move. See Julia G. Besancon-Alford, "Bartlett: A Model Manufacturing Town," *Pulaski County Historical Review* 42 (Summer 1994): 48.

25. Fletcher, "Reminiscence," 261.

26. Michael McNeely, interview by author, 30 Jan. 1995, Little Rock, Ark. Michael McNeely is the historiographer of the Diocese of Arkansas. His information on the "purge" is taken from the oral history of Root's descendants.

27. *Arkansas Churchman,* Sept. 1889, quoted in Ellen M. H. Cantrell, comp., *Annals of Christ Church Parish of Little Rock, Arkansas, from A.D. 1839 to A.D. 1899* (Little Rock, Ark.: Arkansas Democrat Co., 1900), 273–74.

28. Ibid., 279–82.

29. *Anglo-Saxon Churchman,* 1890, quoted in Cantrell, *Annals,* 282–83.

30. Wallace Carnahan, farewell address to Christ Church, Little Rock, quoted in Cantrell, *Annals,* 297. Carnahan considered his tenure at Christ Church to be the pinnacle of his career, but he had little to say of his tenure there out of deference to Ellen Cantrell's history. See Wallace Carnahan, *Odd Happenings* (Jackson, Miss.: Tucker Printing House, 1915).

31. *Anglo-Saxon Churchman,* Sept. 1890, Arkansas History Commission, Little Rock, Ark., 5. The Diocese of Arkansas responded to Carnahan's criticisms by establishing the *Diocese of Arkansas,* a church paper dedicated to the defense of the sacraments as a means of spiritual regeneration and a rebuttal to the more mainstream Protestant evangelism of the *Churchman.* See "Holy Baptism or New Birth," *Diocese of Arkansas,* Jan. 1890, Arkansas History Commission, Little Rock, Ark., 3. It is impossible to determine if Pierce used the *Diocese of Arkansas* as a forum on the race issue, because the January 1890 edition, which would appear to be the only copy in existence, makes no mention of the controversy surrounding St. Philip's. However, it is very unlikely that

Pierce, who habitually eschewed public comment on race matters, would have used the *Diocese* in defense of black participation in the Arkansas convention.

32. Pierce Diaries, entries for 17–19 Apr. 1890; Douglass I. Hobbs to the Bishops and Standing Committees of the American Church, 28 Feb. 1898, bound volume of letters pertaining to the election of the Right Reverend William M. Brown, Bishop William A. Leonard Papers, Archives of the Episcopal Diocese of Ohio, Trinity Cathedral, Cleveland, Ohio, hereafter cited as Leonard Papers.

33. Bragg, *History*, 157.

34. Ibid., 153. To quote the memorial from the Conference of Church Workers, "What is the position of colored men in this Church?" (*Journal of the General Convention* [1889]: 266).

35. Bragg, *History*, 182–83.

36. *Church Advocate*, July 1914, 2.

37. Ibid., Jan. 1918, 3–4. Florida was the other diocese to send a black delegate to the 1889 General Convention.

38. Witsell, *History*, 73–74; D. I. Hobbs, "To the Bishops and Standing Committees of the American Church," 28 Feb. 1898, Leonard Papers.

39. D. I. Hobbs, "To the Bishops and Standing Committees of the American Church," 28 Feb. 1898, Leonard Papers.

40. Henry N. Pierce, "Bishop's Address," *Arkansas Journal* (1897): 16, 31–37; McDonald, *Harvest*, 133–37.

41. William M. Brown, *My Heresy: The Autobiography of William Montgomery Brown* (Galion, Ohio: Bradford-Brown Educational Co., 1931), 20–26.

42. Ron Carden to Michael Beary, 4 Jan. 1999, author's private correspondence. Although Carden's biography of Brown is not yet complete, Carden is by far the most thoroughgoing researcher of Brown's life, to date. See also Henry N. Pierce, "Account of Election of Brown," William Montgomery Brown Papers, Ohio Historical Society, Columbus, Ohio, MSS 780, box 2, folder 1.

43. Although Brown graduated from Bexley Hall, he was, for some reason, denied a Bachelor of Divinity Degree. This could have happened one of two ways. In 1892, the seminary revised its somewhat daunting prerequisites for a B.D., namely, a Master of Arts degree or seven years in the pastorate, in favor of conferring the B.D. on all "candidates 'who shall have satisfactorily completed the full course of this seminary'" (Richard M. Spielmann, *Bexley Hall: 150 Years—A Brief History*, Special Collections, Olin Library, Kenyon College, Gambier, Ohio, 34–35). Having entered the seminary as early as 1880, Brown was either grandfathered out of the change or simply failed to meet its requirements. His lack of sustained pastoral experience by reason of his burgeoning missionary work may have mitigated against him, or his heavy reliance upon tutorials in his academic endeavors, or both. Brown acknowledged that he took "shortcuts" academically (Brown, *My Heresy*, 20–26). He had a thinly disguised contempt for educational standards which failed to acknowledge what he would call the practicalities of successful ministry (Ron Carden to Michael Beary, 4 Jan. 1999, author's private

correspondence). Carden states, "Brown did not consider himself an alumnus of Bexley Hall."

44. Brown, *My Heresy,* 16–21, 23–26.

45. Phillipians 1:15–18, NRSV (New Revised Standard Version).

46. 1 Timothy 3:1–6, NRSV.

47. Although the *Arkansas Journal* indicates that Brown won the clergy by winning nine out of sixteen votes, and Margaret McDonald duly notes the fact in her history of the diocese, Bishop Pierce notes in his diary that one clergyman claimed to have changed his vote, giving Brown a total of ten clerical votes (Pierce Diaries [1897], 350). Nevertheless, the *Journal* figures were and have remained the official tally.

48. Fon Louise Gordon, *Caste and Class: The Black Experience in Arkansas, 1880–1920* (Athens: University of Georgia Press, 1995), 33, 92, 149. Speight, who served the Little Rock Police Department for thirty-two years, was also on the planning committee for the statewide 1897 Emancipation Celebration.

49. Pierce Diaries (1897), 350.

50. Earl F. Woodward, "The Brooks and Baxter War in Arkansas, 1872–1874," *Arkansas Historical Quarterly* 30 (Winter 1971): 321.

51. "In respect to the allegation of Colonel Whipple . . . strongly supported by Governor Jones, that I had been elected by the colored vote, I ascertained that this vote was given to me at both [conventions]" (William M. Brown, "To the Bishops and Standing Committees of the American Church," 15 Feb. 1898, Archives of the Episcopal Diocese of Maryland, Baltimore, Md., hereafter cited as Maryland Papers).

52. Pierce Diaries (1897), 351–53; *Arkansas Gazette,* Dec. 2, 3, 4, 6, 1897; W. M. Brown, "To the Bishops and Standing Committees of the American Church," 15 Feb. 1898, Maryland Papers.

53. W. M. Brown to W. A. Leonard, 12 Oct. 1897, Leonard Papers.

54. William A. Leonard cover letter to bound volume of materials relating to Brown's election, Leonard Papers; W. M. Brown to W. A. Leonard, 1 June 1898, ibid.

55. Brown, *My Heresy,* 3–26.

56. H. N. Pierce to W. M. Brown, 24 Jan. 1898, Leonard Papers.

57. D. I. Hobbs, "To the Bishops and Standing Committees of the American Church," 28 Feb. 1898, Leonard Papers; W. M. Brown, "To the Bishops and Standing Committees of the American Church," 15 Feb. 1898, Maryland Papers; "Protest against the Approval of the Election of the Consecration of Archdeacon William M. Brown as Bishop Coadjutor of the Diocese of Arkansas," a brief in the private collection of the Reverend Joseph B. Tucker, Pine Bluff, Arkansas; W. M. Brown to D. I. Hobbs, 21 Mar. 1898, Leonard Papers; W. M. Brown to Rev. Lockwood, 29 Jan. 1898, ibid.; W. M. Brown to John M. Daggett, 27 Apr. 1898, ibid.

58. Henry N. Pierce to W. M. Brown, 26 Apr. 1898, William Montgomery Brown Papers, Ohio Historical Society, Columbus, Ohio, MSS 780, box 2, folder 1.

59. William M. Brown, "An Explanatory and Historical Statement Regarding the Boston Incident," in William M. Brown, "Bishop's Address," *Arkansas Journal* (1904):

63. According to Ron Carden, Miss Miriam Sayre was one of several readers employed by the elderly Brown after diabetes had debilitated his eyesight. Miss Sayre reports that Brown complained that he was dogged on the "Negro question" from the outset by reason of the role played by the "black vote" in his election (Carden to Michael Beary, 4 Jan. 1999).

60. Brown, "Bishop's Address," *Arkansas Journal* (1904): 63.

61. McDonald, *Harvest,* 139–40.

62. Ibid., 141.

63. William M. Brown, "Episcopal Charge to the 1902 Council," *Arkansas Journal* (1902): 75–78; see "An Episcopal Mistake," *Living Church,* 10 Aug. 1901.

64. "Proceedings of the Thirtieth Annual Council," *Arkansas Journal* (1902): 18.

65. J. Percy Robottom and W. D. Williams, "Record of a Parish Meeting," in William M. Brown, "Bishop's Address," *Arkansas Journal* (1903): 70.

66. Ibid.

67. A. M. Cole and J. A. Buchanan to William M. Brown, 28 May 1902, in Brown, "Bishop's Address," *Arkansas Journal* (1903): 69.

68. Brown, "Bishop's Address," *Arkansas Journal* (1903): 74.

69. E. M. Sadler's analysis of Little Rock churches, in *Indianapolis Freeman,* 21 Sept. 1901, quoted in Willard B. Gatewood Jr., *Aristocrats of Color: The Black Elite, 1880–1920* (Bloomington: Indiana University Press, 1990), 95; "The 1905 'New Handy Map of Little Rock,'" *Pulaski County Historical Review* 34 (Spring 1986): 90–92.

70. Gordon, *Caste and Class,* 12. The *Arkansas Journal* bears witness to Gibbs's standing in Little Rock. He is identified merely as "Judge Gibbs" at the St. Philip's conference, which would imply that he required no introduction (Robottom and Williams, "Record of a Parish Meeting," in Brown, "Bishop's Address," *Arkansas Journal* [1903]: 72).

71. Brown, "Explanatory Statement," *Arkansas Journal* (1904): 80.

72. Theodore Schroeder, *The Bishop of Bolsheviks and Atheists* (Detroit, Mich.: By the author, 1922), 11.

73. Brown, "Explanatory Statement," *Arkansas Journal* (1904): 64.

74. Ibid.

75. Ibid., 66.

76. Ibid., 66, 68.

77. *Church Advocate,* Jan. 1916, 3.

78. In 1903, the Reverend David Le Roy Ferguson, son of the Reverend Joseph Samuel Ferguson, was a brand new deacon just out of the Episcopal Theological School, Cambridge, Massachusetts. Stowe's *Clerical Directory* tells us that he spent the first months of his ministry in Little Rock, but does not say in what capacity. Ferguson was a native of Ohio with no readily visible Arkansas connections other than knowing the former archdeacon of Ohio. It appears that Brown recruited the younger Ferguson to Little Rock out of his old diocese, but Ferguson was not inclined to stay. Brown makes no mention of him in his reports to the Arkansas convention.

79. Brown, "Explanatory Statement," *Arkansas Journal* (1904): 81; *Church Advocate,* Feb. 1918, 3.

80. *Church Advocate,* Mar. 1908, 2.

81. Ibid. (Aug. 1914): 2.

82. Brown, "Explanatory Statement," *Arkansas Journal* (1904): 76.

83. Ibid., 84–85.

84. William B. Mitchell, "Bishop's Address," *Arkansas Journal* (1946): 25.

85. Gavin White, "Patriarch McGuire and the Episcopal Church," *Historical Magazine of the Protestant Episcopal Church* 38 (June 1969): 109–11; see also Randall K. Burkett, *Garveyism as a Religious Movement: The Institutionalization of Black Civil Religion* (Metuchen, N.J.: Scarecrow Press, 1978), 723.

86. Donald Wilson, telephone interview by author, 11 June, 1991, Palm Coast, Fla., transcript. The late Reverend Donald Wilson was the retired rector of St. James's, Baltimore.

87. *Church Advocate,* Mar. 1908, 3.

88. Ibid., 1–2.

89. Ibid.

90. George A. McGuire, "Second Annual Missionary Report," *Arkansas Journal* (1907): 90.

91. Ibid.

92. William M. Brown, "Bishop's Address," *Arkansas Journal* (1907): 55.

93. McGuire, "Second Report," *Arkansas Journal* (1907): 91.

94. McDonald, *Harvest,* 162; *Church Advocate,* Mar. 1908, 1–2.

95. *Church Advocate,* July 1907, 1.

96. Ibid., Mar. 1908, 1–2. To cite a similar example from another diocese, black clergy in the Diocese of East Carolina continued to enjoy all the rights of white clergy in the East Carolina convention, but the convention habitually stifled any measure that might result in increased black representation. Should there be an increase, said Bishop Robert Strange of East Carolina, "The diocese will exclude all of them from its [convention]" (Bishop Robert Strange, "Missionary Districts for the Negroes—The Case Stated," *New York Churchman,* 14 Sept. 1907, 369–70, quoted in David E. Finch, "Little Rock's Red Bishop Brown and His Separate Black Church," *Pulaski County Historical Review* 20 [Sept. 1972]: 28).

97. H. Lewis, *Yet with a Steady Beat,* 86.

98. See Harold T. Lewis, "Efforts to Evangelize the Freedmen," ibid., 47–61, and "West Indian Anglicans: Missionaries to Black Episcopalians," 86–108; *Church Advocate,* July 1907, 1; ibid., Mar. 1908, 1–2; McGuire, "Second Report," *Arkansas Journal* (1907): 84–86.

99. McGuire, "Second Report," *Arkansas Journal* (1907): 84.

100. George A. McGuire, "Missionary Report," *Arkansas Journal* (1906): 77.

101. Ibid.

102. McGuire, "Second Report," *Arkansas Journal* (1907): 85.

103. Ibid., 86.

104. Dorothy B. Wise, "St. Mary's Episcopal Church, 1905–1966," *Garland County Record* 26 (1985): 17.

105. McGuire, "Second Report," *Arkansas Journal* (1907): 86.

106. See Bragg, "The Matter of Self-Support," *History,* 244–50.

107. William M. Brown, "My Speech in the House of Bishops," in William M. Brown, "Bishop's Address," *Arkansas Journal* (1908): 67.

108. *Church Advocate,* Mar. 1908, 4.

109. McGuire, "Second Report," *Arkansas Journal* (1907): 91.

110. Ibid.

111. *Church Advocate,* Mar. 1908, 4.

112. According to the stereotype, southern "converts" are more racist than the people they are trying to emulate. This was Brown (Schroeder, *Bishop of Bolsheviks,* 11).

113. McGuire, "Second Report," *Arkansas Journal* (1907): 89.

114. "From the beginning of their work in the Freedom schools after the Civil War, the Woman's Auxiliary had proved to be the Episcopal Church's most consistent supporter of work among the Negroes" (Mary S. Donovan, *A Separate Call: Women's Ministries in the Episcopal Church, 1850–1920* [Wilton, Conn.: Morehouse-Barlow, 1986], 126–27).

115. *Church Advocate,* Mar. 1908, 4.

116. William M. Brown, *The Crucial Race Question* (Little Rock, Ark.: Arkansas Churchman's Publishing Co., 1907), 248–49

117. Brown, "Speech in the House of Bishops," *Arkansas Journal* (1908): 69.

118. *Church Advocate,* Mar. 1908, 4.

119. Ibid., June 1908, 2.

120. William M. Brown, "Resignation of Archdeacon McGuire," in Brown, "Bishop's Address," *Arkansas Journal* (1908): 56.

121. Roker had an altercation with Bishop Demby and Bishop Thomas C. Casady of Oklahoma in the late 1920s, as described in chapter 4. Perhaps as a result of that experience, he left the pastoral ministry for several years, returning to Arkansas in 1940 to serve St. Andrew's in Pine Bluff (1940–42) and St. Mary's in Hot Springs (1942–51). Roker was particularly inclined to intellectual pursuits and accumulated several degrees.

122. Brown, *My Heresy,* 45; William M. Brown, *Heresy: "Bad Bishop Brown's" Quarterly Lectures, No. 1, The American Race Problem* (Galion, Ohio: Bradford-Brown Educational Co., 1930), 34.

123. Harold T. Lewis, interview by author, 17 Sept. 1992, New York, transcript.

124. See H. Lewis, "George Alexander McGuire and the African Orthodox Church," *Yet with a Steady Beat,* 100–106; See also Burkett, "Sect or Civil Religion: The Debate with George Alexander McGuire," *Garveyism as a Religious Movement,* 71–110."

3

A Marked Man:
The Election of Bishop Demby

In early 1917, three bishops of the Province of the Southwest, an area encompassing Texas, Missouri, Arkansas, Kansas, Oklahoma, and New Mexico, asked the Reverend Edward T. Demby if he wanted to be the suffragan bishop for "colored work" in the Southwest. The Right Reverend James R. Winchester, Demby's old friend and bishop of Arkansas, led the delegation. Demby turned them down. "I told them frankly that I had [no such] ambition; that I could not accept; that I was satisfied being the Archdeacon of the Negro Work of the Church in the Diocese of Tennessee and as the principal of [Hoffman-St. Mary's Industrial Institute] together with community activities in Memphis for which I was responsible [and which] needed my direction, and therefore could not accept the honor."[1] It was a disappointment for Winchester, who had highly recommended Demby to the other members of the group: Bishops James Wise of Kansas, Francis K. Brooke of Oklahoma, George H. Kinsolving of Texas, Sidney C. Partridge of West Missouri and Daniel S. Tuttle, presiding bishop and bishop of Missouri. However, since his diocese was to be the instrument of election, the bishop of Arkansas had the initiative.

Reconciled to the failure of Bishop Brown's Arkansas Plan, Arkansas's Episcopalians were ready to try another experiment in segregation under their new bishop. In the wake of the stormy exits of Bishop William M. Brown and Archdeacon George A. McGuire, Winchester strove to impart a less racist, more sympathetic, and more constructive frame of mind to the evangelization of black Arkansas.

Winchester's upbringing did much to shape his attitude. Born in 1854, he was a southern aristocrat who spent his childhood on a Maryland plantation in the company of numerous slaves. As a result, he carried with him a belief in the ability of Christianity to redeem otherwise adverse relationships between the races and eventually eliminate evil practices, slavery included. His childhood remembrances have that same almost ethereal quality characteristic of Demby's childhood remembrances: "Having been brought up on a Christian

plantation with slaves about me (an inheritance for generations), I saw nothing but loving regard on the part of all. There was a Christian sentiment that
pervaded the plantation and the whole neighborhood. For any child to have
been disrespectful to any of the older colored folk meant correction from our
parents."[2] Winchester exemplified the benign paternalism characteristic of his
class and region. He reveled, for instance, in the Daughters of the Confedera-
cy, those "splendid women, holding up the best traditions of our forefathers.
The purest American blood flows through Southern veins, and the highest
chivalry animates the men of the Southland."[3] His outlook on race was reminiscent of that of Bishop Frank Gailor of Tennessee, in that, while he advocated segregation, he took a deep personal interest in his clergy, whatever their
color. However, he was not the dogmatist on race that Gailor was. Nor did he
have the strong personality of his old bishop. Like Demby he preferred to lead
by pious example.

Confident of Christianity's power to enhance race relations, Winchester
occasionally took an unconventional approach in promoting black ministries
when he thought it in everyone's best interests, a trait going back to his early
days as a priest. While serving at St. John's, Wytheville, Virginia he led an unusually integrated congregation (c. 1878). The church sponsored both a white
and a black school in its basement, held in the afternoons and mornings, respectively. The worship services were joint, but segregated, with the black communicants occupying a gallery. The Reverend J. H. M. Pollard, a young black
priest who went on to be archdeacon of "colored work" in North Carolina,
was in charge of the growing black contingent. Pollard delivered a sermon that
marked "the first time in the history of Virginia that a colored clergyman has
preached to a white congregation in an Episcopal church."[4] He utilized St.
John's to conduct evangelistic meetings in the evenings, adding numerous
black communicants to the mission. All of these activities were sponsored by
Winchester with the wholehearted support of the white congregation of St.
John's. George F. Bragg duly noted Winchester as a friend to black ministries,
as did his protégé, the Reverend Cassius M. C. Mason of All Saints', St. Louis.[5]
On the other hand, the bishop of Arkansas sometimes acted without due consideration for the repercussions of his actions, which meant that his well-
intended initiatives sometimes fell far short of their goals. The black suffragan
plan is a prime example.

Winchester did not set out to elect a black suffragan immediately; rather,
he tried to strengthen the remnants of the Afro-American Convocation. In 1911,
the eight "colored" missions of Arkansas were served by one black priest, the
Reverend John H. Simons, priest-in-charge of St. Andrew's, Pine Bluff, and

three lay readers—C. Elmo Dubisson of St. Philip's in Little Rock, Percy L. Dorman of St. Augustine's in Fort Smith, and Daniel E. Johnson Sr. of St. Mary's in Hot Springs.[6] Dubisson was a merchant from a family of morticians. Although he had aspired to Holy Orders, and had been a postulant since 1911, he never quite made the transition to the vocational ministry. In the summer of 1913, Winchester had suspended him for four weeks due to some unspecified "charges," but he was quickly exonerated.[7] Apparently Dubisson experienced a change of heart about the vocational ministry in 1917, and asked that his name be withdrawn from the list of postulants. He remained a pillar of St. Philip's for practically all of his adult life. Among the lesser items of Bishop Demby's collected papers is a list of the "Three Great Heroes of the Christian Faith." Demby, who did not elaborate on why he designated these three men, named Dubisson along with two other black laymen of long acquaintance.[8] Dorman was the supervisor of black schools in Arkansas. During the First World War, he was field representative to the Arkansas Council of Defense, the state arm of the Council of National Defense. In the latter capacity he fell under the criticism of some black Arkansans, because his job, other than marshaling support for the war in the black community, was to counsel returning African American soldiers toward a peaceful return to accommodation. Dorman also made a name for himself as editor of two black Little Rock newspapers, the *Arkansas Survey* and the *Arkansas Survey-Journal*. He, along with the formidable John E. Bush, wrote a history of the Mosaic Templars, the most successful black business venture in Arkansas, to date.[9] When Dorman was not working for the government or the schools, or publishing, or writing, he was another pillar of St. Philip's, Little Rock, which he served as senior warden at least once.[10] Daniel E. Johnson was the same Daniel E. Johnson of Demby's Colorado days. Ecclesiastically speaking, he was on the rebound. Having been disciplined in 1900 and subsequently deposed from the ministry, Johnson became a public school administrator in Columbus, Ohio, then reemerged as St. Mary's lay reader in the latter days of Bishop Brown's Arkansas Plan. Winchester gave oversight of the black missions to the Very Reverend Edwin W. Saphore, a white archdeacon heretofore associated with white missionary work under the Brown administration. Saphore's three years of supervision were a stopgap measure, intended to keep the black missions solvent until the arrival of black clergy.

In Winchester's early years, a shortage of money hampered all missionary work in Arkansas. This was largely due to Bishop Brown. Brown's habit had been to create missions and erect church buildings that were not warranted by the minimal response of the local communicants. His maxim, "An empty

hive is an opportunity to collect a swarm of bees," had translated into a swarm
of nonviable mission properties. Thus, in 1913, the diocese struggled with about
a three-to-one ratio between churches and missionary enterprises versus clergy.
As a corollary, the diocese could not physically maintain the multitude of vacant or nearly vacant properties spawned during the Brown administration.
Formerly Brown supplemented money for these enterprises from a myriad of
sources, his own pocketbook among them, but in his absence the fallacy behind their existence was apparent. Bishop Winchester and the Arkansas convention were faced with an immediate need to eliminate and consolidate missionary work. In so far as the money shortage affected black ministries, the
$1,800 annual appropriation that Brown secured from the national church
remained unchanged until 1922.

In 1914, Winchester appointed Johnson archdeacon of "colored work" in the
Diocese of Arkansas. Johnson, having been restored to the priesthood by the
bishop of Ohio in December 1913 and sporting a new Doctor of Divinity degree, assumed charge of St. Mary's, Hot Springs, that same month. The church
had just burned in the cataclysmic fire that destroyed downtown Hot Springs.
Johnson's industry in procuring a new building, hand-in-glove with the Reverend A. R. Llwyd, rector of St. Luke's (white) Episcopal Church, apparently
persuaded Winchester to appoint him archdeacon. At about the same time,
Winchester ordained the Reverend Daniel E. Johnson Jr. to the ministry and
placed him in charge of St. Philip's, Little Rock.

Johnson Sr. was a man after Winchester's heart; the black counterpart to his
own upbringing, the confirmation of Christian triumph over social proclivity. Said Johnson,

> My wife and I were born slaves—one in the city and one in the country, about
> fifty miles apart, and yet we were of pious Christian parents, and were both bap-
> tized in our infancy. Of course, were not our owners Christians? Was it not their
> duty to teach our parents, who served them faithfully? . . . Mutual love and in-
> terest between servant and served—the most natural thing in the social world and
> one of the most beautiful—is still possible. It is bred, born, nurtured by a recog-
> nition and improvement of the religious lives of those who have daily contact.[11]

He was also an accommodationist and a sleuth. In his 1916 and 1917 reports
to the Arkansas convention, Johnson expounded the philosophy that under-
lay his work. In the 1916 report, he perceived that the Episcopal Church was
losing ground in the religious education of blacks in Arkansas to "Baptists,
Presbyterians, Quakers, and four different kinds of Methodists," not to mention Roman Catholics. In response he suggested that since the resources of the

Afro-American Convocation were so limited, perhaps the white communicants of the church who had the greater resources should personally undertake the evangelizing of African Americans in the course of their everyday activities, beginning with their servants. He cited the precedent of his own childhood, as quoted above. Should white Episcopalians heed the challenge, said Johnson, they would save many blacks from the "infidelity" of "denominational" Christianity, not to mention the "blinding superstition" of Roman Catholicism. Essentially, he challenged the white assembly to spend more on black ministries or do their own evangelization.[12] In like manner, he played upon their fears in his 1917 address and laid out a strategy for evangelizing black Arkansans. The answer to the paucity of black ministries in Arkansas, he said, lay in institutional work among black children: "The number of churches (literally thousands of them in Arkansas alone) and the denominational prejudice found even in rural districts leave only one door open, but the most effectual—that is, reach them by way of the children." He suggested the Diocese of Arkansas sponsor a black orphanage in rural Arkansas. Furthermore, with Winchester's blessing, he made an appeal for a black suffragan bishop for Arkansas. The black suffragan, he predicted, would be the most effective measure of all. He would offer black Episcopalians a more comprehensive church life, a true counterpart to the white church with its auxiliaries and brotherhoods. More importantly, a black bishop would be a deterrent to demagoguery in the Black Belt of the South by providing "sane religious training." A black suffragan would impart the dignity and edification of the church to heretofore unreachable masses of African Americans. "Give us the suffragan bishop; he will have more influence over the Negro than all the politicians, demagogues, and Kaisers left in the world." Johnson followed this appeal to self-preservation with an observation intended, no doubt, for those white Arkansans still hoping for the establishment of Bishop Brown's separate black Episcopal denomination. Reconcile yourselves, he said, in so many words, to the fact that the existing black membership in the Episcopal Church "cannot be legislated out."[13]

Johnson's arguments were hardly representative of the status of the suffragan bishop plan in the church-at-large, where it was widely regarded as "too little or too much." The church's most outspoken black leaders opposed it for being overly servile while the more overtly racist members of the white leadership opposed it for being a sort of black Episcopal Trojan horse. For instance, when the suffragan plan was first broached as an alternative to the missionary district plan, the Reverend George F. Miller, president of the Conference of Church Workers, foresaw a black bishop totally lacking in the "power of decision and initiative." "It is beyond the comprehension of some of us," he said, "if not all of us, how any man could so far be oblivious of his personal dignity and the exaltedness of the apostolic office as to kneel for consecration on such ignominious terms."[14]

The 1907 General Convention defined the conflict over the suffragan plan, a conflict personified by the emerging schism between Bishop Brown and Archdeacon George A. McGuire. Prior to the convention, Brown declared the suffragan to be no more than a glorified archdeacon, preferring, instead, the establishment of a separate black denomination with its own black bishops. The missionary district plan, he said, was unacceptable in that it promoted racial intermingling in the highest councils of the church. McGuire, as previously noted, espoused the suffragan plan, but only out of expediency. However, in the March 1908 issue of the *Church Advocate,* wherein he announced his disillusionment with Brown and exit from Arkansas, McGuire reversed himself and concurred in Brown's judgment of the suffragan office. The glaring inadequacies of the black suffragan plan, said McGuire, made it all the more urgent for everyone to rally to the missionary district campaign. Meanwhile, the Reverend George F. Bragg used the *Church Advocate* to disparage the black suffragan in terms that, historically speaking, have come to represent the black opposition. He spoke prophetically of the "suffering bishop," a title he alternated with "dummy bishop" over the next decade.

The first serious attempt to elect a black suffragan after the 1910 ratification of the legislation ended in defeat in the Diocese of South Carolina. Once again, representatives of both races ridiculed the plan, but for radically different reasons. The Reverend Joseph H. Woodward, a white South Carolina rector, wrote a lengthy polemic comparing a black bishop to "an educated parrot" in the eyes of non-Christians in the South. Yet he feared the black suffragan for his possible encroachment upon segregation and white supremacy far more than he feared any problems of credibility.[15] Contrariwise, a black communicant of St. Mark's, Charleston, speaking from the pages of the *Church Advocate,* dubbed the black suffragan a "puppet bishop," an Episcopal extension of traditional black servility.[16] Ultimately, the debate itself mitigated against the suffragan plan in the South, where its authors had assumed it would be enacted. Black contempt for the plan elicited by the South Carolina debate further alarmed those white supremacists opposed to the election of black bishops in any form. They perceived from the black reaction that the real issue was not one of electing black bishops to minister to black communicants, which the plan would have allowed; rather, black Episcopalians were intent on nothing less than equality. Thus, despite the fact that the suffragan plan was the only means of electing black bishops, nobody really wanted it.[17]

Therefore, the compromise of 1907 lay dormant until 1917, when the Arkansas convention, carrying forward the vision of Bishops Brown and Winchester, reacted to several unforeseen developments and elected the first black suffragan. In 1915, Winchester and the other bishops of the Southwest had declared their intent to secure a black missionary bishop to serve the blacks throughout the province.[18] The two strongest proponents for this movement were Winchester and the bishop of Texas, George H. Kinsolving. Although Kinsolving, as previously noted, had a reputation for black advocacy, he had reached the conclusion that the Conference of Church Workers was right: the church must elect black bishops, even at the price of segregation. In fact, he had championed their cause before the House of Bishops at the 1907 General Convention, urging his fellow bishops to enact the missionary district plan. Bragg praised him for his efforts on behalf of a losing cause.[19] In 1916, Kinsolving, Winchester, and Bishop Joseph B. Cheshire of North Carolina rallied to the missionary bishop legislation at the General Convention in St. Louis. However, despite some vociferous lobbying on their part, the convention denied the measure again. A committee appointed to investigate the relative merits of the missionary district and suffragan plans delivered a majority report in favor of the missionary district plan. But the peculiar combination of white supremacists and those opposed to segregation being written into church law once again blocked its passage. The minority report, which insisted that the suffragan bishop plan be attempted before any other plan could supersede it, won out. Afterwards, Bishops Cheshire and Kinsolving conferred privately with a representative of the Conference of Church Workers. The counsel of the bishops to the conference representative was that the suffragan plan, flawed as it was, would have to be attempted and its viability, or inviability, demonstrated, before any further legislative progress could be made at the General Convention. Bishop Winchester concurred in their opinion, and the Conference of Church Workers gave grudging consent. It would just have to be tried.[20]

The synod, or biennial convention, of the Province of the Southwest took place at Little Rock early in 1917 and passed the two following resolutions:

1. . . . that if the diocese of Texas or Arkansas or any other diocese in this province is willing to elect a suffragan bishop, we the representatives of the dioceses and missionary districts comprising this province do hereby heartily approve of such an election and pledge ourselves to cooperate with the Diocese of Texas or other diocese electing a Negro suffragan, and will place the work among the Negroes in our respective jurisdictions under the care and supervision of such bishop.

2. And further, we will request the General Board of Missions to appropriate the sum of $3,000 for the support of such bishop.[21]

Once the practicalities were set in motion, it only remained for one of the dioceses to volunteer for the experiment. By virtue of the particular bishops involved, the more receptive attitude of southern black churches toward segregation, and the distribution of the African American population in the Southwest, the lot naturally fell to either Texas or Arkansas. Ordinarily, Kinsolving would have taken the lead, being the more established leader in the field, but in 1917 the elderly bishop of Texas was already asking his diocese for a coadjutor. Therefore, he exempted himself, leaving Arkansas as the logical choice.[22]

Having passed the initiative to Winchester, the southwestern bishops sent a delegation to interview his candidate of choice, the Reverend Edward T. Demby. Demby possessed a substantial, though very localized, reputation as a priest and educator. Most importantly, he had demonstrated a unique ability to turn lemons into lemonade; that is, he had mastered the art of accommodation and progress. Demby, like all black priests of his time and region, walked a fine line, trying to maintain the respect of both races. Too much accommodation could transform a viable black leader into an "Uncle Tom" and lose him the respect of the black community, not to mention his parishioners. Too much assertiveness, on the other hand, could be construed as "uppity," which could cost him respect and support from the predominantly white church and the white community at large. The challenge, of course, was to retain one's self respect and simultaneously develop self-reliant black churches. Demby was better at this than most. He was, in the eyes of the bishops, "safe," yet progressive. His chief liabilities were his nonaffiliation with the Conference of Church Workers, which might cause problems with the church's black leadership, and, less importantly, his decidedly high churchmanship.

It would appear that the bishops, despite having coalesced with the conference at the 1916 General Convention, still acted out of a certain naiveté. They knew the man they wanted and they went out and recruited him without due consideration of national black opinion. While there is also the possibility that they were deliberately excluding the Conference of Church Workers in order to recruit a "safe" suffragan, it is abundantly clear the whole thing boiled down to the relationship between Winchester and Demby. The bishop of Arkansas believed his old friend could impart the harmony they knew in Tennessee to the "Negro work" of an entire province. Of course, all of this was moot in early 1917, for Demby, as previously noted, declined the invitation. Instead, he gave the delegation the names of three black priests he considered worthy of the position—the Reverend George F. Bragg Jr., the Reverend James S. Russell, and the Reverend Hutchins C. Bishop.

Bishop had been the rector of St. Philip's, Harlem, since 1886. He was probably the one person most responsible for the phenomenal growth of that parish over the intervening thirty years; a growth expressed in communicants, property, and various ministries to the community. He had southern roots, going back to ancestors who were members of historic St. James's, Baltimore. Furthermore, he was raised in the Chapel of St. Mary the Virgin, Baltimore's second black Episcopal church, and served as rector to St. Mark's, Charleston, before coming to New York. He was the first black graduate of New York's General Theological Seminary.[23]

Bragg, the rector of St. James's, Baltimore, since 1891, was probably the best known of the three candidates. Besides editing the *Church Advocate,* the unofficial organ of the Conference of Church Workers, he had been secretary to the same body for all but three of the previous thirty-four years. His deportment, as recorded in the group photos taken at the annual meetings of the conference, outwardly reflected his place within the organization. He generally sat front and center where he would, from time to time, fold his arms, cross his legs, and look singularly at ease. In other words, he looked as important as he was. Bragg was, arguably, the preeminent black clergyman in the Episcopal Church in 1917. However, he was also a vociferous opponent of Jim Crow as it encroached upon the life of the church, and, by reason of this, was a candidate in name only. For instance, in speaking of South Carolina's unsuccessful attempt at electing a black suffragan, Bragg was contemptuous of the South Carolina plan in a way that foreshadowed Demby's troubles. The black suffragan, he said, "would be the Suffragan Bishop of South Carolina, and being subject to the diocesan convention, his place would be in the diocesan convention, and in the chancel, next in honor and dignity to the bishop of the diocese."[24] Many white Southerners predicated their approval of the suffragan plan on the condition that this very situation would be avoided. Bragg was not safe.

Russell was a man revered by one and all as an especially pious man, an educator, and a builder of churches. He graduated with the first class of Bishop Payne Divinity School, contributed to the formation of no fewer than thirty-six churches, and won his greatest recognition as the founder and president of St. Paul's Normal and Industrial School in Lawrenceville, Virginia. According to the Reverend Harry Rahming, one of the more celebrated black priests in the generation before the civil rights movement, Russell was "the voice of the Negro clergy and congregations in the South."[25] Having served as archdeacon of the Diocese of Southern Virginia under Bishop Alfred M. Randolph, previously mentioned in connection with the rise of Jim Crow in the southern dioceses, Russell had few peers in the art of accommodation and progress.[26] He and Demby were the front runners.

Bishop Winchester, Archdeacon Johnson, and the actions of the General Convention and synod prevailed at the Arkansas convention of 1917, and the first black suffragan bishop was duly elected. Archdeacon Johnson was nominated, but withdrew his name. Subsequent to the 1917 convention, he became involved with YMCA work in conjunction with the United States Army at Camp Pike, Arkansas, and preferred to remain in that role. The ballot, therefore, consisted of Bragg, Russell, and Demby. Either Demby had experienced a change of heart since his Tennessee interview or Winchester simply nominated him, hoping an electoral victory would persuade him to come to Arkansas in spite of his reservations. In any event, Russell won the Arkansas election and, for that matter, was the preliminary choice for black suffragan in North Carolina the following year. However, he declined both positions in order to remain at Lawrenceville.

Winchester called a special convention for December 1917 in order to elect a second candidate. With Russell out of the picture, Demby became the obvious choice and entered the national limelight for the first time. George F. Bragg "wrote a very fine article," to use Demby's words, about the archdeacon from Tennessee in the December 1917 *Church Advocate.* Thus, it looked as though he had the endorsement of the Conference of Church Workers.[27] At the December convention, Demby was chosen unanimously on the first ballot and this time he accepted the call. However, the bishop-elect, titled "Suffragan Bishop for Work among the Colored People in Arkansas and the Province of the Southwest," had two more hurdles to clear. Church law required that he, like all bishops, must have the consent of a majority of the standing committees of the Episcopal Church and a majority of the bishops in order to be consecrated. The period of consent, often little more than an exercise in protocol, tested Demby's ability to endure and prevail in the face of intense scrutiny—an ability he would need again and again in the years to come.

Initially, reaction to the election was very positive. Demby received congratulatory letters from a myriad of black and white clergy from all over the country and from a host of his former parishioners. Many boasted that they, like Winchester, had envisioned him as a bishop long before the fact. Many encouraged him to accept the election, citing, among his many qualities, the fact that he had always conducted himself as a "Christian gentleman." This was said primarily in reference to his behavior, but it referred to his demeanor as well. Demby looked and sounded the part. Indeed, there is a consensus among those who knew him that he had a sort of "regal bearing" that did not betray the stress or the frustrations inherent to his ministry.

Demby's initial refusal of the office could be cited as evidence of his poise and a personal ambition divested of destructive self-interest. He certainly wanted to be a bishop, but he was in no hurry. Likewise, after he was elected, he accepted the election within the week, but basically kept the news to himself. Apparently he was content to wait and see what the mail would bring. His scrapbooks suggest that most of his friends and colleagues found out about the election via the church press. Once the word was out, however, there was plenty of encouragement to take the post, in addition to several requests for speaking engagements, plenty of unsolicited advice, and a few requests for personal favors. For instance, as soon as Demby accepted the election, Winchester and Archdeacon Johnson immediately enlisted his aid in removing Rev. Daniel E. Johnson Jr. from Arkansas to Tennessee. On Demby's recommendation, Bishop Gailor appointed the junior Johnson to be the new principal of Hoffman-St. Mary's, thereby filling Demby's vacant chair. This move, incidentally, divested the Diocese of Arkansas of one of its two black priests, a most urgent adjustment in light of the fact that the Southwest Province did not, as yet, have money to pay the bishop-elect.[28]

The overriding theme of the letters congratulating Demby was exhortation, calling upon him to be an example to both races, dispell the myth of black inadequacy for the episcopate and draw black people into the church. Perhaps the Reverend E. Robert Bennett, a black priest in Buffalo, New York, best exemplifies this:

> Your wisdom and experience will remind you that from now on you are a marked man, bearing the burden of your whole people. Every word and act will from now on, either weigh for or against us. Be not afraid, remember, you do not stand alone, a whole race watches and prays. You are also surrounded by an innumerable company, all ready and anxious to help keep you steadfast, the Christ Himself supporting you in his everlasting arms. Your are chosen by God to give the lie to our defamers and detractors, your excellent common sense will stand you in good stead. I know you feel the heavy responsibility, I know you almost doubt your sufficiency for the great task that is before you, it is because you are fit and ready that such meekness fills your being. Remember Moses and take courage. I shall offer a monthly Eucharist on your behalf.[29]

Other leading figures in the Conference of Church Workers also lauded Demby's election. Russell sent an early communication, as did Archdeacon Henry L. Phillips Sr. of the Diocese of Philadelphia, former mentor to George A. McGuire and, along with Bragg, a perennial patriarch of the nation's black clergy. He called Demby the "right man in the right place."[30] The Reverend

James R. Satterwhite, whom Rahming described as one of the "actual leaders of the conference," rejoiced to learn that Demby accepted the election and answered "God's call."[31]

Bragg, however, could not bring himself to accept the election of a man not affiliated with the Conference of Church Workers without protest. His initial reaction, as recorded in a letter to Demby, was cordial but carried an understated opposition to the election: "The only regrettable thing, it seems to me, is that it should so happen that the first man so elected should be distinguished as one, who all these years, has held aloof from his brethren of the Conference of Church Workers, who, more than others, have, by their continuous education of the church, made such an election possible. So far as myself is concerned, my congratulations are genuine and hearty; for, I have long ago assured myself that I was entirely out of consideration, because of my persistency in the advocacy of the measure."[32]

This was the calm before the storm. It would appear that Bragg spent the last weeks of December scrutinizing Demby's career and concluded that Arkansas had chosen the wrong man for several reasons, including the one previously stated. So, when the *Living Church* announced Demby's acceptance in early January, Bragg dispensed with subtleties and openly opposed Demby's consecration. He drew up the January 1918 issue of the *Church Advocate* with the intent of blocking Demby's confirmation by the House of Bishops and circularized the bishops with copies of the same, duly highlighting all materials pertaining to the bishop-elect. He basically presented Demby as a man of extremes, a bull in the china shop of black Episcopal ministries. First and foremost, said Bragg, Demby is relatively unknown to the Conference of Church Workers and is certainly not our choice. Yet one should not be misled into believing Demby to be "timid" merely because he "has held aloof from his brethren of the Conference of Church Workers." "There is hardly a more radical 'race' man among us than he." Bragg substantiated this charge with excerpts from the *The United States and the Negro,* discussed at length in chapter 1. He quoted Demby's rousing condemnations of Jim Crow contrivances, political disfranchisement, dehumanizing racist propaganda, Booker T. Washington, and industrial education. Demby, continued Bragg, is as extreme in his churchmanship as in his political views. Father Demby is the "'most Catholic' of all his brethren in the priesthood." Bragg declared that Demby's churchmanship was so esoteric as to be a detriment to the cause of evangelism—a complaint reminiscent of Bishop Brown's rationale for "deritualizing" the Diocese of Arkansas after the death of Bishop Henry N. Pierce. The nation's first black bishop, said Bragg, should be a staunch "middle of the road" man.[33] In summary, according to Bragg:

> Father Demby is a good, able, strong man. While we are far from being "advanced" as he is in churchmanship, yet we are of an extremely tolerant mind; however, we are sure that extreme churchmanship will never win the race. And with respect to his views on the late Dr. Washington, we have always thought very differently. But Father Demby has just as much right to his views as any other man. That has been our fault all along. We have been frank and outspoken. Yet, as the columns of the "Advocate" will abundantly witness, we have, almost scrupulously, confined ourselves to our ecclesiastical relations, avoiding things political. Soon he will be the interpreter of what we have consistently advocated for nearly thirty years, and no man will give him more hearty and sincere support than ourself.[34]

All of the charges, save one, can be seen as specific to Demby. However, the controversy regarding Demby's churchmanship could also be described as symptomatic of the West Indian "liturgical invasion," discussed in chapter 2. Indeed, some black priests celebrated Demby's election as a "triumph for the high church party."[35]

Bragg followed this long exposition on Demby's disqualifications with a rather transparent attempt to discredit him for being an Episcopal convert. In a snippet entitled "The Two Archdeacons," he noted, matter-of-factly, that Archdeacons Daniel E. Johnson of Arkansas and Edward T. Demby of Tennessee, were former A.M.E. "traveling preachers." Then, immediately below "The Two Archdeacons" he inserted another snippet, "Accessions from the Denominations," which included the following italicized remark: "In our book, 'Afro-American Church Work,' published in 1904, we give the names of *eleven* men who had been deposed from our ministry between 1886 and 1904, and, with only *one* exception, they came into the church from other bodies."[36] Johnson, for those in the know, was one of these. Would Demby be another?

Demby was livid but, constrained by habit and the wisdom of his years, he wrote Bragg nothing in response and made no public defense. Winchester reassured him, "I cannot think the article will ultimately affect you in the least, and I beg you not to lose your temper . . . we shall trust God that all will be righted. . . . Give a man rope enough sometimes and he will hang himself."[37] Demby mulled over Bragg's accusations, decided some of them were true, anyway, and, as for the others, he would explain when and if called upon to do so. This was not to be a repeat of the election of William M. Brown. In Demby's own words: "I was asked to express myself as to the things that the Rev. Dr. Bragg said and wrote, but I would not for fear that I might weaken his opposition, because what he said and wrote were true. I knew too well by personal experience that right always triumphs."[38] Taking comfort in the sufferings of the Apostle Paul, as recorded in 2 Corinthians 11:26–28, Demby awaited developments with the knowledge that, if he were ever to be a bishop, this was the sort of hardship he might expect. "In journeyings often, in perils of waters, in perils of robbers, in perils by mine own countrymen, in perils by the heathen, in perils in the city, in perils in the wilderness, in perils in the sea, in perils among false brethren; in weariness and painfulness, in watchings often, in hunger and thirst, in fastings often, in cold and nakedness. Beside those things that are without, that which cometh upon me daily, the care of all the churches."

In due time, an inquiry from Frederick F. Reese, bishop of Georgia, afforded Demby the opportunity to make a timely and effective defense. Reese asked pointedly if Bragg's accusations were true. If they are true, said Reese, "I cannot vote for your confirmation, and will ask my brother bishops to do likewise."[39] Demby responded: "I have read [Dr. George F. Bragg's] most unchristian, selfish, pusillanimous, and exhorable [sic] attack upon me . . . I can only say as the author of 'Science and Christian Ethics,' that 'The truly cultivated mind will not regard disagreement as sufficient cause for enmity.'" Demby denied that he had been driven by "animosity or hatred" to make his Key West speech of 1907 and "neither do I entertain such now, if so I am not fit to be a communicant, to say nothing of being a priest in the Church of God."[40] And as to the essentials of the Key West extract, Demby responded:

1. I believe in my race, and that it has a future worthwhile in America, not, however, without the sympathetic support of the white friends in every section of our National Commonwealth.
2. I do not believe my people are being justly treated.
3. I believe every American citizen's vote should be protected.
4. As to the education of my people, I believe they should have a Christian, vocational, and a literary training to fit them for an intelligent, industrial, and permanent citizenship.
5. As to my views about the late Dr. Booker T. Washington, I believe in his line of endeavor, he was the world's greatest apostle of industrial education, and among the great men of my race.

During the last ten years, my opinions with reference to the non-essentials of the extract, because of my personal work in public charity and sociological movements for the uplift of my people, are not now in harmony with my present views.[41]

Reese replied, "You will get my vote and I will not fail to ask my brother bishops to do likewise."[42]

Ultimately, the January *Church Advocate* turned in Demby's favor. It inspired a multitude of character witnesses to rally to his side, Bishops Winchester and Gailor among them. Gailor's February 2 letter to the *Living Church* praised his archdeacon for "his prudence and good common sense as well as . . . his loyalty, faithfulness, consecration, and high Christian character." "I have never heard a word from white people," said Gailor, "that was not commendatory of him."[43] Winchester seconded Gailor's observations in the February 16 issue of the *Living Church*. He also challenged Bragg's charges that Demby's election was essentially an ex parte action, excluding the church's black leadership from the process. The Arkansas convention, said Winchester, "had letters from most of the colored clergy of the Province of the Southwest, besides unsolicited letters from every section of the country, suggesting him as most acceptable to his people. The emphasis of the many letters was his sound judgement and Christian character." An unidentified man described as "one of the best of the colored laymen in the church" wrote Winchester a glowing letter in praise of Demby, which he quoted: "Archdeacon Demby . . . is safe and the most unassuming man I ever met among our people." Clearly, if Demby had a flaw, it was that he did not assert himself enough.[44]

The campaign to block Demby's consecration backfired among the black clergy, as well. The Reverend John Albert Williams of the Church of St. Philip the Deacon, Omaha, Nebraska, wrote Bragg a letter, castigating him for his method of protest and forwarded a copy of the same to Demby. Regionally speaking, Williams was a very important person. He was the only black priest in what may have been the most colorblind diocese in the United States.[45] In 1918, he was secretary-registrar to the Diocese of Nebraska where he, like Rahming, had the distinction of serving on the Board of Examining Chaplains of his diocese in this, the heyday of Jim Crow. In addition to his parochial and diocesan duties, he was editor of the *Omaha Monitor,* a black national weekly. He upbraided Bragg for acting "contrary to [his] usual open, above-board, and manly method of fighting." "Disapproving of [Demby's] election, as, of course, you have a perfect right to do, it would have been far better in my judgement, to have frankly stated your objections than to have pursued the indefensible method of professing friendship for him and confidence in his sincerity and integrity while stabbing him in the back." Williams vouched for Demby's "sanctifying common sense" with regard to his high church inclinations and expressed his "regret [over] the attack, because it does not do you credit."[46] Demby received another letter "from one of our leading priests who asked me to withhold his name." The writer expressed concern that the white readership of the *Church Advocate* might be swayed by thinking that the *Advocate* represented the "entire colored priesthood, which is not the case." Regarding the charge that Demby had held himself "aloof" from the Conference of Church Workers, the priest in question vented his own grievances against the conference: "I want to say that your spiritual life has been greatly benefitted by such absence, as it is nothing but a wrangle, sarcasm and snobbishness all thro' and I am done with the conference and there are many good, quiet, and intelligent men among us who have the good judgement to stay away from it."[47] Henry L. Phillips was indignant at Bragg. He wrote Demby: "I have just finished reading that *damnable* article about you in the Advocate. As I understand it (I do hope I am wrong) it is simply a dastardly attempt to influence Standing Committees [against] your confirmation. I don't believe it will succeed."[48] Phillips, the beloved rector of W. E. B. Du Bois, also knew Demby through the Boulé.

The net result of Bragg's protest was to cause a substantial delay in Demby's confirmation process. One of the few bishops who refused consent, interestingly enough, was Bishop William B. Cheshire of North Carolina, one of the primary advocates of the suffragan experiment. He was of the opinion that publicly contested episcopal elections are inherently bad ones and should not be confirmed. In 1897, he had refused consent to William M. Brown on the same grounds.[49] In the end, practically all of the bishops and standing committees gave their consent and Demby's consecration was slated for 29 September 1918, the Feast of St. Michael and All the Angels.

However, before closing on Bragg-Demby, it would be remiss not to point out that they are remembered in black Episcopal circles as friends. Although Bragg was not present at Demby's consecration, he invited Demby to preach at St. James's, Baltimore, shortly thereafter. The church, according to the Reverend Edward E. Willett, was "crowded to the steps—the impression made was most remarkable, so much so, some of the vestry [of St. James's] said to the bishop and I quote, 'The things that we have said about you are all false, untrue; how evil some people who call themselves Christians can be.'"[50] Said Demby, "I ever remained a true friend of the Rev. Dr. Bragg. I ever admired him until the end."[51] There is an old story, as told by Bishop Orris G. Walker of Long Island, that Bragg undermined Demby's high churchmanship while the latter was staying at St. James's rectory. Demby was in the habit of keeping his fast until he had celebrated the Eucharist every Sunday morning. Bragg, however, prepared something especially enticing for breakfast. As the aroma wafted up through the house, Demby eventually succumbed and joined the Braggs for breakfast.[52]

Demby's troubles, however, were just beginning. The bishops of the Southwest Province had gone ahead with the suffragan plan without giving their black congregations due consideration in the matter. Consequently, the majority of the black churches outside of Arkansas balked. While the clergy, as Winchester said, wholeheartedly approved of Demby, many of them opposed the suffragan bishop plan on principle. After all, none of them, save Daniel Johnson in his address to the Arkansas convention, even participated in the election. The Reverend M. E. Spatches, Demby's colleague from Key West days, was one of the dissidents. Spatches, who was priest to the Church of the Ascension, Kansas City, Kansas, could not abide the plan despite his personal admiration for Demby. The fourteen black churches in the dioceses of Texas, West Texas, Oklahoma, Eastern Oklahoma, Kansas, West Missouri, and Missouri felt only an indirect connection to the election and the experiment as a whole.[53] According to Rahming, the black congregations in Kansas, West Missouri, and Missouri found distant oversight by a bishop located in Little Rock, Arkansas, unacceptable—especially under the conditions of the suffragan bishop plan. Demby had no salary and no budget with which to help them. Most of them were missions, dependent to some degree on the support of their bishops, and were not prepared to relinquish that relationship, let alone pay Demby a salary. Furthermore, no convention in the province allowed Demby voting rights. And, of course, neither did the House of Bishops. The churches in question were being asked to forsake their fully vested white bishops and, in some cases, their equal standing in their respective diocesan conventions, in order to cast their lot with a largely titular black bishop from a another diocese, a diocese whose two hundred disenfranchised black communicants were distributed among four missions.

By contrast, St. Augustine's, Kansas City, Missouri, had two hundred communicants and All Saints', St. Louis, had four times that many. Together, they numbered more black communicants than the rest of the province combined. St. Augustine's and All Saints' opposed the suffragan plan for many reasons, but mainly because they opposed segregation. A body that encompassed many of the black elite of St. Louis, All Saints' was largely the work of Bragg's protégé, the Reverend Cassius M. C. Mason. The thriving parish was little more than a dream when Mason arrived in 1880, a layman with a stammer and no postsecondary education. Eventually, however, Bishop Tuttle of Missouri came to hold Mason in high esteem and counted him a friend. Mason died in 1917, but not before aligning his parish solidly against the suffragan bishop plan. St. Augustine's concurred. Both congregations were assimilationist in outlook and refused to be "Jim Crowed."[54] Both enjoyed the attention of their white bishops who worked out of their respective localities, an advantage also shared by St. Simon's, Topeka. Consequently, the black churches of Missouri and Kansas asked their respective bishops for exemption from the plan and got it. By the time of Demby's consecration, it was understood that he operated outside of Arkansas only with the consent of the bishop of the particular diocese he was visiting and the permission of the individual churches, as well.[55]

Judging by their lack of resistance, the dioceses of Oklahoma and Texas were more amenable to the plan. Texas's archdeacon for "colored work," the Reverend George G. Walker, was very pro-Demby, as was Bishop Kinsolving.[56] Oklahoma, however, was a different matter. Bishop Brooke of Oklahoma was, as Demby said, one of those bishops principally interested in the plan, but he died in 1918. With the death of Brooke, Bishop Theo G. Thurston of the Missionary District of Eastern Oklahoma became bishop of all of Oklahoma. Thurston had always opposed the suffragan plan as contrary to orthodox Episcopal government and he intended that his black churches should be exempt. "When the suffragan bishop became a reality," writes Samuel L. Botkin in *The Episcopal Church in Oklahoma,* "Eastern Oklahoma's white bishop insisted Negro congregations who so desired should remain as regular members of the District of Eastern Oklahoma."[57] Consequently, Demby lost one additional congregation with the broadening of Thurston's jurisdiction, the Church of the Redeemer in Oklahoma City. In January 1918, when Demby's election was under attack, Winchester had exhorted the bishop-elect: "We are going to try, by God's grace, to make Arkansas a center of light and life to the people." It came true, but in a way that he never intended.[58]

Despite their misgivings, the priest and vestry of All Saints', St. Louis, agreed to be the site of Demby's consecration—with the understanding that this was only a matter of convenience based on the size of the church and not an acknowledgment of Demby's authority. The Reverend D. R. Clarke and his vestry specified beforehand that they were not bound to Demby's support or office by having the ceremony within their walls.[59]

The Feast of St. Michael and All the Angels arrived with a joy and splendor that belied the turmoil of the previous nine months. Church dignitaries and well-wishers from near and far filled the church to capacity. Of the bishops who recruited Demby, Bishops Winchester, Wise, Tuttle, and Partridge were present to join in the laying on of hands. Gailor, who preached the sermon, also joined in, along with the Right Reverend Frederick S. Johnson, bishop coadjutor of Missouri, and Bishop Edwin W. Saphore, Arkansas's white suffragan bishop. Henry Phillips Sr. was present, as was the Reverend Shelton C. Bishop, son of Hutchins Bishop. Bennett made the trip from Buffalo, as did most of the black clergy of the Southwest Province and Tennessee. Henry

Phillips Jr., a vestryman at All Saints', helped Clarke organize the service. Phillips was a teacher at the Sumner School, the St. Louis equivalent to Washington's M. Street High School or Philadelphia's Institute for Colored Youth. Clarke was a protégé of Henry Phillips Sr.[60]

It was a joyous and impressive ceremony, pleasing the Dembys to no end, save for one discordant note. For all his previous experience as a dark man in a notoriously bluevein establishment, nothing was more surprising than the reaction of some parishioners of All Saints'. Demby recalls a group so distraught by his complexion "that they hysterically cried."[61] Indeed, if one looks at the group photograph of clergymen gathered before All Saints', Demby, at first glance, appears to be the only black priest. However, a closer inspection reveals that there are many African Americans in the photo.

Before the happy throng disbanded, there was one problem yet to be resolved. The Dembys did not have a home, or, to be more specific, the Southwest Province had not provided a place for them to live. The Diocese of Arkansas was charged with providing a residence, but the who and how of paying for it was as yet undetermined. The day after the consecration, some concerned parties arrived at a temporary solution. The central figure was the aforementioned Harry Rahming. In September 1918, Rahming was a newly ordained deacon in charge of St. Augustine's. He was awed and somewhat puzzled that the bishop of West Missouri, Sydney Partridge, had brought him to St. Louis as his chaplain. His unspoken question was answered, however, in the course of a comically transparent conversation. Sequestered with Rahming, Henry Phillips Jr., Archdeacon Johnson, and the Reverend James H. King of Kentucky, Clarke broached the news of the Dembys' housing dilemma. Phillips said that he might have a solution. King and Johnson nodded in agreement. Rahming asked, "How?" Phillips recalled Bishop Demby's tenure at St. Augustine's. Could not the Dembys stay temporarily as paying houseguests in the home of one of their old St. Augustine's parishioners? After all, they were so well liked there. Rahming made a call and Phillips was proved correct. The Dembys were overjoyed with the arrangement and resided for four months in Kansas City.[62]

Although Bishop Demby's home was in Kansas City, he spent most of the academic year 1918–19 touring the East Coast and in Texas. Once again, he was dean to Paul Quinn College, Waco, Texas. This seems to have fulfilled at least two or three purposes with the Dembys—a place to live, a salary, and another degree. Demby lacked what some Episcopalians regard as an academic prerequisite for the bishopric, a doctorate of divinity, but Paul Quinn awarded him an honorary D.D. after his year of service. Presumably this Texas hiatus was also designed to allow time for the southwestern bishops to put Demby's house, literally and ecclesiastically, in order. However, little had changed in the way of the black suffragan's circumstances by the spring of 1919, when he began work in earnest. Demby had a house in Little Rock in need of repairs and no salary other than the $1,800 national appropriation for "colored work" in Arkansas, which he had to share with Archdeacon Johnson.

On the heels of Demby's election, the Diocese of North Carolina elected the country's second black suffragan, the Right Reverend Henry B. Delany of North Carolina. Consecrated six weeks after Demby, Delany was the North Carolina counterpart to Demby and Russell. He was vice principal of St. Augustine's Normal and Industrial Institute, Raleigh, North Carolina, where he had spent practically all of his adult life, and archdeacon for "colored work" in North Carolina. Unlike Demby, he was a member of the Conference of Church Workers, but he was not a controlling figure in that organization. Delany's chief assets were his conservative churchmanship and his ability to get things done without rankling the white establishment. His chief liability was that some of his peers considered him too "safe." Nevertheless, Delany's election and consecration were glaring contrasts to Demby's experience. The black clergy of North Carolina participated in Delany's election, and his consecration was the highlight of the annual meeting of the 1918 Conference of Church Workers. Likewise, Delany's fiscal situation was a dramatic improvement over that of Demby, and most of the black churches of North Carolina were well-established missions that acknowledged his authority. It was widely understood that both men were elected because they were perceived as nonthreatening accommodationists. Consequently, they both had to cope with the knowledge that some black Episcopalians perceived them as "Uncle Toms."[63]

How could the bishops of the Southwest Province have been so negligent in the matter of electing the country's first black bishop? Historically speaking, race relations in the Episcopal Church have been defined by the white majority, which has, in turn, reflected the values of country. We might call the southwestern bishops of 1918 enlightened "white moderates," to borrow a term from Martin Luther King Jr. They really wanted to see a burgeoning of black ministries in their region, and they really believed that a separate but equal arrangement, via the missionary district plan, would bring it about; the blacks would have a fully vested black missionary bishop and the national church would foot the bill. By embracing the missionary plan, they acknowledged that the key to the establishment of independent black churches was and is black initiative—not white paternalism. However, with the failure of the plan at the

1916 General Convention, they reverted to a more paternalistic scheme in hopes that it might ultimately justify passage of the missionary district plan. But they failed to count the cost.

The problem is that paternalism begets paternalism, just as segregation begets segregation. With Demby in hand, so to speak, but lacking a national appropriation to support his ministry, the urgency to establish independent black churches and organize them into a de facto missionary district withered in the heat of the day. The bishops were in favor of the plan only so long as it was budgeted by the Department of Missions; they were not prepared to pay for it or implement it against the wishes of their black communicants. In summary, they opted for the suffragan plan without asking the black churches in the region if they wanted it, elected their man without serious regard for the wishes of the Conference of Church Workers, and were less than conscientious in providing for the cost of his ministry. They left Demby hanging. Implicit in every oversight was the idea that the opinions of black people did not really matter, that the deference and attention to detail that would normally accompany the election of a white bishop or the administrative reorganization of several white churches was not exercised. The black clergy and the black churches of the Southwest, which were all missionary dependencies, save one, were seen as objects. Hence the driving force behind the dogma of self-sufficiency preached incessantly by Demby, Bragg, and their colleagues.[64] Black Episcopal history, as described by Harold Lewis in his *Yet with a Steady Beat,* is the gradual emergence of African Americans to a place of recognition in the Episcopal Church. Slowed to a great degree by dependence on white philanthropy and the paternalism that accompanied it, black Episcopal history could also be described as the gradual emergence of African Americans to a place of recognition with the help of, and often in spite of, high-minded white authorities. Such was the election of Bishop Demby.

So, why did he take the job? Certainly he had been thinking about the bishopric for his entire career. It was the next logical step and he was ready. Every charge given to Edward T. Demby had blossomed under his hand—and he had always left them in bloom. The interview in Tennessee may have started him thinking along these lines, which would explain why he allowed his name to be on the Arkansas ballot in the first place. Moreover, in all and through all runs the very subjective matter of calling, seemingly affirmed by the very passive way in which he won his office. In spite of his contested election and handicaps of his office, Demby believed it was God's will that he be E. Robert Bennett's "marked man."

NOTES

1. Edward T. Demby, "Off of the Record since 1939," MS, James Weldon Johnson Collection, Yale Collection of American Literature, Beinecke Rare Book and Manuscript Library, Yale University, New Haven, Conn., 397, hereafter cited as Demby, "Off of the Record."

2. James R. Winchester to Scipio Jones, 13 July 1927, Bishop Edward T. Demby File, box 13, RG 282, James R. Winchester Papers, Archives of the Episcopal Church, U.S.A., Austin, Tex., hereafter cited as the Winchester Papers. It appears that this letter relates to the repairs to Bethel A.M.E. church, Little Rock, necessitated by the Carter lynching described in chapter 4. Jones was a trustee of Bethel and the NAACP attorney who led the successful defense of twelve black men imprisoned for their alleged participation in the infamous Elaine Riot of 1919. (See Richard C. Cortner, *A Mob Intent on Death: The NAACP and the Arkansas Riot Cases* [Middletown, Conn.: Wesleyan University Press, 1988].) In the wake of the Carter lynching, black and white religious and civic leaders were anxious to coalesce and prevent any further outbreaks of mob violence in Little Rock.

3. *Arkansas Churchman*, 15 Dec. 1925, 3.

4. Giles B. Cooke to James R. Winchester, quoted in James R. Winchester, "A Black Skin and a White Soul: Uncle Leonard Harris," article clipped from unidentified newspaper, n.d., 305, Winchester Papers. Pollard was a pioneer in black ministries. He served in South Carolina and North Carolina consecutively after his early career in Virginia. When he took his seat in the 1887 South Carolina convention, it sparked the confrontation described in chapter 2.

5. George F. Bragg, *History of the Afro-American Group of the Protestant Episcopal Church* (Baltimore: Church Advocate Press, 1922), 158.

6. Simon's brief and uneventful sojourn in Arkansas preceded his elevation to the pastorate of St. Thomas's, Chicago, one of the more prestigious black churches in the Midwest.

7. "Register of W. M. Brown, 1896–1916," Episcopal Church Records of Arkansas, microfilm, roll 1, item 7. Bishop Brown's register also served as Bishop James R. Winchester's register during the early years of his episcopate.

8. E. T. Demby, "Great Heroes of the Christian Faith," MS, Demby Family Papers, Manuscripts, Archives, and Rare Books Division, Schomburg Center for Research in Black Culture, New York Public Library Astor, Lenox, and Tilden Foundations, New York, box 1, folder 7, hereafter cited as Demby Family Papers.

9. Fon Louis Gordon, *Caste and Class: The Black Experience in Arkansas, 1880–1920* (Athens: University of Georgia Press, 1995), 76–77, 128–30; see C. Calvin Smith, "John E. Bush: The Politician and the Man, 1880–1916," *Arkansas Historical Quarterly* 54 (Summer 1995): 115–33.

10. Bush began the Templars as a society to aid the sick and bury the dead, but it exceeded his expectations to become the most influential fraternal and benevolent

society in the Little Rock's black community. The Templars' success propelled Bush to the upper echelon of Booker T. Washington's National Negro Business League.

11. Daniel E. Johnson Sr., "Report of the Archdeacon of Colored Work," *Journal of the Annual Convention of the Protestant Episcopal Diocese of Arkansas* (1916): 92, hereafter cited as *Arkansas Journal;* Gordon, *Caste and Class,* 76–77.

12. Johnson, "Report," *Arkansas Journal* (1916): 91–93.

13. Daniel E. Johnson Sr., "Report of the Archdeacon of Colored Work," *Arkansas Journal* (1917): 78–83.

14. George F. Miller, "Missionary Episcopate as a Method of Evangelism," in *Black Gospel/White Church,* ed. John M. Burgess (New York: Seabury Press, 1982), 34, quoted in Harold T. Lewis, *Yet with a Steady Beat: The African-American Struggle for Recognition in the Episcopal Church* (Valley Forge, Pa.: Trinity Press International, 1996), 77.

15. Joseph H. Woodward, *The Negro Bishop Movement in the Protestant Episcopal Diocese of South Carolina* (McPhersonville, S.C.: By the author, n.d. [c. 1916]), 43.

16. E. C. Gaillard, "A Negro Suffragan—A Puppet Bishop," *Church Advocate,* Jan. 1912, 3.

17. David M. Reimers, "Negro Bishops and Diocesan Segregation, 1870–1954," *Historical Magazine of the Protestant Episcopal Church* 31 (Sept. 1962): 235; *Church Advocate,* July 1914, 1; ibid., Jan. 1912, 3; ibid., Mar. 1908, 3.

18. *Church Advocate,* Apr. 1915, 1; James R. Winchester, "The Work among the Colored People in Arkansas," a 1915 report to the Arkansas convention, Winchester Papers; J. R. Winchester to Mrs. Roberts, 23 June 1915, ibid.

19. George F. Bragg praises Kinsolving for his efforts on behalf of black ministries at least five times (*History,* 154–55, 169, 177, 182–83); *Church Advocate,* Jan. 1918, 3–4.

20. Bragg, *History,* 154–56; James R. Winchester, letter to the editor, *Living Church,* 25 Sept. 1937, 358; Donald Wilson, telephone interview by author, 2 July 1991, Palm Coast, Fla., transcript. The Reverend Donald Wilson was an acquaintance of Bishop Demby who shared a common friendship with the Reverend George M. Plaskett, a close friend of Demby. Plaskett says, via Wilson, that Demby and his peers were well aware that the black suffragans would fall short of the authority and prestige that other bishops enjoyed. Failure in this sense was implicit and understood by the first bishop-elect at the time of his consecration. However, it remained to see what could be made of the opportunity despite of the limitations of the office.

21. Edward T. Demby to William P. Witsell, 5 Dec. 1922, Collected Papers of the Reverend William P. Witsell, Archives of the Diocese of Arkansas, Trinity Cathedral, Little Rock, Ark., hereafter cited as the Witsell Papers.

22. Margaret Sims McDonald, *White Already to Harvest: The Episcopal Church in Arkansas, 1838–1971* (Sewanee, Tenn.: University Press for the Episcopal Diocese of Arkansas, 1975), 191–92.

23. Willard B. Gatewood, *Aristocrats of Color: The Black Elite, 1880–1920* (Bloomington: Indiana University Press, 1990), 74, 278–279, 257.

24. Bragg quoted in *Church Advocate,* July 1914, 1.

25. Harry Rahming to Thomas S. Logan Sr., 10 May 1978, private correspondence of the Reverend Canon Thomas S. Logan, hereafter cited as Rahming letter.

26. Bragg, *History,* 174; *Washington Afro-American,* 26 Nov. 1932; see Roberta Arnold, *A Man and His Work: The Life Story of James Solomon Russell, Founder of the St. Paul Normal and Industrial School, Lawrenceville, Virginia,* pamphlet commemorating the fiftieth anniversary of St. Paul's (Lawrenceville, Va.: St. Paul's Normal and Industrial School, 1938).

27. Demby, "Off of the Record," 505.

28. Anna M. Skillern to Edward T. Demby, 17 Dec. 1918, Collected Papers of Edward T. Demby, St. Matthew's Episcopal Church, Wilmington, Del., hereafter cited as the St. Matthew's Papers; Daniel E. Johnson Sr. to E. T. Demby, 14 Dec. 1917, ibid.; George L. Neide to E. T. Demby, 1 Jan. 1918, ibid.; R. W. Bagnall to E. T. Demby, 2 Jan. 1918, ibid.; Fred Garrett to E. T. Demby, 2 Jan. 1918, ibid.; John Q. Taylor to E. T. Demby, 1 Nov. 1918, ibid.; James R. Winchester to E. T. Demby, 12 Dec. 1917, ibid.

29. E. Robert Bennett to Edward T. Demby, 22 Dec. 1917, St. Matthew's Papers. George F. Bragg would like to have seen Bennett elected suffragan bishop ("The Selection of Suffragan Bishops," *Church Advocate,* Feb. 1918, 2).

30. James S. Russell to Edward T. Demby, 22 Dec. 1917, St. Matthew's Papers; Henry L. Phillips to Edward T. Demby, 27 Dec. 1917, ibid.

31. Rahming letter; James R. Satterwhite to Edward T. Demby, 11 Jan. 1918, St. Matthew's Papers.

32. George F. Bragg to Edward T. Demby, 22 Dec. 1917, St. Matthew's Papers.

33. *Church Advocate,* Jan. 1918, 1–2.

34. Ibid.

35. J. R. Lewis to Edward T. Demby, n.d., St. Matthew's Papers; Fred A. Garrett to Edward T. Demby, 15 Dec. 1917, ibid.

36. *Church Advocate,* Jan. 1918, 2.

37. James R. Winchester to E. T. Demby, 10 Jan. 1918, St. Matthew's Papers.

38. Demby, "Off of the Record," 398.

39. Ibid.

40. E. T. Demby to Frederick F. Reese, 11 Jan. 1918, St. Matthew's Papers.

41. Ibid.

42. Demby, "Off of the Record," 398.

43. Thomas F. Gailor, letter to the editor, *Living Church,* 2 Feb. 1918, St. Matthew's Papers.

44. James R. Winchester, letter to the editor, *Living Church,* 16 Feb. 1918, St. Matthew's Papers.

45. In 1903, the Reverend George F. Miller, president of the Conference of Church Workers, stated the following: "Only in the Diocese of Nebraska has the matter of color or or lineage had no repressive or restrictive force; there alone, of this vast territory, has a brother, despite his color and in virtue of his merit, risen to place and been accorded due recognition" (William M. Brown, "Bishop's Address," *Arkansas Journal* [1903], 74).

46. John Albert Williams to George F. Bragg, 9 Jan. 1918, St. Matthew's Papers.

47. Anonymous to E. T. Demby, Jan. 1918, St. Matthew's Papers.

48. Henry L. Phillips to E. T. Demby, 5 Jan. 1918, St. Matthew's Papers. "When Archdeacon Henry Phillips, my last rector, died," writes W. E. B. Du Bois, "I flatly refused again to join any church or sign any church creed" ("My Character," in *W. E. B. Du Bois: Writings* [New York: Literary Classics of the United States, 1986], 1124–25).

49. Demby, "Off of the Record," 397–98; J. B. Cheshire to W. T. Capers, 25 Aug. 1932, Witsell Papers.

50. Demby, "Off of the Record," 505.

51. Ibid., 398.

52. Orris G. Walker, interview by author, 15 Sept. 1992, New York; Carl Black, interview by author, 14 Sept. 1992, New York; Donald Wilson, telephone interview by author, 11 June 1991, Palm Coast, Fla.

53. Rahming letter; Montraville E. Spatches to E. T. Demby, 22 Dec. 1917, St. Matthew's Papers; Harry E. Rahming, "Church Work among Negroes: A Plea for Recognition of Negro Leadership," *Living Church*, 4 Aug. 1928, 463–64.

54. Rahming letter; Gatewood, *Aristocrats of Color*, 277.

55. Rahming letter; Rahming, "Church Work among Negroes," 463–64.

56. George Gilbert Walker to J. R. Winchester, n.d., in *Facts Associated with the Ordination and Consecration of Edward Thomas Demby*, comp. Antoinette M. R. Demby (Little Rock, Ark.: Episcopal Diocese of Arkansas, 1927), 22, box 13, Winchester Papers, hereafter cited as *Facts*.

57. Samuel L. Botkin, *The Episcopal Church in Oklahoma* (Oklahoma City: American Bond Printing Co., 1958), 78.

58. James R. Winchester to E. T. Demby, 11 May 1918, St. Matthew's Papers.

59. Rahming letter.

60. A. Demby, *Facts*; James A. Williams, "First Negro Bishop for American Church," *Omaha Monitor*, 12 Oct. 1918, 1, Winchester Papers; Rahming letter; Gatewood, *Aristocrats of Color*, 195, 216; Gavin White, "Patriarch McGuire and the Episcopal Church," *Historical Magazine of the Protestant Episcopal Church* 38 (June 1969): 111. Saphore was elected at the same convention that elected James S. Russell in 1917.

61. Demby, "Off of the Record," 112.

62. Rahming letter.

63. Ibid.; Rahming, "Church Work among Negroes," 463–64; Dennis Wilson, telephone interview by author, 6 June 1991, Palm Coast, Fla.; Thomas S. Logan Sr., interview by author, 19 Oct. 1995, Yeadon, Pa.

64. See Bragg, "The Matter of Self-Support," *History*, 244–50.

4

Bricks without Straw:
The Ministry of Bishop Demby, 1918–32

In 1919, Bishop Edward T. Demby began his ministry with the hope that his office would be short-lived. The Episcopal Church, he believed, had ignorantly withheld the missionary district plan from its black communicants. Furthermore, there had been no concerted effort to win the 1,850,000 blacks living in the Province of the Southwest to the Episcopal Church. All of that, he hoped, was about to change. Demby looked upon his election as a mandate to educate the church on the needs of blacks in the Southwest and demonstrate how much could be accomplished with even the limited amount of episcopal authority exercised by a suffragan bishop. The industry and especially the self-reliance of black Episcopalians would be manifested to the church-at-large; the General Convention would see its duty, constitute a missionary district from the Seventh Province, and elect a black missionary bishop to supervise the work. Demby hoped to be that bishop. Having laid the framework for progress, the church would, at last, stop being so tight-fisted and contribute generously to the creation of black schools, colleges, hospitals, and orphanages in the Southwest. This was the plan.

The plan, however, ran contrary to the need. Demby knew that he could not succeed in the Southwest unless he could convey a greater vision for black ministries on the part of the Episcopal Church. And the most important element of that greater vision, other than the election of black bishops, was institutional development. The establishment of schools, hospitals, and orphanages would better enable him to make a legitimate call upon African Americans to lay aside their prejudices against the Episcopal Church and heed its presentation of the Gospel. The black population of Arkansas, for instance, was the same population that had resisted Archdeacons George A. McGuire and Daniel E. Johnson Sr. before him—a people generally inclined to reject the Episcopal Church for reasons of race and religious background.[1] Elsewhere in the province, where the climate of opinion was much the same and his jurisdiction had been compromised, the establishment of black Episcopal institutions could mean a new credibility for his office—and the church—in the eyes of the black community. To put the problem in its simplest terms, Demby needed to succeed in order to win appropriations, but he needed appropriations in order to succeed.

Demby expounded on the price of progress before the Arkansas convention, noting that the national church appropriated less than $7,000 for "Negro work" for the entire Southwest in 1918. "Can you wonder," he said, "that so little has been done or is being done for my people in this great territory?" In response, he called for five projects totaling $39,000 to "place the Episcopal Church before the colored people of Arkansas in a real sense" and an additional $250,000 dollars to do the same thing throughout the province.

A Fund for Constructive Work $100,000
A Church Orphanage $25,000
A Fund for a Training School for Missionary Priests . . $25,000
A Parochial School Fund $50,000
A Church Hospital $50,000

Given this kind of investment, said Demby, "within a few years the work that we now have would be self-supporting." It was a vision so aggressively autonomous that he felt it needed qualification: "A separate Colored American Episcopal Church in America[?] No, never! The Episcopal Church must remain One, and United, Apostolic, and Catholic."[2]

Demby's early ministry, from 1919 to 1922, was more a question of survival than of success. George F. Bragg's *History of the Afro-American Group of the Protestant Episcopal Church,* published in 1922, gives us some idea of the demographic challenges Demby encountered, as well as some comparative information on the black suffragan experiment in the Southeast. Bragg presents the following statistics for Province of the Southwest:

Diocese	Congregations	Communicants
Kansas	4	155
Missouri	1	412
West Missouri	2	150
Oklahoma	2	82
Arkansas	5	158
Texas	4	99
West Texas	1	22
Dallas	1	8

Using Bragg as a rule of thumb, we see that Demby was, technically speaking, shepherd to twenty churches and over one thousand communicants in the early years of his ministry. Bragg's figures, however, are very ambiguous, because they do not reflect the jurisdictional caveats that accompanied Demby's election, as discussed in chapter 3. Probably half of the churches actually acknowledged his authority. In all of the eight dioceses, save one, the black churches were treated individually; in Arkansas they were grouped into a convocation. By contrast, Bishop Henry B. Delany, Demby's counterpart in the Province of Sewanee, exercised jurisdiction over the black churches in North Carolina and, eventually, South Carolina as well. In 1922, that area embraced 3,123 black communicants and sixty-six congregations, a flock roughly three times the size of Demby's. Average congregations in both jurisdictions numbered about fifty communicants, but Delany's jurisdiction was more established, more moneyed, more populous, and more concentrated than Demby's. To further illustrate the disparity, the Carolinas boasted several parochial schools and two black Episcopal institutions of higher learning—St. Augustine's College, Raleigh, North Carolina, the oldest and most prestigious of the black Episcopal colleges, and Voorhees Normal and Industrial School, Denmark, South Carolina. St. Augustine's and St. Paul's Normal and Industrial School in Lawrenceville, Virginia, were the colleges of choice for southern blacks aspiring to the ministry. The "ordination pipeline," so to speak, ran from St. Augustine's and St. Paul's to nearby Bishop Payne Divinity School in Petersburg, Virginia. The Southwest Province, on the other hand, had nothing to compare with the Carolinas; no black Episcopal colleges, no black seminaries, and only one black parochial school. Nevertheless, Demby and Delany were equal and united in one respect. They were both at pains to demonstrate that blacks could make capable bishops, a point very much at issue. Many whites opposed blacks in the episcopate because they believed that the first two black bishops of the Episcopal Church, James Theodore Holly, bishop of Haiti, and Samuel David Ferguson, bishop of Cape Palmas, Liberia, were failures. Off the record, both black suffragans believed that racism often rendered them subordinate to white clergy who were manifestly inferior.[3]

Having completed his brief tenure at Paul Quinn College in the spring of 1919, Demby threw himself into establishing a self-supporting episcopate. He immediately encountered a shortage of money. The Dembys' house on Cross Street in Little Rock was in a lamentable state, and the bishop's salary was more a source of wonder than of income. The black missions of Arkansas, newly designated the Colored Convocation in place of Bishop Brown's Afro-American Convocation, were in considerable debt and were not, as a rule, in the habit of paying their priests. Nevertheless, by the end of 1922, Demby had four of them paying $300–$400 per annum to their clergy, paying their utilities as well, and, in three cases, paying toward the Nation-Wide Campaign and the convocation assessments. He reported to a national representative, "There are no colored missions in the province doing as much to help themselves than our missions in Arkansas." St. Andrew's, Pine Bluff, which Demby deemed the best of the Arkansas missions, had a debt of $3,000 at the time of Demby's consecration. By December 1922 the debt had been eradicated by $1,000 in donations from the congregation, assistance from the Board of Missions, and help from the American Church Building Fund Commission—an agency of the Episcopal Church empowered to finance the purchase and construction of church property—and the Double Temple Society. This represents 75 percent of the original debt of the Arkansas missions.[4] As for his house, Demby would spend a considerable amount of his own stipend over the next eight years in order to make it "habitable."[5]

Given the fiscal situation, Demby found it nearly impossible to find and keep clergy. Except for the short tenures of the Reverends William E. DeClaybrook and E. A. Christian, Archdeacon Johnson was Demby's sole clerical assistance until he transferred to the Diocese of Springfield in 1920. Winchester ordained DeClaybrook, a New Zealander with a D.D. from the University of China, to the diaconate and the priesthood in 1918. DeClaybrook served St. Mary's in Hot Springs until early 1919, when he transferred to the Diocese of Texas. Christian, who held an M.A. from Lincoln University and an S.T.B. from Lincoln Seminary, was ordained in 1916. He was a missionary to the dioceses of West Texas and Oklahoma during the First World War until he, like Daniel Johnson Sr., took up YMCA work in connection with the armed forces. He appears to have served St. Philip's, Little Rock, less than a year (1919–20) before transferring to the Diocese of Western Michigan. After the departures of Johnson and Christian in 1920, Demby was the sole black cleric in Arkansas for several months.

He did not fare much better with his first Arkansas ordinand, the Reverend John H. Jones. Jones was reared and educated an Episcopalian in the Southeast, attended St Paul's College, Lawrenceville, Virginia, and Oberlin. He served St. Augustine's, Fort Smith, as a catechist until Demby ordained him to the diaconate in April 1921. He then served St. Augustine's in his new capacity for another year and a half, at which time he left the diocese. He returned to St. Augustine's in 1923 and transferred to North Carolina in 1924, where he had the distinction of being ordained to the priesthood by the church's other black suffragan, Bishop Delany. Nor did Demby have good luck with subsequent assistants. In 1922, Demby ordained Bernard G. Whitlock to the diaconate and the priesthood. Whitlock came to Arkansas a candidate for holy orders from the Diocese of Southwestern Virginia. A graduate of Bishop Payne Divinity School, he served St. Mary's until 1923, when he transferred to Emmanuel Church, Memphis. It would appear from the *Arkansas Journal* that money problems mitigated against Whitlock's continued ministry in Arkansas. The Reverend Royal S. Hoagland served St. Philip's, Little Rock, from 1922 to 1924. The Reverends A. M. Forsythe, E. Seiler Salmon, and John R. Brooks briefly assisted the work in Arkansas between 1924 and 1927. Thus, in the early years of Demby's episcopate, Arkansas acquired a reputation as a place for black clergy to begin their ministry or to work while on their way to somewhere else. Demby termed them "birds of passage." During this period, he assumed the roles of bishop, priest, organist, missionary, lay reader, catechist, Sunday school teacher, and sometimes janitor, exhibiting a positive outlook and cheerful disposition that won him the enthusiastic allegiance of many laymen.[6] Said George Black of St. Andrew's, Pine Bluff: "Bishop, you are a peculiar bishop, without a priest or deacon to help you and the people indifferent, a stranger in a strange field and among a strange people; your task is a most difficult one to which the church has called you; you were not even introduced to us, in all you are a man of faith, and may the Lord be with you—without you we would have no persons for baptism and confirmation, and few services, then are you good enough to do so many things that the people ought to do; the work that you are now doing is what is called making bricks without straw."[7]

Measures were taken ad hoc to relieve his money problems. The Reverend John Boden of Christ Church, Little Rock, moved that the 1920 Arkansas convention begin the collection of an annual offering for "Negro work"—a promising gesture, but not much more than that. At the 1921 convention, the Reverend C. P. Parker of St. Paul's, Fayetteville, made a similar gesture and netted $328. White Episcopalians throughout the Southwest contributed to Demby's work in the form of gifts. Unfortunately, the dioceses of the Southwest also preferred to give gifts and refused to make his ministry a budget item. Money trickled in from Woman's Auxiliaries and clergy outside the diocese, especially in the North and East. Bishop Winchester, a sympathetic but less than commanding figure, contributed what help he could. Meanwhile, Demby continued to receive his salary piecemeal. The province's original request for $3,000 per annum had been made specifically for the Reverend James S. Russell. When Russell declined the Arkansas election, the province issued a second request based on Demby's election, which ended up on a prioritized list. In other words, his salary was tabled. In 1920, a second and more urgent appeal met with the same fate. The realization that he had no salary eventually moved the province to "emergency action," and for the years 1921 and 1922 Demby's salary was paid by subscriptions from all the various dioceses, a total of $3,000 in 1921 and $2,400 in 1922. Giving, of course, was hampered by the fact that many of the dioceses had compromised Demby's jurisdiction at the outset. They were using him very little, or not at all, and contributed to his stipend only by reason of their original agreement. Demby's reports to the Arkansas convention, which he drew up for the benefit of Arkansas, the province, and the Board of Missions, detailed every nickel and postage stamp of a ministry that showed every sign of perishing, notwithstanding his attitude.[8]

The money situation began to improve in 1921. After a consultation with George Black, Demby resolved to take up fund-raising in earnest. Although he was never at ease with aid in any form, his aversion to soliciting money gave way to the realization that if the Colored Convocation were ever to be financially independent, he must be a more aggressive fund-raiser, or at least give his work a higher profile. He presented his vision and his plight to the entire church in the form of a pamphlet, *The Mission of the Episcopal Church among the Negroes of the Diocese of Arkansas.* He wrote to drive home two points. First, the blacks in the Southwest were in dire need of the ministry of the Episcopal Church, a missionary work no less important than its counterparts in "China, Japan, Africa, the Philippines, the Canal Zone or Brazil."[9] Second, he needed help. Contributions began coming in with greater regularity and in greater amounts. Likewise, in 1924, he proposed an annual offering for "colored work" as part of his report to the Arkansas convention and continued to do so for several years thereafter. Although the annual offering never materialized, the situation at the parochial level grew more generous. In those cities where a white and a black church were located, namely, Little Rock, Fort Smith, Pine Bluff, Hot Springs, and Forrest City, the local white churches made it a practice to aid their black counterparts across town. Simultaneously, Demby's speaking engagements skyrocketed from a previous high of about 125 in 1919 to 218 in 1924. The 464 addresses he made in 1926 were more than the total number from the first four years of his episcopate.

The problem with Demby's fund-raising, other than the disparity between what he needed and what he raised, was that it continued to elicit one-time gifts. True, as of January 1922, the Department of Missions of the National Council raised the annual appropriation for "colored work" in Arkansas from $1,800 to $2,400, but this was the exception and not the rule. Almost none of Demby's receipts consisted of budgeted items that he could program into his own budget. Mortified at this continued hand-to-mouth existence, Bishops James Wise of Kansas and James R. Winchester of Arkansas reinitiated the drive to get an appropriation for Demby's salary from the Department of Missions of the National Council, the successor to the Board of Missions. In 1922, they enlisted the aid of the province's newly appointed representative to the council, the Reverend William P. Witsell of St. Paul's, Waco, Texas. Witsell argued Demby's case before the council, citing the considerable number of bricks Demby had made thus far without the benefit of straw, and the pittance, relatively speaking, that he received from the National Council versus the council's much larger contribution toward Bishop Delany's ministry in the Southeast. According to Witsell, the Southwest Province, which constituted Demby's jurisdiction, and the Carolinas, which constituted Delany's jurisdiction, each had about 1.5 million black people. However, the similarities ended there. The Episcopal churches, black and white, were older and far more numerous in the Carolinas. Therefore, the fiscal foundation for black ministries was correspondingly larger. Institutional work in the Episcopal Southwest had nothing to compare with many black parochial schools and several colleges in the Southeast. Why then were the Carolinas appropriated $21,634 for black ministries in 1923 and the Seventh Province a mere $6,800? Why did the Province of Sewanee, comprising all the dioceses of the southeastern states, receive $10,000 for educational work while the Southwest Province, which had twice requested a salary for Bishop Demby, received no provincial appropriation of any kind?[10] At last, the council heeded the disparity and granted Demby's salary, pared down to $2,800 per annum, effective 1 January 1923. However, any appraisal of Demby's salary should be seen in light of the fact that he always felt compelled to contribute money from his stipend to defray the costs of convocation business. From time to time, his reports indicated that the balance of the Colored Convocation's outlay was paid by a donation from their bishop.

During this time, Demby traveled the Southwest, visiting black missions and addressing church groups, civic groups, and black institutions of higher learning. His activities alternated between winning souls and raising money, but his primary goal was to convey a black episcopal presence to his widely scattered flock. In October 1920, for example, he toured the Diocese of Texas in company with Archdeacon George G. Walker of Texas. While visiting Texas's black churches, he addressed assemblies at Texas College in Tyler, Paul Quinn College in Waco, the Colored High School in Waco, and Galveston's city auditorium. Despite the fact that he was well received wherever he went, the jurisdictional compromise of 1918 remained in effect during these travels, as indicated by this 1923 retrospective: "I have offered my service to each of the Bishops of the Province . . . I have been a number of times in the dioceses and missionary districts of the province not, however, on ecclesiastical matters, but as a member of my race to learn the mind of the people with reference to the church, and I am glad to say the future is bright; each bishop of the province should have more help from the Department of Missions."[11] He confirmed black Episcopalians in the Southwest in the same way he confirmed black Episcopalians anywhere else outside of Arkansas: "on the invitation of the rectors and missionaries and with the [consent of their bishops]." The deployment of black clergy remained the prerogative of each southwestern bishop, with Demby acting only in an advisory role, if any.

Otherwise, he toured the nation, speaking, preaching, confirming, baptizing, marrying, burying, ordaining. Once again, he strove to convey a black episcopal presence; a unifying figure among black Episcopalians and a precursor of better things yet to come. Black Episcopal churches capitalized on his visits in order to evangelize the black community, coalesce with local white Episcopalians, and improve relationships to the white community at large. Mrs. Demby would assist him by speaking to women's groups. The significance of Demby's speaking engagements can be seen in a letter from Jefferson S. Coage, a longtime friend and one of the more prominent African American employees of the federal government in the 1920s. "The people of Delaware, your native state, are proud of you. Immediately after your address to the graduates of Howard High School last June, the *Every Evening,* a daily paper, the oldest in Delaware, commented editorially on your address. This comment has brought about a more friendly feeling between the two races in Delaware. This is the first time that a column in this paper on the editorial page has been given to a member of our group. See what Christian culture and training will accomplish."[12]

In September 1919, Demby had the unexpected pleasure of ceremonially violating the color line in the name of a more catholic church. The Diocese of Tennessee elected the Reverend Troy Beatty of Grace Church, Memphis, to be Bishop Thomas F. Gailor's new coadjutor. Beatty, an old friend of Demby's, invited Arkansas's black suffragan to say the Litany at his consecration and participate in the laying on of hands.

On a less celebratory note, Demby's ambiguous relationship to the Conference of Church Workers was resolved at the October 1919 conference held in Cleveland, Ohio. In the words of the Reverend Harry Rahming, the 1919 conference "was really a power struggle in respect as to what colored bishop was the voice of the colored clergy and congregations so far as the church was concerned."[13] The traditional leadership of the conference believed Bishop Delaney too easily manipulated by southern bishops and considered Bishop Demby an unknown quantity. After Cleveland, it was widely understood that both Demby and Delany were outside of the power structure of the Conference of Church Workers.

The second period of Demby's ministry, from 1923 to 1932, could be described as the years of conspicuous growth. With his budgetary restrictions somewhat eased and his reputation spreading, the convocation began to build momentum. Arkansas's black Episcopalians established a kindergarten and a parochial school and eliminated the original debts on the black missions. Furthermore, the missions substantially assisted their priests by providing more adequate housing and related expenses, and embellishing their salaries, which no longer came from the missions themselves but from the National Council. In 1925, the National Council increased the appropriation for "colored work" in Arkansas from $2,400 to $3,700. This enabled Demby to pay each of Arkansas's black clergy about $600 per annum, which the missions were expected to match. Mrs. Demby and Mrs. George Black of Pine Bluff organized and presided over the "Convocation Branch of the Woman's Auxiliary" through the 1920s. The auxiliary, which met concurrently with the annual meeting of the Colored Convocation, raised substantial sums of money for the convocation and contributed loyally to the national Woman's Auxiliary. Of the approximately $900 raised from January 1923 to May 1924, $523 went to work in Arkansas, $135 went to the Nation-Wide Campaign quota, and the rest was distributed to missions, education, charity, and the United Thank Offering. St. Agnes's Guild, a ministry to the sick in each mission, was especially popular with the auxiliary. Mrs. Demby reported regularly to the Woman's Auxiliary of the Diocese of Arkansas, the counterpart, it would appear, to her husband's role in the Arkansas convention.[14] Bishop Demby held teaching conferences in Little Rock for all the black clergy and lay workers of the Southwest Province, Tennessee, and Mississippi. By 1927, the convocation's only noteworthy debt was the balance owed on a $2,800 loan to Christ Church School from the American Church Building Fund Commission, an item apparently cleared up by 1929. Demby publicized his progress via the *Southwest Churchman*, the official organ of his office.

His efforts to find and keep quality clergy were finally blessed with success. All the comings and goings of 1919–27 yielded two long-term clergy—Demby's right and left arms, so to speak. The Reverend Melbourne B. Mitchell arrived in Arkansas, like Whitlock and Jones, via the Virginia connection. Born in Boston and raised in Rhode Island, Mitchell graduated from Bishop Payne Divinity School in 1924 and came to Arkansas a candidate for holy orders. Demby immediately ordained him to the diaconate and put him to work at St. Augustine's, Fort Smith. The following year, Demby ordained Mitchell to the priesthood and transferred him to St. Mary's, Hot Springs, which he served until 1927, at which time he transferred back to St. Augustine's. Two years later, he transferred from the diocese. The Reverend James H. King arrived in 1921, a forty-six-year-old native of North Carolina, educated at St. Augustine's College and Bishop Payne Divinity School. Having served churches in Georgia and Kentucky, King was chaplain and vice-principal to Hoffman-St. Mary's Industrial Institute for three years prior to transferring to Arkansas.

In portrait, King habitually wore the dour expression of a man whose best friend has recently departed this life, but his behavior was that of an extrovert. If he had had a second calling it would have been that of a salesman, attorney, or politician. One of the more popular anecdotes told about him illustrates the point. King, who was not a teetotaler, was on a business trip when the call of nature compelled him to use the restroom at a roadside tavern. The clientele greeted him with excruciating silence as he passed through the front door. Having spotted his collar, they cupped their hands around their drinks and averted their eyes. He contemplated the situation while secluded in the restroom, and decided to have some fun. As he exited the still deadly quiet establishment, he stopped at the front door, turned to face the cowering merrymakers, and rebuked them. "Gentlemen," he said in his sternest ecclesiastical voice, "I hope you can hide that from God!" He strode to his vehicle without another word, his grim demeanor giving way to side-splitting laughter as the car pulled out onto the highway.[15]

King possessed an unusual grasp of human nature and a shrewd ability to turn people in the way he wanted them to go, be they black or white. Like Demby, he came to Arkansas an assimilationist and a proponent of working within the system rather than challenging it directly, an advocate of parochial/industrial education with an eye to its long-range benefits. He reasoned that a child's moral and intellectual development probably would not enable him to assimilate into a white-dominated society, but at least it might establish him as a good citizen and empower him to find a more prosperous niche within the caste system. He strove to imbue young black people with enough education and, especially, moral stamina to "do well in life" in spite of racial indignities.[16] "If they take away your dignity," he would say, "it means nothing."[17] King, who habitually praised and quoted Booker T. Washington, was more of a genuine proponent of Tuskegee than was Demby. Such was the genius behind the establishment of Christ Church Parochial and Industrial School.

The date of King's first visit to Forrest City is lost. He may have come in company with Professor Todd Alston, son of the Reverend Ossian P. Alston and an instructor at Hoffman-St. Mary's, and Demby. He seems to have played a part in the selection of the church site. Beginning in the summer or fall of 1921,

King visited Forrest City on the weekends, alternating his work schedule at Christ Church with that of Hoffman-St. Mary's. He preached at a little one-room chapel erected by Demby with the help of the Woman's Auxiliary of the Diocese of Pennsylvania. Leading citizens of Forrest City, white and black, welcomed Demby and King in anticipation that they would erect a second "Hoffman-St. Mary's" within their municipality. The families of Scott Bond, a locally renowned African American landowner and entrepreneur, and W. H. Purifoy, the superintendent of St. Francis County's black schools and a fixture in the struggle against lily-white Republicanism in Arkansas, exemplify Forrest City blacks who welcomed the establishment of Christ Church Mission and, most especially, Christ Church Parochial and Industrial School. The Reverend Jeremiah Wallace, rector of the Church of the Good Shepherd, Forrest City's white Episcopal Church, was Demby's enthusiastic liaison to the white community.[18]

King wasted no time in organizing "Father King's school," as the residents of St. Francis County preferred to call it. Rather than wait for Demby to procure funding, he took matters in hand and began teaching a class of ten children. Simultaneously, his bold and compassionate manner made a favorable impression upon the community. He won the hearts of Sarah Strong, and her daughters, Emma, Annie, Suzie, and Dora, and her granddaughter, Murtha, when he rescued a funeral gone awry. The Strongs became the nucleus of a small but zealous congregation determined to minister to the community by way of a school.[19]

Christ Church was a congregation distinct from the black Episcopal stereotype. Unlike St. Philip's, Little Rock, Christ Church did not have a reputation for professionals and blueveins. Nor was it made in the image of St. Augustine's, Fort Smith, and St. Cyprian's unorganized mission in Helena, churches composed of the "best people" in their respective communities. Christ Church, apart from the faculty of the school, was a mission consisting of poor and very black people, a high proportion of whom were single mothers who made their living as domestics.

From 1924 to 1931 the school and its personnel took on the dedicated, if not sacrificial, character that became its trademark. A loan from the American Church Building Fund Commission and some local fund-raising enabled Demby and King to erect a combination rectory and school adjacent to the chapel for $4,500. On 3 January 1924, Demby conducted the service of blessing and Christ Church Parochial and Industrial School opened its doors to sixty-five students and two teachers, Father and Mrs. King. When the National Council increased its annual appropriation for Arkansas in 1925, King was able to hire two additional teachers—Ruth Norment, one of the more qualified black instructors in the Forrest City School District, and Bedonia McKenzie. Each drew $300 per annum, but McKenzie drew her salary by way of a 50/50 arrangement between the National Council and the Diocese of Arkansas. The $150 paid on McKenzie's half-salary constituted Arkansas's only budgetary outlay for the Colored Convocation during Bishop Demby's tenure.[20] Lois Lockhart, a United Thank Offering social worker from Pine Bluff, joined the school in 1929. She was a graduate of the Bishop Tuttle School of Social Work, affiliated with St. Augustine's Normal and Industrial School in Raleigh. When she died in 1931, she was replaced by Inez Middleton, another Tuttle School graduate and a native of North Carolina. The UTO social workers received about $600–$700 per annum, but paid the school $300 per year for room and board.[21] The Kings did not draw teaching salaries. Alston, who joined King in the move from Mason to Forrest City, taught music at the school on a part-time basis but was generally not on the payroll.[22]

Christ Church Parochial and Industrial School was widely regarded as the best education available to St. Francis County's black children until its closure in 1968. Its success was predicated on academic discipline and the sheer weight of personal attention each student received. By 1927, it was filled to capacity and essentially remained that way for the remainder of its existence. The one hundred or so students of Christ Church School received rigorous instruction in the "three Rs," plus domestic science, carpentry, mechanics, secretarial work, and even waiting on tables. The alumni were renowned for their "good citizenship" by the white community. Like all schools created in the image of Tuskegee, it prospered in part because it represented the status quo.

Demby lamented his inability to do more for King's school but rejoiced at its example of black enterprise. With only enough money appropriated to pay the salaries of the instructors, the school forged ahead in the spirit of its founder, supporting itself by way of tuition, a thrift shop, the sale of rugs and chicken dinners produced by the domestic science department, and a canning barter system instituted by Mrs. James H. King, the former Nina Pearl Fields of Mason, Tennessee. Mrs. King's barter system enabled Christ Church to maintain a school lunch program during the Great Depression. In 1932, Christ Church consolidated its work with that of Hoffman-St. Mary's, presumably in the interest of remaining solvent. Affiliation with Hoffman-St. Mary's meant indirect affiliation with the American Church Institute for Negroes. Nine major ACIN institutions survived the first five years of the depression, debt free, on the strength of appropriations from the National Council, local (diocesan) support, consolidation, and community support like that engendered by King.

Ultimately, the flagship of the Colored Convocation would survive the national cataclysm without incurring any substantial debts.[23]

In 1930, Demby heralded a ten-year plan to make Arkansas's black missions into self-sufficient parishes, add three new chapels, and transform Christ Church School into the premier Christian missionary institution among Arkansas's African American population, a prototype for the entire Southwest Province. His great hope was that he might expedite self-support, "the salvation of the church work in Arkansas," through an annual offering, or perhaps by a gift from a wealthy donor.[24]

There were five organized missions in Arkansas. They were St. Andrew's in Pine Bluff, St. Mary's in Hot Springs, St. Philip's in Little Rock, St. Augustine's in Fort Smith, and Christ Church in Forrest City. There were three or four unorganized missions or "preaching stations," chief among them St. Cyprian's in Helena. Demby bought land at Peace, Cleveland County, with the intent of establishing a church and a second parochial and industrial school, but shortages of money and personnel hampered his plans and the Peace mission never came to pass. All of the Arkansas churches experimented with parochial education. Mrs. P. L. Dorman, and a postulant, Ira S. Ashe, were the people most responsible for the establishment of kindergarten at St. Philip's. The convocation numbered about four hundred communicants at its peak, with about twice that many baptized members. The structures were all relatively small churches, St. Philip's in Little Rock being the largest of the five and St. Andrew's in Pine Bluff being the most expensive. St. Andrew's was worth about $12,000, or three times the value of any other black Episcopal structure in Arkansas. Numerically, St. Mary's in Hot Springs, with its eighty-plus communicants, was the largest mission. In keeping with Bishop Demby's taste in liturgy, all of the missions were very "high," save perhaps Christ Church, which was more understated than its sisters but still high in comparison to many of Arkansas's white Episcopal churches.

Bishop and Mrs. Demby frequently remarked how the ministry in Arkansas was hampered by the Great Migration. For instance, the bishop reported forty members "lost by moving away" in 1922–23. Reporting "migratory" losses to the Arkansas convention not only presented a more objective standard by which to gauge the strength of his ministry, it probably won him a measure of compassion from the all-white assembly. The Great Migration was not popular among white Arkansans, especially in the bottomlands of southern and eastern Arkansas where cotton was still king and the labor force must necessarily be large and inexpensive. When local newspapers published articles pertaining to the Great Migration, the stories were invariably calculated to discourage African Americans from leaving. For instance, the front page of the *Forrest City Times Herald* of 17 May 1923 described the betrayal of "Negroes Fleeced by Labor Agents." The so-called promised land special, said the *Herald*, never arrived at Grady, Arkansas, quashing the northbound hopes of "over 500" African Americans and bilking them out of their train fares. Likewise, other *Herald* stories like "The Other Side of Life in Detroit, Michigan," and "Negro DIES from Cold" described the lonely and miserable fate of those blacks who had the misfortune to actually arrive in the big, impersonal northern cities.[25]

Demby tried repeatedly and unsuccessfully to start a training school for clergy, with the intent of raising up a more sedentary "native ministry" in the region.[26] He alternated between Little Rock and Memphis as possible sites for the school, but neither location attracted a viable underwriter. Therefore, he was compelled to recruit candidates with the intention of sending them east to Bishop Payne Divinity School in Petersburg, Virginia. Ultimately, no native Arkansans matriculated into the Episcopal ministry during his tenure.[27]

Demby faithfully promoted the program of the Episcopal Church with regard to black ministries. In 1922, for instance, the Department of Missions and Church Extension published a book by Bishop Theodore D. Bratton of Mississippi titled *Wanted—Leaders!* Bratton was alarmed at the dearth of black Episcopal leadership in the South arising from the lack of recognition given to black Episcopalians. The outlook for church growth among the black population was grim. So, he wrote *Leaders!*—a polemic accompanied by a study guide—with the intention of educating white Episcopalians and recruiting black clergy. The Reverend George F. Bragg praised Bratton for his efforts on behalf of black Episcopalians and even invited the bishop of Mississippi to write the introduction to his own *History of the Afro-American Group of the Protestant Episcopal Church,* published the same year. Demby endorsed Bratton's book before the Arkansas convention and had his churches participate in the study. He also challenged them to contribute toward the work of the national church in spite of their limited means. He faithfully promoted the evangelical Forward Movement.

The last years of the twenties, 1927–29, were a period of continued growth, but under a different kind of duress. The General Convention of 1925, scene of Bishop William M. Brown's final deposition from the ministry, directed the presiding bishop to appoint an evaluation committee for the purpose of laying out a more comprehensive strategy for missionary work. The committee collected and analyzed data on all of the various missionary and educational enterprises of the Episcopal Church. This necessarily brought Demby's ministry under their scrutiny. The Reverend E. P. Dandridge, a future bishop of Tennessee and a representative of the committee, sent Demby a long list of questions pertinent to the church's work among the black population in the United States. This provided Demby an opportunity to vent some frustration accumulated during his thirty years in the Episcopal ministry and especially his experiences as a bishop. "The policy of the church with reference to her mission to the Negroes," Demby declared, "is to manifest as little interest as possible in them, and because of this attitude our Negro work is a religious tragedy. . . . THE CHURCH IS NOT DOING ENOUGH for the Negroes in the South." He listed three immediate needs for the success of black ministries in the South: (a) a field secretary for "Negro work" in the pay of the National Council, (b) a class A parochial school adjunct to every black mission in a large city, and (c) "partial scholarships for boys of high school age who will give themselves to Christ for the ministry of the church and full scholarships when they enter the seminary."[28] Demby wrote specifically of problems encountered in the Diocese of Arkansas. He informed Dandridge that his aspirations for black ministries were hindered by financial problems peculiar to the Arkansas, incorrect information circulating about work among African Americans in Arkansas, and the unwillingness on the part of white Episcopalians to engage in joint activities with black Episcopalians.

The Arkansas convention of 1927, held at St. Mary's, El Dorado, graphically demonstrates the detrimental effects of the color line as it bore upon Demby's ministry. In the months prior to the convention, Bishop Winchester was beset by an organizational crisis. Winchester desperately wanted to put the diocese on a more sound financial footing and bring it into compliance with the program of the national church. He had at his disposal Rev. William P. Witsell, mediator of Bishop Demby's 1922 salary dispute. Witsell was the new rector of Christ Church, Little Rock. He had prepared an armload of legislation and he and Winchester awaited the first opportunity to enact it.

Unfortunately, the convention was postponed twice due to unprecedented flooding in eastern and southern Arkansas. Approximately 20 percent of the state was paralyzed, inundating some towns and reducing the rest to islands connected by railroads and the few highways high enough to constitute a dike, the same floods hailed by W. E. B. Du Bois as a timely incentive for blacks to leave the "hell" of Arkansas, Louisiana, and Mississippi.[29]

Finally the weather cleared, but a new trouble loomed on the horizon. Just days before the convention, the vestry of St. Mary's told Winchester that Bishop Demby and the black clergy must stay away from the convention or there would be no convention. While no one connected with this event specified why St. Mary's took such a radical position, it was undoubtedly inspired by the Carter lynching in Little Rock. On May 1, the *Arkansas Democrat* reported that the body of a small white girl was discovered in the belfry of First Presbyterian Church. Lonnie Dixon, a black man and the son of the church's janitor, confessed to sexually assaulting and murdering the girl. Determined to prevent a lynching, Little Rock's chief of police "spirited away" the Dixons. When the white mob discovered that they had been tricked, they made a furious but futile search all over central Arkansas. For the next two days, Little Rock, a city that prided itself on peaceful coexistence between the races, festered in anticipation of some sort of reprisal by the white community. Todd E. Lewis describes what followed: "Then, on May 4, a middle-aged woman and her daughter reported being attacked by a black man on a road south of town. A posse assembled and by that afternoon had captured John Carter, reportedly a 'halfwit.'" The posse stood aside as a mob lynched Carter, used his body for target practice, and dragged it to the corner of Broadway and Ninth Street, the hub of black Little Rock's black community. The vigilantes erected a pyre fueled with boards ripped off of Bethel A.M.E. Church and burned Carter's body.[30] Meanwhile, black Little Rock was under siege. Merchants like Elmo Dubisson of St. Philip's feared for their businesses as white mobs roamed the streets vandalizing and dispensing violence at random. Little Rock police refused to intervene and the rioting continued for three hours until troops dispatched by the governor arrived on the scene. A quarter of a century later, Bishop Demby described it this way:

> In another city, a Caucasian farm woman was driving with a load of hay, and the horses were frightened at something which was never learned and began to run, the woman crying for help. . . . [She] fell from the wagon when a man, [a] Negro, caught the running horses and asked if he might take her and the wagon where she might say, and [as] he was talking, several men, Caucasians, appeared with sticks, clubs, and knives, exclaiming, "Rape! Rape!! Rape!!! Lynch the nigger." The woman said, "Don't do that. [H]e saved me. He has not touched me. For God's sake don't hurt the man who came to my rescue. . . . The man did not come within five feet of me." But with her pleading the man was tied hand and foot and gagged and taken to a street and lynched by the mob, and the dead body was tied to the end of a wire rope, dragged to the city eight or more miles away to the front of the largest Negro church and burned in the presence of more than a thousand people and all the Negro places of business and recreation halls [were] ordered closed, and all lights in [the black section of town] extinguished for fear of [more] serious trouble. The verdict was that the man came to his death by unknown persons.[31]

Black Arkansans recoiled from the events of 4 May. Some left the state, while others looked for a way to make common cause with white authorities in order to preclude further violence. For example, the sheriff of St. Francis County deputized Rev. James King of Christ Church, Forrest City, making him an honorary deputy of the county. Always a dogmatic advocate of law and order, King began to wield legal authority in—and on behalf of—Forrest City's black community. He sported a badge beneath his jacket and even wore a pistol when the need arose.[32]

The upshot of the Carter lynching, as regards Arkansas's 1927 Episcopal convention, is that it prompted a fanatical enforcement of the color line. The rector of St. Mary's, the Reverend Samuel H. Rainey, opposed the vestry's action. He was of the opinion that the black clergy should not only attend the Arkansas conventions but vote in them as well. Rainey had gone to great lengths to arrange suitable housing for the black clergy and was unwilling to relinquish the point. However, knowing the unpopularity of his position, he confided it only to Winchester and Witsell.[33]

Winchester was stymied. Seeing his plans for reviving the diocese jeopardized, he called in Witsell to help formulate a response to what they both regarded as an unmitigated breach of Christian doctrine, not to mention a violation the canons of the Diocese of Arkansas.

The legal rights and privileges of black Episcopalians in Arkansas were embodied in the "Constitution of the Colored Convocation." This document, written by Bishop Demby and passed into law in 1920, established the legal measure of black participation in the Arkansas convention. According to the constitution, the convocation was to meet separately from the convention. The only person designated to represent the convocation before the white convention was Bishop Demby. He was to deliver his annual report to the convention and all other black clergy were, technically, subject to the same exclusion experienced by George A. McGuire in 1907. In practice, however, Demby always attended in company with the other black priests of Arkansas. Blacks were disfranchised in all cases save one. According to Article 2, in the event that the Arkansas convention was slated to elect a bishop, all of the black clergy were entitled to vote in the election.[34]

Witsell suggested that Winchester make an intermediate response to St. Mary's by having Bishop Demby attend the convention and read his report but in a less conspicuous fashion that was normally done. Winchester decided that Demby should come to the convention, but that a white priest should read his report. Demby complied and was so discreet in attending that most of the white delegates never knew he was there.[35] As for the opening worship service, there was no question of Winchester's challenging Demby's exclusion, because the Carter lynching had reinforced that most hallowed of southern taboos. It was one thing for Demby to appear at the all-male convention; it was another to appear at a worship service where white women were present. The Dixons, after all, had also had a pretext for being in a white church.

Witsell's reputation for executive leadership and his position on the National Council preceded him to the 1927 Arkansas convention. He was, with the possible exception of Bishop Winchester, the preeminent clergyman in Arkansas. He was a South Carolinian by birth, a graduate of South Carolina Military College, Hobart College, and General Theological Seminary. He possessed an honorary Doctor of Divinity from St. Luke's Theological Seminary, University of the South. A church historian of some merit, he was author of *Our Church: One through the Ages*. He was also well known for a second book, *The Bible vs. Evolution*. He was renowned as a leader and organizer, a politically astute churchman with a strong sense of ethics. Through his work on the National Council he enjoyed the respect and friendship of many bishops. He and Rainey were friends, having served together in the Diocese of Texas and being like-minded on many issues.

Witsell had a keen interest in Arkansas's Episcopal history. He was an ardent admirer, personally and historically, of the former rector of Christ Church, Little Rock, the Reverend John Gass. He wholeheartedly agreed with the Christ Church interpretation of Arkansas's 1897 episcopal election. Gass's defeat, he said, was a travesty, the product of lies propagated by Brown's supporters. Witsell's greatest claim to notoriety in Arkansas, prior to moving there, was his role in an abortive attempt to consolidate Christ Church and Trinity Cathedral. In 1916, both churches were without a priest and burdened with debts. Witsell was called in as a third party in an informal attempt to unify the two churches under one priest and thereby remedy the situation. Ultimately, neither parish was willing to sacrifice its sovereignty for unification and the effort foundered.[36] Although Witsell was generally inclined to observe the racial guidelines of each diocese or local church, his position on race relations within the Episcopal Church was the same as Rainey's—blacks were entitled to equality with whites in every respect.

In order to further consolidate his plan for reconstruction and simultaneously rectify the injustice done to Demby, Witsell made Winchester an offer. Christ Church, he said, would host the 1928 convention and he (Witsell) would draw up the agenda for the convention—with this proviso: the black clergy must be present and vested, they must process with the white clergy, and Demby must deliver his report in person and read the epistle at the opening service.

Winchester agreed. Chronically ill, he was relieved to have someone else take charge of the convention.[37]

The customary rights and privileges of black Episcopalians in the Arkansas convention, such as Demby's occasional leadership in the opening worship service and the attendance of other black priests, were established in one of two ways: by the will of the bishop of the diocese or by the will of the host parish. It was the responsibility of the diocesan bishop to draw up the programs for the services of the convention. Winchester sometimes asked Demby to read the epistle, a role that not only put the black suffragan at the forefront of the service but also placed him ahead of the white congregation at the distribution of the Eucharist—a situation fraught with possibilities, and most of them unpleasant. Moreover, Demby's experiences with regard to convention worship services were consistent with the pattern of urban versus rural Jim Crow; that is, he encountered less discrimination in the city than in the country, which is true of the South in general and Arkansas in particular.[38] The Arkansas convention journals record only one instance in Demby's entire episcopate when he assisted in a service outside of Little Rock's two major churches, that being the 1923 convention held at St. John's Church in Helena. This is more than a little surprising in view of Helena's "unreconstructed" reputation.[39] In the scheme of Arkansas history, Helena has been the epitome of the plantation economy and traditional southern values. The site of a battle adjunct to Ulysses S. Grant's Vicksburg campaign, Helena boasts no fewer than seven sons who became Confederate generals. Of all the churches where Demby might lead a convention worship service in 1923, St. John's would have to have been near the bottom of the list. We note that there is no record of any trouble in connection with the St. John's convention, but we also note that this was the last time that Winchester designated Demby as a worship leader on his own initiative.

Five years later, at Christ Church, Little Rock, Demby read the epistle again, but only at Witsell's insistence. With Presiding Bishop John G. Murray in the chancel, the 1928 convention passed without incident, the only wrinkle being in the preparation of the luncheon. Some of the women of Christ Church did not want to serve the black priests. Witsell recalls, "I told them just to fix the table and I would serve the Negro brethren. That brought them to their senses and all went nicely."[40] The 1927–28 episode was, for Witsell and Demby, the beginning of a lasting friendship. Witsell brought to Demby not only advocacy but solace, consolation, and counsel during the bleakest periods of the bishop's ministry. The Reverend Donald Wilson, heir, by way of the Reverend George K. Plaskett, to some of Demby's more private thoughts, affirms that this is true. When asked if there were any white Arkansas clergy that Demby regarded as a friend, Wilson replied without hesitation, "Oh, yes, Dr. Witsell."[41] In August 1928, Demby wrote Winchester: "I have just met the Rev. Dr. Witsell. I must say the more I come in touch with him, the more I am convinced that he is a true friend of all peoples . . . had we a few more like him [in] the Province of the Southwest our church work among the colored people would go over big."[42]

Unfortunately, the conventions of 1927 and 1928 also had the following repercussions for Witsell and Demby. Witsell was acknowledged as an unusually capable but not altogether welcome addition to the Arkansas clergy. The obvious and disproportionate authority of this newcomer, as compared to that of other parish priests of long standing, aroused some professional jealousy among the clergy and the ire of some laymen. Some alleged that he was a de facto bishop with aspirations to ultimately fill Winchester's shoes. Undoubtedly he contributed to that image by compelling everyone to accept, or forbear, Demby's participation in the Arkansas convention. Had Winchester insisted on parity and respect for the black clergy, instead of Witsell, it would have been a momentous gesture. As it was, Witsell was only one priest among many, albeit a powerful one. To put it another way, Episcopalians of this era acknowledged the customary right of each church to treat black Episcopalians in the fashion deemed proper by that church. Despite their opposite intentions, both Witsell and the vestry of St. Mary's, El Dorado, demonstrated that this was still true—even at the convention level. In this way Witsell's advocacy of Demby merely affirmed the status quo. Moreover, Witsell had played the advocate for Demby before the Arkansas convention and they became fast friends during the summer of 1928. For good or ill, they were subsequently identified with one another, a fact not fully appreciated until Article 2 of the Constitution of the Colored Convocation thrust the black clergy into the vortex of the political struggle of 1931–32.

All of the predominantly white Protestant denominations possessing a substantial black contingent during the twenties and thirties experienced racial friction as they tried to extend hospitality to black delegates at church conventions. The northern Methodists, Presbyterians, and Baptists, as well as as the Congregationalists, ran afoul of Jim Crow contrivances, especially when their national bodies convened. Hotel accommodations and entertainment were often at issue, but the preeminent consideration was the common meal. Eating together had an implication of fraternization and social equality that the more purely ecclesiastical affairs of conventions did not. The South, to be sure, had not forgiven Theodore Roosevelt for his "scandalous" repast with

Booker T. Washington in 1901.[43] The northern Methodists, who enacted their equivalent of the missionary district plan in 1920 with the election of two black bishops, discovered that only resolution and foresight could prevent racial conflict at integrated social gatherings. In 1926, a Washington, D.C., hotel was the scene of a banquet held in honor of the bishops of the Methodist Episcopal Church. The two black bishops and their wives were barred from entering by the hotel management. Thereafter, careful planning of integrated facilities was the order of the day.[44] The Congregationalist experience was very similar to that of the Methodists. Even when they prearranged for integrated facilities, the proprietors would sometimes balk when the blacks arrived.[45] The northern Presbyterians encountered their own version of the problem in successive Jim Crow altercations during the late twenties and early thirties. The three most notorious incidents were: (a) a gathering at Hood College in Maryland, when a black delegate was barred from a "dinner meeting," (b) an incident at the 1928 General Assembly in Tulsa, and (c) an incident in connection with the 1932 General Assembly in Denver.[46]

The epidemic of Jim Crowism in the Episcopal Church made matters of hospitality toward black delegates a worrisome affair at integrated church gatherings. Archdeacon George A. McGuire spoke at length to the 1906 Arkansas convention to the effect that segregation is the best policy when it comes to the entertainment of blacks, because it precludes racial antagonism. Indeed, defiance of the color line was rare and only the powerful could indulge in it unscathed. In 1907, for example, John Pierpoint Morgan rallied Wall Street and almost single-handedly saved the United States from a stock market crash. That same year, Morgan also attended the tumultuous Richmond General Convention as a delegate from the Diocese of New York. One evening, he and his dinner guest, Bishop Samuel Ferguson of Liberia, motored together through downtown Richmond for all the world to see. Generally speaking, however, the white majority dictated matters of hospitality, which resulted in a good many racial indignities at those special events that drew the two races together.

Black Episcopalians, as a rule, chose to endure racial indignities patiently, preferring instead to reserve their right to protest for more purely ecclesiastical matters. Not only would it have been futile to challenge matters of hospitality, the angry backlash from white communicants would only have served to reinforce the color line in the ecclesiastical arena. The Philadelphia Divinity School episode provides a good example. In February 1933, the *Crisis* published a letter from the Reverend John A. Howell, the white rector of St. Michael and All the Angels, a black Philadelphia church. The letter was an indictment of the "Jim Crow table" at Philadelphia Divinity School. According to Howell, when the white seminarians insisted that the black seminarians should eat at a separate table, the blacks were asked for their opinion. But the black students, and especially those from the South, feared repercussions from the bishops who sponsored them, so they refrained. However, one of them had a change of heart and, although he did not protest, he made the Jim Crow table public knowledge. The black clergy of his diocese protested to their bishop and Howell publicized the situation via the *Living Church*. Subsequently, the black seminarian was dismissed and the table remained in place.[47] The Reverend Canon Thomas S. Logan, a future president of the Conference of Church Workers and a senior at nearby Lincoln University in 1933, recalls, "The whole thing was perceived by black Episcopalians as another affront by the white establishment. Most of us thought it best to ignore it and go on, as one usually did with such things."[48]

Jim Crow was de rigueur at when it came to common meals at diocesan conventions. Roberta Church of Emmanuel Church, Memphis, recalls a Tennessee convention wherein the black clergy were relegated to a children's Sunday school room for their meals—complete with child-sized tables and chairs.[49] The Reverend James W. Temple of Kansas, who joined the ministry during Bishop Demby's tenure, recalls that the black clergy of Kansas were Jim Crowed at luncheons and banquets held in the church proper. However, if the meals were removed to hotels or restaurants, the arrangement was usually integrated, the explanation being that a public place offered greater anonymity, while an integrated eating arrangement in the church could be construed as a statement on behalf of fraternization and equality.[50] Finally, segregated eating arrangements could be more ingrained than ecclesiastical segregation. They were the last vestiges of Jim Crow to be dispensed with in the dioceses of Alabama and Arkansas.[51] The segregation of Episcopal hospitality during the twenties and thirties may have been taken for granted, but it was a grave matter to violate it.

Arkansas convention problems aside, Bishop Demby spent the years of 1927 and 1928 in a vigorous defense of his ministry. Since 1918, he had faithfully observed the abbreviated jurisdiction as it was handed to him at his consecration. When he traveled in the Province of the Southwest, he operated with no more authority over the black congregations outside of Arkansas than black congregations anywhere else in the United States. He could preach, confirm, consecrate, ordain, teach, raise and dispense funds, encourage, and organize, but only with permission of the local white bishop—and the local black church. When the evaluation committee sent out by the 1925 General Convention brought this to light in its February 1927 report, it immediately threatened Demby's fiscal lifeline. Since the bishop's ministry did not live up to the original agreement upon which his salary was predicated, the National Council indicated that either Demby should perform a greater ministry to the Southwest Province or receive less money from the council. Demby responded by altering his report to the 1927 Arkansas convention, making his title conform to his limitations. In place of the ecclesiastically correct "Report of the Suffragan Bishop for Negro Work in the Diocese of Arkansas and the Province of the Southwest," he substituted the politic "Report of the Suffragan Bishop for Negro Work in the Diocese of Arkansas."[52] Likewise, when the synod of the Southwest Province convened in November 1927, it acknowledged its error and called upon its member dioceses to utilize their black suffragan.

The year 1927 was rough. It began with a debilitating traffic accident. Driving from Little Rock to Memphis, Bishop and Mrs. Demby "narrowly escaped death when their car was struck and thrown into a ditch."[53] Apparently Mrs. Demby capitalized on her prolonged convalescence to compile a pamphlet commemorating her husband's 1918 consecration. Her decision to celebrate the ninth year of his episcopate instead of the customary tenth anniversary can best be explained by the fact that 1927 was also their twenty-fifth wedding anniversary, and he probably needed the encouragement anyway. Beset by an Arkansas convention that did not want him, the routine difficulties inherent to his ministry, and the scrutiny of the national body, Demby struggled to maintain his habitual positive outlook. It appears that Witsell encouraged him to offer his services more aggressively to the bishops of the Southwest Province and counseled the bishops to solicit his help.[54]

Following the November synod, Demby embarked on a two-month tour of the dioceses of Texas, Oklahoma, and Kansas at the request of their respective bishops. He baptized and confirmed the children of William H. Bright-Davies at St. Augustine's Mission, Galveston, Texas. Bright-Davies, a native of British West Africa whose educational pedigree included tutorials in London and Oxford, would eventually become one of the more influential black priests in the United States. Demby also confirmed Florence G. Arrington of St. Philip's, Muskogee, Oklahoma. Florence was the mother of Daniel M. Arrington, the first black civil engineer to graduate from the University of Michigan, and the grandmother of the Reverend Nan Arrington Peete, a renowned innovator of outreach ministries in the Episcopal Church.[55]

Concurrent with his whirlwind tour of the province in late 1927, Demby distributed his second nationwide fund-raising pamphlet: *The Mission of the Church among Colored People in the Diocese of Arkansas and the Southwest*

Province. Mission would appear to be Mrs. Demby's second compilation of 1927. Eager to emphasize his achievements despite the losses of the Great Migration, she reported the following statistics for the first nine years of her husband's episcopate:

3 deacons and 3 priests ordained
265 baptisms in Arkansas
365 confirmations in Arkansas
104 confirmations in the province
203 confirmations outside of the province
62 received from the Roman Communion
over $8,000 paid against mission debts together with improvement taxes
1 church built, 1 combination rectory/school built, and 3 churches consecrated
$12,600 paid towards building and repairs
9 convocations and 2 teaching conferences held
over $5,000 paid out of Demby's "own small stipend" towards repairing his home and expenses related to his ministry
$22,825 raised from the missions in Arkansas
a debt of less than $2,000

Beginning with *Mission,* Demby began a four-year campaign to make the Episcopal Church aware that he was committed to a program of developing self-sustaining black ministries in the Southwest—not an altogether new theme, of course, but one he wanted to make sure that the church acknowledged. Judging by his choice of words, it would appear that he came to the realization that his ministry was being undermined by the ubiquitous image of African Americans as lazy and incompetent. White Episcopalians, we may deduce from Demby's remarks, viewed the continuing dependence of black missions in the Southwest as the fulfillment of the old stereotype, and withheld their support accordingly. Demby was determined to quash their misconceptions by publicizing the "heroic" efforts at self-reliance on the part of his churches. Just as he took his "bricks without straw" image from George Black of St. Andrew's, Pine Bluff, Demby capitalized on the remark of an Arkansas priest to establish his new theme in *Mission:* "Bishop Demby," said the unidentified man, "you are teaching us the lesson of SELF HELP." From 1927 to 1931, the terms "self-help" and "self-support" peppered his reports and public addresses.

In 1928, the new bishop of Oklahoma, Thomas C. Casady, reversed the policy of Bishop Theo Thurston and called upon Demby to help pastor his black priests. For instance, when Casady was confronted with a dispute between the Reverend Augustus C. Roker and Roker's congregation, Church of the Redeemer, Oklahoma City, the bishop asked Demby to investigate. Since leaving Arkansas and Bishop William M. Brown, Roker had enjoyed a successful ministry in Oklahoma. He founded and served St. Philip's, Muskogee, from 1910 to 1926, moving on to the Church of the Redeemer in 1927. By the spring of 1928, however, something was clearly amiss at Redeemer. Some of the leading laymen complained to Casady that their new priest was not up to the task of extending the Episcopal Church to Oklahoma City's black community. Casady looked to Demby for clarification, which Demby provided in a manner as convoluted as his office: "If there is a 'mysterious difficulty' at the Church of the Redeemer it is due to the lack of intelligent information of the church, her program, and without a definite and constructive parochial policy for the extension of the Episcopal Church in Oklahoma City among the colored people, hence without aggressive vision—there must be more tangible expression of initiative and producible ability on the part of our missionaries if we are to get results."[56] Demby was in a quandary. He could play the inquisitor but not the pastor. He could report on Roker but lacked the pastoral intimacy that would have enabled him to take Roker into his confidence and either resolve the situation at Redeemer or help Roker with a transfer. Initially, he counseled the congregation to rise above their differences with their priest. However, upon closer inspection—and contrary to Casady's opinion—he eventually had to admit that he believed the laymen were right: it was time for Roker to leave Redeemer.[57] Casady responded by broadening Demby's powers, asking that the suffragan counsel Roker and try to bring about a transfer. But Roker apparently would have none of it, being absent during Demby's next two visitations. Meanwhile, Demby deliberated on placing him in Pennsylvania, Tennessee, and Texas while he looked for a suitable replacement. No movement was forthcoming, however, and the two parties must have reached some sort of rapprochement, because Roker remained at Redeemer until 1932—at which time he took an eight-year hiatus from the Episcopal ministry.

Concurrent with the Roker episode, Demby procured a clergyman for St. Thomas's, Tulsa, which proved to be an equally complicated and tedious process. Demby had overseen the organization of St. Thomas's personally and was justifiably proud of Oklahoma's newest congregation. For the time being, he gave the Reverend H. C. Banks, priest-in-charge of St. Philip's, Muskogee, additional responsibilities at St. Thomas's. Banks was well received and there was even speculation that he might become St. Thomas's full-time priest. Then he ran afoul of some of its leading members and the situation began to look like a reprise of Roker versus Redeemer. In fact, one prominent member of St. Thomas's told Demby that Banks "was not the man to extend the church in

Tulsa."[58] Demby investigated the problem and felt compelled to remove Banks from St. Thomas's, but the similarities to Redeemer end there. He retained a high opinion of Banks and saw to it that he remained at St. Philip's. Demby continued to peruse candidates for St. Thomas on behalf of Casady until the Reverend James E. Stratton assumed charge of St. Thomas's in the summer of 1930.[59]

Despite the unpleasant nature of the events at Redeemer and the difficulties Demby encountered in finding a priest for St. Thomas, Tulsa, the net result of these ministrations was that Casady placed greater trust in Demby and substantially supported his ministry in Oklahoma. To cite two examples, Casady subsidized new and improved structures for St. Philip's, Muskogee, and especially St. Thomas's, Tulsa. St. Thomas celebrated the completion of a brand new $8,000 structure in 1930.[60]

Even with all of its ups and downs, the clerical situation in Oklahoma was an improvement on the situation elsewhere in the province. After visiting the four black churches in Kansas in July and August 1928, Demby observed that "Bishop [James] Wise needs what we need in Arkansas, men and funds, indeed this is true throughout the Province of the Southwest: in the Diocese of Kansas there is only one colored priest."[61] Demby's travels laid bare his other, nonpolitical, impediment to ministering to his huge jurisdiction, namely, money. He wrote Casady in 1928: "I hope to be able to go to the General Convention, but there is nothing certain about it. I have had to use so much of my small stipend to help here and there in the work, especially incident to my own entertainment in visiting the work generally in the province."[62]

In February 1928, Demby published an apologetic in defense of his ministry in the *Arkansas Churchman,* giving an account of his travels and statistical evidence of the overall progress of black ministries in the Southwest. He stated unequivocally, "For the most part in Arkansas, I have been making bricks without straw, building single-handed with patience and faith with the belief [that] some liberty-loving churchmen concerned in the extension of the church among the colored people will ere long hear and respond to the Macedonian cry."[63] True to form, he did not mention specifically the jurisdictional compromise of 1918, nor the absence of a salary from the Board of Missions for the first four years of his ministry.

At about the same time, the findings of the evaluation committee began to generate an intense and widespread debate that would continue into the General Convention in October. In June, an editorial in the *Living Church* put Demby in an unfavorable light by contrasting his ministry with Bishop Delany's "considerable" success in the Carolinas:

It is pointed out that the National Council pays the entire salary of a Negro suffragan bishop "who is understood to be charged with the promotion under the diocesan bishops of the work in the Province of the Southwest," yet after nine years of this experiment the number of Negro missions, clergy, and communicants under his charge is negligible. We may suggest the question whether, in the event that the Province of the Southwest does not desire to lay greater stress upon this work, it might be feasible (with the consent of all concerned) to transfer the Negro suffragan to a center in the Gulf states where the Negro population is at its height, and our work among the population is almost negligible.[64]

Speaking to the 1928 Arkansas convention, Demby called the evaluation committee's analysis "a splendid piece of work," but "some of its findings . . . are questionable. . . . [Nevertheless], the subcommittee strikes at the root of the whole question with reference to the colored work, in saying 'it is practically the unanimous opinion that the church is not doing enough for the Negroes in the South.'"[65] In August, he wrote Winchester a more forceful message, thanking him for his support, disputing the findings of the evaluation committee with regard to his episcopate, and suggesting that the Episcopal Church's alleged concern for black ministries was exaggerated. He quoted a letter he received from an unidentified black clergyman: "[Dear Bishop Demby] If you had done no more than the establishment of Christ Church Parochial and Industrial School your efforts have been a success under the conditions under which you have had to work and the assistance you have received."[66]

Several black priests, most notably the Reverend Harry Rahming, jumped to Demby's defense. Since appearing as the junior black clergyman at Demby's consecration, Rahming had evolved into a priest of considerable stature in the Diocese of Colorado. In 1924 Bishop Irving P. Johnson appointed him secretary to the Board of Examining Chaplains, the body in each diocese that scrutinizes candidates for the ministry. Rahming's elevation to the board, let alone his secretaryship, represented a coup for black clergy. Only two black priests in the entire nation served on their boards of examining chaplains in 1928. Johnson counseled Rahming, "Harry, we won't have any trouble so long as you pass them, but the moment you flunk one of them, we are going to have plenty of trouble, because for a colored man to flunk a white man is like a Harvard College graduate being flunked by a Kentucky Hill Billy [sic], but I think you can handle it."[67] The report of the evaluation committee provided Rahming an opportunity for a scathing, but eloquent, critique of the white Episcopal perspective on black Episcopal ministries. His rebuttal, which appeared in the August Living Church, had nothing but praise for Demby. "All through the province he is loved, honored, and respected." He responded to the comparison of Demby's and Delany's ministries: "Had the same conditions and opinions existed in the jurisdiction of the late Bishop Delaney that exist in the Province of the Southwest, the results would have been exactly the same." Rahming cited Demby's problems of jurisdiction as a severe deterrent to effective work and laid the blame at the feet of the white authorities who failed to consult the black constituents of the province before electing a black suffragan. Furthermore,

> The churches in the province were in a state of dilapidation; there were few colored clergy, and these were very poorly paid; only one Negro school in the entire province, and the colored population woefully ignorant of the Episcopal Church. What the Suffragan Bishop of Arkansas needs, and what his friends and the parts of the province under his jurisdiction seek, is not his transfer to some other province, where he will receive as little aid as he has in the past, but money to build schools, churches, and a hospital, and sufficient money to pay a decent wage to the clergy.[68]

Rahming's rebuttal elicited at least one positive response. He all but named All Saints', St. Louis, as the primary stumbling block to the implementation of Demby's greater jurisdiction. In early 1929, All Saints' invited Demby back to the church of his consecration. The bishop led a retreat and confirmed twenty-three people.[69] It meant a great deal to him and he needed the encouragement. Not long thereafter, he and Mrs. Demby were seriously injured when they were struck by another car.

In August, the *American Mercury* brightened their convalescence with an article, "We Elect a Bishop," a satire on the foibles of Episcopal elections written by Nelson A. Crawford. Bishop Delany having died in 1928, Crawford looked to Demby for an example of black Episcopal bishops. The suffragan bishop of Arkansas, he said, was a particularly compelling figure:

> Nobody enjoys being a bishop more than does a Negro, and after seeing one of them celebrate Pontifical High Mass in the midst of an array of black acolytes, glittering candles, and clouds of incense, I am inclined to think nobody is better qualified. . . . In point of fact, the average colored communicant in the South knows much more theology and liturgics than his white brother. Entertaining, but not altogether palatable to Southern tastes is the fact that the Right Rev. Edward Thomas Demby, the colored suffragan of Arkansas holds more degrees than any Southern white bishop and most Northern ones. Bishop Demby holds a B.D. from Wilberforce University, an S.T. D. from the University of Chicago, a D.D. from Paul Quinn College, a Litt. D. from Selma University, and a Mus. B. and LL. D. from Oskaloosa College.[70]

Demby's unremitting struggle for credibility and finances disgusted black Episcopalians. The Reverend Edgar C. Young of Philips Brooks Memorial Chapel, Philadelphia, addressed the Conference of Church Workers in October 1928, praising the African Orthodox Church of George A. McGuire in contrast to the Episcopal Church, which conferred second-class status on its black bishops. "Suffragan bishops," he declared, "will not do."[71]

Nevertheless, when the dust cleared, Demby had conducted a successful defense of his ministry. The 1928 General Convention took no action on the report of the evaluation committee and the National Council's appropriations for "colored work" in Arkansas continued to climb. The dioceses of the Southwest rendered him a greater acknowledgment and the nation's black clergy realized the need to close ranks around their only representative in the episcopate. A "non-player" in the Conference of Church Workers since 1919, Demby presided over the 1931 national conference in Denver. Presumably, Harry Rahming, the host pastor, made certain of it.

Aside from his rebuttal to the evaluation committee and the burgeoning ministry of Christ Church Parochial and Industrial School, Demby's most important achievement of the late 1920s was the recruitment of two excellent clerics to Arkansas—the Reverend George Gilbert Walker and the Reverend Robert Josiah Johnson. Both men had served in the Southwest Province for many years before coming to Arkansas. Johnson came to St. Mary's, Hot Springs, in 1930, after a long tenure in Kansas, where he pastored St. Augustine's in Wichita (1923–25) and the Church of the Ascension in Kansas City (1925–30). As Demby's earlier remarks would indicate, Johnson was the only black clergyman in Kansas for at least part of his Kansas experience. Although born in Connecticut, he trod the same academic route as James H. King, graduating from St. Augustine's College and Bishop Payne Divinity School before he obtained a D.D. from Western University in Kansas City. His forte was social outreach. Previously mentioned in connection with Demby's travels in Texas, Walker was the archdeacon for "colored work" in the Diocese of Texas (1917–21). He also served the Church of St. Simon the Cyrenian in Topeka for the five years prior to Demby's election (1912–17). His academic credentials were no less impressive than Johnson's. A Canadian with a B.A. and an M.A. in law from King's College, London, he graduated from General Theological Seminary in 1912. He became the leading man of letters in Arkansas's Colored Convocation, being the editor of the *Colored Churchman,* its monthly newsletter. Walker was also the convocation's chief political activist, having joined with Dr. J. M. Robinson and others to form the Arkansas Negro Democratic Association in 1928. Spurred to action by the ascendancy of lily-white Republicanism and the Carter lynching of 1927, Robinson, Walker, and their colleagues were determined to break up the white hegemony of Arkansas's Democratic Party and give black Arkansans the opportunity for meaningful participation in state politics.[72] Walker answered the call to St. Philip's, Little Rock, in 1928. Together with Demby and King, Walker and Johnson formed a cadre of well-educated, seasoned professionals capable of leading the convocation through the Great Depression.

In the broader sense, however, Demby continued to look upon his progress relative to his two major goals: (a) the organization of the Southwest Province into a black missionary district, and (b) the election of a fully vested missionary bishop who would, in all likelihood, be himself.[73] Winchester was equally resolute about Demby and the missionary plan, having watched his black suffragan perform admirably for over a decade. Thus, no one was more shocked and disappointed than Demby when Winchester announced to the 1931 Arkansas convention that he was resigning due to poor health.

The outstanding quality of the relationship between Demby and Winchester during their long sojourn together was the genuine affection that they bore for one another, a relationship that extended beyond Winchester's retirement. They were very similar in temperament. Both men preferred to bring about change without confrontation. Winchester, like Demby, believed that people were best persuaded by forbearance, moral suasion, and pious example. Likewise, they both projected their better qualities onto other people. Winchester fully expected the Province of the Southwest to live up to its commitment to Demby. Similarly, he did not anticipate the jurisdictional problems of 1918. To put it another way, Winchester's idealism betrayed Demby, but Demby forgave him—if, indeed, he ever blamed him in the first place. Demby had his own idealism to contend with. He truly believed that he could educate the white Episcopalians of the Southwest Province and the national church into a wholehearted support of his ministry. Unfortunately, Demby's subsequent experiences paralleled those of Booker T. Washington. To amend the words of historian J. C. Furnas: "The truth was that Washington's [or Demby's] self-reliant confidence, assuming proudly that demonstrated worth would eventually get spontaneous recognition, was an unjustified compliment to the human race, a shameful failure of its white division."[74] Both bishops continued to hold on to the missionary district plan as the best option for the development of black ministries. Winchester argued its merits as late as 1937 when he penned a pro-district article for the *Living Church*. Demby stood by the plan until his retirement in 1939. Perhaps nothing better illustrates their relationship than fact that they remained friends in 1932, even though they found themselves on the opposing sides of a bitter internecine struggle in Arkansas. Demby wrote Winchester in 1933, "I have never regretted anything so much as when you resigned as our Right Reverend Father-in-God, then retired and left the diocese."[75] Theirs was the parting of kindred spirits.

In summary, Demby was a called to do a great deal with very meager resources and look good while doing it. For those who paid attention and were not blinded by racial prejudice, his accomplishments were exemplary, but for the majority he remained an anomalous figure with an ambiguous jurisdiction and a record of dubious accomplishments. It was painfully evident from the inception of Demby's ministry that only a small minority of white ecclesiastics were truly in favor of the black suffragan plan because it held out the promise of greater black ministries. Most whites were not concerned and were just glad to have the blacks at a distance. And, of course, the white Episcopalians had the money. Then again, the Colored Convocation of Arkansas was a vast improvement over the Afro-American Convocation of Arkansas that preceded it. In 1931, Demby understood this, and, as he looked about with his habitual optimism, he saw that he was enjoying greater recognition among black Episcopalians and greater recognition in the Arkansas convention. If only the Diocese of Arkansas would elect the right man to follow Winchester, that upward curve might continue in spite of the Great Depression.

NOTES

1. George A. McGuire, "Second Missionary Report," *Journal of the Annual Convention of the Protestant Episcopal Diocese of Arkansas* (1907): 87–91, hereafter cited as *Arkansas Journal*; David E. Johnson Sr., "Report of Archdeacon," *Arkansas Journal* (1916): 93. Demby was especially antagonistic toward the traditional black emotional religious experience, as he considered it to be a placebo in the place of genuine self-improvement. See Edward T. Demby, "Off of the Record since 1939," MS, James Weldon Johnson Collection, Yale Collection of American Literature, Beinecke Rare Book and Manuscript Library, Yale University, New Haven, Conn., 88–89, 106, hereafter cited as "Off of the Record."

2. Edward T. Demby, "Report of the Suffragan Bishop," *Arkansas Journal* (1919): 48–51.

3. "The Need of Reorganization," *Church Advocate*, Jan. 1914, 2; ibid., Apr. 1915, 2; William M. Clark, "No Negroes Fit for the Position of Bishop," ibid., Aug. 1915, 1; ibid., Jan. 1916, 3; "The Negro's Training in Servility to the White Man," ibid., Feb. 1918, 2; E. T. Demby, "Bishop Demby's Comments," *Little Rock Colored Churchman*, Christmas, 1930, 4, Bishop Edward T. Demby File, box 13, RG 282, Bishop James R. Winches-

ter Papers, Archives of the Episcopal Church, U.S.A., Austin, Tex., hereafter cited as the Winchester Papers; Sarah Delany and A. Elizabeth Delany, *Having Our Say: The Delany Sisters' First One Hundred Years*, ed. Amy Hill Hearth (New York: Kodansha International, 1993), 116; Nelson A. Crawford, "We Elect a Bishop," *American Mercury*, 17 Aug. 1929, 428, Demby Family Papers, Manuscripts, Archives, and Rare Books Division, Schomburg Center for Research in Black Culture, New York Public Library Astor, Lenox, and Tilden Foundations, New York, box 1, folder 1, hereafter cited as Demby Family Papers. "I could tell it wasn't easy for [Bishop Demby]," recalls his niece, Dorothy Demby. "He would contrast his academic qualifications with those of the white clergy who served with him. After all, he had to overachieve in order to have equity. He commented that he had to cope with less qualified people" (Dorothy Demby and Elizabeth Demby Payne, interview by author, New York, 14 Oct. 1995, transcript).

4. Edward T. Demby to William P. Witsell, 5 Dec. 1922, and attached Report to the National Council, Collected Papers of the Reverend William P. Witsell, Archives of the Diocese of Arkansas, Trinity Cathedral, Little Rock, Ark., hereafter cited as the Witsell Papers.

5. Antoinette M. R. Demby [?], *The Mission of the Church among Colored People in the Diocese of Arkansas and the Southwest Province* (n.p., 1927), 3, Bishop Edward Thomas Demby Papers, St. Matthew's Episcopal Church, Wilmington, Del., hereafter cited as St. Matthew's Papers. By 1927, Demby had spent more than $5,000 of his salary to make his Little Rock home "habitable."

6. Edward T. Demby, "Report of the Suffragan Bishop," *Arkansas Journal* (1923): 56–57; ibid. (1925): 51; ibid. (1927): 74.

7. Ibid. (1923): 56. Demby does not identify the "bricks without straw" speaker, but I have concluded that it was George Black, based on a very similar communication autographed by Black (George Black to Edward T. Demby, 12 Nov. 1922, St. Matthew's Papers).

8. E. T. Demby to W. P. Witsell, 5 Dec. 1922, and Witsell's attached Report to the National Council, Witsell Papers.

9. E. T. Demby, *The Mission of the Episcopal Church among the Negroes of the Diocese of Arkansas* (n.p., 1921), 5, black notebook, box 2, Demby Family Papers. Demby made at least four nationwide canvasses, in 1921, 1927, 1930, and 1938. When soliciting money, he was prone to draw comparisons between the generous support given overseas missionary work and the lackadaisical support given domestic black ministries. This, as Harold Lewis points out, was a two-edged sword. Highlighting disparities between the two fields might compel the church to contribute more toward black ministries, but it also reinforced the idea of blacks as a sort of alien subculture within the church, a local manifestation of the "white man's burden" (Harold T. Lewis, *Yet with a Steady Beat: The African-American Struggle for Recognition in the Episcopal Church* [Valley Forge, Pa.: Trinity Press International, 1996], 130).

10. E. T. Demby to W. P. Witsell, 5 Dec. 1922, Witsell Papers.

11. Demby, "Report," *Arkansas Journal* (1923): 58.

12. Jefferson S. Coage to E. Thomas Demby, 30 July 1927, in *Facts Associated with the Ordination and Consecration of Edward Thomas Demby,* comp. Antoinette M. R. Demby (Little Rock, Ark.: Episcopal Diocese of Arkansas, 1927), 25–26, Winchester Papers; see also "Bishop Demby Holding Mission at Christ Church," *Forrest City Times Herald,* 19 Feb. 1925, 5.

13. Harry E. Rahming to Thomas Logan Sr., 10 May 1978, private correspondence of the Reverend Canon Thomas Logan Sr., Logan Residence, Yeadon, Pa.

14. According to Marguerite Gamble, a lifelong member of Trinity Cathedral, Little Rock, Mrs. Demby attended meetings of the Little Rock Rotary Club, which was "not always a popular move" (Marguerite Gamble, interview by author, 14 May 1991, Little Rock, Ark., transcript).

15. Emery Washington, interview by author, 25 Mar. 1995, St. Louis, Mo., transcript.

16. "Father King Dies," *Arkansas Churchman,* Sept. 1955.

17. Charlene Shaw Neal, interview by author, 21 May 1995, Forrest City, Ark., transcript.

18. Edward Norman, "The History of Christ Church and Christ Church Parochial and Industrial School (Christ Church School), Forrest City, Arkansas, 1921–1982," MS, 1982, records of Christ Episcopal Church, Forrest City, Ark., 1; Dora Strong Dennis, interview by author, 14 May 1995, Forrest City, Ark., transcript; Dora Strong Dennis, telephone interview by author, 4 July 1995, Forrest City, Ark., transcript; Emery Washington, interview by author, St. Louis, Mo., 25 Mar. 1995, transcript; Todd E. Lewis, "Booker T. Washington and His Visits to Little Rock," *Pulaski County Historical Review* 42 (Fall 1994): 61; Charles J. Rector, "Lily-White Republicanism: The Pulaski County Experience, 1888–1930," ibid. 42 (Spring 1994): 9; A. Demby, *Facts,* 28, Winchester Papers. A pamphlet celebrating Demby's first nine years in the episcopate, *Facts* includes a congratulatory letter issued by the laity of Christ Church and other Forrest City blacks, a veritable who's who of Forrest City's black upper class. See also Michael J. Beary, "Birds of Passage: A History of the Separate Black Episcopal Church in Arkansas, 1902–1939," M.A. thesis, University of Arkansas, 1993, 55–58. Born into slavery in Mississippi, Scott Bond owned twelve thousand acres of fertile bottom land at the time of his death, operated six cotton gins and a lumber business, furnished the Rock Island [Railroad] Line with gravel from a pit on his property, grew peaches and apples commercially, and operated a mercantile store in Madison (Robert W. Chowning, *History of St. Francis County, Arkansas [through] 1954* [Forrest City, Ark.: Times Herald Publishing Company, 1954], 152–56).

19. Dora Strong Dennis, interview by author, 14 May 1995, Forrest City, Ark., transcript.

20. Beary, "Birds of Passage," 52; "County Examiner's and County Superintendent's Register of Black Teachers' Licenses, 1919 and 1920," Records of the St. Francis County Board of Education, St. Francis County Courthouse, Forrest City, Ark. Norment had the distinction of holding a state professional license for four years instead of the standard two-year license accompanied by qualifying test scores.

21. Beary, "Birds of Passage," 50–54. Born in Columbia, South Carolina, Middleton was basically an orphan. She was educated at St. Mary's School in Wilmington, N.C., and St. Augustine's Normal and Industrial School, Raleigh, N.C. After one year of college at St. Augustine's she entered the Bishop Tuttle School of Social Work affiliated with St. Augustine's. Upon graduation, she came to Arkansas because there were no openings in North Carolina. She succeeded the late Lois Lockhart, another Tuttle School graduate and a native of Pine Bluff, Arkansas. In addition to her teaching duties, Middleton spearheaded the Christ Church Woman's Auxiliary, taught Sunday school, directed the choir, and served as vice-principal of Christ Church School. She retired to North Carolina in 1952 (Inez Middleton, interview by Joyce Howard, Dec. 1981, Raleigh, N.C., transcript).

22. Alston received $10.00 for his services in 1926, his only record of payment via the National Council. Domestic and Foreign Missionary Society of the Protestant Episcopal Church in the United States of America, *Annual Report of the Board of Missions (National Council) of the Protestant Episcopal Church* (Fenalong, N.Y.: Domestic and Foreign Missionary Society, 1926), 295. A lay missionary, contractor, carpenter, and music instructor, Alston preceded King to Forrest City. It was he and Norman Otto Peoples who drew up the plans for the chapel and erected it. He contributed his musical expertise to the chapel and school. Dora Strong Dennis, telephone interview by author, 4 July 1995, Forrest City, Ark.; Ethel B. Driver, telephone interview by author, Forrest City, Ark., 14 May, 1995.

23. Norman, "History of Christ Church," 2; Margaret Sims McDonald, *White Already to Harvest: The Episcopal Church in Arkansas, 1838–1971* (Sewanee, Tenn.: University Press for the Episcopal Diocese of Arkansas, 1975), 205; Dora Strong Dennis, telephone interview by author, 22 May 1995, Forrest City, Ark., transcript; Emery Washington, interview by author, 25 Mar. 1995, St. Louis, Mo., transcript; Ethel B. Driver, interview by author, 14 May 1995, Forrest City, Ark., transcript; Inez Middleton, interview by Joyce Howard, Dec. 1981, Raleigh, N.C., transcript; Minnie Shaw Warren, interview by author, 21 May 1995, Forrest City, Ark., transcript; Charlene Shaw Neal, interview by author, 21 May 1995, Forrest City, Ark., transcript; *The Mission of the Protestant Episcopal Church in the Province of the Southwest and the Diocese of Arkansas among the Colored [Negro] People*, a fund-raising booklet celebrating Bishop Demby's twentieth year as bishop, (n.p., 1938), box 2, Demby Family Papers; Wallace A. Battle to Edward R. Embree, 20 Dec. 1935, Reverend Wallace Battle Correspondence, Julius Rosenwald Fund Archives, Amistad Research Center, Tulane University, New Orleans, La. In order to put tuition payments in perspective, consider that Christ Church School operated on $238.46 for 1940, apart from salaries and special gifts. Approximately one-third of the operating budget was raised by tuition payments.

24. E. T. Demby, "The Colored Work in the Southwest," *Arkansas Churchman*, Feb. 1928, 7.

25. "The Other Side of Life in Detroit, Michigan," *Forrest City Times Herald*, 26 May 1923, 1; "Negro DIES from Cold," 3 Jan. 1924, ibid., 5; Bishop Theo Thurston of Okla-

homa "regretted the inability of the Church to stabilize Negro congregations, stating that 'our colored brethren seem to be of a roving disposition'" (Samuel L. Botkin, *The Episcopal Church in Oklahoma* [Oklahoma City, Okla.: American Bond Printing Co., 1958], 28).

26. Demby, "Report," *Arkansas Journal* (1925): 51.

27. "And This Is the Record," *Church Advocate*, Feb. 1920, 2; *Arkansas Journal* (1920): 52.

28. E. T. Demby to E. P. Dandridge, 9 June 1926, "Off of the Record."

29. According to the *Crisis*, relief funds intended for black refugees were being distributed inequitably between white and black flood victims (quoted in W. E. B. Du Bois, *W. E. B. Du Bois: Writings* [New York: Literary Classics of the United States, 1986], 1218–19.

30. Todd E. Lewis, "Mob Justice in the 'American Congo': 'Judge Lynch' in Arkansas during the Decade after World War I," *Arkansas Historical Quarterly* 52 (Summer 1993): 156–58, 170–71, 177. See also James R. Eison, "Dead, but She Was in a Good Place, a Church," *Pulaski County Historical Review* 30 (Summer 1982): 30–42; Du Bois, *Writings*, 68.

31. E. T. Demby, "Off of the Record," 69–70. Remembering the Carter lynching and similar events that made the decade after the First World War so notorious for racial violence, Demby remarked, "It is said by not a few Caucasians that when Negroes speak in defense of their people . . . that they always have a 'chip on their shoulders.' However, if they had to endure what the Negroes do, they would not have a chip on their shoulders, but heavy stones" (ibid., 70). Perhaps there is no better example of "heavy stones" than Richard Wright, author of *Native Son* and "Bright and Morning Star." Wright lived in the vicinity of Elaine, Arkansas, in 1916, three years before the infamous Elaine Riot. When his uncle was lynched, Wright and his mother fled to West Helena for fear that there might be repercussions on the extended family. The "white fear," said Wright, "was upon the land." See Addison Gayle, *Richard Wright: Ordeal of a Native Son* (Garden City, N.Y.: Anchor Press, Doubleday, 1980), 15–19. Demby heartily endorsed *Native Son* as an accurate portrayal of the dilemma of blacks in America and, especially, the South. Demby, "Off of the Record," 65. For a more detailed description of the Elaine Riot, see Lee E. Williams and Lee E. Williams II, *Anatomy of Four Race Riots: Racial Conflict in Knoxville, Elaine (Arkansas), Tulsa, and Chicago, 1919–1921* ([Hattiesburg]: University and College Press of Mississippi, 1972). See also Richard C. Cortner, *A Mob Intent on Death: The NAACP and the Arkansas Riot Cases* (Middletown, Conn.: Wesleyan University Press, 1988). Although he was not quite as outspoken as Bishop Thomas F. Gailor of Tennessee, Bishop Winchester also published a condemnation of lynching (James R. Winchester, "On Peonage and Lynching," article published in unidentified newspaper, n.d., Winchester Papers).

32. Demby, "Report," *Arkansas Journal* (1927): 74–75; McDonald, *Harvest*, 206; Reverend Thomas S. Logan to Michael J. Beary, n.d., author's private correspondence.

33. Carolyn R. Harris, interview by author, 1 Mar. 1991, Fayetteville, Ark., transcript.

34. "Constitution of Negro Convocation," *Arkansas Journal* (1933): 82–85. Bishop Demby habitually substituted "Negro" for "colored" in all titles relative to his ministry, "Negro" being widely regarded as the more progressive nomenclature for black people. Hence the change from the original "colored" to "Negro" in the title of the constitution. (See also n. 23 above, where Demby has made a similar change in a title.)

35. Apparently Demby stayed just long enough to hear his report, then left. W. P. Witsell, "My Contact with Some High Points of the History of the Diocese of Arkansas, 1927–1957," MS, Archives of the Diocese of Arkansas, Trinity Cathedral, Little Rock, Ark., 4–5; Edwin W. Saphore, "Ecclesiastical Authority Addresses Bishops," *Arkansas Churchman*, Sept. 1932, 8–9; Carolyn R. Harris, interview by author, 1 Mar. 1991, Fayetteville, Ark., transcript.

36. McDonald, *Harvest*, 190–91.

37. Witsell, "High Points," 5.

38. John W. Graves, *Town and Country: Race Relations in an Urban-Rural Context, Arkansas, 1865–1905* (Fayetteville: University of Arkansas Press, 1990), 225, 226.

39. George K. Cracraft, interview by author, 10 Aug. 1991, Little Rock, Ark., transcript. Judge Cracraft is a product of St. John's, Helena. Marguerite Gamble, interview by author, 14 May 1991, Little Rock, Ark., transcript. Ms. Gamble is a lifelong member of Trinity Cathedral, Little Rock, and has some personal familiarity with the racial climate of Episcopal Arkansas in Demby's day.

40. Witsell, "High Points," 5.

41. Donald Wilson, telephone interview by author, 2 July 1991, Palm Coast, Fla., transcript.

42. E. T. Demby to James R. Winchester, 10 Aug. 1928, Witsell Papers.

43. See Willard B. Gatewood Jr., *Theodore Roosevelt and the Art of Controversy: Episodes of the White House Years* (Baton Rouge: Louisiana State University Press, 1970), 32–61.

44. David M. Reimers, *White Protestantism and the Negro* (New York: Oxford University Press, 1965), 104–8. Bishop Robert E. Jones, the first black bishop in the Methodist Episcopal Church, had an advantage over Demby when it came to integrated facilities. Jones, whose jurisdiction also included Arkansas, was so light complected he could "pass" for white and ride in Pullman cars. Demby, of course, had to take the Jim Crow car. See Walter N. Vernon, *Methodism in Arkansas, 1816–1976* (Little Rock, Ark.: Joint Committee for the History of Arkansas Methodism, 1976), 309–10.

45. Reimers, *White Protestantism*, 104.

46. Ibid., 106; "Presbyterians Won't Permit J. C. in Fort Worth," *Washington Afro-American*, 15 Oct. 1932, 23; "Uphold No Jim Crow Edict," *Pittsburgh Courier*, 9 Nov. 1932, 10.

47. John A. Howell, "The Church and Black Folk," *Crisis*, Feb. 1933, 32.

48. Thomas S. Logan Sr., interview by author, 19 Oct. 1995, Yeadon, Pa., transcript.

49. Roberta Church, interview by author, 17 Aug. 1994, Memphis, Tenn., transcript.

50. James W. Temple, telephone interview by author, 1 Dec. 1991, Los Angeles, Calif., transcript. Reverend James Temple was a student at Bishop Payne Divinity School in the early 1930s, where he received financial assistance from Bishop Demby. I take my interpretation of the Kansas "peculiarity" from Ms. Roberta Church (Roberta Church, interview by author, 30 July 1994, Memphis, Tenn., transcript).

51. Harold T. Lewis, telephone interview by author, 20 Oct. 1992, New York, transcript.

52. Demby, "Report," *Arkansas Journal* (1927): 73.

53. *Arkansas Churchman*, Jan. 1927, 3.

54. Thomas C. Casady to W. P. Witsell, 5 Oct. 1927, Collected Papers of Rt. Rev. Thomas C. Casady, Bishop Edward T. Demby File, Archives of the Episcopal Diocese of Oklahoma, Oklahoma City, Okla., hereafter cited as Casady Papers; E. T. Demby to T. C. Casady, 5 Oct. 1927, ibid.; W. P. Witsell to T. C. Casady, 6 Oct. 1927, ibid.; E. T. Demby to T. C. Casady, 29 Dec. 1927, ibid.

55. E. T. Demby to T. C. Casady, 29 Dec. 1927, Casady Papers; Phoebe Arrington, interview by author, 18 Oct. 1995, Brooklyn, N.Y., transcript; Marjorie Nichols Farmer, "Different Voices: African American Women in the Episcopal Church," in *Episcopal Women: Gender, Spirituality, and Commitment in an American Mainline Denomination,* ed. Catherine M. Prelinger (New York: Oxford University Press, 1992), 232, 233.

56. E. T. Demby to T. C. Casady, 13 Apr. 1928, Casady Papers.

57. Ibid.

58. E. T. Demby to T. C. Casady, 3 Jan. 1930, Casady Papers.

59. One of the candidates Demby contemplated for priest of St. Thomas's was the Reverend F. Norman Fitzpatrick, a graduate of General Theological Seminary whom he had ordained to the priesthood. Fitzpatrick had been the center of a stormy and somewhat bizarre episode for black Episcopal ministries in Oklahoma. At the time of Demby's consecration, he had been in charge of Redeemer Church in Oklahoma City. Later on, says Demby, Fitzpatrick left the Episcopal Church to become a Roman Catholic and tried to proselyte members of Redeemer to Oklahoma City's black Catholic church. By January 1930, however, he had reversed himself and was once again in Demby's good graces. Demby recommended Fitzpatrick for the pastorate of St. Thomas's, but the post went to the Reverend James E. Stratton. Unfortunately, Stratton's happy association with St. Thomas's ended suddenly in March 1932, when he died of an illness. Stratton's death left Oklahoma with no black clergy at a time when Casady's and Demby's resources were badly depleted by the Great Depression. They had little power to recruit. The Reverend Shirley G. Sanchez of St. Augustine's, Fort Smith, transferred to St. Thomas's five months later, but the move proved to be counterproductive for Demby's ministry in Oklahoma, because Demby and Sanchez were not on good terms, for reasons given in chapter 6. Sanchez's move gave the Diocese of Oklahoma one badly needed black clergyman and helped to relieve Demby of one disputatious relationship in Arkansas, but it was not conducive to his oversight of Oklahoma. E. T.

Demby to T. C. Casady, 26 May, 6 July, 21 Nov. 1928, 23 Mar., 4 Apr., 24 June 1929, Casady Papers.

60. E. T. Demby, "Colored Work in the Southwest," *Arkansas Churchman,* Feb. 1928, 6–7; E. T. Demby to T. C. Casady, 27 Apr. 1928, 17 Apr., 27 Dec. 1929, 3 Jan. 1930, Casady Papers; Mr. Popkin to T. C. Casady, 14 Jan. 1931, ibid.; *Oklahoma Churchman,* Oct. 1932, 4.

61. E. T. Demby to James R. Winchester, 10 Aug. 1928, Witsell Papers.

62. E. T. Demby to Thomas Casady, 1 Aug. 1928, Casady Papers.

63. Demby, "Colored Work in the Southwest," 6.

64. *Living Church,* 9 June 1928, 184.

65. Edward T. Demby, "Report of the Suffragan," *Arkansas Journal* (1928): 27–28.

66. E. T. Demby to James R. Winchester, 10 Aug. 1928, Witsell Papers.

67. Harry E. Rahming to Thomas S. Logan Sr., 10 May 1978, private collection of Rev. Canon Thomas S. Logan Sr., Logan residence, Yeadon, Pa.

68. Harry E. Rahming, "Church Work among Negroes: A Plea for Recognition of Negro Leadership," *Living Church,* 4 Aug. 1928, 463–64.

69. Edward T. Demby, "Report of the Suffragan," *Arkansas Journal* (1930): 32; Demby, "Off of the Record," 112.

70. Crawford, "We Elect a Bishop," 427–28.

71. Monroe V. Work, ed., *Negro Yearbook: An Annual Encyclopedia of the Negro, 1931–1932* (Tuskegee, Ala.: Negro Yearbook Publishing Co., 1932), 256–57.

72. Rosemary White and Charles White, interview by author, 26 Mar. 1997, Little Rock, Ark., transcript; John Kirk, "Dr. J. M. Robinson, the Arkansas Negro Democratic Association and Black Politics in Little Rock, Arkansas, 1928–1952," *Pulaski County Historical Review* 41 (Spring 1993): 6.

73. E. T. Demby, "Bishop Demby's Comments," *(Little Rock) Colored Churchman,* Christmas 1930, 4, Winchester Papers; J. R. Winchester, "Bishop Winchester on Colored Missionary Bishops," clipping, ibid.

74. J. C. Furnas, *The Americans: A Social History of the United States, 1587–1914* (New York: G. P. Putnam's Sons, 1969), 853.

75. E. T. Demby to J. R. Winchester, 23 Dec. 1933, Winchester Papers.

5

The Newport Incident

In the summer of 1932, Arkansas Democrats rallied to the populist rhetoric of Senator Huey P. Long of Louisiana and elected Hattie Caraway of Jonesboro to the United States Senate. Long and Caraway stumped the state in a whirlwind campaign replete with a blue cadillac, blaring sound trucks, a cadre of bouncers and baby rockers, a Bible, a throat atomizer, a pistol, loads of sentiment, and Herman Deutsch of the *Saturday Evening Post* to record it all. Caraway, an incumbent by virtue of an emergency election following the death of her husband, won the Democratic nomination outright during the second week of August. After the formality of the November election, she became the first woman regularly elected to the United States Senate.

The Democratic stump of August was still smoking when Arkansans learned of another precedent-setting election in their midst. According to the state's two leading newspapers, the Episcopal Church in Arkansas had convened in May and elected one of its own priests, Dean John Williamson of Trinity Cathedral, Little Rock, as the new bishop of Arkansas. However, two white priests and a black bishop, the Right Reverend Edward T. Demby, intended to nullify that election. The grounds for nullification, they said, was "racial discrimination" in connection with the election and the Holy Communion that preceded it. Arkansans were incredulous. What could have happened at a church convention to so embolden a black clergyman that he would risk public protest and why would two white clergymen back him up? In the South of 1932, writes John Egerton, "The highest virtues were honor and duty, loyalty and obedience. Every member of society—man and woman, white and black—knew his or her place, and it was an unusual (not to mention foolhardy) person who showed a flagrant disregard for the assigned boundaries and conventions."[1]

Nevertheless, the fight was on and the press, both secular and religious, publicized the quagmire of accusations, rebuttals, and recriminations on into the fall. In late September, the belligerents essentially took their quarrel "inside" in the interest of preserving the church's image and the electoral hopes of the bishop-elect. In November, the higher powers issued their verdicts: Franklin Delano Roosevelt became the new president of the United States and the black bishop and the two white priests won their case with the national church—the House of Bishops overturned the Arkansas election. Friends of the bishop-elect, mortified and stunned, vowed to elect him again and continued to try for six more years. Ultimately, the Episcopal Diocese of Arkansas reconciled itself by electing a bishop from outside the diocese in 1938. As if on cue, Arkansas Episcopalians involved in the 1932 episode suppressed mention of it by a mutual and unspoken agreement. By 1941 a majority of those intimate with the events had retired, died, transferred, or were deposed. They left behind three convoluted and incomplete versions of what we will call the Newport incident; three stories that conform to party lines and come down to us embellished in the course of countless potlucks and dinner parties. One school, by far the most vocal among white Arkansans, alleges that Demby's protest was the machination of the Reverend William P. Witsell, rector of Christ Church, Little Rock. Witsell, runner-up to Williamson in the May 1932 election, allegedly persuaded Demby and others to make a mountain out of a racist molehill. This view is most pronounced among those Episcopalians of long affiliation with Trinity Cathedral. A second Arkansas school suspects that Demby was correct but sees no reason to raise an old, divisive issue for which there is no conclusive evidence. Their usual response is silence in the face of the first school. The third school is that of the black clergy, nationally speaking. They believe Demby's case was valid but needs work. Margaret Sims McDonald, whose *White Already to Harvest: The Episcopal Church in Arkansas, 1838–1971*, is the most comprehensive history of the diocese to date, summed up the episode this way: "With charges and counter-charges in the press and with no original documents to check against, the matter is left at this point, except to say that while 'racial discrimination' seemed to make wider news waves, some news items did stress the fact that the diocese already had three bishops drawing salaries and/or honorariums and it was not financially able to support another."[2] Witsell, being a principal in the conflict, wisely abstained from comment in his *History of Christ Episcopal Church, Little Rock, Arkansas, 1839–1947*, save for the following: "In the convention held at St. Paul's church, Newport, May 11, 1932, the matter of electing a bishop was again brought up, but the result was such a sharp controversy, and since the action of the convention was not confirmed by the House of Bishops, we refrain from going into any details although at some expense of complete historical records."[3] Their disagreement over records and their disinclination to comment, especially on the race issue, betray the volatile nature of the topic. Both authors were too close chronologically and personally to the event to make anything but the most ambiguous comments.

As it turns out, Witsell was correct about the abundance of historical records. He had in his possession about five hundred documents, mainly personal correspondence, bearing on the episode. The collected papers of the Reverend William P. Witsell are a consolidation of Witsell's voluminous records, together with a smaller collection compiled by his close friend and chancellor of the Diocese of Arkansas, Deadrick Cantrell, and some of Demby's correspondence. The information contained therein is explicit and relatively unguarded, a veritable clinic in ecclesiastical politics, all racial considerations aside. Practically every Episcopal bishop who served in the 1930s is represented in the Witsell papers. In addition, there is a substantial amount of material to be found in the papers of the Arkansas Executive Council, which is primarily the correspondence of the Tom Wood, acting chairman of the Arkansas Executive Council in 1932. The executive council papers, which are equally candid, represent the views of those opposed to Witsell and in favor of the 1932 election. Mrs. McDonald either missed these or deemed them insufficient for the purpose.

In 1989, the Arkansas Episcopal election of 1932 reemerged in reference to the election of the Right Reverend Barbara Harris, suffragan bishop of Massachusetts. Harris, a divorced black woman, was the first priest of her gender to be elected bishop in the Episcopal Church. Her controversial, precedent-setting election prompted speculation that she might fail of national confirmation even if she won the Massachusetts election. Searching about for a historical precedent to Harris's possible rejection, writers rediscovered the Arkansas election, another milestone in black Episcopal history.[4] But the record of that failed election remains essentially as its authors left it in 1938, a mess. So what happened in 1932 and, most especially, what happened at that May convention to start it all?

The short version of 1932 is as follows. The Diocese of Arkansas elected the Very Reverend John Williamson, an Arkansas priest, as its bishop, only to see his election vetoed by the House of Bishops. Jaundiced by an infamous segregated communion episode, a racist ticket, Arkansas's questionable ability to pay his salary, and doubts regarding his executive ability, Williamson's election failed. Although it was one of several church-related racial incidents of its day, it is the only racial incident in the history of the Episcopal Church to prompt intervention by the national body. Yet this was far more than a racial incident; here was a diocese at war with itself. Every conceivable impediment to effective church government complicated the 1932 Annual Convention of the Diocese of Arkansas. Rivalries, personal and intrachurch, permeated the proceedings, accompanied by a general spirit of insubordination and a lack of money. Everyone, it seems, wanted to steer the ecclesiastical ship of state through the convention—except the ones with the authority to do so. Ultimately, the racial protest revealed the schismatic character of the diocese, which, more than any other factor, assured Williamson's defeat. This, in synopsis, was the Newport incident.

The longer version of 1932 begins with the ever-encroaching spread of Jim Crow and the unprecedented violence visited on black people in the decade following the First World War. As always, oppression of African Americans in the country at large gave sanction to the same attitude in the Episcopal Church. Uncertain as to whether or how to make a fight, the church's forty thousand black Episcopalians and their white allies had no effective strategy for bringing the church to terms with its very worldly outlook on race. True, the omnipresent struggle for the missionary district plan continued at the General Conventions of the twenties and thirties, conceding segregation in the name of black equality and recognition at the church's highest levels, but the plan was mired in debate. Meanwhile, at the sub-General Convention levels of the church most people made a stand for catholicity only when they had no alternative, when some measure or practice or deed flagrantly violated the church's professed all-inclusiveness in the name of white supremacy. If the protest became public knowledge via the secular press, the result was nothing short of sensational. Black people, after all, were supposed to accept their lot in life without protest. Their white advocates enjoyed more freedom of speech, but not that much more. They too had to count the cost. Thus, those incidents that did occur had a precedent-setting value in a church otherwise subdued by the attitude of the country, and none more than what the *Church Advocate* termed the "Southern Florida Outrage" of 1921.[5]

According to Gavin White, "Archdeacon P. S. Irwin, an Irishman and a missionary to Bahamian immigrants in the Missionary District of South Florida, was tarred and feathered by a gang of local patriots" as punishment for encouraging black insubordination.[6] Afterwards, Irwin was spirited out of Miami on the pretext that his continued presence might cause violence to his flock. The police were unable to apprehend his assailants, which compounded the outrage of the *Church Advocate,* the *Living Church,* and Bishop Cameran Mann of South Florida. "If Liberian officials can protect missionaries and Miami officials cannot," asked the *Living Church,* "[who] has the higher civilization?"[7] The violence was particularly galling for Mann, who had promoted Irwin's ministry on the same grounds that Bishop William M. Brown, Archdeacon George A. McGuire, Bishop James R. Winchester, Archdeacon Daniel

E. Johnson Sr., and Bishop Edward T. Demby had promoted black ministries in Arkansas; namely, that the ministrations of the Episcopal Church produced law-abiding black citizens. Addressing the South Florida convention the following year, Mann insisted that his former archdeacon was not guilty of fomenting social rebellion, called for justice on Irwin's behalf, and adjured the assembled delegates that it was their "duty to encourage Negroes to rise in the world, and, as for religion, 'they are entitled to as full membership in the Catholic Church as we are.'"[8] "It was a courageous thing to say in Miami," writes White, "but Mann was aware as was everyone else that he did not carry his people with him, and it seems to have been felt that Irwin received what he deserved."[9]

A series of three dramatic incidents between 1929 and 1932 further demonstrated to Episcopalians and the nation at large that the Episcopal Church was, in various places, integrated beyond the realm of social acceptability. New York City was the scene of two well-publicized racial incidents, the first in St. Matthew's, Brooklyn, in September 1929. Commonly known as the Blackshear incident, it was a tour de force for ecclesiastical segregation, or, to put it another way, Black Thursday played havoc on Wall Street while "White Sunday" triumphed on the other side of the East River. The southern-educated rector of a white New York City church, the Reverend William Blackshear, successfully expelled the growing West Indian contingent of St. Matthew's. Technically, the blacks were not members of St. Matthew's, but they were too numerous and too faithful to remain visitors indefinitely. On 15 September, Blackshear, speaking from his pulpit and via the church bulletin, told the newcomers that they should attend one of the nearby black churches and discouraged them from further attendance at St. Matthew's. Nevertheless, eleven blacks attended St. Matthew's the following Sunday while plainclothes New York police detectives stood by to "prevent any demonstrations."[10] Twenty-five Ku Klux Klansmen allegedly attended the same service with the intent of thwarting a rumored demonstration by blacks, which is not unlikely considering that the Knights of the White Camelia exercised a conspicuous presence on Long Island in the 1920s.[11] Blackshear's brazenness embarrassed many northern white Episcopalians and infuriated black Episcopalians everywhere. James Weldon Johnson, secretary of the NAACP and a leading man of letters in the Episcopal Church, called upon St. Matthew's vestry to force Blackshear's resignation. The vestry, however, stood with their rector and effectively prevented intervention from any quarter, including Blackshear's superior, Bishop Ernest M. Stires of Long Island. The major Episcopalian periodicals at once criticized and agreed with Blackshear. The *Living Church* argued for segregation—with exceptions. Segregation was practiced, said the Milwaukee paper, "for the mutual comfort and well being of both [races]."[12]

In its more immediate significance, the Blackshear incident demonstrated that a church could practice blatant segregation with impunity so long as the vestry formed a united front. Segregation, traditionally regarded as the prerogative of the local church, now enjoyed a quasi-official sanction. The incident also showed white southern Episcopalians that many white northern Episcopalians shared their desire for segregation, although northerners generally preferred greater discretion.

The second incident, the forced desegregation of All Souls', Harlem, in 1932, incorporated many of the Blackshear elements, although with a radically different outcome. Again, a formerly all-white New York City parish became the unlikely church home of a large contingent of West Indian immigrants. Again, there was a written attempt on the part of the white-controlled church to expel the newcomers and send them to a nearby black church. Again, the NAACP entered the fray, blazing away at the proponents of segregation. But there the similarities end. The white rector of All Souls', the Reverend Rollin Dodd, was an Englishman who welcomed the blacks with open arms. The new arrivals were made members of the church and constituted 75 percent of the congregation by October 1932, when the disposition of the church's endowment finally propelled the race controversy to its climax.

All Souls' was a beautiful structure reflecting the tastes of the stylish and prosperous all-white congregation that had built it. It enjoyed a commensurately munificent endowment of $131,000, making it fiscally independent of the weekly offering. In mid-1931, a majority of the all-white vestry determined that the blacks must go; otherwise they would eventually share in the government of the church and control of the endowment. The vestry insisted that Dodd write Bishop C. B. Colmore of Puerto Rico to the effect that the bishop should send no more transfers of membership to All Souls'. According to the vestry majority, Dodd claimed to have complied in this.[13] Having assumed as much, the vestrymen were stunned by the rector's open defiance later that same year when he began protesting their "racial discrimination." Dodd compounded their outrage with an anti-divorce-and-remarriage sermon in the spring of 1932. The sermon constituted a personal affront to the senior warden, or chief vestryman, of All Souls', Manuel Roure, whose daughter had recently divorced and remarried. She was also a parishioner of All Souls', and, to make matters worse, her new husband was himself a vestryman. Coincidentally, Roure and his son-in-law were leading the fight to exclude the blacks from the church. They looked upon Dodd's sermon as the last straw and resolved to overrule him with regard to the West Indians. In June 1932 a majority of the vestry closed ranks with them to preserve the endowment from future black influence. They approached Dodd's superior, Bishop William T. Manning of New York, for a solution. Apparently Manning agreed to open St. Monica's, a defunct black mission near All Souls', as a black alternative. Taking this as a mandate to "Blackshear" the West Indians, the vestry went one step further and tried to expel them by distributing cards to them on Sunday, 10 July, at the morning service. The cards brazenly instructed the blacks to cease attending All Souls' and remove themselves to St. Monica's. Upon reading one of the cards, Dodd vehemently defied the vestry's action—during the service. His wife and his son, who was also a vestry member, joined him. Likewise, Dodd exhorted the black parishioners to disregard the cards, which they did. Due to the absence of Manning, who had gone abroad, the issue remained deadlocked though the summer and into the fall. Seven of the twelve vestrymen were bent on expulsion of the West Indians, while the other five supported Dodd wholeheartedly. According to the *New York Times,* the seven were, to use the modern parlance, "white flight" commuters who lived in the suburbs, while the five actually lived in Manhattan. Almost all of All Souls' 250 parishioners supported Dodd. Those opposed, counting the seven vestry members, numbered about twenty-five. Thus, the segregationists had the money and the political majority; the integrationists had the church. In early September, the vestry asked for Dodd's resignation when he refused to hold separate services for the blacks. They withheld his salary, but Dodd ignored them for the time being. Manning sent his assistant, Suffragan Bishop Charles K. Gilbert, to arbitrate the dispute, but to no avail. In early October, the vestry closed the church, ostensibly for repairs to the sanctuary. Dodd and company countered by worshiping in the church's basement, but removed to a nearby lecture hall when the vestry locked them out of the basement, as well. A battle of words ensued between the two parties in the press. Roure maintained that safety was the preeminent issue, the building being in a dangerous state of disrepair. He alleged that Dodd was withholding information from city inspectors that would back him up. Dodd maintained that the repairs were neither coincidental to the schism nor crucial to the safety of the congregation; it was a case of racism, pure and simple.[14]

The decisive element of the All Souls' incident proved to be Bishop Manning, a small, frail-looking man who possessed in determination and authority what he lacked in stature. He was, like Dodd, a hard-liner against divorce and remarriage, the most pervasive moral issue of the day. As noted in chapter 2, Manning had "cut his teeth" on black ministries, so to speak, while a young curate at Emmanuel Church in Memphis.[15] Over the course of his ministry, he had earned a reputation as a champion of black ministries. Demby called him "one of the tried and true bishops of the Church who are deeply concerned in the Church's success among the Colored people."[16] With the closure of All Souls', Manning laid plans to force the integration issue. He told Dodd to hold his ground. Dodd, in turn, encouraged his flock to persevere in the face of the vestry's actions. Manning confided to Dodd that he planned to act, but wanted to time his actions in order to amass public support.[17]

The showdown came on Sunday morning, October 23. Manning, Dodd, a majority of All Souls' parishioners, the New York press, several of New York's finest, and a locksmith "broke in" to All Souls'. Once inside, Manning delivered his sermon from a jury-rigged pulpit in the aisle, set against a backdrop of scaffolding and debris. The sermon, an exposition of the "divine vision of the Holy Catholic Church," unqualifiedly placed Dodd in the right and the vestry majority in the wrong.[18]

Not persuaded of Manning's theology or authority, the vestry locked the church up again, only to witness a second break-in the following Sunday, October 30. This time Dodd and Denzil Carter, a black seminarian attending All Souls', supervised the action. Acknowledging the futility of resistance in light of Manning's position, the vestry majority threatened legal action against the bishop. The threat, however, proved to be an empty one and they eventually left All Souls', taking the endowment and a tiny minority of the congregation with them. Simultaneously, several black members of All Souls' responded by forming a "committee to keep the wolf away from the rector's door," in order to preserve Dodd's salary and expedite the transition to black leadership of the church.[19] Dodd and All Souls' researched the successful financial practices of nearby churches of various denominations and came up with a viable plan for the support of the church. Thus, they mastered fund-raising and survived divestiture.[20] Walter White, successor to James Weldon Johnson, lauded Manning, as did many Episcopal clergy across the nation.[21]

Be that as it may, All Souls' did not have the precedent-setting value that Blackshear did, or, at least, not immediately, because it ran contrary to the social norm. Opponents and proponents understood it to be the exception to a rule as old as Absalom Jones and St. George's Methodist Church—a rule which remained solidly in place: a few black visitors in a white church may be permissible, but a growing black membership is not.[22] Marguerite Du Pont Lee, matriarch to Wilmington's first Episcopal family, scolded both sides in the All Souls' incident from the pages of the *New York Churchman:* "If today the neighborhood is largely occupied by those of the colored race, the trouble is quickly solved by the others finding houses of worship elsewhere." This, she said, would spare the church the indignity of a public dispute. As for Bishop Manning's stand on orthodoxy, she would remind him that the church is also a hub of social functions, functions "which give ample opportunity for the formation of intimate friendships. Are Bishop Manning and the editor of the [New York] *Churchman* prepared to face this problem? Let us worship Paul's Unknown God sanely—Crocodile tears on behalf of our colored brother are totally uncalled for."[23] White clergy of other denominations generally acknowledged Manning's orthodoxy but questioned the wisdom of his actions. Black Episcopalians rejoiced over All Souls', but saw it as mainly a local victory, because segregation and racism were too entrenched in the church and society to be much affected by the forced desegregation of one Manhattan parish. Presumably Manning and those sympathetic to his stand hoped that the example of All Souls' would help dissuade more West Indian Anglicans from joining George A. McGuire's African Orthodox Church.[24]

Yet Manning was not quite the unyielding, mace-wielding crusader for racial justice that legend has made him. He was at least as calculating as he was bold. He had several advantages that Bishop Stires of Long Island did not enjoy in 1929. The KKK, for example, might be a force on Long Island, but they were certainly not a factor in Harlem. Likewise, Manning capitalized on the fractured vestry of All Soul's, the presence of an overwhelming black majority in the church, public opinion, and the stubbornness of Dodd to win the issue. In fact it was Dodd—and perhaps Demby—who were most responsible for Manning's stand. Note that Manning never took issue with Roure's public statement regarding the opening of St. Monica's, and neither did Dodd, for that matter. Apparently Manning agreed to open St. Monica's in the hope it that would placate the vestry of All Souls', but he had not reckoned on the vestry's brutal attempt to capitalize on his concession or Dodd's equally bold defiance of 10 July. When he returned from his sabbatical, the fat was in the proverbial fire. Furthermore, events in Arkansas may have have helped to stiffen Manning's resolve. While he was on vacation, Bishop Demby, another old Gailorite, had openly challenged the racist conduct of the Arkansas episcopal election of 1932.

The third incident of the segregation trilogy began at St. Paul's Church, Newport, Arkansas, in May 1932 and ran concurrently with the All Souls' crisis through the summer and fall of 1932. Far more complicated than All Souls' and Blackshear, Newport is best understood as the story of three conventions and the three leading candidates for bishop of Arkansas.

The Right Reverend Edwin Warren Saphore was the Ecclesiastical Authority, or acting bishop, of Arkansas in 1932. He was a seventy-one-year-old missionary, who, according to McDonald, "dreamed dreams, but was now past the age when he could see visions."[25] A quiet and passive man in most circumstances, his greatest strength lay in his will to persevere. Above all, he wanted to be bishop of Arkansas before he retired, a resolve that only seemed to grow with age. He felt that he deserved the higher office as a reward for his long and faithful service to the diocese, which had literally been in his debt for many years. He was accustomed to being paid in arrears.[26]

Saphore was a contemporary of Winchester in age and of Demby in length of ministry in the Episcopal Church. He had been priest to several parishes in the Diocese of Central New York (1898–1908), and an instructor at St. Andrew's Divinity School, Syracuse, New York (1900–1903). In 1909, Bishop William M. Brown appointed him archdeacon for "white work," an office he maintained for the next eight years. From 1911 to 1914, Saphore doubled as archdeacon for "colored work," an experience that seems to have imbued him with a genuine sympathy for black ministries. His other specialties under Winchester's administration were the supervision of white missionary work among the isolated missions of the diocese and the ministry to college students at the University of Arkansas at Fayetteville. In 1932, he was particularly active with the Winchester School for Mountain Boys affiliated with St. Barnabas's Mission at Havana, Arkansas. Located deep in the Ouachita Mountains west of Little Rock, the school was the counterpart of the Helen Dunlap School for Mountain Girls located near Fayetteville in northwest Arkansas. Both schools provided a parochial education to children who otherwise lived the sort of poverty and isolation generally associated with "hillbillies" of the Ozark Plateau and the Appalachians.[27]

The head of the Winchester School was the Reverend Gustave Orth, locally revered as "the Apostle of the Mountain."[28] It appears that Orth was an unpolished "preacher," in the popular sense of the word, but with an unusual inclination toward social work and ritualized worship. One detractor would later complain of his "outbursts" at diocesan functions.[29] Orth was also a permanent deacon; that is, he was ordained to the lesser order with the understanding that he would not advance to the priesthood. Ordained by Winchester, he had served the Helen Dunlap School before being transferred to Havana. In all diocesan matters, Orth's loyalties lay with Saphore, who had been his chief intermediary with the diocese for twenty years. Saphore, whose wife did not accompany him to Arkansas, lived at the Winchester School when he was not billeted at the Little Rock YMCA. Havana was his refuge and Orth his friend. When the school burned in 1932, Saphore's papers burned with it.[30]

More important to Saphore's episcopal ambitions was the Reverend Charles

F. Collins of St. Luke's, Hot Springs. Collins was central in all attempts to elect Saphore to Winchester's vacant post, while Orth, politically speaking, was extremely loyal but more of a peripheral figure. Having graduated from Bishop Brown's Arkansas Theological Chautauqua School, Collins entered the Arkansas ministry two years after Saphore's transfer to Arkansas. His early appointments were missions under Saphore's supervision. The two men developed a fast friendship, which bore fruit for Saphore in the stormy 1930s.

Saphore had many opponents who felt that his lack of administrative ability, in particular his lack of vision and will, combined with his advanced years, precluded his election. Nevertheless, he faithfully executed many duties rightly belonging to Winchester, who was chronically ill during the last years of his episcopate. From 1930 onward, Saphore shouldered a workload comparable to that of a bishop coadjutor about to succeed his diocesan. According to McDonald, the salary shifting from Winchester to Saphore made possible by Winchester's retirement "made the figures meet the facts."[31]

Unfortunately, Winchester's retirement only aggravated the money situation as it bore upon the election of his successor. Encumbered by the general economic decline associated with the Great Depression, Arkansas, which had never successfully paid the salaries of its two white bishops, now assumed the responsibility for Saphore's salary, Winchester's honorarium, and the salary of Winchester's successor. The obvious solution was to elect Saphore and shorten the payroll, but this, in the opinion of many Arkansans, would mean a continuation of the lackadaisical course the diocese had been following since the decline of Winchester's health. This, they said, was no solution at a time when the diocese needed a firm hand. Thus, Saphore's salary became an impediment to a satisfactory election.[32]

The 1931 Arkansas convention, assembled at Trinity Cathedral, arrived at a gentleman's agreement in order to cope with the money problem. A majority believed that it was imperative to proceed with the election of a new bishop, but that the election should be restricted, unofficially, to priests already resident in Arkansas, because Arkansas's clergy, having been appraised of the financial situation, would be more sympathetic. An "in-house" election, reasoned its advocates, would enable the diocese to pay a substandard salary to the bishop-elect while an "outside" candidate would probably find the salary too small, reject the call, and perhaps embarrass the diocese. Thus the convention, reflecting a particularly strong impetus among the laymen, resolved to elect an Arkansas priest as its new bishop at a special convention slated for 14 October.[33]

The 1931 Arkansas convention was especially significant for Demby and the

Colored Convocation. First and foremost, Winchester's retirement crippled advocacy for the convocation within the diocese. Therefore, it behooved Demby and his colleagues to vote for a new advocate from among those Arkansas priests most likely to be elected. The finger naturally pointed at Witsell, a proven friend serving his last year on the National Council. As Demby had already discovered in 1922, Witsell had clout with the New York office when it came to missionary work. Secondly, the black priests of Arkansas, heretofore a quiet novelty at each convention, were suddenly center stage—for two reasons. First, Saphore delegated to Demby the honor of reading the Gospel at the opening service of the convention, a promotion from Demby's very occasional reading of the epistle. As gospeler, Demby was second only to the celebrant (Saphore) in the order of service. Second, the black clergy, who now numbered five, including Demby, constituted a political presence for the first time. By the terms of Article 2 of the Constitution of the Colored Convocation the black clergy were disenfranchised from all actions of the Arkansas convention save for the election of bishops. In 1931, they constituted a quarter of the clerical vote in the upcoming special convention. When one considers that episcopal elections in Arkansas were established by a simple majority in each of the two orders, clerical and lay, a black caucus could expedite or even deny an election. Therefore a a pro-Witsell black caucus was a near certainty. The Reverends James H. King of Christ Church in Forrest City, Robert J. Johnson of St. Mary's in Hot Springs, and George G. Walker of St. Philip's in Little Rock were loyal to Demby and well-informed in this regard. The newest member of the convocation was the Reverend Shirley G. Sanchez of St. Augustine's, Fort Smith. Sanchez had transferred from Alabama to St. Augustine's in 1931. A Jamaican by birth, he had attended St. Paul's Normal and Industrial School, Lawrenceville, Virginia, before graduating from Bishop Payne Divinity School in 1926. Sanchez was a generation removed from King, Walker, and Johnson by age and vocation. That fact, coupled with his late arrival, made him more of a peripheral figure to the convocation. Nevertheless, he was inclined to join them in support of Witsell.

But Witsell was not certain that he wanted to be a candidate. The 1931 Arkansas convention was the scene of open hostility directed toward the priest and delegates of Christ Church. Based on documentation pertaining to the 1932 controversy, we can safely assume that members and allies of Trinity Cathedral were in the vanguard of the assault. They were unified in their belief that Christ Church and Witsell exercised an inappropriate amount of influence in the diocese and expressed their discontent in two ways. Officially, they routed Christ Church and pro–Christ Church delegates from the Executive Council, the body charged with carrying out the will of the convention. Unofficially, they snubbed and were unabashedly rude to Witsell.[34] After the convention, Winchester observed, "Witsell, the devil seems to have gotten into that convention. I do not know how he got there, but he certainly seems to have been there." The Very Reverend John Williamson, dean of Trinity Cathedral, confided to Witsell, "I think you and Christ Church got a dirty deal." Witsell sent a letter to Winchester shortly thereafter to air grievances and announce that, inasmuch as Christ Church was resented for its influence, it no longer assumed any responsibility for the activities of the diocese.[35]

While some convention antipathy is attributable to the ongoing rivalry between Little Rock's two parishes, it would appear that most of it was aimed at the rector of Christ Church personally. Witsell, in his zeal to correct wrongs and otherwise help direct the diocese during the previous five years, had created enemies. His weakness and his strength were the same. If he saw an item that needed correcting, his usual response was to throw himself wholeheartedly at the problem until he succeeded in rectifying it, personalities notwithstanding. Witsell's advocates considered him visionary, industrious, organized, intelligent, and ethical—sometimes to the point of charging windmills.[36] His detractors believed he was an Episcopal Machiavelli—heavy-handed, conceited, ambitious, and manipulative. His demeanor contributed to that image. He could be insufferably brusque to those whose judgment he did not respect, a fact to which he was somewhat blind; blind to its ramifications, if not to its existence. Yet a good many Arkansans were not offended by his manner and deemed his very businesslike approach just the remedy for the disorganized, financially embarrassed, and somewhat insubordinate condition of the diocese. Contrary to the allegations of his detractors, Witsell was not, in fact, a law unto himself. He sought council with regularity from those clergy whose judgment he respected. In summary, he was a love-or-hate candidate in the Diocese of Arkansas and may well have been its best candidate for bishop.[37]

Witsell's foremost adversary in diocesan affairs was Thomas E. Wood, a Little Rock attorney and chapter (vestry) member of Trinity Cathedral. As of 1932, Wood had served as secretary of the Arkansas convention for seventeen years, spent six years as chairman of the Executive Council, and had considerable experience editing the *Arkansas Churchman,* the official organ of the diocese. He had a reputation for being overbearing and insubordinate, a layman with an inordinate amount of influence in Saphore's administration. He was solidly behind the cathedral and the bishop versus Christ Church and Witsell. Wood was a vitriolic speaker and writer when angered and pursued his course with the firm conviction that it rested on higher motives. He was typical of

Witsell's opponents, who preferred to work against him without direct confrontation. Witsell's enemies feared him as much as they disliked him.[38]

In May 1931, a contingent of well-wishers led by another Little Rock jurist, Deadrick H. Cantrell, pressed Witsell to be their candidate for bishop. Cantrell was "old Christ Church" and chancellor of the Diocese of Arkansas, not to mention a vociferous ally of his priest. Witsell declined Cantrell's initiative in light of the bad blood, old and new, between Christ Church and Trinity Cathedral. He did not want to suffer the same "travesty" as the Reverend John Gass, who endured the "slings and arrows of outrageous misrepresentation" in the 1897 election. However, subsequent conferences with the Right Reverend James DeWolf Perry, presiding bishop of the Episcopal Church, and the Right Reverend W. T. Capers, bishop of West Texas, persuaded Witsell that he should at least allow his supporters to nominate him. The Witsellites, to coin a phrase, were delighted and Cantrell became Witsell's ex officio campaign manager among the laity.[39]

The Reverend Samuel H. Rainey, previously mentioned in connection with the 1927 episode at St. Mary's, El Dorado, was Witsell's champion among the Arkansas clergy. Rainey, who had relocated to St. Paul's, Fayetteville, reveled in the executive ability of the man he always addressed as "Dr. Witsell." Their friendship was helped along by the fact that Rainey also had a reputation for being "his own man." He was not averse to conflict if he felt that he was in the right, as is evident from his calling to St. Paul's in 1928. According to his daughter, Carolyn Rainey Harris, St. Paul's invited him to be their priest with the understanding that he would be given great latitude in governing the church. However, the vestry reneged on the understanding before the Raineys had even moved into the rectory. So, with the car still packed and a wedding to conduct back in El Dorado, Rainey and family took off. Rainey made it clear that St. Paul's could either adhere to the original agreement or the wedding would become a permanent change of address. St. Paul's complied and Rainey returned.[40]

Coincidentally, Rainey was, like Witsell, at odds with Tom Wood. The Executive Council, feeling the pinch of the Great Depression, had discontinued publication of the *Arkansas Churchman* in 1930 in order to save money. At the time, Wood, who edited the *Churchman*, was absent from the council and Rainey was acting chairman in his stead. Wood returned to find his cherished paper gone. He felt that Rainey had taken advantage of his absence to suspend publication and had unjustly blamed him for the *Churchman*'s financial problems.[41]

Other than Rainey, the most stalwart of the white pro-Witsell priests was Rainey's neighbor to the south, the Reverend W. S. Simpson-Atmore. Atmore, as he was usually called, was the English warden of the Helen Dunlap School at Winslow. He concurred in Rainey's judgment of Witsell and delighted in Witsell's national prominence, because of the additional leverage that it might give Arkansas's missions in dealing with the National Council. He also concurred with Witsell and Rainey regarding black equality in the Arkansas convention. Having served the Diocese of Springfield in 1903, Atmore was working alongside Demby for perhaps the second time in his career.

Atmore had his own problems with diocesan authorities. The Helen Dunlap School had received two sterling evaluations by the national church since the 1931 convention and he was understandably proud of his school and liked to boast of it at every opportunity. William G. Thayer, special representative of the National Council, wrote Atmore: "You are the stuff of which heroes are made and deserve much stronger support than you have received."[42] But the boasting, they soon discovered, was a preliminary to demands for more money. Specifically, the diocese had lapsed on its payments to the church pension fund on Atmore's behalf, a problem endemic to Arkansas during the Great Depression. Atmore, however, was nearing retirement and was not content to suffer quietly with his colleagues. He wanted his payments made current and felt that was the least the diocese could do in light of the success of his school—success, he might add, against great financial handicaps. To put it succinctly, Atmore's righteous indignation made him unpopular in Little Rock in spite of his achievements.[43]

Witsell anticipated the worst of Episcopal politics in 1931 and tried to avoid even the appearance of campaigning, or in any way drawing attention to himself. He eschewed speaking engagements at other Arkansas churches and otherwise let his friends do the talking. He resigned his post with the National Council—a move he had been contemplating for some time. Yet he did not go far enough. It looks as though his advocates among the bishops may have inadvertently damaged his cause by their enthusiastic assistance. Bishop Capers, or "Oddie," as Witsell called him, was a staunch ally of his former priest. He wrote a letter of recommendation on behalf of Witsell, as did Bishop Thomas F. Gailor of Tennessee and Bishop Perry, for presentation at the special convention. Then Capers went a step further, canvassing for Witsell among individual Arkansas clergymen. He lionized Witsell in letter to Reverend E. W. Mellichampe of St. John's, Helena, an old family acquaintance. Simultaneously, he asked Gailor to write Reverend William T. Holt of St. Paul's, Newport, as well as Mellichampe, on Witsell's behalf. Gailor knew both men by way of their service in Tennessee. Capers also asked Bishop Theodore D. Bratton to write the Reverend Elnathan Tartt, rector of St. Paul's, Batesville, and a former priest of Mississippi. Events would prove that Capers's door to door lobbying probably backfired. Witsell and Capers assumed that these three priests, all recent arrivals to Arkansas, were nonaligned politically and therefore might be receptive. But that view naively omits the political climate of Arkansas in general and Trinity Cathedral in particular. From the outset, Witsell was on trial for "purple fever," as it is sometimes called. His opponents anticipated intrigue, manipulation, and unbridled ambition on his part. As a result, the bishops' letters may have been viewed by their recipients as corroborative evidence. Eventually, Tartt, Holt, Mellichampe, and Reverend Charles D. Lathrop, of St. John's, Fort Smith, would unite to defeat Witsell and elect Dean Williamson of Trinity Cathedral.[44]

Tartt, Mellichampe, Lathrop, and Holt represented a new and influential clerical faction in Arkansas. Winchester's waning leadership during his final years resulted in greater authority at the parish and committee level, an excellent opportunity for new priests to achieve quick prominence. Therefore, despite their short tenure in Arkansas, these four quickly established themselves among the governing bodies of the diocese. Their names appear on the Executive Council, the Standing Committee, the Board of Examining Chaplains, the Committee on Constitution and Canons, and as delegates to the biennial Provincial Synods and the General Convention of 1931. Holt and Mellichampe were more outspoken than the other two. Holt was a tall, white-haired man whose best known work outside of his pastorate were his labors on behalf of children with physical handicaps. His mercurial temperament made him the clerical counterpart of Tom Wood. His sympathy with the cathedral, coupled with an adversarial relationship to Witsell, emerged sometime prior to the 1932 convention. Mellichampe is remembered for his missionary work to isolated communities on the Mississippi River. He was considered a leader among clergy. He was, like Witsell, a native of South Carolina, but differed radically on racial matters. In fact, he despised Witsell's open fraternization with Demby and some other black clergy, which he witnessed at an unspecified convention. He concealed his indignation from Witsell. It seems that Lathrop may have opposed Witsell's election primarily for aesthetic reasons. Lathrop's judgment of candidates for bishop fluctuated between the superficial and the intuitive. A candidate, he believed, must first look and sound like a bishop. That being established, one must look to one's gut feelings from personal encounters with the individuals. This is not to say that Lathrop disregarded a candidate's record or education, but he would not seriously consider them until the candidate had passed on appearance and intuition. Therefore, he considered Witsell, who was somewhat hampered in public speaking by a bulky hearing aid, less desirable that Dean Williamson of Trinity Cathedral, who, by all accounts, looked and sounded the part. Tartt would appear to differ from the other three in that he was more purely pro-Williamson than they were. There is no record of his having openly criticized Witsell; nor were there any allegations that he did so. Likewise, Tartt exercised less political influence upon his congregation than Holt, Lathrop, and Mellichampe exercised upon theirs.[45]

A fifth priest Williamson could count on in a runoff with Witsell was the Reverend Cornelius C. Burke of St. Andrew's, Marianna. Like Williamson, Burke, who sported the traditional round hat of the English clergy, hailed from the "mother country." Like Charles Collins of St. Luke's, Hot Springs, Burke's ministry dated back to Bishop Brown and the Arkansas Theological Chautauqua School. Williamson had additional linkage with Burke via Tom Wood, whose family had moved from St. Andrew's, Marianna, to Trinity Cathedral, Little Rock.

Perhaps the earliest omen of the upcoming election was the hearing aid episode of August. Some propaganda was spread about to the effect that Witsell was going deaf. This report, construed from an unguarded comment by Witsell's doctor, was disseminated by Witsell's opponents. Witsell located the origin of the rumor and Cantrell fired off a letter of inquiry. The doctor apologized for having discussed the matter with a third party, explained that he had been misquoted, and wrote a letter to Cantrell, a formal rebuttal to the "deaf" rumors. Cantrell came to the October Special Convention armed with the rebuttal and the prognosis of two other physicians.[46]

The 1931 Special Convention, the second Arkansas convention held at Trinity Cathedral in six months, did not elect a bishop. Rather, it brought about a coalescing of three distinct factions behind three front runners. Saphore was nominated by Collins and seconded by Lathrop. He enjoyed the loyal support of those churches which he had helped to organize. Williamson was nominated and seconded by the lay representatives of Trinity Cathedral. Rainey nominated Witsell, seconded by Cantrell. Witsell's strength among the white delegates included representatives from Rainey's present and former churches, namely, St. Mary's in El Dorado and St. Paul's in Fayetteville. St. Mark's in Hope was also decidedly pro-Witsell.

Proceeding to the election, it appeared for a time that it was to be a race between Saphore and Witsell. Holt and Mellichampe disdained the partisanship of Arkansas ecclesiastical circles and nominated a colleague from their Tennessee days and a future bishop of Pennsylvania, the Reverend Oliver J. Hart of Chattanooga. Their out-of-state initiative, however, made hardly a ripple in the three-fish pond. The seventh ballot established Williamson as a solid third contender. He had the largest number of lay votes and Witsell had the largest number of clerical votes, being the favorite of eight out of twenty-one priests present. Saphore enjoyed a significant following in each order. The convention adjourned and reconvened later that evening. The lay delegates moved that the ballot be restricted to the three front-runners, but the clergy balked and the election was postponed until the 1932 regular convention. Holt invited the delegates to decide the issue at St. Paul's, Newport, in May 1932. Witsell, for one, was glad to remove the contest from Trinity Cathedral.

The proceedings of the Special Convention brought both good and bad tidings for the black clergy. Once again, Saphore appointed Demby gospeler at the opening service. Saphore, unlike Winchester, was a dogmatic traditionalist when it came to the worship of the convention. He believed that bishops, be they black or white, belong in the chancel and should lead in the service. Thus, Demby, who had never served in the chancel consecutively, was a novelty on the verge of becoming a tradition. On the surface of it, Saphore's boldness seems out of character. Yet, in light of his determination that clerics like himself be recognized for long, faithful, and unheralded service—and his aforementioned sympathy for black ministries—perhaps it is not so surprising. Aware that some Episcopalians viewed him and Demby as something less than genuine bishops, Saphore's "promotion" of Demby probably represented his own vindication as well. Saphore also shared Demby's awkwardness, being another assistant-bishop-in-limbo, waiting to see what the new administration would bring. However, on a more mercenary note, Saphore may have been looking for black votes, which, taken in light of his behavior over the whole of the 1931–35 interregnum, is a plausible interpretation. And he may have succeeded. Indeed, some white lay delegates actually believed the black clergy were in Saphore's party.[47] However, others, being more astute in their observations, surmised that the black caucus was an integral part of Witsell's clerical superiority. Hereafter, the race to be bishop of Arkansas took on definite racial overtones. One parishioner of St. Paul's, Newport, would write Demby in 1932: "Your faction tied up two conventions—was that not enough?"[48]

The months between the October 1931 Special Convention and the May 1932 Annual Convention were spent in political consolidation among those in favor of Witsell's election and those opposed. Given the "in-state" nature of the election, there were only two candidates who could oppose Witsell with any hope of success: Williamson and Saphore. This put the anti-Witsell faction in a quandary, because to elect either man was to deny the pretext for the election, namely, strong leadership. Everyone, including Witsell, considered Williamson an endearing, gentle man.[49] He was an accomplished Rotarian and a truly gifted master of ceremonies. He had a paternal quality that attracted people and a fine speaking voice. On the other hand, he was, like Saphore, a passive and indecisive man, who habitually acquiesced to the will of his congregation. His organization and decision-making skills were the antithesis of Witsell's. One lifelong parishioner of Trinity declared, "If you could have merged the better qualities of the two men into one candidate, you would have had a bishop."[50]

The signal event of this "Phony War" period in Arkansas's Episcopal Church was an attempt by Bishop Saphore to secure his election to diocesan by way of a political exchange with Witsell.[51] In March 1932, Saphore confided to Rainey that he did not want to retire without first being elected bishop of Arkansas, and that he had a proposition for Witsell. If Witsell would help him get elected at Newport, he would retire after not more than two years in office and assist Witsell in succeeding him. Such a plan had actually been discussed by Bishop Capers and Witsell in January, but Witsell had discarded it as unethical. In the meantime, however, a rumor circulated by the opposition probably made its way to Saphore's ears. According to the grapevine, should Witsell be elected bishop of Arkansas at Newport, he would "cut the throat" of Bishop Saphore, that is, force him into retirement.[52] Thus, it seems likely that the fear of "Bishop" Witsell, combined with Saphore's own ambition, inspired Arkansas's white suffragan to try and "cut a deal." Saphore even confided to Rainey that if the Newport election should turn into a Williamson vs. Witsell runoff, he would throw his support behind Witsell, whom he regarded as Arkansas's best candidate for bishop. Williamson's election, he said, would be a "calamity." Rainey relayed the suggested compromise to Witsell, who declined in practice what he had already declined in theory. Nevertheless, Witsell and company held onto the runoff proviso. Already on the winning track after the October convention, they arrived at Newport justifiably optimistic and ripe for disappointment.[53]

Saphore had a change of heart after Witsell declined his offer. A few days before the convention, Witsell persuaded Williamson and Saphore to join him in excusing themselves from the assembly at the time of election. This, said Witsell, would eliminate any appearance of electioneering on the part of the major candidates and allow the delegates more freedom of action. Citing the intensely partisan climate, Witsell suggested that it was more important how the election transpired than who was elected. Saphore agreed to the plan, while Williamson "tied a string," said Witsell, to his agreement. However, as Saphore and Williamson rode the train to Newport on the morning of the convention, they decided against the united exit. When combined with the other events of 11 May, this gesture suggests that the two of them may have arrived at an agreement whereby the lesser candidate would come to the aid of the greater in the event of a runoff with Witsell.[54]

Bishop Demby, meanwhile, deliberated on a very different kind of "deal." In the first week of May 1932, he discovered that the black priests were not entirely welcome at Newport. On 1 May, Saphore issued a letter to Holt, enclosing his program for the convention. Saphore designated Demby to lead in the opening service for an unprecedented third time in a row. He also delegated authority to Holt to make "any additions you may wish to include."[55] The bishop said he would try to come early enough to go over the program with Holt before the convention. The vestry of St. Paul's, Newport, met at a local bank sometime shortly after Holt's receipt of the letter. Led by William A. Billingsley, president of the bank and senior warden of St. Paul's, they insisted that Holt make some changes in the program and conduct of the opening service. Most importantly, Bishop Demby's name was to be struck from the list of those assisting the celebrant. An African American distributing the elements of communion to white people, they said, was intolerable. Holt was more or less told to make the arrangements and notify Demby of the same. Therefore, Demby received a letter, dated 4 May 1932, composed by Billingsley and Holt but signed by Holt.[56] The first two paragraphs were devoted to a welcome and a tribute to mutual cooperation and respect between the races in language reminiscent of the *Living Church*'s evaluation of the Blackshear affair:

> We are making every effort that you and your clergy may be comfortable and happy. . . .
>
> Both of us are spiritually representative of our respective races and will of course cooperate in the desire to have a harmonious convention wherein there will be a greater realization of our opportunities.

Then, Holt uneasily got to the point: "There is no objection to the convocation sitting in the church and voting, I hear, but there might be some feeling about the two races taking Holy Communion together. I have a beautiful chapel, which I use frequently, in the church crypt [basement]; would it be agreeable for you to celebrate for your people there? I will be present with you and assist you in the celebration."[57]

Aside from the obvious unwillingness to celebrate the Eucharist with—and at the hands of—black people, it appears that the motivation for this action had, at its roots, the same southern taboo that had guided the actions of St.

Mary's, El Dorado, in 1927, namely, the prohibition against placing black men and white women in social proximity. Oral history holds that one particularly influential female parishioner of St. Paul's was adamant that there be no African Americans at the opening service. This accords with the actions of the vestry, which did not attempt to deny Demby's rights with regard to the convention. Conventions, proper, were all male. Usually, women could attend, but only as spectators or designated representatives of the Woman's Auxiliary, which convened separately. Worship services and luncheons, however, were another matter. Be that as it may, total exclusion was an extraordinary measure, even by the standards of the day. Southern Episcopalians generally resolved misgivings over black participation in the Eucharist by having the blacks receive the elements last—not excluding them altogether.[58]

It is difficult to exaggerate the dread, and, therefore, the anger, that could be engendered among whites by an ecclesiastical violation of racial decorum. For instance, when Bishop Henry B. Delany died in 1928, Bishop William A. Guerry of South Carolina tried to revive the campaign for a black suffragan in South Carolina. As a result, he was assassinated in his office by his perennial opponent on the issue, the Reverend Joseph H. Woodward.[59] Woodward, who committed suicide afterwards, saw a precedent in the election of black suffragans that could ultimately threaten the white women of the Episcopal Church. In his opinion, segregated black bishops could lead to nonsegregated black bishops who might take advantage of white women. White women, said Woodward, are possessed of a very receptive frame of mind toward the counsel of bishops and would be placed in an unnatural and subordinate role to black men. Thus, he deemed the black suffragan debate to be "at the bottom . . . a sex problem."[60] Moreover, as noted in connection with the El Dorado incident, many southern Episcopalians passionately adhered to the belief that segregation, ecclesiastical or otherwise, guaranteed the sanctity of southern womanhood in the face of the innate licentiousness of African American men.

The Newport vestry had, as justification for its actions, the precedent set at St. Mary's, El Dorado, and the unwritten law that segregation of worship services is not a matter of legalities or the inherent rights of Christians; rather it is a matter dictated by local custom. And, of course, the Blackshear incident may have served as a second precedent.

Holt's letter placed Demby between the proverbial rock and a hard place. The suggestion of a basement communion service for the blacks deserved a flat "No," but the fact that Holt would go so far as to put his suggestion in writing indicated that he was under considerable pressure. An abrupt reply from Demby would only increase racial tension at St. Paul's, with unpredictable results. In that event, the convocation's bias toward Witsell could be his—and their—undoing. Holt was known to be opposed to Witsell's election. Weighing his very limited options, Demby sent Holt this reply on 7 May:

> I am of the opinion that the things of which you write are questions of interpretation and pronouncement by the acting bishop (the Rt. Rev. Edwin Warren Saphore, D. D.) of the diocese, and yet while the matters in question are among the inherent rights and privileges of the children of God in the One Holy Catholic and Apostolic Church, you and I know the attitude of some people who call themselves Christians when Negro churchmen (be they bishops, priests, or laymen) are [to be considered] within the equation of the Christian reflection and affability, however, I will assure you nothing will be done, to make the Convention non-harmonious on our part.[61]

Taken in light of his later comments, it is clear that Demby intended this to be a very gentle denial of Holt's suggestion and a referral to Saphore for a resolution of the problem—in other words, a polite "no."

Holt, however, construed this tangled sentence to be Demby's intention to comply with his request and notified his vestry of the same. Demby's habitual, and perhaps compulsory, verbosity aided the white rector's self-deception. Quite possibly Holt concealed the letter from his vestrymen because of Demby's manifest anger regarding "the attitude of some people." He was, after all, a host trying to maintain order and prevent conflict. Be that as it may, the vestry approached the convention with the understanding that Demby had written Holt a letter "conceding" the "wisdom" of Holt's plan.[62]

As for Demby's suggestion that Holt consult Saphore, events suggest that Holt and his vestry had a strategy to secure the cooperation of both bishops, predicated on assumptions about the character of both men and a time element. John Dollard, in his contemporary *Caste and Class in a Southern Town,* demonstrates that southern blacks, when confronted with white "aggression" (Holt's letter), must either accommodate white people or, by refusal to do the same, risk the appearance of active protest, an impracticality which whites generally construed as black "aggression."[63] Demby, for this and other reasons previously cited, tried to accommodate Holt by promising not to disturb the convention and constructing a deliberately vague refusal. Nevertheless, he had a reputation for accommodation and forbearance in such matters, a trait which undoubtedly encouraged Holt and his vestrymen to believe they had struck an agreement with him. They saw in Demby's letter not only the cooperation they desired but the black acquiescence they were accustomed to as well. Resistance on Demby's part was inconceivable. As for Saphore, it was imperative that he be kept in the dark as long as possible. He enjoyed a good rapport with the black clergy and might try to resist their exclusion from the opening service. However, he could be pressured at the last minute if the plan were "dropped" on him in the same fashion that the El Dorado vestry had challenged Winchester in 1927. Even better, whereas Winchester had had days to respond, Saphore would have to act in hours or even minutes. And, to cap it all off, as soon as Holt informed Saphore of Demby's "compliance," they could be doubly sure of Saphore's acquiescence.

The false expectations of all parties crashed headlong into each other just prior to the opening service of the convention. The previous day, Demby had briefed the black clergy on the situation as they awaited their train at Union Station in Little Rock. Therefore, when they assembled outside St. Paul's Church on the morning of 11 May and discovered that Holt still intended to go through with the basement communion, they were not caught totally unawares. They suppressed their outrage while Holt showed them the basement chapel, a gesture that clearly implied Saphore's knowledge of the arrangement. One assumes that Demby must have inquired of Holt whether the rector had taken his advice and consulted Saphore, but there is no documentation of such a conversation. Holt could have responded in at least two ways without resorting to a bold-faced lie. He could have laid claim to delegated authority or he could have merely indicated that Saphore would be celebrating upstairs and let Demby draw his own conclusions. We do not know what transpired, but we do know, via Demby's memoirs, that he was told that Saphore would celebrate for the white people upstairs while he (Demby) celebrated for the blacks downstairs.[64] Gazing at the makeshift altar, the exposed pipes, the concrete floor, and the apprehensive looks of his subordinates, Demby recognized a scandalous "interpretation and pronouncement by the acting bishop."[65]

Holt's hopes were dashed when the blacks conferred among themselves and declined. Demby recalls: "It was decided—because of the condition of the place where we were told to celebrate the Body and Blood of Christ, and the uncatholic proceeding of the whole affair, and with justice to the race which we represent, it would not be wise for us to carry out the idea of the Rector and [we] did not."[66] Holt hoped for some alternate plan from Demby, but the bishop did not offer one and the matter was left unresolved.[67]

By this time the convention was assembling for the opening service. Proceeding directly to the church from the railroad station, Saphore arrived out of breath and totally ignorant of Holt's plan. He perused the order of worship and noticed that Demby's name had been struck. Having guessed that St. Paul's had asserted its customary right to segregate, he assumed his responsibility for the program of the convention, spotted the clique of black priests outside of St. Paul's, approached Demby, and "informed him," to use Saphore's words, that there had been a change of plan. Thus, he unknowingly and inadvertently reaffirmed what Demby already "knew"; the segregated communion, albeit the design of Holt, had the official sanction of the acting bishop, and, with him, the Diocese of Arkansas. A poised but angry Demby replied that he was aware of the change, being so informed by a "disagreeable" letter from Holt. Although they had barely broached the issue, their conversation was interrupted by the immediate need to form up the procession and begin the service. Saphore moved on, shaking hands and tending to last-minute details while acolytes, choir members, flagbearers, and ushers sorted themselves out. Inside the church the walls reverberated to the prelude as the organist invited a very full house to worship.[68]

Demby was thunderstruck by Saphore's undisguised "complicity" and could only wonder what awaited the black clergy inside the church. Once again, he weighed his options and tried to find an unoffensive yet not-so-demeaning way for the black clergy to participate in the opening service of the Sixtieth Annual Convention of the Diocese of Arkansas. Manifestly unwelcome at the upstairs service, they must, thought Demby, find a way to get through the next hour without further controversy. Above all, the white delegates must not feel threatened by their actions. Witsell's election was at stake and future of the Colored Convocation with it. So, what were the black clergy to do upon entering the church? Should they receive communion anyway? No. Saphore had made that clear already. What about marching in and taking their seats with the rest of the clergy? After all, they had to sit somewhere. That being the case, the black clergy needed to find some unobtrusive way to march in, be seated, and remain seated while the white clergy communed at the altar rail. It would be very difficult for four priests and especially one bishop, resplendent in episcopal robes, mace, and miter, to be unobtrusive anywhere, let alone up front among the clergy, but not nearly so awkward as celebrating the communion in the basement of the church. This, we may infer, was Demby's strategy. It also follows that he communicated it to Walker, King, Sanchez, and Johnson, necessitating what must have been a hasty, hushed, and very deliberate conference in St. Paul's courtyard to the south side of the main entrance. Breaking the huddle, so to speak, they joined the procession. The prelude concluded, the bell began to ring, and the black priests braced themselves for the unexpected. It came.

The organist struck up the opening hymn and the procession moved ponderously into the church. Simultaneously, the parties who insisted on the sep-

arate communion for the blacks realized that their plan had gone awry and
they were in imminent danger of an integrated communion service. According to oral tradition, just as Demby entered the church, he was told, on the
initiative of the aforementioned matriarch of St. Paul's, that the blacks were
expected to sit at the back of the church. Demby complied, signaling for his
four colleagues to follow him. Consequently, the tail of the procession stalled
as the body moved on, leaving a gap between the last white priest and Saphore,
who brought up the rear in what we may call suppressed dismay.[69]

The climax of the service was, of course, the Eucharist, as described in the
introduction to this book. As the line of communicants played out, the black
clergy continued to sit. Holt had made the assumption that they would commune as Demby thought best. He looked up with alarm when they did not
come forward, took Saphore aside, and suggested that the white suffragan
beckon them to come to the rail. Saphore did so.[70]

It would seem, as many whites would argue later on, that the black clergy
now had their opportunity to join in the Eucharist but failed to take advantage of it. However, that is to ignore the ecclesiastical miscarriage leading up
to the service. In order to understand what happened next, one must, in the
words of Harper Lee, "put on" Demby's "skin." Demby understood that the
two white clergymen were naively adding insult to injury. Having failed to
exclude the black clergy from the service altogether, Saphore and Holt now
condescended to invite them to the Eucharist, as if to say, "It's all right. We've
had a change of heart. You may come up after all." So, for a few awkward
moments Saphore held the paten aloft and Demby counseled his subordinates
to stay put. With that, the white suffragan closed the service, and, he hoped,
the issue. Afterwards, Holt took Demby aside to express his regrets that the
bishop "did not commune," not, as some understood it, to apologize. Demby, who was not prepared to enter into a discussion on catholicity, said that
everything was "satisfactory."[71]

The worshipers left the church and the delegates conducted the preliminary
business of the convention. All unpaid assessments for the support of the diocese owed by various churches were remitted due to the economic depression, thereby allowing all of the delegates present to vote. This was Witsell's
first defeat of the day. He and the Christ Church delegates were adamant that
voting rights should be tied to assessments having been paid in full, depression or no. For them, it was another chapter in the perpetual discord over
Christ Church's disproportionate share of the diocesan budget. It also shows,
by the way, that Christ Church's intention to shun the diocese had not mate-

rialized. The better strategy, they had decided, was to persevere with the diocese and, hopefully, elect Witsell.[72]

At one o'clock, the delegates adjourned to a luncheon at the First Christian Church across the street. The luncheon was the scene of a poignant episode that simultaneously advanced the cause of catholicity and probably did the convocation untold harm in the election to follow. As the ladies of First Christian Church went about their catering, the black clergy took their accustomed place at the Jim Crow table. However, some white delegates became hostile toward them. We may guess that it was an expression of racism compounded by electoral tension and the fact that the blacks had disrupted the opening service with what some white delegates must have regarded as a "sullen" and incomprehensible protest.[73] The black clergy were noticeably ill at ease until a white woman, Mrs. Mildred Dorsey, intervened on their behalf. Dorsey, an eighty-one-year-old pillar of St. Paul's, crossed the room, introduced herself, and asked if she might join them. As Demby and company rose with amazement to greet their unexpected guest, the effect on the whole gathering was immediate and salutary. Everyone was put at ease, or in their place, as the case may be, for the remainder of the luncheon.[74]

In her boldness Mrs. Dorsey took advantage of several exemptive peculiarities in the code of racial relations, as well as her own reputation. The daughter of James E. Wilmans, a prosperous landowner and steamboat entrepreneur of antebellum Jackson County, she was a locally renowned woman of letters, a doctor's widow with a reputation for good works and sound character, and the matriarch of one of Newport's older, wealthier, and more educated families. Her nephew, James E. Wilmans, was a prosperous landowner and operator of one of the larger cotton gins in the area. He was also a vestryman of St. Paul's. Thus, though a young white woman, or a white man, or a person of questionable reputation, or a recent arrival could expect censure, ostracism, or even exile for such an act, Mrs. Dorsey was safe. Cotton, or delta, towns were indulgent of women like her, preferring to say, if indeed anything need be said, that they are "eccentric" in their behavior toward blacks.[75] Her paternalism, however, was several degrees removed from that of her peers in that she apparently possessed a more genuinely egalitarian spirit in race matters. Standing on the platform of the Newport railroad station, she lamented that a "man as educated as Bishop Demby should be confined to the Jim Crow car. He should be allowed to ride in the Pullman."[76]

The convention reconvened at 2:30 in the afternoon. Saphore made his opening address, followed by Demby, who delivered his annual report. Demby's report was typical of him, being an apologetic for the rate of black church growth, followed by a record of black Episcopal progress in Arkansas: "Notwithstanding the continued and depressed economic, commercial, and vocational condition, the Negroes, who are suffering more than any other American race group are evidencing faith, fortitude, the spirit of Christian democracy, racial fellowship, etc." In all and through all was Demby's omnipresent sermon on the "catholicity and apostolicity" of the Episcopal Church. The appendant "official acts" section gave evidence of the same, namely, that he experienced less restrictive fellowship in the church at large. Demby laid particular emphasis on a Special Meeting of the House of Bishops, which he attended as the guest of Bishop Stires of Long Island, and a funeral of a black priest in which he and Bishop Thomas Casady of Oklahoma officiated jointly, accompanied by several priests of both races.[77]

After fixing the salary of the bishop-elect, the convention began the election process. Colonel Carroll Armistead, a parishioner of Rainey's, nominated Witsell, seconded by John Barlow of St. Mark's, Hope. Holt nominated Williamson, seconded by Wood. Collins nominated Saphore, seconded by Judge E. P. Toney of Emmanuel, Lake Village, one of Saphore's former charges. The Reverend H. A. Stowell of Trinity, Pine Bluff, rounded out the in-state candidates. The only out-of-state candidate was Oliver Hart, nominated once again by Mellichampe.

Witsell secured the clerical vote on the fifth ballot by capturing ten out of nineteen clerical votes cast. That being established, the convention set aside the clerical vote and proceeded on a "laity only" ballot. Unable to secure a lay majority on the sixth ballot, the Witsellites moved to adjourn for supper and reconvene later that evening.

The recess, on motion of Judge Talbot Field of St. Mark's, Hope, was, to quote Witsell, a "tactical blunder."[78] Field wanted to use the time to canvass for Witsell, who was still nine votes shy of a lay majority. It was the opposition, however, who capitalized on the recess. Tartt, Wood, Lathrop, Holt, and Mellichampe used the interval to do some passionate lobbying on behalf of Williamson and against Witsell. Following up several preconvention themes, Holt and Mellichampe did considerable damage to Witsell's cause among the laity. They accused Witsell's supporters of dirty politics, claimed that Witsell, if elected, intended to remove Saphore, and resurrected the issue of Witsell's supposedly poor health. But Mellichampe's activities, if those of no one else, had a direct bearing on the fortunes of the Colored Convocation. He propagated fears among the laity that Witsell, if elected, would "raise the Negroes to equality with the whites" in the Arkansas convention and force integrated seating arrangements upon the delegates. Naturally, the unpleasant luncheon just concluded at First Christian Church played into his hand, as did Witsell's black advocacy at the 1928 Arkansas convention. Mellichampe duly noted that Witsell was riding to power on the strength of five black clerical votes. Lay members of the Witsell party would later report that their candidate had been stigmatized as a "nigger lover."[79]

By the time the convention reassembled at eight o'clock, Witsell's momentum was gone and so was his "ace in the hole." To the dismay of Rainey, Witsell, and Cantrell, Williamson consolidated a lay majority on the eighth ballot by virtue of a mass defection from Saphore's camp.

Deadlocked between a lay majority candidate and a clergy majority candidate, the election began anew. This time, the delegates nominated four additional candidates, Mellichampe among them. Interestingly enough, Mellichampe did not decline the nomination in the interests of Williamson's election, as one might suppose. Similarly, Holt seconded the nomination of an out-of-state candidate nominated by Stowell. One of Williamson's parishioners nominated an out-of-state candidate, seconded by Barlow from the Witsell camp. Field acted in kind, nominating yet another out-of-state candidate. It seems that both sides had a lucid moment in which they recognized the folly of the "in-house" rule. Having seized the momentum from Witsell, his opponents hesitated to follow through; electing Williamson was secondary to defeating Witsell.

It was then that the Witsellites inspired Williamson's victory by trying to avoid it. Following the new nominations, a group of laymen fired a blunderbuss of motions in order to postpone the election until another convention or recess until the next day. Nominators of Mellichampe and Saphore contributed to the cause, but most conspicuous among the "postponers" was Grover T. Owens, a parishioner of Witsell's. Owens presented a motion that would have created "a committee to investigate the qualifications of available men and report to the next convention."[80]

Always on the lookout for Witsell's machinations, Holt took the floor and implored the delegates to finish the election. There was, he said, "a conspiracy to elect Dr. Witsell or adjourn the convention" and "that the convention was being conducted on lines unworthy of men of God."[81] He claimed to have proof of the same and lambasted Witsell's proponents for political misconduct, impugning Witsell by implication. Incensed at Holt's allegations, Armistead and Field took the floor in defense of their candidate. Armistead, an aged United States Army veteran of quick temper, issued a "dignified but unmistakable denial,"[82] while Field, who shared Holt's determination not to adjourn without an election, did likewise.[83] According to Witsell, the wives of the delegates also contributed to the fracas by manipulating events from the "galleries."[84] The convention, to quote Cantrell, took on the aspect of a "ward meeting," the shouting going on unabated while Saphore and Williamson looked on stoically.[85] Once order was restored, Holt won his case with the convention and Owen's motion for postponement failed, 40-24. This would be a fight to the finish.

The election resumed with both orders voting again. Witsell's clerical majority wavered on the ninth ballot, declining from ten to seven. The seven, presumably, were Demby, King, Johnson, Walker, Sanchez, Simpson-Atmore, and Rainey. Mellichampe won eight lay votes on the same ballot, a revealing development in light of its timing and his racist propaganda. The anti-black impetus, like the in-house election impetus, was basically a lay movement. Williamson won the clergy on the tenth ballot and the laity overwhelmingly on the eleventh, making him the winner. Armistead made a successful motion for a unanimous election.

Leaving St. Paul's on the night of 11 May, Demby spoke with Holt, who was still concerned over the opening service. According to Holt, Demby expressed "complete satisfaction with the entire convention,"[86] which a relieved Holt took to be the end of a regrettable and altogether avoidable episode. For Demby, however, this was but one more exercise in survival. He regarded Holt as a mere agent of Saphore, the person truly responsible for the communion episode, and, by the precedent it established, the racial overtone of the entire convention. For him, the quarrel was between the black suffragan and the white suffragan. Besides, Mrs. Demby had had an accident of some kind and he needed to go to her.[87]

Demby congratulated Williamson and Demby, Walker, and King signed slips of paper, thereby affixing their signatures to Williamson's "Testimonial of Election," a document certifying their belief in the qualifications of the bishop-elect. Sanchez and Johnson did not sign the testimonial by reason of an early departure on behalf of Mrs. Demby. However, subsequent events would indicate that they were probably acting in protest of the election and Mrs. Demby's problem gave them an opportunity to excuse themselves without making a statement or gesture to that effect.[88]

Witsell did not congratulate the bishop-elect or sign the testimonial. He was appalled at the conduct of the election and believed Williamson incompetent for the higher office. Thinking that perhaps Witsell forgot to sign the testimonial, Wood visited him shortly after the convention in hopes of procuring his signature. Despite his adversarial relationship to Witsell, he knew it would be unwise to submit Williamson's election to the national church without the endorsement of Arkansas's best known and most highly esteemed priest. So, testimonial in hand, Wood arrived at Christ Church. Witsell lost no time in clarifying his position. This, he said, was no oversight. He would add, "No one could see the slightest trace of the Holy Spirit in the convention, and the result had been obtained without any assistance from Him, and there was a good deal of evidence, both before and during the convention . . . of another sort of spirit." Witsell sent his nemesis away empty-handed.[89]

Rainey subsequently withdrew his signature from the testimonial, explaining that he had signed it in a spirit of unanimity, not fully understanding that his signature constituted a personal endorsement of Williamson's qualifications. Embittered by Rainey's and Witsell's actions, Wood wrote Stowell, who replied that he agreed with them as regarding Williamson but thought that it would have been better for Rainey not to withdraw his name. Showing the wisdom of his years, Stowell added that he had not voted for any of Arkansas's leading candidates for bishop. Thus, Rainey and especially Witsell further damaged the credibility of a document signed only by a bare majority of the delegates present. Williamson's "Testimonial of Election" became an oxymoron: an endorsement of his qualifications and a liability to his election.[90]

Meanwhile, Holt tried to patch things up. He wrote Witsell a letter, explaining that his actions in the convention were "actuated by my sincere belief that I was doing my duty." He then tried to console the defeated candidate, a particularly ill-timed and misguided gesture.[91] Witsell wrote a three-page rebuttal, saying, among other things:

> While writing to you I wish to also to say that the one thing that deeply distressed me was your telling so Godly a man as Bishop Demby that he could not come to your altar to receive the Holy Communion. . . . It seems to me an outrage against the catholicity . . . of the church. How any man can think that the Holy Spirit is with him in such an attitude is wholly impossible for me to understand. What possible injury to anyone's feelings could have been done by allowing this bishop and his priests to come to communion after all the white people had communicated? Such a method is thoroughly approved in old South Carolina and Virginia. The claim for the Spirit's guidance in your other methods is about on the same level, in my opinion.[92]

Witsell also wrote bishops Gailor, Perry, and Capers an account of the convention—a condemnation of its actions with this postscript: "It grieves me greatly to say that our good Bishop Demby and four Negro priests of the diocese in attendance with him . . . for the purpose of participating in the election were told by the rector, Rev. Wm. T. Holt, that they were not expected to partake of the Holy Communion. What an outrage against the catholic spirit and teaching and heritage of the church."[93]

Christ Church, which had threatened a boycott after the 1931 Annual Convention, eschewed a similar declaration after the 1932 convention but minimalized its role in the Diocese of Arkansas. Christ Church members resigned their diocesan posts, beginning with Cantrell's resignation as chancellor shortly after the convention. At the June meeting of the Executive Council, Witsell resigned his new appointment. Holt, who was also on the council, moved that Witsell's resignation be accepted. When Moorehead Wright, one of Witsell's parishioners and another newly elected to the council, submitted his own resignation, Holt moved that Wright's resignation be accepted—"with regret."[94] Christ Church contributions toward the work of the diocese, normally 20 to 25 percent of the annual budget, dropped off precipitously. Among the reasons given were the remission of diocesan assessments at Newport and the fact that Christ Church, like those churches whose debts were remitted, also suffered from the Great Depression.[95]

Withdrawal, however, was a luxury that Bishop Demby did not enjoy. Two of his priests, outraged at the conduct of the convention, threatened to leave the diocese. In view of Demby's struggles to find and keep clergy, this would have visited a small catastrophe on his head. Simultaneously, Saphore gave Demby no leeway in which to act. Had he inquired into Demby's silent protest at the back of St. Paul's Church and made some effort at reconciliation or appeasement, it might have enabled Demby to let the matter pass. But Saphore was silent, which made his culpability all the more obvious. He could not be allowed to ignore the significance of Newport upon the convocation. The black clergy had been humiliated and Demby had to act in their defense, knowing full well that white reaction would play havoc with, if not destroy, his ministry in Arkansas. "We just got to thinking about it after the election and finally decided the issue was too important to overlook," he said. "Such action in this day and time, is preposterous."[96] Sometimes Paris is not worth a Mass.

NOTES

1. John Egerton, *Speak Now against the Day: The Generation before the Civil Rights Movement in the South* (New York: Alfred A. Knopf, 1994), 19.

2. Margaret Sims McDonald, *White Already to Harvest: The Episcopal Church in Arkansas, 1838–1971* (Sewanee, Tenn.: University Press for the Episcopal Diocese of Arkansas, 1975), 217.

3. William P. Witsell, *A History of Christ Episcopal Church, Little Rock, Arkansas, 1839–1947* (Little Rock, Ark.: Christ Church Vestry, n.d.), 143.

4. Emmet C. Smith, "It Happened in 1932: The Story of a Man Who Was Elected Bishop, but Did Not Receive Necessary Consents," *Living Church*, 29 Jan. 1989, 9–10.

5. "Southern Florida Outrage," *Church Advocate*, Sept. 1921, 1; see also *Living Church*, 19 Nov. 1921.

6. Gavin White, "Patriarch McGuire and the Episcopal Church," *Historical Magazine of the Protestant Episcopal Church* 38 (June 1969): 125.

7. *Living Church*, 10 Sept. 1921, quoted in White, "Patriarch McGuire," 125.

8. *Journal of the Annual Convention of the Missionary District of South Florida* (1922): 44–46, quoted in White, "Patriarch McGuire," 125.

9. *Journal of the Annual Convention of the Missionary District of South Florida* (1924), quoted in White, "Patriarch McGuire," 125.

10. David M. Reimers, *White Protestantism and the Negro* (New York: Oxford University Press, 1965), 101.

11. In 1925, Elizabeth Delany, a Harlem dentist and daughter of the Right Reverend Henry B. Delany, was nearly accosted by the KKK on Long Island. Wearing their traditional white robes, Klansmen were stopping cars exiting a Long Island beach and making the black occupants get out. Bessie and her boyfriend raced around the roadblock and escaped (Sarah Delany and A. Elizabeth Delany, *Having Our Say: The Delany Sisters' First One Hundred Years*, ed. Amy Hill Hearth [New York: Kodansha International, 1993], 139).

12. *Living Church*, 5 Oct. 1929, p. 752, quoted in Reimers, *White Protestantism*, 102.

13. A survey of the collected papers of Bishop Colmore indicates that Dodd never wrote Colmore in this regard. Nor is there correspondence in the collected papers of Bishop William T. Manning at General Theological Seminary to indicate otherwise. Bishop C. B. Colmore Papers, Puerto Rico Papers, Archives of the Episcopal Church, Austin, Tex.; Bishop William T. Manning Papers, boxes 13–15, St. Mark's Library, General Theological Seminary, New York.

14. *New York Times*, 24, 25, 26, 30, 31 Oct. 1932; *New York Churchman*, 29 Oct. 1932; *Washington Afro-American*, 17 Sept., 22, 29 Oct. 1932; ibid., 29 Oct. 1932; *Pittsburgh Courier*, 9 Nov. 1932.

15. Roberta Church, interview by author, 17 Aug. 1994, Memphis, Tenn., transcript.

16. E. T. Demby to James R. Winchester, 10 Aug. 1928, Collected Papers of the Reverend William P. Witsell, Archives of the Diocese of Arkansas, Trinity Cathedral, Little Rock, Ark., hereafter cited as Witsell Papers.

17. Dennis Wilson, telephone interview by author, 2 July 1991, Palm Coast, Fla., transcript; James E. Lindsley, *This Planted Vine: A Narrative History of the Episcopal Diocese of New York* (New York: Harper Collins, 1984), 288.

18. *New York Times*, 24 Oct. 1932, 1, 3.

19. Ibid., 31 Oct. 1932, 17.

20. The Reverend Dennis Wilson, a retired priest and a former rector of St. James's, Baltimore, and St. Matthew's, Wilmington, Delaware, was a young parishioner of All Souls' in 1932. He witnessed Bishop Manning's break-in. According to Wilson, "The All Souls' incident prompted many whites to leave the parish. Fr. Dodd, who had previously been allocated the entire budget on January 1 every year, suddenly had to raise

funds. He consulted the heads of [some non-Episcopal churches] in New York City and came up with a plan to survey the members with envelopes and offerings. The next year, he had a surplus of money to run the church and pay his salary. . . . [The incident] was a coming of [the black contingent] into their responsibility" (Dennis Wilson, telephone interview by author, Palm Coast, Fla., 2 July, 1991, transcript).

21. *New York Times,* 31 Oct. 1932, 14–15.

22. Thomas S. Logan Sr., interview by author, 19 Oct. 1995, Yeadon, Pa., transcript; Dennis Wilson, telephone interview by author, 2 July 1991, Palm Coast, Fla., transcript.

23. Marguerite Du Pont Lee, letter to the editor, *New York Churchman,* 12 Nov. 1932, 2.

24. Thomas S. Logan Sr., interview by author, 19 Oct. 1995, Yeadon, Pa., transcript; Dennis Wilson, telephone interview by author, 2 July 1991, Palm Coast, Fla., transcript; White, "Archdeacon McGuire," 133–34.

25. McDonald, *Harvest,* 214.

26. W. P. Witsell to Charles Clingman, 8 Apr. 1935, Witsell Papers; Marguerite Gamble, interview by author, 14 May 1991, Little Rock, Ark., transcript; Clark Wood, interview by author, 10 Aug. 1991, Little Rock, Ark., transcript. Gamble is the daughter of W. R. Gamble, treasurer of Trinity Cathedral. The Gambles were faithful members of Trinity Cathedral and personal friends of Dean John Williamson, whom Marguerite called "Uncle John." Wood was the son of Tom Wood and assisted his father in printing the fiery rebuttals that peppered the *Arkansas Churchman* in the fall of 1932.

27. McDonald, *Harvest,* 213–15.

28. Ibid., 196.

29. H. A. Stowell to W. P. Witsell, 7 June 1938, Witsell Papers.

30. W. P. Witsell to Frank W. Creighton, 6 Feb. 1933, Witsell Papers.

31. McDonald, *Harvest,* 214. McDonald asserts that "Arkansas assumed responsibility for Demby's house," which, in turn, had a detrimental effect on Saphore's salary. However, the diocese, as noted in chapter 4, assumed the debt but did not actually pay on the balance for at least a decade.

32. According to the Reverend Hanson A. Stowell, Winchester's salary put a considerable strain on the diocese, even before the elections of Demby and Saphore (H. A. Stowell to W. P. Witsell, 26 May 1927, Witsell Papers).

33. William T. Capers to bishops, 29 Aug. 1932, Witsell Papers; John W. Naylor to W. P. Witsell, 14 May 1938, ibid.

34. W. P. Witsell to W. G. McDowell, 29 Aug. 1932, Witsell Papers; W. P. Witsell to Clinton S. Quin, 13 Feb. 1935, ibid.; Deadrick H. Cantrell to C. D. James, 13 June 1932, ibid. Based on the alignment of churches and personalities in the 1932 debacle, the shift away from Christ Church's influence can readily be seen at the 1931 annual convention. Prior to the convention, there were fourteen members of the executive council, six of whom could be described as friends or allies of Christ Church and especially of Witsell. This figure includes Winchester and Witsell himself. After the 1931 convention, however, that number was reduced to one member, Col. C. D. James of St. James's, Eureka Springs. Thus the election of Williamson at the 1932 convention

could be described as the second stage in a campaign to reduce the influence of Christ Church.

35. W. P. Witsell to J. R. Winchester, 13 Aug. 1932, Witsell Papers.

36. W. T. Capers to W. P. Witsell, 18 Nov. 1933, Witsell Papers.; W. T. Capers to W. P. Witsell, 24 Nov. 1933, ibid.

37. Randolph R. Claiborne to T. E. Wood, 26 Aug. 1932, Executive Council Papers, Archives of the Diocese of Arkansas. Trinity Cathedral, Little Rock, Ark., hereafter cited as Executive Council Papers; T. E. Wood to James De Wolfe Perry, 29 Aug. 1932, ibid.; W. P. Witsell to William G. McDowell, 29 Aug. 1932, Witsell Papers.

38. T. E. Wood to William T. Holt, 17 Sept. 1932, Executive Council Papers; T. E. Wood to Hanson A. Stowell, 17 Sept. 1932, ibid. Here we have two instances where Wood took the initiative in the deployment of clergy, a clear encroachment of Saphore's powers but one that the latter must have allowed.

39. W. P. Witsell to W. G. McDowell, 29 Aug. 1932, Witsell Papers.

40. Carolyn Rainey Harris, interview by author, 1 Mar. 1991, Fayetteville, Ark., transcript.

41. T. E. Wood to Samuel H. Rainey, 25 Aug. 1932, Executive Council Papers.

42. William G. Thayer to W. S. Simpson-Atmore, 29 Mar. 1932, Executive Council Papers.

43. Hanson A. Stowell to T. E. Wood, 4 Nov. 1932, Executive Council Papers; Executive Council of the Episcopal Diocese of Arkansas, minutes, 11 Oct. 1932, ibid.; W. S. Simpson-Atmore to Deadrick H. Cantrell, 10 June 1932, Witsell Papers; Carolyn R. Harris, interview by author, 1 Mar. 1991, Fayetteville, Ark., transcript.

44. W. T. Capers to Edwin W. Mellichampe, 4 Sept. 1931, Witsell Papers; W. T. Capers to Theodore Du Bose Bratton, 4 Sept. 1931, ibid.; W. T. Capers to Thomas F. Gailor, 4 Sept. 1931, ibid.

45. Holt was president of the Arkansas Society for Crippled Children. See Clyde Martin, "A Dream Realized—Arkansas Society for Crippled Children," *Arkansas Historical Quarterly* (Winter 1946): 371. Mellichampe saw Witsell fraternizing with Demby and his colleagues at either the 1930 Synod of the Southwest Province, or the General Convention of 1928, or the General Convention of 1931. W. T. Capers to W. P. Witsell, 24 Nov. 1933, Witsell Papers; W. P. Witsell to James D. Perry, 13 May 1932, ibid.; W. P. Witsell to W. T. Capers, 7 Sept. 1931, ibid.; Joseph B. Tucker, interview by author, 1 Oct. 1991, Pine Bluff, Ark.; Charles D. Lathrop to W. P. Witsell, 13 May 1938, Witsell Papers; Elnathan Tartt to Samuel H. Rainey, 3 May 1932, ibid.; Edward T. Demby, "Report of the Suffragan Bishop," *Journal of the Episcopal Diocese of Arkansas* (1932): 33, hereafter cited as *Arkansas Journal.*

46. W. P. Witsell to W. P. Capers, 12 Aug. 1931, Witsell Papers; W. P. Witsell to D. H. Cantrell, 13 Oct. 1931, ibid.

47. "Chapter Endorses Dean Williamson," *Arkansas Gazette,* 18 Aug. 1932; W. P. Witsell to T. F. Gailor, 16 May 1932, Witsell Papers. The black clergy closed ranks behind Witsell at Newport, but only as the election narrowed down to a runoff with Williamson.

48. Lily Billingsley to E. T. Demby, 15 Aug. 1932, Witsell Papers. See also W. P. Witsell to T. F. Gailor, 16 May 1932, ibid.

49. W. P. Witsell to W. G. McDowell, 29 Aug. 1932, Witsell Papers. In 1938, Williamson deemed a certain priest a poor choice for the next bishop of Arkansas because the man in question was "hard to know." Witsell responded to Williamson's observation with one of his own: "If a man is hard for Williamson to approach then I am afraid that he [the candidate] is thoroughly reserved" (W. P. Witsell to Charles D. Lathrop, 17 May 1938, ibid.).

50. Marguerite Gamble, interview by author, 14 May 1991, Little Rock, Ark., transcript.

51. W. P. Witsell to T. D. Bratton, 15 June 1933, Witsell Papers; W. P. Witsell to Milton A. Barber, n.d. [1933], ibid. W. T. Capers to W. P. Witsell, 8 Jan. 1932, ibid.; W. P. Witsell to W. T. Capers, 19 Jan. 1932, ibid.; W. T. Capers to W. P. Witsell, 21 Jan. 1932, ibid.; W. P. Witsell to W. T. Capers, 28 Mar. 1932, ibid.; S. H. Rainey to D. H. Cantrell, 30 Mar. 1932, ibid.

52. W. P. Witsell to Thomas F. Gailor, 16 May 1932, Witsell Papers.

53. W. P. Witsell to T. D. Bratton, 15 June 1933, Witsell Papers.

54. Ibid.

55. Edwin W. Saphore to William T. Holt, 1 May 1932, included in the brief "In Re: Consent of the Bishops of the Church to the Election of the Very Reverend John Williamson as Bishop of Arkansas," Executive Council Papers, hereafter cited as "In Re."

56. E. T. Demby to W. T. Holt, 7 May 1932, "In Re"; W. A. Billingsley to Standing Committee, 17 Aug. 1932, ibid.; W. T. Holt to William T. Capers, 15 Aug. 1932, Witsell Papers; Shirley G. Sanchez, letter to editor, *Living Church,* 10 Sept. 1932, 447.

57. W. T. Holt to E. T. Demby, 4 May 1932, "In Re."

58. Mildred W. Page, interview by author, 11 May 1991, Newport, Ark., transcript; W. P. Witsell to W. T. Holt, 17 May 1932, Witsell Papers; W. P. Witsell to W. G. McDowell, 29 Aug. 1932, ibid. Total exclusion from the Eucharist, even for southern black Episcopalians long accustomed to the practice of whites first/blacks last, was a relatively rare offense which justified complaint. Sarah (Sadie) Delany recalls attending a service conducted by her father, Bishop Henry B. Delany, Demby's counterpart in North Carolina: "One time, not long after Papa was consecrated to the bishopric, he did a service at Christ Church in Raleigh. It was a white, segregated church. Our family attended, and do you know what happened? We had to sit in the balcony, which was built for slaves! And we were not given the privilege of Communion. Ooooh, that makes Bessie [her sister, A. Elizabeth Delany] mad. At the time, she wanted to make a fuss, but she did not, because she did not want to embarrass Papa" (Delany and Delany, *Having Our Say,* 116). The Reverend Canon Thomas Logan, a pioneer in the development of racially integrated congregations in the Philadelphia area, sums it up this way: "I believe the issue, at heart, is the common cup and the disdain of some white people to take the cup after a black person. I'm sure there's more to it, but I believe the problem

is actually on that level" (Thomas S. Logan Sr., interview by author, Yeadon, Pa., 19 Oct. 1995).

59. Robert W. Prichard, *A History of the Episcopal Church* (Harrisburg, Pa.: Moorehouse Publishing, 1991), 215, 226.

60. Joseph H. Woodward, *The Negro Bishop Movement in the Protestant Episcopal Diocese of South Carolina* (McPhersonville, S.C.: By the author, n.d. [c. 1916]), 30. In a study of southern culture contemporary with the Newport incident, John Dollard observed, "It has sometimes seemed [as though black and white] conflict centers around social, and ultimately sexual, contact" (*Caste and Class in a Southern Town* [1937; reprint, Garden City, N.Y.: Doubleday and Co., 1957], 91).

61. E. T. Demby to W. T. Holt, 7 May 1932, "In Re."

62. L. Billingsley to E. T. Demby, 15 Aug. 1932, Witsell Papers; "Diocesan Bodies Uphold Election," *Arkansas Gazette,* 19 Aug. 1932.

63. Dollard, *Caste,* 250–53, 265, 287.

64. Edward T. Demby, "Off of the Record since 1939," MS, James Weldon Johnson Collection, Yale Collection of American Literature, Beinecke Rare Book and Manuscript Library, Yale University, New Haven, Conn., 68, hereafter cited as "Off of the Record"; W. P. Witsell to W. T. Holt, 17 May 1932, Witsell Papers; Shirley G. Sanchez, letter to the editor, *Living Church,* 10 Sept. 1932, p. 447; Mrs. O. E. Jones Sr., interview by author, 3 Aug. 1992, Batesville, Ark., transcript.

65. E. T. Demby to bishops, 2 Aug. 1932, Witsell Papers.

66. Ibid.

67. W. T. Holt to W. T. Capers, 15 Aug. 1932, Witsell Papers; L. Billingsley to E. T. Demby, 15 Aug. 1932, ibid.

68. Edwin W. Saphore to bishops, *Arkansas Churchman,* Sept. 1932, 8–9.

69. There are at least two other possible scenarios. Having resolved to sit out the celebration of the Eucharist, Demby and company may have been trying to enter the church—less their regalia—and simply take a seat at the moment they were confronted by the unidentified messenger. Then again, they may have been notified outside of the building while the procession was forming up. I contend that Demby, by force of habit and in the absence of any specific direction from Saphore, would follow standard liturgical procedure as nearly as he possibly could, that is, he would process. Based on his earlier conclusions regarding Saphore and the basement communion, Demby would have perceived a seating directive from an usher of St. Paul's as one more racial indignity sanctioned by Arkansas's acting bishop, regardless of when and where it happened. Demby unequivocally asserts that he was told not to commune.

It is testimony to the power of suppression by mutual consent, as well as as the all-male composition of the vestry and convention, that the actions of one woman parishioner of St. Paul's are remembered by several of her fellow parishioners as "the" racial offense of the 1932 convention. According to Mrs. Mildred W. Page, niece of Mildred Dorsey, oral tradition holds that the black clergy were intercepted as they entered the church and essentially told to sit on a back pew. The Eucharist planned for the basement and the entry of racism into the election process have either been forgotten or continue to be suppressed. The memories of other contemporary white Arkansas Episcopalians of the events at Newport are generally vague to nonexistent. There is no record of Bishop Demby broaching the issue publicly after August 1932. He preferred to confide in the Reverend George Plaskett of New Jersey, a dear friend who kept that confidence. I have been unable to locate any black Arkansas Episcopalians with a knowledge of the incident, save the Reverend Emery Washington, who discovered it among the Witsell Papers. Mildred W. Page, interview by author, 11 May 1991, Newport, Ark.

70. W. T. Holt to W. T. Capers, 15 Aug. 1932, Witsell Papers; L. G. Billingsley to E. T. Demby, 15 Aug. 1932, ibid.; E. W. Saphore to bishops, *Living Church*, 17 Sept. 1932, 471–72; S. G. Sanchez, letter to the editor, ibid., 10 Sept. 1932, 447.

71. S. G. Sanchez, letter to the editor, *Living Church*, 10 Sept. 1932, 447; T. E. Wood, "Letter of Transmittal," 20 Aug. 1932, "In Re."

72. W. P. Witsell to C. S. Quin, 13 Feb. 1935, Witsell Papers.

73. Lily G. Billingsley to Edward T. Demby, 15 Aug. 1932, Witsell Papers.

74. Mildred W. Page, interview by author, 11 May 1991, Newport, Ark., transcript.

75. Dollard, *Caste*, 65, 76–77, 81–82; Mildred W. Page, "Mildred Ann Wilmans Dorsey," *Stream of History* 26 (Fall 1989): 3. The two works by Mildred Dorsey are reprinted posthumously as appendixes to Mildred Page's article—"Bridges," ibid.: 4–5, and "Jackson County as It Used to Be," ibid.: 6–9. I do not offer this analysis to suggest that Mrs. Dorsey was anything less than courageous and compassionate; rather it is an attempt to explain why she could break with white solidarity and still retain her place in the community. In his memoirs, Demby quotes a white woman employed as an instructor at a black university and, consequently, disowned by her southern family: "I am not allowed to enter the home of my birth, and all because I am teaching Negroes and live in the institution with them" (Demby, "Off of the Record," 67). Social status, moral reputation, gender, and age were Mrs. Dorsey's allies.

76. Mildred W. Page, interview by author, 11 May 1991, Newport, Ark., transcript.

77. Demby, "Report," *Arkansas Journal* (1932): 31–34.

78. W. P. Witsell to W. T. Capers, 13 May 1932, Witsell Papers.

79. W. P. Witsell to Thomas F. Gailor, 16 May 1932, Witsell Papers; W. P. Witsell to William T. Capers, 13 May 1932, ibid.; William P. Witsell to James De Wolf Perry, 13 May 1932, ibid. As previously noted, all documents indicate that Tartt's participation in this intense, last-minute lobbying was strictly pro-Williamson in nature. Witsell's informants portrayed Holt and Mellichampe and, to a lesser extent, Lathrop, as the chief culprits (Elnathan Tartt to William T. Holt, 18 Aug. 1932, Executive Council Papers). Shortly after the convention, Holt wrote a misguided letter of consolation, to which Witsell responded with an accusatory letter, enumerating all of the anti-Witsell propaganda just cited. He omitted, however, the "nigger lover" charge, which would indicate that Mellichampe, who would be more brazenly racist at the 1933 Arkansas con-

vention, was at the heart of that particular accusation (W. P. Witsell to W. T. Holt, 17 May 1932, ibid.).

80. "Proceedings," *Arkansas Journal* (1932): 17.

81. L. G. Billingsley to E. T. Demby, 15 Aug. 1932, Witsell Papers.

82. D. H. Cantrell to James R. Winchester, 11 Aug. 1932, Witsell Papers.

83. "Chapter Endorses Dean Williamson," *Arkansas Gazette,* 18 Aug. 1932, 1, 7.

84. W. P. Witsell to Hanson A. Stowell, 16 May 1938, Witsell Papers.

85. D. H. Cantrell to James R. Winchester, 11 Aug. 1932, Witsell Papers.

86. "Minister Defends Election of Bishop," *Arkansas Gazette,* 16 Aug. 1932.

87. Shirley G. Sanchez to W. T. Holt, 14 May 1932, "In Re."

88. E. T. Demby to bishops, 2 Aug. 1932, Witsell Papers; Shirley G. Sanchez to the Arkansas Executive Council, 19 Sept. 1932, Executive Council Papers.

89. W. P. Witsell to William G. McDowell, 29 Aug. 1932, Witsell Papers.

90. L. G. Billingsley to E. T. Demby, 15 Aug. 1932, Witsell Papers; Samuel H. Rainey to T. E. Wood, 20 May 1932, Executive Council Papers; H. A. Stowell to T. E. Wood, 25 May 1932, ibid.

91. W. T. Holt to W. P. Witsell, 14 May 1932, Witsell Papers.

92. W. P. Witsell to W. T. Holt, 17 May 1932, Witsell Papers.

93. W. P. Witsell to James DeWolf Perry, 13 May 1932, Witsell Papers; W. P. Witsell to W. T. Capers, 13 May 1932, ibid.; W. P. Witsell to T. F. Gailor, 16 May 1932, ibid.

94. Minutes, Arkansas Executive Council, 3 June 1932, Executive Council Papers.

95. The diocesan assessment controversy culminated in a confrontation between Christ Church and Saphore described in chapter 7. Bishop Clinton S. Quin of Texas acted as an arbitrator. W. P. Witsell to C. S. Quin, 13 Feb. 1935, Witsell Papers.

96. "Minister Defends Election of Bishop," *Arkansas Gazette,* 16 Aug. 1932, p. 1.

6

Dogfight

It didn't matter if Dean Williamson or Dr. Witsell won the election; it
was bound to be a dogfight either way.

—Marguerite Gamble interview

In 1932, Winslow straddled one of the most rugged stretches of highway in
Arkansas. If one were to drive northward from Fort Smith, the nexus of the
Arkansas/Oklahoma state line, to Fayetteville, home of the University of Arkansas and city central to northwest Arkansas, one would pass through Winslow on the way down from Boston Mountain into Fayetteville. Winslow, to
quote the *W.P.A. Guide to 1930s Arkansas,* was the "highest . . . incorporated
town in Arkansas, [located] at the crest of the divide between the watersheds
of the White and Arkansas Rivers."[1] The St. Louis-to-California Butterfield
Stage Line, which followed this precipitous route between 1856 and 1861, inspired many a "religious experience" among its passengers. A stereotypical
Ozark landscape, the area around Winslow was heavily wooded, rugged, and
isolated. A rail connection to Fayetteville somewhat ameliorated the isolation
during the era in which the Episcopal Church maintained a school and a mission at Winslow, but it was nonetheless a region of poor hill people; subsis-
tence farmers and loggers who scraped a living from the roof of Arkansas. It
was a land of majestic views, dense virgin forests, and rushing ice-cold rivers
encased by rock bluffs—a post card to beckon summer travelers up from the
steamy heat of the flatlands and, for the Episcopal Church in Arkansas, a call
to ministry.

In 1903, the Dunlaps of Winslow bequeathed ten acres of land atop Boston
Mountain and a summer hotel building to the Diocese of Arkansas in memory of their granddaughter, Helen. Following her tragic death, they offered the
property to Bishop William M. Brown in order that he use it to establish a girls'
school in Helen's name. Brown capitalized on the offer and launched the Helen
Dunlap School for Mountain Girls in company with St. Stephen's Mission. It
closed for a time due to a lack of funds, then reopened under Bishop James R.
Winchester in the 1920s. By 1932 it was a much lauded missionary work, as well
as an Episcopal retreat center for Arkansas and the Province of the Southwest.
It was also a major casualty in the political cataclysm of 1932, which is under-

standable in light of its significance to the protest against Dean John Williamson's election. This is where the protest began.

As previously mentioned, the Southwest Province held a biennial synod to coordinate missionary activities within the region. The Young People's Service League of the province held a corresponding meeting every synod year. In 1932, the YPSL convened at Winslow during the first week of July. Leading the gathering were the vanquished white clergy of Arkansas's May episcopal election: the Reverend William P. Witsell and his closest allies, the Reverends W. S. Simpson-Atmore and Samuel H. Rainey, and the Right Reverend William T. Capers, bishop of West Texas and president of the Province of the Southwest. It was an opportune moment for the four of them to assess the situation in Arkansas, lay out a strategy to cope with the results of Newport, and otherwise comfort and encourage one another. While they were sequestered in Atmore's residence, the tenor of their meeting changed radically when Capers produced a letter he had recently received from Bishop Edward T. Demby.[2] A landmark document in black Episcopal history and Episcopal government in general, it is worth quoting in full in what we believe to be its original form:

Dear [Bishop Capers],

Just before the diocesan convention of the church of the Diocese of Arkansas which met at St. Paul's Parish, Newport, Arkansas, May 11th, the rector (the Rev. W. T. Holt) wrote me in this wise:

"There is no objection to the convocation sitting in the church and voting, I hear, but there might be some feeling about the two races taking Holy Communion together, etc."

On the arrival of the Negro clergy on the morning of the convention in conference it was decided—because of the condition of the place where we were told to celebrate the body and blood of Christ, and the uncatholic proceeding of the whole affair, and with justice to the race which we represent, it would not be wise for us to carry out the idea of the rector and [we] did not.

This attitude has already handicapped my efforts to extend the church among my people in the Diocese of Arkansas—likewise in other dioceses of the province where my services are being used. Personally I have said nothing in regard to the matter before this, which means that if this is to be the attitude of the church towards my people, I had just as well leave the field. The effect of the action on the colored work in this diocese, the Province of the Southwest, and the whole American church is already working a great hardship, and two of my men are anxious to leave their work in this diocese because of the attitude taken at the [convention].

The reception of the Holy Communion under this racial condition was of course declined, as I have said by my clergy and myself, the working out of which meant to my mind nothing less than our Excommunication. And let me say that action was taken not alone by Mr. Holt, for the services at a diocesan convention are always arranged for by the Ecclesiastical Authority, and in this case were actually made by such Ecclesiastical Authority (Bishop Saphore).[3]

Aside from the plain message of the text, the construction of this letter betrays the peculiarities of Demby's situation and that of southern black Episcopalians in general. First of all, this letter was a note in a bottle. Uncertain as to where or how he might obtain remedial action, Demby addressed his complaint to his nominal superior, Capers. In his capacity as president of the Province of the Southwest, Capers had no means of redress at his disposal, but he might have been able to advise a course of action or act as Demby's advocate with the Diocese of Arkansas. By directing his protest to Capers, Demby implied first that Bishop Edwin W. Saphore, being culpable, could not be trusted to grant a fair hearing. Second, Demby admitted that the indignation of two of his subordinates, presumably Reverends Shirley G. Sanchez and Robert J. Johnson, spurred him to action. Dogged by a history of transient priests, or "birds of passage" as Demby called them, the prospect of losing two clergy over racial injustice was not to be borne. Feeling very much alone and at the end of his Episcopal rope, the nation's only black bishop believed that his Christianity, not to mention his ministry, had been ecclesiastically invalidated at Newport. The same held true for his subordinates. Therefore, he had nothing to lose in protesting. A third fact which literally jumps off the page is this: Demby makes no attack on Williamson's election. One will note that the racial overtones of Williamson's election go unmentioned, as does the connection between the Reverend William T. Holt and Williamson. It was Holt who wrote the exclusionary letter and Holt who spearheaded Williamson's election. Why not attack Williamson's election by way of Holt? Clearly, this was not Demby's intention. The "election connection" was too ill-defined for a black man initiating a formal protest in a region where black people did not protest.

When faced with the possibility of a public altercation with white people, black southerners generally sought out white advocates, sometimes referred to as "white angels," to help them.[4] But Demby's "white angel," so to speak, was Witsell, runner-up to Dean Williamson. Drawing Witsell into the fray would jeopardize the protest from the outset, reducing it, in the eyes of some Episcopalians, to a transparent case of "sour grapes" and manipulation on Witsell's part.

Therefore, Demby narrowed his attack to things apolitical and documented. The issue, he decided, must be the integrity of that most sacred of Christian mysteries, the Eucharist—not the political fortunes of the Colored Convocation. And, by virtue of Holt's letter of 4 May, the proposed communion in the basement was an established fact. Likewise, in a church manifestly committed to the principle of government by bishops, the culprit must be Saphore. He must not be allowed to distance himself from his actions by attributing them to one of his subordinates. To blame anyone other than the Ecclesiastical Authority would not only miss the point, it would escalate the conflict, inviting personal recriminations and perhaps an explosive racial confrontation—all to no good end. Demby was determined to confine the dispute to the upper echelons of the church. So, without anyone's knowledge, white or black, he wrote Capers and hoped for counsel and justice and maybe some reading between the lines.

Existing correspondence suggests that Capers, pursuant to the Winslow conference, advised Demby to go ahead and make the connection between the Eucharist and the election, thereby bringing the character of Williamson's election into question, and submit the completed text to Presiding Bishop James D. Perry. The four white clergymen, Capers, Atmore, Rainey, and Witsell, were in agreement with Demby's summation; Newport could not be overlooked and Demby had more to lose in holding his tongue than in protesting. That being the case, Williamson's confirmation process presented Demby with the appropriate means of redress. Not only would rejection by the House of Bishops be just compensation for a tawdry and unchristian election, it would spare Episcopal Arkansas from a tawdry and unchristian administration. In communicating with Demby, it would appear that Capers deliberately omitted any mention of Witsell's participation in order to maintain a political quarantine around Demby's act.[5] Demby responded to Capers's suggestion with the following paragraph, which concluded the final circularized version of his letter.

> The program of the proceedings of the Annual [Convention] of the Diocese of Arkansas is as a matter of fact always mapped out by the Ecclesiastical Authority, and as I have said was so done in this case, and therefore, the responsibility attaches itself to the Ecclesiastical Authority as one who arranges the proceedings of the [convention]. This, Rt. Rev. Sir, is therefore a diocesan action. I ask, Bishop, that you give this matter your grave consideration when the matter of confirming the election by the convention of the Rev. John Williamson to be Bishop of Arkansas is brought to your attention.

Upon reading Demby's letter, Atmore and Rainey had composed a joint letter of their own; a letter intended to provide the linkage between what Demby could say and what he could not. They, likewise, pointed to the communion incident, Saphore's alleged knowledge of the same, and, consequently, the diocesan authority behind it. Then they added this parenthetic observation: "It is a significant fact that it was generally known that Bishop Demby was not in favor of the election of Dean Williamson who was being supported by the rector of the parish, Rev. W. T. Holt [,] who gave Bishop Demby the notice of denial of the communion." Having essentially accused Saphore of complicity against the black priests and bishop on Williamson's behalf, Rainey and At-more drew a broader connection, "We are of the opinion that these things injected an unworthy, uncatholic, and unchristian mind and spirit into the convention which were manifested . . . in the election of the bishop, and viti-ated them all." Recapitulating the relationship between Demby and Holt, and Holt and Williamson, they concluded: "This establishes the direct connection between those responsible for the election and the outrage against both the rights of a section of the convention and the true catholicity of the church. This, it seems to us is the real, vital point at stake." Williamson's complicity, they admitted, was an unknown quantity, "but we do not think that has any par-ticular relevancy to the essential point stated above." The Simpson-Atmore/Rainey letter also closed with a request for the bishops' "grave consideration" and a warning that Williamson's confirmation would place "the future of this diocese" in jeopardy.[6]

In late July, Capers and Witsell kept up a correspondence regarding the let-ters of protest, which depicts the relationship between the five men, as well as the course of events. For instance, Witsell wrote Capers the following remarks about Demby:

> May I say just a word in regard to your estimate of him. From this association with him and much conference about his work, I have come to the conclusion that he is a very godly man, thoroughly devoted to his work and really has sound ability. . . . he is doing as good a piece of work for his people as [the distribution] of funds and other circumstances, which he cannot control, will allow. You know what an uphill work it is for the church to get ahold of the imagination of the Negro race, which is so susceptible to emotionalism, rather than the solid presentation of the Gospel, such as the [Episcopal] Church offers. I have found Bishop Demby a real man and never dodges issues. Between you and me, he is far superior to the oth-er suffragan in every way.[7]

Capers drew up the final draft of the Atmore-Rainey circular and forward-ed a copy of their letter, in tandem with Demby's, to Perry. Perry responded by saying that he was in "hearty sympathy and agreement . . . with the prin-ciples which they have stated," but that they must write each bishop individ-ually.[8] He also dropped a hint that they must hurry, because he was about to distribute the official notices regarding Williamson's election.[9] Thus, even as Tom Wood reveled at Williamson's quick approval by the church's standing committees from the pages of the July *Southern Churchman*, Demby, Simpson-Atmore, and Rainey printed the letters that would ultimately lead to the nullification of the dean's election. On 2 August, they mailed them in tandem, a copy of each to all seventy-three bishops of the Episcopal Church. Rainey and Simpson-Atmore also sent copies to Witsell's parishioner and ally, Deadrick Cantrell, saying, "The pot will soon boil."[10]

Meanwhile, the dissidents received some unexpected assistance from Bishop G. A. Oldham of the Diocese of Albany, New York. Oldham, who issued his own circular on 4 August, insisted that the Diocese of Arkansas was already receiving an inordinate amount of money from the National Council. "To administer this diocese, which is actually smaller than Trinity Parish, New York, there is beside the retired bishop, a bishop suffragan, a Negro suffragan, and now the proposal is to elect a diocesan. It is indeed hard to see, whatever the area and conditions may be, why a single bishop could not administer such a diocese with comparative ease and have a good deal of time to spend elsewhere."[11] Oldham urged his fellow bishops to follow his example and not consent to Williamson's election.

Upon receipt of the Demby and Atmore/Rainey letters, Cantrell issued several letters of his own in support of the protest, and, most notably, a letter to the retired bishop of Arkansas, James R. Winchester. Foreseeing that the diocesan authorities would try to persuade Winchester to support Williamson's election, Cantrell tried to preempt the "Reds," as he called them.[12] He recapitulated the grounds for the protest, but misquoted the Atmore/Rainey letter to the effect "that Dean Williamson was also aware of the refusal of Mr. Holt to permit the colored clergy to have communion in his church." Of all the protests disseminated by the Arkansas opponents of Dean Williamson's election, this is the only instance where the dean is portrayed as having a hand in the communion episode. Indeed, this unsubstantiated remark may have backfired, contributing to Winchester's decision to defend Williamson in the latter days of the struggle. We may be sure that Winchester, who was very fond of his former dean, thoroughly scrutinized any allegation aimed at him. Otherwise, Cantrell lambasted Holt for his "attack . . . upon Dr. Witsell" at Newport and Saphore and Williamson for their complacency regarding the same. As for Williamson, Cantrell insisted that he lacked the qualifications for the office of bishop. He wrote: "If Dean Williamson should be confirmed as bishop, the effect on the diocese will not be overcome in twenty-five years."[13] Witsell, who was also privy to the letters of 2 August, wrote Winchester in a sim-

ilar vein. He and Cantrell urged Winchester to remain neutral in the fight that
was sure to come.[14]

Open conflict began on 14 August. Having obtained copies of the Winslow
circulars, an infuriated Tom Wood read them to the stunned congregation of
Trinity Cathedral at the Sunday morning service and publicized them the following day via the *Arkansas Gazette* and the *Arkansas Democrat,* the state's two
leading newspapers.

The *Arkansas Democrat* grasped the national significance of the protest and
dispatched a reporter to interview Demby, who was presiding over the Thirteenth Annual Convocation of Colored Churchmen and Colored Churchwom-
en of Arkansas at nearby St. Philip's, Little Rock. Demby reiterated his objections to Dean Williamson's election, citing especially the "unfair . . . spirit" of
the proceedings. Said Demby, "If I were in Dean Williamson's place, I would
have refused the election of a convention held in such a spirit as that." Demby
added that he had already received twenty responses from bishops in agreement with his protest and quoted, as an example, Bishop William G. McDowell of Alabama, who wrote: "I did not believe that such a thing could happen
in the church. I for one shall not rest until this wrong has been righted." Demby
also produced the Oldham circular, quoted above, bringing to light the diocese's money/bishop troubles. The *Democrat* also broached the internal political issue, closing the article, entitled "Negro Bishop's Stand Backed by His
Church," with this observation: "Persons who refused to be quoted have said
that the objection to Dean Williamson's election was the result of dissatisfac-
tion of supporters of certain other candidates."[15]

Perhaps the most significant aspect of this article, other than its equanimi-
ty, is what it did not say. While it headlined the convocation's endorsement of
Demby, it eschewed printing the actual resolution of endorsement, which the
convocation passed by acclamation. Introduced by P. L. Dorman, senior warden of St. Philip's, the resolution included the following: "We regard this act
of Bishop Demby as an example of rare courage in the face of certain peculiar
conditions existing in this section of our country. . . . We stand solidly behind
our bishop in resenting the uncalled-for conduct of the convention at New Port
[*sic*]. We realize that there was no other course for Bishop Demby to pursue if
he would retain the respect of members of the church, both white and colored,
who subscribe to the spirit of our church."[16]

Emboldened by Demby's stand, the convocation's carefully worded protest
went beyond the immediate offense and challenged the notion of white supremacy that lay behind it. The *Democrat,* it would seem, eschewed the resolution
as too volatile, as did all the other Arkansas newspapers. The two church week-

lies most widely read in Arkansas, Milwaukee's *Living Church* and Richmond's *Southern Churchman,* apparently did likewise, if indeed they ever knew of it. Ultimately, the resolution was published in the *New York Churchman,* which reprinted it as part of an article describing the events of the Thirteenth Annual Convocation. The New York weekly also noted that the Reverend Wallace Battle was in attendance. Battle, the field secretary for the American Church Institute for Negroes, was the most highly placed black administrator in the Episcopal Church at that time. Cast primarily in fund-raising role, he could hardly risk comment on Demby's protest—and did not.

The inaction of Battle, the unprecedented and recalcitrant protest of Demby, and the convocation's resolution of support exemplify southern race relations as described by sociologist John Dollard in his *Caste and Class in a Southern Town,* a book Demby considered a definitive study of southern culture. The price of white supremacy, writes Dollard, is unremitting suppression of practically any black gesture that could be construed as discontent with the status quo. Such gestures, wrote Dollard, are usually construed as black "aggression" by the whites and invite retribution from the white community, which has at its disposal every legal and monetary means of control—not to mention the specter of clandestine violence.[17]

Ironically, it was Judge Talbot Field of Hope, Witsell's ally at Newport, who made the most threatening public indictment of Demby. Writing in response to the *Gazette* article described above and a second article appearing the following day, Field condemned Demby's actions in the *Gazette* of 18 May:

> I consider the letter written by the Rev. W. T. Holt to Bishop Demby very unfortunate. However, I think that it is child's play for such a protest to be made now. The colored bishop was certainly aware of his rights as a churchman, and when he refused to accept the invitation to . . . the Holy Communion . . . he not only waived his right, but also waived his right to lead his race by not setting an example to them by taking advantage of their rights. If he felt aggrieved at the letter received by the Rev. Mr. Holt, he should have called the convention's attention to it. He had ample opportunity when he made his report, and many other times. . . . [Demby's protest] is a dangerous spark for race strife and should be extinguished at once.[18]

Fortunately for Demby, Field's inflammatory statement, predicated, as it was, on an extremely altruistic scenario, failed to provoke an incident.

Far from attacking Demby along racial lines, the diocese strove to thrust aside the race issue by attacking the alleged motive behind the protest. Speaking to the secular press, diocesan officers played down the "Negro question" in favor of what they believed to be the real issue, namely, the bitterness of the defeated candidate, William P. Witsell. In addition to the nebulous *Democrat* accusation from "persons who refused to be quoted" mentioned above, Holt bluntly and publicly accused Witsell of fomenting the protest out of his bitterness over having lost the election. Holt's accusation, which appeared in the 17 August issue of the *Gazette,* elicited a public denial of the same from Demby in the next day's paper: "I desire to say that my letter of protest to the House of Bishops was not prompted by the Rev. William P. Witsell, the rector of Christ Church, this city, nor anyone in his parish, nor did he or they know anything about it."

Holt's interpretation is very important, because it stuck. His is the view that has remained in the minds of most Arkansas Episcopalians who have any familiarity with the episode and are inclined to talk about it. It is the story that the uninitiated are most likely to hear. The 1932 episode has come down to us basically as the "Witsell conspiracy." This interpretation is also important in that it is, racially speaking, a Trinity Cathedral reprise of the Christ Church protest of 1890–98. To recapitulate the Christ Church protest as recorded in chapter 2, the Christ Church congregation believed that blacks ought not to be included in the Arkansas convention because of their "conspicuous incapacity for the difficult task of ecclesiastical legislation and their susceptibility to manipulation."[19] Bishop Henry N. Pierce, chief advocate of Arkansas's black Episcopalians, would not yield the point, which prompted a six-year Christ Church boycott of the Arkansas convention. Christ Church rejoined the convention in 1896, presumably in hopes of electing a new bishop more amenable to its views on the color question. However, the Very Reverend William M. Brown, who was, for all intents and purposes, Pierce's "man," defeated the Reverend John Gass, rector of Christ Church—by one black lay vote in each order. For Gass's supporters, the election represented a terrible vindication of the 1890 boycott. Thus, the 1932 election was a painful turnabout for Trinity Cathedral and a demonstration of how little things had changed with regard to the "Negro question." The proponents of Dean Williamson's election alleged that Demby was a mere puppet of Witsell, who had manipulated him into attacking Williamson's election. It would seem that they never seriously entertained the possibility that Demby might be justified in his complaint and capable of protest independent of Witsell. The Witsell conspiracy, therefore, is more than just an unabashed indictment of Witsell's character; it is also a barometer of the prejudice against Demby and his race. In the shadow of each controversy, 1897 and 1932, lurks the stereotype of the ignorant, incompetent, and servile African American.

So what was Witsell's relationship to the actions of Demby, Rainey, and Simpson-Atmore? Witsell and Demby undoubtedly had some contact after Newport, as indicated by Witsell's remarks about the communion episode in the weeks immediately following the convention. Witsell's outrage could only have compounded Demby's own, which undoubtedly would have encouraged the bishop to act. Witsell may even have suggested that Demby write Capers. Undeniably, Witsell knew of Demby's actions at least as far back as the Winslow conference, which would make Demby's remarks to the *Gazette* a bold-faced lie—unless Capers "leaked" Demby's plans to Witsell. This would seem to be the case. However, the substance of the Witsell Papers, whence most of this information was gleaned, indicates that Witsell and his parishioners wanted anything but another fight in the summer of 1932. They had washed their hands of the diocese, insofar as it was possible, and resolved to let the government of Episcopal Arkansas go its own way. Witsell did not propagate the protest; he dreaded it. Once the protest began, however, he became less recalcitrant. He consulted Bishop Thomas F. Gailor of Tennessee as to a course of action, and Gailor advised him to "keep quiet and do nothing."[20]

For a few weeks, Witsell was content to follow Gailor's advice, until it became apparent that there was more to be lost in avoiding controversy than there was in joining in the protest. The political quarantine, after all, was doing nothing to inhibit the emergence of the "Witsell conspiracy." Likewise, as the diocese launched its counterattack, Rainey and Simpson-Atmore began to resent Witsell's reluctance to join in.[21] His critics, however, merely took this as a sign that he was acting in character by using the protesters as pawns. The Reverend Randolph R. Claiborne, father of the future bishop of Georgia, was a wholehearted believer in Witsell's culpability. A former Arkansas priest with an adversarial relationship to Witsell and a low opinion of Rainey, Claiborne wrote the following: "Two weeks ago Bishop Green [the Right Reverend William Green, bishop coadjutor of Mississippi] asked me about the Arkansas affair. I had not heard of it. He told me of the Demby letter, and of Rainey and Simpson-Atmore. Right off the bat I told him of the man [Witsell] who I believed to be behind the whole thing and that these two were proteges. . . . He came to Ark. expecting to be bishop; acted like he *was,* saw the error. But could not conceal his ambitions."[22] Claiborne made it a point to disseminate the conspiracy theory among the bishops of his acquaintance, which probably occasioned the following remark from Bishop Walter Mitchell of Arizona, brother of the Reverend Richard B. Mitchell, future bishop of Arkansas. He told Witsell: "I heard somewhere on one of my trips out of state, that it was thought that you had accepted Christ Church with the expectation of succeeding Bishop Winchester!"[23] Privately, Holt dubbed the protesters the "Triumvirate" and Wood labeled them the "Three Horsemen."[24] Publicly, Wood utilized Demby's remark, as recorded in chapter 5, about the deliberations that led to the protest and lampooned the "Conferites" from the pages of the September *Arkansas Churchman.*[25]

Although the conspiracy theory quickly became the party line at the diocesan offices, it won few adherents among the bishops. Bishop Harry T. Moore of Dallas would seem to be an exception and Bishop Greene, mentioned above, may have been swayed by Claiborne's interpretation. Be that as it may, Witsell continued to enjoy an overwhelming respect in the House of Bishops. He was personally acquainted with most of its members, as the communication with Mitchell would indicate, and they did not believe him so "small" as to try to discredit Williamson's election merely because Williamson was the victor. Indeed, Wood and Holt did untold damage to Williamson's chances by propagating the conspiracy theory. For example, Presiding Bishop Perry received the following communication from Wood in late August: "As a matter of fact there is no strife in this diocese, there is just one big 'sore toe' [Witsell] and a few satellites trying to circumvent the will of the diocesan convention without regard to the welfare of the church. . . . From now on my lance is unsheathed in the name of a militant church to cleanse the Temple of God of those who would use it for personal ambition."[26] Such unguarded remarks naturally brought into question the character of Arkansas's diocesan government and, with it, the 1932 convention. They also reflected badly on Williamson, who, by his silence, demonstrated either his agreement with the actions of Wood and Holt or his inability to control them. Both interpretations cast doubt on his qualifications for bishop, making him appear either spiteful, or weak-willed, or both. Witsell's alleged deviousness and manipulative powers so preoccupied the minds of his enemies that they lost sight of their goal and their role.

There was no conspiracy theory, however, pursuant to the official defense of Williamson's election, a brief entitled "In Re: Consent of Bishops of the Church to the Election of the Very Rev. John Williamson as Bishop of Arkansas." As of 14 August, with Saphore absent in New York, Wood assumed the unofficial mantle of chief advocate of the diocese and mobilized it to action. A self-styled defender of the faith, he saw in Williamson's defense nothing less than a "calling." Assisted by Saphore, Holt, and the somewhat reluctant Reverend H. A. Stowell, the Little Rock attorney arranged for emergency meetings of the Standing Committee, the Executive Council, and the Chapter of

Trinity Cathedral in the week of 14–20 August, all ex parte meetings held at Trinity Cathedral. Upon the completion of the deliberations, Wood consolidated the findings of the three committees, along with some pertinent correspondence, into "In Re" and distributed copies to every bishop in the church. Wood's "Letter of Transmittal" summarized Williamson's defense along these lines:

> From this evidence you will learn, first, that there was no racial feeling entering into the election of a bishop at the convention; second, that the colored suffragan and the four Negro clergy were not excommunicated; third, that one of the Negro priests who attended the convention and who has since left the diocese did so not by reason of anything that occurred at the convention according to his own word; fourth, that the Ecclesiastical Authority (the Rt. Rev. Edwin W. Saphore) had nothing to do with that part of the diocesan program of the communion service, neither did the bishop-elect, the Very Rev. John Williamson have any knowledge of the attempted arrangement; fifth, that there is no merit in the protest sent to you by the Rt. Rev. E. Thomas Demby and the Rev. S. H. Rainey and Dr. W. S. Simpson-Atmore.[27]

While resolutions from the three committees consolidated arguments for Williamson's defense, Wood utilized several letters to expand on particular points. In order to emphasize the parochial nature of the segregated communion, he devoted one page to a letter from W. A. Billingsley, senior warden of St. Paul's, Newport. Billingsley explained that Holt was "authorized and directed" by St. Paul's vestry to write Bishop Demby a letter "stating some of the problems which would arise and requesting his suggestions as to how they might be avoided, and also to make [a] suggestion as to a possible solution." Billingsley asserted that Saphore and Williamson knew nothing of the arrangement and concluded with the implication that Demby was a cad:

> We desired to make the colored clergy comfortable and happy and we [the vestry of St. Paul's] were most eager to avoid their being offered any indignity.
> If Bishop Demby had acted as a gracious guest, he would have discovered a gracious host; if any censure is to be directed toward St. Paul's Parish, then we must be condemned for the attempts to be a gracious host. This is a purely local affair and has nothing whatever to do with the diocese or the convention or the election of Dean Williamson.[28]

Although Wood mentioned in the "Letter of Transmittal" that Holt spoke with Demby after the service to express his "regret" that the black bishop did not commune, there was nothing else in "In Re" to suggest either regret or sympathy toward Demby and certainly nothing to suggest an apology. The tenor of the brief was solidly in keeping with the tone of Billingsley's letter—defense and counterattack.

Wood included copies of the original exchange between Holt and Demby, plus correspondence from two other black clergymen, with the intention of defending Holt's character and leveling another attack on Demby. First and foremost, Wood offered three communications by and with the Reverend Shirley G. Sanchez, formerly of St. Augustine's, Fort Smith. Sanchez's first entry was a thank-you letter to Holt and St. Paul's for the hospitality extended to the convocation at Newport, which included this remark: "I hope that all the parishes and missions will rally to Dean Williamson after his consecration and that the strong spirit of division which have [sic] manifested itself so far, will be overcome."[29] Holt replied to Sanchez on 16 May:

> I was glad that I had a chat with Bishop Demby before he left. He understands my position now and I do hope that you will join in with him and Father King and myself and others in our efforts to find a means of larger co-operation [sic] of our two races in the extension of Christ's kingdom.
>
> The Executive Council elected me to head the Department of Missions and I was also appointed on the Committee on Constitution and Canons. I hope this may put me in the position to give Bishop Demby additional help in his efforts to provide adequate support for and [generate] more interest in his work. It would be a fine thing if the clergy in the Afro-American Convocation would have a con-ference some time [sic] which would take the nature of a "retreat." At that time we could take up the matter of bettering racial relations in the Grace of our Lord

The Sanchez trilogy closed with a letter addressed to Williamson, dated 1 August. In it, Sanchez announced his appointment to St. Thomas's, Tulsa, replac-ing the priest that Demby buried in March. The move, said Sanchez, offered him a raise in salary, which he badly needed. The letter ends: "I am hoping that you have definite word as to your consecration. I wish for you, God's blessing and success in the work and office which await you." Sanchez's communica-tions were fortuitous for the diocese. They demonstrated that at least one black priest approved of Williamson's election and harbored no resentment regard-ing the convention. They also indicated a genial relationship between Holt and one of Demby's priests—with a suggestion of Holt's ongoing and genuine concern over Demby's reaction to the events of 11 May, namely, that Holt was not the dyed-in-the-wool racist that the Winslow letters would seem to indi-cate. Most importantly, the letters proved that Sanchez's expressed reason for leaving Arkansas was money—not Newport.

The Sanchez trilogy of "In Re" would be incomplete, however, without the contextual information provided via a communiqué from Sanchez to the Arkansas Executive Council in September. Seeking redress for a debt he incurred while priest-in-charge of St. Augustine's, Sanchez laid his case before the council and vented his unmitigated fury at Demby: "I took up the matter of [St. Augustine's] inability to pay me several times with [Demby], but it has always been to my grief, for he lacks a sense of duty. This was what caused me to leave the Diocese of Arkansas and not anything that took place at Newport, as seemed to have been inferred. It was impossible to accomplish anything at Fort Smith, due largely to his attitude."[30]

The Reverend E. J. Lunon, dean of Jackson African Methodist Episcopal Seminary, Shorter College, Little Rock, was the second black clergyman quoted in defense of Williamson's election. In a letter to Holt, Lunon endorsed Holt and Williamson, culminating with a personal attack on Demby. Lunon, who doubled as minister to St. Luke's A.M.E. Church, Newport, wrote the following:

> You know my interest in the members of my own race; inasmuch as I took great pains in seeing that Bishop Demby and the other colored clergy were properly entertained [at Newport]. I know your interest in my race by your eagerness to see that the colored clergy were well cared for. I can [sic] not understand Bishop Demby's attitude. . . . I am sure that if Bishop Demby had entered into conference with you and had made the effort to co-operate with you in solving the problem presented by the participation of the two races in a church service, you would have avoided the unhappy issue which has now arisen. It seems to me that Bishop Demby has acted hastily or has been misguided by wrong advice and influence.

Lunon lionized Holt for his efforts to minister to the black populace as president of the Arkansas Crippled Children's Society. Then he paid homage to the virtues of joint labors between black and white Christians, enterprises carried forth without any violation of "racial integrity." This "fellowship of the Spirit," wrote Lunon, "would help us to avoid all the sad situations that arise from any efforts toward 'social equality' or 'white supremacy.'" He interrupted what may be described as a recapitulation of the Atlanta Compromise to say this of Demby: "The effect of Bishop Demby's attitude is to perpetuate the old fallacy of the colored people seeking to mingle with the whites at the expense of their racial pride and self respect. Bishop Demby would force his way among the whites."[31]

Lunon's words are representative of an attitude common among members of all-black churches with regard to African Americans who chose to remain in predominantly white churches. The Reverend George F. Bragg, for instance, once engaged a prominent A.M.E. clergyman in a public debate on this very issue via the pages of his *Church Advocate*.[32] Harold Lewis contends that the scrutiny of black Christian America is part and parcel of the black Episcopal experience: "Most black Christians in the United States are the spiritual sons and daughters of [Richard] Allen. [Therefore] black Episcopalians often find themselves in a defensive posture. Their authenticity and even their integrity as Christians are almost routinely brought into question. They must answer allegations of 'Uncle Tom-ism.' They have been accused of selling their birth right for a mess of pottage of rather dubious value."[33]

"In Re" closed with a rebuttal to the fiscal objections of Bishop Oldham. The Executive Council passed a resolution intended to correct Oldham's figures. Citing Oldham's inclusion of Demby's entire salary in the national appropriation to Arkansas, they pointed out that Demby's jurisdiction included the entire Southwest Province. Hence, only a just proportion of his salary rightfully belonged to Arkansas. The council also noted that Bishop Saphore had voluntarily cut his own salary in order to accommodate Williamson's salary-to-be. In conclusion, they gently insisted that the diocese's money affairs were essentially internal matters, which is to say, "please stop meddling."[34]

With the counterattack thus launched, Wood disseminated copies of "In Re" to all of the bishops and hoped and prayed that the diocese had acted in time.

Rainey and Simpson-Atmore responded to "In Re" with a second circular to the bishops in which they reaffirmed the allegations in their original circular. They implored the bishops to disregard Holt's "parochial" defense of the communion incident. Demby issued a similar circular on 26 August, reaffirming his original protest and noting that the deliberations surrounding "In Re" were ex parte. This was his last public statement regarding the 1932 controversy.[35]

Holt, meanwhile, circularized the bishops on his own, describing himself as a victim of circumstances beyond his control in an "entirely parochial" matter. Citing the enclosed copy of his 4 May letter to Demby, Holt argued that he signed the letter only at the request of the vestry and out of courtesy to Demby. It was, said Holt,

> our effort to meet the issues of the race question in a manner satisfactory to the colored clergy. . . . If Bishop Demby had debated the question, offered a solution other than the one I suggested, or had shown any inclination to help us solve the problem of race relationship, before the convention, he would have done a great service to his race and our diocese. As it is, now, nearly three months after the diocesan convention, he comes forward in his attitude of wounded majesty—aided, of course, by two white clergymen—and by an ingenious process of reasoning tries to make a case against Dean Williamson's election.

The Newport rector insisted that the black clergy had not acted in keeping with the "spirit of hospitality and fellowship" extended to them, however irregular that hospitality might have been. They were not, argued Holt, "denied the privileges of the altar," but eschewed the proposed separate communion service and a second offer at the end of the regular service by their own choice. He concluded, "It would be a calamity to this diocese if these three men should be able thwart Dean Williamson's election."[36]

Capers also joined the fray, publicly speaking, on 19 August. Writing in his capacity as president of the Province of the Southwest, he issued a circular to the bishops. He ascribed Arkansas's problems in large measure to a leadership vacuum now several years old. Despite Williamson's better qualities, wrote Capers, that vacuum would continue with Williamson "even if he had the united effort of the clergy and the laity of the diocese behind him," which, of course, he did not. Therefore, according to Capers, Williamson should not be confirmed.[37] Capers also responded to Holt's circular by writing Holt a private rebuttal. Regarding the communion episode, Capers announced his willingness to concede Holt's point about the ignorance of Saphore and Williamson, a concession which implicitly denied Demby's assertion to the contrary. Otherwise, he granted the Newport rector no quarter and ignored the latter's remarks about the participation of St. Paul's vestry. They could not share in the rector's responsibility, however demanding they may have been. Capers pointed to the fact that Holt had actually raised the "color line" by trying to arrange a separate Negro service in the name of avoiding the "color line." In summary, he asserted that Holt's circular, with its enclosure, merely reaffirmed his original judgment against Dean Williamson's election, to wit, "[it] has created a disastrous division in the diocese and therefore his election should not be confirmed."[38]

Capers's letter elicited an acidic rebuttal from Holt, wherein he insisted that the protest of 2 August constituted the true raising of the "color line." Otherwise, Holt delved into the relationship between Capers and Witsell: "do you mean that if we do not elect your nominee [for bishop of Arkansas] that you will stir up trouble in the diocese and prevent any other bishop being elected?" The Newport convention, said Holt, was a victory of the laity over the Witsell "machine." He closed with a cascade of blistering irony aimed at Capers, who had earlier declared his intention to "offer the church in Arkansas such help as I am able to give." After suggesting ways in which Capers might "help" Witsell, Demby, Rainey, and Simpson-Atmore, Holt vented his frustration with the congregation of St. Paul's: "I would like to have your help in teaching my people to be more sociable to the colored race." For Holt, 1932 was a protracted lesson in futility.[39]

Wood, meanwhile, engaged Rainey and Atmore in a debate via the mails, allowing him the opportunity to air some long-standing grievances against them. "I have refrained for five years, as Chairman of the Executive Council of the diocese, from replying to or noticing the small and unrighteous things that have been done to prevent the harmonious functioning of the council or church life, but the time has come when some friend of the church must stand up for constituted authority in this diocese, and the welfare of the cause in this diocese calls for a reprimand of the tactics of you two conspirators."[40] It would seem that Rainey and Atmore tried to establish a more open, deliberative tone with the authorities in Little Rock during the last half of August but were thwarted by Wood, who repeatedly deduced what he believed were their true intentions.[41] Wood and Holt regarded the new thrust from the northwest as a ridiculously belated attempt at protesting through channels in order to give the protest legitimacy. Holt wrote Rainey and Atmore that inasmuch as they had already subjected the Diocese of Arkansas to scandal and tried to bring down Williamson's election, "you should at least have the decency to keep to yourselves."[42] Wood, who enjoyed at least the tacit approval of Bishop Saphore for his part in the debate, ceased writing at Stowell's suggestion: "In such matters correspondence . . . but fans the flame and goes on indefinitely with no result."[43] Likewise, Stowell told Rainey and Atmore: "It will be well to stop the controversy between us and wait for the action of the bishops."[44]

Hanson Stowell is an interesting figure in that he tried desperately to find a middle ground in the 1932 controversy. At that time, he was the senior resident clergyman in Arkansas and his tenure extended, like that of Saphore, Burke, and Collins, back to the days of "bad Bishop Brown." He was the sagacious, portly, white-haired priest of possibly the most prestigious Arkansas church outside of Little Rock—Trinity Church, Pine Bluff. Although he was a venerable figure among the Arkansas clergy, he was not identified with the diocese's warring factions and placed a distant fourth among the candidates for bishop at Newport. He enjoyed at least as much political influence as Holt and Wood, if not more, by virtue of being president of the Standing Committee and a member of the Executive Council.

Stowell supported Williamson out of loyalty to the diocese, but he disapproved of Williamson's election for three reasons. First, he eschewed the politically volatile "in-house" election and voted only for non-Arkansas candidates at Newport. The diocese, he knew, was asking for trouble by insisting that one of its own be elected. Second, he did not believe Williamson qualified for the office of bishop. Speaking to the emergency meetings of the Standing Committee and the Executive Council, pursuant to the publication of "In Re," Stowell stated the following: "I did not vote for Dean Williamson and I disapprove of the election but I signed the testimonial on the democratic principle of yielding to the will of the majority and, if the bishops confirm the election, I will be loyal to the electee and do all I can to aid him in his work."[45] He had a corresponding disdain for the circularizing of 2 August, citing it as a breach of protocol. The problem, he said, should have been submitted to diocesan authorities instead of the House of Bishops. Although Stowell had served the Diocese of Springfield concurrently with Demby and Atmore in 1903, Demby was no more than an acquaintance in 1932 and Atmore represented an unpleasant but necessary relationship. In his capacity as the Arkansas Executive Council's chairman of religious education, Stowell commerced regularly with Atmore, whom he considered too abrasive for his office. As for Demby, Stowell basically agreed with the diocese's arguments in "In Re" regarding the treatment of the black clergy at Newport; it was a parochial matter. He volunteered no critique of Arkansas's black suffragan, save that he disapproved of the bishop's "method" of protest.[46] Above all, he abhorred the publicity surrounding the controversy and made it his business to restrain the pen of Tom Wood. Third, Stowell emphatically agreed with Bishop Oldham; the Diocese of Arkansas was already financially overburdened with bishops and should in no wise elect another. Having heard this criticism of Arkansas at more than one General Convention, Stowell declared that "one [b]ishop can easily perform all the work among the whites and the [N]egroes [of Arkansas] and this has always been the case. I feel sure that [this] is the matter which makes the [b]ishops hesitate about ratifying the election and that the controversies which have arisen—controversies which under other circumstances would have had little influence—add something to the case."[47]

Stowell found the middle ground very slippery. Bishop Harry T. Moore of Dallas, a pro-Williamson bishop, wrote Stowell to inquire as to the identity of the Executive Council member who dissented from the council's resolutions in defense of Williamson's election. The dissenter, of course, was Stowell, who objected to the following resolution: "That in the consecration of the Very Rev. John Williamson to be Bishop of Arkansas this council is of the opinion that the work of the church will be strengthened and advanced."[48] Stowell wrote Moore this contrite reply: "I should not confess the sin of any other individual but I am free to admit my own. I am the guilty person to whom you refer."[49]

While Moore may have been piqued at Stowell for his lack of solidarity, he was indignant at Capers for circularizing against the Arkansas election. He circularized the bishops with a rebuttal to Capers's circular, saying that the bishop of West Texas had exceeded his authority as president of a province by trying to nullify Williamson's election. Capers, he implied, was meddling. He attacked the substance of Capers's protest as opinionated and unsubstantiated, concluding with a thinly veiled accusation, presumably in reference to Capers's relationship to Witsell. "If the Bishop of West Texas is in possession of any facts involving the character or integrity of Mr. Williamson, I would plead with him to present them to us for our own information and as a means to our wise decision. In case there are no such facts which can be presented to us, then one would be entitled to assume that there were other reasons, perhaps other motives; and if this be true, we are equally entitled to know these facts."[50]

Witsell reluctantly entered the public debate in late August. Having reconciled to and even rejoiced at Christ Church's recent disavowal of the Diocese of Arkansas, Witsell came to realize that he must come to the aid of his three allies or be found unworthy of their friendship. During the summer and fall of 1932, Witsell, who had a summer house north of Fayetteville, visited the Raineys at St. Paul's rectory.[51] He also had occasion to speak with Demby after the protest was launched. Demby, Atmore, and Rainey beckoned Witsell morally, if not literally, from the other side of the Rubicon where their reputations and their ministries hung in the balance. Witsell, of course, realized that his joining the protest would stigmatize it with a decidedly political angle in the eyes of some Episcopalians. However, a letter from Bishop William G. McDowell of Alabama helped him "go public." McDowell wrote: "Recently in a group of bishops your action in refusing to sign the testimonials of election was brought up. We could not believe that this was merely the spite of a defeated candidate. The church has reason to believe that you are a well balanced and Christian man. We felt you must have some good reasons for withholding your signature, and if so, that you should make them known to the church, or at least to the bishops who are now called upon to judge the election. . . . The friends of Dean Williamson have circularized the church. We need the other side."[52]

Witsell responded with a five-page letter, essentially a revision of a letter sent to Bishop F. F. Reese of Georgia, which was, in turn, essentially a revision of the aforementioned letter sent to Winchester. Witsell recounted the events leading up to Newport and the activities of 11 May. As touching upon Demby's protest of the communion episode, Witsell unequivocally aligned himself with Demby. "In my opinion, the inherent spiritual rights of this bishop and four priests were violated, and they were unnecessarily and pitilessly humiliated, and the real brotherhood of the priesthood before the altar denied. Not one of them would have objected if they had been requested to come to

the communion railing together after all the white people had communed."
Regarding Demby's accusation of Saphore and the "*the diocesan attitude at that
convention,*" Witsell wrote, "It seems as if there is to be a conflict between state-
ments of Bishop Demby and others. I do not hesitate to say that I believe Bishop Demby." He concluded, "The crucial point . . . is . . . the fact that those
responsible for the outrage . . . are those responsible for the election."[53]

Perhaps nothing about the McDowell circular, other than its support of
Demby, is so descriptive of Witsell as his remarks pertaining to Williamson and
the confrontation that eventually resulted. Witsell listed the various reasons
he thought Williamson unsuited for the office of bishop and recapitulated a
conversation with the dean to the same effect. He noted Stowell's dissent, as
cited above, and added, "The feeling of the dean's incompetency for the episcopate, I am told, was shared by quite a number of people in his own congregation."[54]

When Williamson learned of the letter at the end of September, he was aghast
at Witsell's humiliating critique. He drove over to Christ Church, apparently
with the intention of obtaining an explanation—if not an apology—and a copy
of the letter. Witsell was uneasy but resolute. He delayed, took counsel with
Capers and Perry, and, following their advice, decided to refuse Williamson
the letter. Two days later, he visited the cathedral in order to give Williamson
his decision, but Williamson announced that he had already obtained a copy
and intended to employ it in some public sense. Ultimately, its contents were
never made public.[55]

In closing the McDowell letter, Witsell cited Wood and Holt for their vindictive and very public handling of Williamson's defense. He was especially
critical of Wood, whom he described as "an unsuccessful politician and law-
yer, not even able to maintain an office." Since both of them were identified
with Williamson, said Witsell, "this playing to the galleries and misleading the
public mind will be continued [in the event of] Dean Williamson's consecration."[56] At McDowell's suggestion, Witsell distributed his letter to a select
majority of the bishops.[57]

Two more circular letters, written on behalf of Williamson's election, were
distributed to the bishops during the ninety day period of confirmation. Having agonized over Arkansas's situation for two months, Winchester distributed a circular in October, a letter in praise of Dean Williamson and silent on
all other points. Winchester's sentiment was refreshing for its less partisan
approach, but it was too little, too late.[58] Saphore wrote a more controversial
letter in early September. In it, he disputed the money protest of Bishop Oldham, pled ignorance of the communion arrangement at Newport, and paid

special attention to the precedent set at El Dorado in 1927. Saphore noted that neither Demby nor Rainey protested the events at El Dorado.[59] All in all, Saphore's letter sounds like a more tactful recapitulation of Tom Wood's arguments. For instance, Wood wrote Rainey in August:

> Why, Mr. Rainey, if you are so concerned about the treatment of the convention to your colored brethren, did you not make a halloa in 1927. You, Mr. Rainey, will remember that while you were rector of St. Mary's, El Dorado, in 1927 your vestry sent a letter of complaint about the presence of Bishop Demby even within the church. As a result, your beloved colored brother was not even permitted to attend the convention or to enter the church where the convention was held that year. And you were the rector of that church. "Thou art the man." Your consciousness of your responsibility to your church at this time in a matter of this kind is more than passing strange.[60]

As this comparison and a multitude of other documentation indicates, Wood clearly had Saphore in tow during this period. Nevertheless, he wholeheartedly disapproved of Arkansas's acting bishop. Wood wrote Presiding Bishop James D. Perry a letter in support of Williamson, "a live, energetic, and gracious spiritual leader," and in rebuttal to Bishop Oldham's charges of fiscal irresponsibility. In the course of making his defense against Oldham, Wood pronounced this judgment on Saphore and Demby: "If the great body of the communicants of the church in this diocese could receive any suggestion as how it could be relieved of the two suffragan bishops it would welcome the information. Bishop Saphore does not accept the intimation that he resign. His work certainly does not justify his elevation to the bishopric. . . . As for Bishop Demby, if he ever had any usefulness, he has wholly destroyed it in this diocese."[61]

The Arkansas controversy made news in the major church papers, usually in the form of letters to the editor and reprints of the various circular letters. It was covered in New York's *Churchman,* Richmond's *Southern Churchman,* Chicago's *Witness,* and Milwaukee's *Living Church.* The two most prominent papers, the *Churchman* and the *Living Church,* took opposing sides on the issue. The *Churchman* published mainly those items written by or on behalf of the protesters. It did, however, include a letter written by Bishop H. H. Fox of Montana in defense of Arkansas and its money problems. It appears that Fox, who was Witsell's roommate at General Theological Seminary in New York, refused consent to Dean Williamson's election.[62] Nevertheless, as bishop of a vast but sparsely populated missionary district, he sympathized with Arkansas on the money question and asked the *Churchman* to publish his rebuttal to Bishop Oldham's circular. Oldham had complained that Arkansas and nine other missionary dioceses or missionary districts, Montana included, shared the onus of having two or more bishops, while the thickly populated Diocese of Albany managed with one. Fox embarked on a long defense of Montana and its sister dioceses in the West, but not before a word or two on Arkansas's suffragan bishops. Having been a suffragan himself, he empathized with Saphore's "uncomfortable position": "You [Bishop Oldham] are absolutely right in saying that there is no need of two bishops [Saphore and Williamson] to minister to nineteen parishes and fourteen missions in Arkansas. . . . But evidently Bishop Saphore cannot be elected bishop." As for Demby, he "is accredited to Arkansas only because the church does not permit an unattached, if I may use the phrase, bishop. . . . He is a bishop of the Seventh Province and he cannot therefore be considered a Bishop of Arkansas."[63] Clifford P. Morehouse, editor of the *Living Church,* decided in favor of the dean's election in a 10 September editorial.[64] He cited Shirley Sanchez's letter to the editor in the same issue as a compelling factor. Sanchez understood that Holt had apologized to Demby for the proposed communion in the basement. "That," said Sanchez "should have closed the matter."[65]

In late September, Bishop Perry urged Morehouse and other editors of major Episcopal periodicals to refrain from publishing further commentary on the Arkansas troubles. Publicity, he said, only inflamed passions and inspired further controversy. It appears that everyone complied.

The *Arkansas Churchman,* resurrected by Wood in August, was not so easily subdued. Wood and Holt, editor and associate editor respectively, used the diocesan paper as a forum for the defense of Williamson's election. Fearing Wood's proclivity for public debate, Stowell wrote him in late August, "I hope that the [September] issue of the *Arkansas Churchman* will contain no mention of the recent upheaval re the Newport convention and the election there made."[66] Wood responded: "There is the other side to contemplate, I know—those who shrink from any kind of fight think that it is un-Christian, just as if the truth of God was not something worth trying to preserve. . . . I would rid this diocese of its Judas Iscariots. . . . I am debating the question and will pray over it."[67]

Despite his anger, Wood had all but decided to take Stowell's advice, when Bishop Capers's circular to the bishops came across his desk. Wood explained to Stowell, "Knowing the connections and spirit that prompted this attack, I consider that I would be untrue to my church and unmindful of the best interest of my diocese, did I not reply editorially to this presumptuous circularization."[68] Thus, the September issue of the *Arkansas Churchman* was permeated with invective, Capers being the target of choice. "When, pray, did Bishop Capers of West Texas, get to be the guardian of the internal affairs of the Diocese of Arkansas?"[69] Wood, however, gradually acknowledged that Stowell was probably right and Bishop Perry, visiting Little Rock in September, made it clear that each new disputation only mitigated against Williamson's confirmation by the House of Bishops. After September, Wood basically contented himself with an occasional thinly veiled barb at Capers or Demby.[70] Meanwhile, Witsell utilized the September issue as a ready-made second circular to the bishops; an exposé of the spirit behind Williamson's election.

September was also the month that diocesan authorities launched their attacks on Rainey and Atmore. Persuaded that both priests ought to be removed from their posts, they successfully terminated Atmore's position with the Helen Dunlap School and nearly expelled Rainey from St. Paul's, Fayetteville.

In early September, the diocese laid plans to fire Atmore.[71] The pretext for firing him was that his participation in the August protest had deeply offended the Woman's Auxiliary of the Diocese of Arkansas, the most important contributor to the school's operating expenses, and the Daughters of the American Revolution, a lesser contributor whose involvement presages, in a small way, the DAR's infamous exclusion of Marian Anderson from a Washington concert hall in 1939. The collective dislike of these two women's organizations for Atmore threatened to be the undoing of financial support for the school. This, according, to Stowell, was the "last straw" for a man not well liked in the diocese otherwise.[72] The next meeting of the Executive Council was unofficially slated to fire him.

Wood, meanwhile, attacked Rainey through an unlikely source. Sue Walker, an elderly matriarch of St. Paul's, Fayetteville, resolved to force Rainey's resignation. She was the sister of J. Vol Walker, a Fayetteville attorney and the champion of a successful struggle to keep the University of Arkansas in Fayetteville. Walker could be described as a aged southern aristocrat. Her reputation, her deportment, and her values were decidedly "Old South." She disliked Rainey for his speech, his taste in literature, his style of ministry to students at the University of Arkansas, and his liberal views regarding blacks. He was, to put it bluntly, a "Yankee."[73] She considered Rainey's protest against the racist character of the Newport convention reprehensible.

In August, Rainey had tried to downplay the race issue by splitting a very fine hair. Writing to the Fayetteville, Fort Smith, and Little Rock newspapers, he declared, "I resent this matter of Mr. Williamson's election being made into a racial affair when it is not. . . . Dr. Atmore and myself have protested against the spirit and attitude injected into the convention [by the race issue]."[74] We may guess from this that Rainey was delineating the destructive partisanship of the convention as the more important issue. And he certainly wanted to avoid the incendiary emotional climate incumbent to a strictly racial interpretation of the protest.

Be that as it may, the fact that two white priests were backing Demby was not lost on "Miss Sue," as she was called. Having invoked the curse of Ham as partial justification for her actions, she began corresponding with Tom Wood in mid-August and together they formulated a plan to force Rainey's resignation from St. Paul's, or, if need be, remove him by force of church law.[75] Walker, acting as a go-between, put the plan in motion. She helped persuade two vestry members of St. Paul's, Victor E. Russum and J. P. Brower, to ally themselves with Wood and the diocese against Rainey. Wood, in turn, gladly provided them with encouragement and information pertinent to their cause. He enjoined Saphore to sanction their actions and Saphore complied. On 9 September, Wood wrote Brower, "Bishop Saphore . . . asks that your vestry take such action in the premises as you deem just and churchly,"[76] and Russum, "Bishop Saphore [requests] your vestry to take what action you deemed the offense would justify."[77] The issue was decided on 14 September at the monthly meeting of St. Paul's vestry. Brower, an attorney and the senior warden of St. Paul's, arrived with a brief of anti-Rainey materials in hand, submitted the same to Rainey and the vestry, and made some pertinent comments. Having concluded his indictment, Brower, or perhaps Russum, moved that St. Paul's notify the Diocese of Arkansas of its condemnation of Rainey's anti-convention activities. Russum, Brower, and a third member voted in favor of the motion. Colonel C. F. Armistead, a veteran of the Newport shouting match, James McIlroy, the junior warden of St. Paul's, and a third member voted against it. Rainey cast the deciding vote in his favor and the motion was defeated, 4-3.[78]

Although he was far from comfortable at St. Paul's for some time thereafter, this was the high-water mark of the attack on Rainey. Contributions fell off in protest of his collaboration with Demby and company, compounded by the general economic calamity sweeping the land. During the winter, Rainey was so deeply moved by the homeless vagabonds moving through the Fayetteville area that he allowed some of them to sleep in the sanctuary of St. Paul's. He felt less generous, however, when the "poor devils" tore up the carpeting for blankets. In August 1933, he wrote Witsell that he had received only $25 toward his expenses for the month. Witsell tried to help him relocate, first to Oklahoma and then to Missouri, but to no avail. Ultimately, the Raineys lived out the remainder of the Great Depression in Fayetteville—long enough to know their enemies as boarders. William T. Holt II attended the University of Arkansas in the mid-1930s. According to Rainey's daughter, Carolyn, he fell out with the cooking on campus and, after a heart-to-heart talk with Mrs. Rainey, moved in with his father's former adversary. Likewise, "Miss Sue," aged and infirm, found herself in need of a better living arrangement and moved in with the Yankee priest and his family, where she spent her remaining days. Carolyn Rainey Harris still has jewelry given to the Raineys by Miss Sue in payment for her long stay.[79]

Returning to the fall of 1932, Williamson invited Bishop Perry to Little Rock for counsel on the election controversy. The presiding bishop attended the joint meeting of the Standing Committee and the Executive Council on 16 September. Wood anticipated that Perry would rebuke the two committees after some fashion, but the bishop restricted his theme to concern for Arkansas's well-being and offered nothing in the way of specific direction except to advise those present that the Diocese of Arkansas should, by all means, stop publishing controversial matter as it only damaged their cause. Afterwards, he spoke to Dean Williamson privately and more directly. He advised the dean that there was almost no chance that the election would succeed and that his best option would be to withdraw his name immediately, rather than let the issue drag on until the 19 November deadline.[80] Williamson then drove Perry over to Christ Church where Witsell, Rainey, Cantrell, and Atmore awaited him. Demby was not present at this meeting.

Meanwhile, the Executive Council went into special session and fired Atmore, effective at the end of the academic year, 1932–33. Telling Atmore, however, proved far more difficult than firing him. The members of the Executive Council could not establish exactly who was responsible for notifying him that he had been dismissed. Stowell finally informed him on 27 September, just two days before the school was to open.[81] The move caught Atmore unawares, quashing his erroneous belief in his secure standing with the school. With his confidence thus shaken, his relationship to the diocese—and that of the school to the diocese—began to deteriorate quickly. He asked that the Department of Religious Education, Stowell's bailiwick, forward enough money to start the term. Stowell replied that the usual procedure was for bills to be paid one month in arrears, a bookkeeping measure instituted by the Woman's Auxiliary. Therefore, Atmore should start the year on credit as he had done in the past and reimbursement would be forthcoming. The warden, however, began to look at the lack of money in light of his dismissal and, no doubt, his preexisting dispute with the Diocese of Arkansas over pension fund payments. He demanded money in hand as assurance that the diocese would continue to pay for the operating expenses of the school. When it did not come, he refused to open the school. During October, a series of misunderstandings and miscues, fueled by Atmore's anger at being fired and the Executive Council's dislike of him, kept the school's doors closed. Atmore composed a circular to the bishops, entitled "To Whom it May Concern: The Closing of the Helen Dunlap School." He argued that his firing and the subsequent closing of the school were the result of the diocese's taking revenge on him for participating in the August protest. Stowell, however, maintained that the council was not being vindictive in its actions:

> I do not regard the action of the Executive Council as one taken in revenge. The most that can be said of it is that his—what I think mean way of trying to defeat the ratification—was a 'last straw.' If he had been loved and respected by the diocese his expression of his opinion in this matter—no matter how disapproved— would have been looked upon as an unjustifiable blunder, but would not have weighed against him to the extent of forfeiting his position. It is because he is not liked and not wanted that his letter told against him.
>
> We all have the right to express our opinions, but we all ought to know what human nature is, especially those of us who are dependent on voluntary support.[82]

Cantrell, Witsell, and Rainey tried to help Atmore defend himself. In response to their appeal, Cantrell's successor as chancellor, Col. C. D. James of Eureka Springs, judged that Atmore was denied lawful preliminary notification of the Executive Council's intent to fire him when it met on 16 September. Therefore, his dismissal was null and the warden was entitled to preliminary notification of any future attempt to fire him. The council gave the required notice of such a meeting to be held on 22 November. Atmore circularized the council with a letter drawn up by Cantrell. It warned the councilmen that the National Council, which paid Atmore's salary, might come to his defense if the Executive Council tried to dismiss him again. It was a hollow argument. On 22 November, three days after Bishop Perry announced that Williamson had been rejected by the House of Bishops, the Arkansas Executive Council met, heard Atmore's defense, terminated him, and officially closed the school. It never reopened.[83]

In October, the Chapter of Trinity Cathedral initiated a grass roots campaign to save Williamson's election. Acting, it seems, in ignorance of the presiding bishop's private conference with Williamson, they circulated pro-Williamson vestry resolutions and petitions among the Arkansas churches. Copies of the completed documents were forwarded to those bishops whose vote was still in question. It is unclear whether the chapter canvassed all the churches in Arkansas, but the surviving vestry resolutions are primarily from churches whose rectors supported Williamson in May: St. John's, Fort Smith; St. John's, Helena; St. Andrew's, Marianna; St. Paul's, Newport; and Trinity Cathedral. Noticeably absent was St. Paul's, Batesville. Elnathan Tartt may have been a Williamson stalwart, but his people were not. None of St. Paul's delegates to the Newport convention signed Williamson's Testimonial of Election and no petition was forthcoming in October. In all, eight parishes and four missions completed the petitions. Running through every document is the affirmation that "the church in Arkansas . . . needs the able and spiritual leadership of Dean John Williamson" whereby "the true democratic form and spirit of the church will be preserved." The petitions emphasized, as Holt and Wood did, that "Dean Williamson's election was the desire of the laity in this diocese and still is." The vestry resolution of St. Paul's, Newport, expanded on the democratic theme by taking a subtle dig at Witsell: "[Williamson] is a man who would strive to build the diocese through the united efforts of his people rather than through his sole personal effort." Vexed and humiliated by the turn of events since May, the Newport vestry dispensed with subtleties and blasted away at "a few insignificant and unimportant clergy, (three Negroes, two white rectors, and one white teacher, six in all), who failed to realize, by reason of the election of Dean Williamson, personal ambitions and therefore seek through misrepresentation to discredit the entire convention."[84]

The October canvass, like all other attempts to defend Williamson's election, was unsuccessful. On 19 November, Perry sent Stowell a telegram: "Am mailing you official notification that only a small minority of bishops have consented and that the election is null."[85] For the congregation at Trinity Cathedral the news came, to quote one devotee of Dean Williamson, "like a bolt out of the blue."[86] At the provincial synod held in St. Louis in October, Holt and Wood had let it be known that they intended to reelect Williamson if the bishops did not confirm him. When their fears became fact, they publicly reaffirmed their intention, setting the stage for another six years of political maneuvering.

The debate over Williamson's election had a revelatory effect on the House of Bishops. The House found itself divided into two opposing schools of thought when it came to the confirmation of bishops-elect. One school, whom we may call the strict constructionists, espoused a very narrow interpretation of the words "meet and fit," as pertaining to the qualifications of bishops-elect. Electees, they said, should be confirmed matter-of-factly unless they are proven to be morally or spiritually unclean. It was their belief that the House of Bishops can and should rely upon the electing dioceses to scrutinize the candidates before presenting them. Therefore, the circumstances of an election are an internal matter for the diocese and irrelevant to the confirmation process of the House of Bishops. The absence of Williamson's culpability in the communion episode, said the strict constructionists, made the race issue irrelevant. Likewise, the strict constructionists asserted that the qualifications of a bishop-elect are also an internal matter, the crucial point being that a diocese knows its needs better than the House of Bishops can. Bishop Robert N. Spencer of West Missouri, a strict constructionist, argued that men who appear to be overrated at the time of election often rise to the challenge and prove themselves worthy of the office, once elected. Bishops Moore of Dallas and Greene of Mississippi also belonged to the strict construction school.[87]

The large majority of bishops in 1932 could be termed "broad constructionists." They took the view that, yes, the circumstances of an election do enter into confirmation judgments. Ironically, they cited as their prime example the case of Bishop William M. Brown of Arkansas, deposed from the ministry in 1925. Brown, after all, accepted the office and won the consent of the House of Bishops amid a storm of controversy in Arkansas. Surely here, if nowhere else, was justification for greater scrutiny of the election process. Compounding this insight were the subsequent Arkansas elections of two suffragan bishops, which were inhibiting, in one way or another, the election of a diocesan bishop for Arkansas. Bishop J. B. Cheshire of North Carolina, one of the few bishops who voted against Demby's consecration, wrote Capers: "I declined to consent to the consecration of Brown; I declined to consent to the consecration of Demby. . . . [As for Saphore], I ought not to have consented to his consecration *and I hope I did not.*"[88] Moreover, broad constructionists were determined that bishops be verifiably qualified for office; to wit, "meet and fit" means not just morally and spiritually clean but competent as well. Said Bishop E. N. Schmuck of Wyoming,

> Unless a man has been involved in a some notorious scandal or [is] a blatant heretic [,] confirmation of the election generally follows without regard to whether a man is [qualified and appropriate for the job] . . . affairs are in a horrible mess in Arkansas and the man chosen should certainly be a capable man to handle the situation.
>
> From [the McDowell and Capers circulars], I gather that Dean Williamson, while having some qualifications[,] is not the man for the situation. This is the thing bishops ought to know before they pass on a man. When the country was smaller . . . it was easy to ascertain, but now since there is such a great body of clergy . . . I believe the time is come that more information should be given about the man personally.[89]

Bishops F. A. Juhan of Florida and F. M. Taitt of Pennsylvania voiced similar opinions.

Black newspaper editors generally waited to see the verdict of the House of Bishops before commenting on the Arkansas controversy, which is indicative of a lack of public commentary on the part of black Episcopal clergy. The *Washington Afro-American* printed a synopsis in December 1932 and the *Crisis* gave it a footnote in February 1933. Black editors had essentially the same problem as white editors: the morass of charges and countercharges and the detection of a direct link between the communion incident and the election. The *Washington Afro-American* and the *Crisis* portrayed Williamson as the perpetrator of the Jim Crow communion.[90] The *Church Advocate,* which George F. Bragg had downgraded to a parish paper for fiscal reasons, refrained from comment.

At what point did Dean Williamson's election fail, or, more specifically, what killed it? Arkansas Episcopalians allied with Trinity Cathedral and of an age to remember the personalities involved believe it was Witsell's protest from beginning to end. The decisive element, they contend, was his influence. This argument naturally renders the protest letters of 2 August, Capers's circular, and the McDowell circular academic, mere escalating stages in a contemptible conspiracy. As for Witsell, he discovered that his parishioners awaited his explanation of the events in order that they, in turn, could defend their church and their rector. So, he drew up his synopsis of the entire episode and published it to the congregation. He explained: the decisive element in bringing down the election was the schism made manifest by the race protest—not the race protest itself. "It is idle," he said, "to talk of the influence of the Negro question as an applicable factor in the situation. There is information to prove that very few, if any of the bishops in casting their vote were governed by that consideration, and furthermore, most to the bishops of the Southern dioceses voted against the confirmation."[91] The McDowell letter was, in Witsell's own estimation, merely a confirmation of judgments already rendered by a majority of the House of Bishops. In other words, the Demby/Rainey/Atmore protest illuminated the schism, which better substantiated nonconfirmation than the race issue alone. The bishops, said Witsell, could plainly see that Dean Williamson's election was not a diocese uniting around its new leader but a mere mastery of one faction over another.

The two interpretations have something in common: they both deemphasize the protest against racial discrimination. Demby's twenty affirmative responses, received by 15 August, constituted 29 percent of the House of Bishops. Yet, this information went largely unheeded in the final analysis of the white combatants, because it was too volatile. Practically everyone wanted to avoid the additional strife inherent to an open acknowledgement of the race issue. It would have done incalculable damage to the effort at reconciliation.

Witsell, of course, had an additional motive in that he was personally concerned with protecting Demby. For the white supremacists in the Episcopal Arkansas it was enough to acknowledge that an African American's protest, be he a bishop or otherwise, could mitigate against the dean's election. To acknowledge that Demby's protest was decisive by way of revealing the schism within the Diocese of Arkansas would have been intolerable. Yet this was the case. As for the bishops themselves, none challenged the validity of Demby's complaint. All acknowledged that exclusion from the Eucharist on racial grounds was patently unchristian. This was a given. They were primarily concerned with placing the responsibility for the exclusion and, more importantly, establishing the relationship between the communion episode and the convention in general, and the election in particular. Demby, they knew, must needs be very careful in his accusation. In this, his reputation served him well. In his sixteen years in the House of Bishops, he had not once taken the floor, although he was entitled to do so. Suddenly, this "good Negro," as some whites praised him and some blacks deprecated him, was trying to bring down an Episcopal election on grounds of racial discrimination.

In the Arkansas controversy of 1932, the bishops enjoyed a unique advantage. They had, by way of the confirmation process, a means to redress a protest of racial discrimination and the ability to do so while remaining relatively anonymous, or, at least, understated. As demonstrated by the Blackshear affair, intervention was well nigh impossible so long as the vestry of the local church remained united. Bishops could condemn racist behavior publicly, but little else. True, they could discipline clergy by exercising their powers of appointment and pecuniary assistance, but these were long-term options with many variables. In light of the unwritten law against meddling in the affairs of other dioceses, the customary prerogative of the local church to segregate according to its own "lights," and the climate of public opinion, it is hard to believe that a majority of them would publicly denounce a diocese or convention for overtly racist behavior. But the confirmation process changed all that, enabling them to vote their consciences without citing their reasons. Only a minority volunteered how they voted and why.[92]

Finally, the anomalous relationship of Bishop Demby and, for that matter, all black Episcopalians to their church is dramatically evident in the 1932 episode. Demby took his stand, the Colored Convocation followed, Sanchez dissented, and the white Episcopalians fought it out while the church's black constituency looked on. Indeed, when researching this episode, I found no Arkansas black Episcopalian with a memory of the event. Outside of Arkansas, their fellow Episcopalians looked upon Newport as a local matter, much like Bishop Manning's break-in at All Soul's—an island of justice in a sea of injustice, an exception to the prevailing trend. Events would prove it was much more than that.

NOTES

Marguerite Gamble is the daughter of W. R. Gamble, a member of the chapter of Trinity Cathedral during the 1932 controversy. The Gambles were close friends of Dean John Williamson and his wife. Williamson was "Uncle John" to Marguerite.

1. Federal Writers' Project of the Works Progress Administration, comp., *The WPA Guide to 1930s Arkansas,* intro. by Elliot West (Lawrence: University Press of Kansas, 1997), 314–15.

2. I am extrapolating on existing information. While we do not have all the details of the meeting, it is obvious from existing documents that Demby's letter was the catalyst for the protest, that it was revealed at the Winslow conference, and that the original letter was intended only for Capers.

3. Edward T. Demby to [Bishop Capers], 2 Aug. 1932, Collected Papers of the Reverend William P. Witsell, Archives of the Diocese of Arkansas, Trinity Cathedral, Little Rock, Ark., hereafter cited as Witsell Papers.

4. John Dollard, *Caste and Class in a Southern Town* (1937; reprint, Garden City, N.Y.: Doubleday and Co., 1957), 212.

5. W. P. Witsell to W. T. Capers, 27 June 1932, Witsell Papers; James De Wolf Perry to W. T. Capers, 26 June 1932, ibid.; William T. Capers to William P. Witsell, 30 June 1932, ibid.

6. Samuel H. Rainey/W. S. Simpson-Atmore to bishops, 2 Aug. 1932, Witsell Papers.

7. W. P. Witsell to W. T. Capers, 27 July 1932, Witsell Papers.

8. James De Wolf Perry to W. T. Capers, 26 July 1932, Witsell Papers.

9. W. T. Capers to W. P. Witsell, 30 July 1932, Witsell Papers.

10. W. S. Simpson-Atmore/ S. H. Rainey to Deadrick H. Cantrell, 6 Aug. 1932, Witsell Papers.

11. G. Ashton Oldham to bishops, 4 Aug. 1932, Executive Council Papers, Archives of the Diocese of Arkansas, Trinity Cathedral, Little Rock, Ark., hereafter cited as Executive Council Papers.

12. D. H. Cantrell to F. B. T. Hollenberg, 11 Aug. 1932, Witsell Papers.

13. D. H. Cantrell to Winchester, 11 Aug. 1932, Witsell Papers.

14. W. P. Witsell to James R. Winchester, 13 Aug. 1932, Witsell Papers.

15. "Negro Bishop's Stand Backed by His Church," *Arkansas Democrat,* 15 Aug. 1932. The *Democrat* has been widely perceived as the more conservative of Little Rock's two major newspapers, because of its coverage of the Little Rock desegregation crisis. However, in 1932, this was not the case. The Reverend Smythe H. Lindsay, Dean Will-

iamson's assistant at Trinity Cathedral, was also employed at the *Arkansas Gazette*, and Tom Wood, who frequented the *Gazette* during the tumult of August, wrote Stowell: "The newspaper boys are in thorough sympathy with the authorities of [the diocese] in this matter" (Thomas E. Wood to H. A. Stowell, 30 Aug. 1932, Executive Council Papers). Lindsay went on to become general editor of the *Living Church*.

16. "Colored Segregation Is Protested," *New York Churchman*, 27 Aug., 1932, 16–17. The Colored Convocation issued a letter to Bishop Capers on the same day, thanking him for his support of Demby (Colored Convocation to W. T. Capers, 15 Aug. 1932, Witsell Papers).

17. Dollard, *Caste*, 317–18, 333.

18. "Chapter Endorses Dean Williamson, *Arkansas Gazette*, 18 Aug. 1932, 1, 7.

19. William P. Witsell, *A History of Christ Episcopal Church, Little Rock, Arkansas, 1839–1947* (Little Rock, Ark.: Christ Church Vestry, n.d.), 72–73.

20. W. P. Witsell to T. F. Gailor, 11 Aug. 1932, Witsell Papers; T. F. Gailor to W. P. Witsell, n.d., ibid. Prior to the Christ Church exodus from diocesan offices in the summer of 1932, Witsell wrote Capers this synopsis of the Newport convention: "The whole thing has clarified the atmosphere for us at Christ Church and puts us in a position to act as we think best without any sort of mist to cloud our apprehension of the facts" (W. P. Witsell to W. T. Capers, 13 May 1932, ibid.).

21. Carolyn Rainey Harris, interview by author, 1 Mar. 1991, Fayetteville, Ark., transcript.

22. Randolph R. Claiborne Sr. to T. E. Wood, 26 Aug. 1932, Executive Council Papers.

23. Walter Mitchell to W. P. Witsell, 3 Oct. 1932, Witsell Papers.

24. William T. Holt to Thomas E. Wood, 12 Sept. 1932, Executive Council Papers; T. E. Wood to Edwin W. Saphore, 20 Aug. 1932, ibid.

25. *Arkansas Churchman*, Sept. 1932, 5.

26. Tom Wood to James De Wolf Perry, 29 Aug. 1932, Executive Council Papers.

27. T. E. Wood, "Letter of Transmittal," 20 Aug. 1932, "In Re: Consent of Bishops of the Church to the Election of the Very Rev. John Williamson as Bishop of Arkansas," Executive Council Papers, hereafter cited as "In Re."

28. W. A. Billingsley to Standing Committee, 17 Aug. 1932, "In Re."

29. S. G. Sanchez to W. T. Holt, 14 May 1932, "In Re."

30. Shirley G. Sanchez to the Arkansas Executive Council, 19 Sept. 1932, Executive Council Papers. The Executive Council declined to act on Sanchez's petition due to its lack of jurisdiction over the churches of the Colored Convocation.

31. E. J. Lunon to William T. Holt, 16 Aug. 1932, "In Re."

32. "Rev. Dr. George F. Bragg of St. James' P. E. Church, This City, Replies to Prof. R. R. Wright, Jr., Editor *Christian Recorder* of A. M. E. Church," *Church Advocate*, June 1919, 1–2.

33. Harold T. Lewis, *Yet with a Steady Beat: The African-American Struggle for Recognition in the Episcopal Church* (Valley Forge, Pa.: Trinity Press International, 1996), 3–4.

34. "Resolution Adopted by the Executive Council of Arkansas In Re Bishop Oldham Letter," "In Re."

35. W. S. Simpson-Atmore/S. H. Rainey to bishops, 22 Aug. 1932, Witsell Papers; E. T. Demby to bishops, 26 Aug. 1932, ibid.

36. W. T. Holt to W. T. Capers [bishops], 15 Aug. 1932, Witsell Papers.

37. W. T. Capers to bishops, 19 Aug. 1932, Witsell Papers.

38. W. T. Capers to W. T. Holt, 23 Aug. 1932, Witsell Papers.

39. W. T. Holt to W. T. Capers, 1 Sept. 1932, Witsell Papers.

40. T. E. Wood to S. H. Rainey and W. S. Simpson-Atmore, 25 Aug. 1932, Executive Council Papers.

41. S. H. Rainey and W. S. Simpson-Atmore to the Standing Committee of the Diocese of Arkansas, 22 Aug. 1932, Executive Council Papers; S. H. Rainey and W. S. Simpson-Atmore to T. E. Wood, 27 Aug. 1932, ibid.; T. E. Wood to S. H. Rainey and W. S. Simpson-Atmore, 31 Aug. 1932, ibid.

42. W. T. Holt to S. H. Rainey and W. S. Simpson-Atmore, 6 Sept. 1932, Witsell Papers.

43. H. A. Stowell to T. E. Wood, 29 Aug. 1932, Executive Council Papers.

44. Ibid.

45. H. A. Stowell to Harry T. Moore, 24 Aug. 1932, Executive Council Papers.

46. Ibid.

47. H. A. Stowell to T. E. Wood, 20 Sept. 1932, Executive Council Papers.

48. Resolutions Adopted by the Executive Council, Diocese of Arkansas, In Re: Consent to Bishop Elect, "In Re."

49. H. A. Stowell to H. T. Moore, 24 Aug. 1932, Executive Council Papers.

50. Harry T. Moore to bishops, 29 Aug. 1932, Executive Council Papers.

51. Rainey's daughter Caroline remembers the sequestered conferences between Rainey, Atmore, and Witsell—primarily because of their inconvenience. While the three clergymen conferred privately in the Raineys' living room, all traffic between bedrooms and kitchen detoured through the yard (Caroline Rainey Harris, interview by author, 1 Mar. 1991, Fayetteville, Ark., transcript).

52. William G. McDowell to W. P. Witsell, 26 Aug. 1932, Witsell Papers. Witsell had already answered a similar request from Peter Gray Sears, representing the Standing Committee of the Diocese of Texas, in June. However, it was intended solely for the committee and Bishop Clinton S. Quin of Texas. W. P. Witsell to W. T. Capers, 25 June 1932, ibid.

53. W. P. Witsell to W. G. McDowell, 29 Aug. 1932, Witsell Papers, emphasis in the original.

54. Ibid.

55. W. P. Witsell to J. D. Perry, 28 Sept. 1932, Witsell Papers; W. P. Witsell to J. D. Perry, 30 Sept. 1932, ibid.

56. W. P. Witsell to W. G. McDowell, 29 Aug. 1932, Witsell Papers.

57. W. G. McDowell to W. P. Witsell, 3 Sept. 1932, Witsell Papers.

58. J. R. Winchester, "A Letter from Bishop Winchester," *Arkansas Churchman,* Nov. 1932, 13–14.

59. E. W. Saphore, "Ecclesiastical Authority Addresses Bishops," ibid., Sept. 1932, 8–9.

60. T. E. Wood to S. H. Rainey and W. S. Simpson-Atmore, 31 Aug. 1932, Executive Council Papers.

61. T. E. Wood to J. D. Perry, 27 Aug. 1932, Executive Council Papers.

62. Although Williamson had the approval of a majority of the church's standing committees by the end of July, the Standing Committee of the Missionary District of Montana refused consent to his election.

63. *New York Churchman,* 24 Sept. 1932, 16.

64. "The Arkansas Election," *Living Church,* 10 Sept. 1932, 451–52.

65. S. G. Sanchez, letter to the editor, ibid., p. 447.

66. H. A. Stowell to T. E. Wood, 22 Aug. 1932, Executive Council Papers.

67. T. E. Wood to H. A. Stowell, 23 Aug. 1932, Executive Council Papers.

68. T. E. Wood to H. A. Stowell, 5 Sept. 1932, Executive Council Papers.

69. "The Plot Thickens—Another Conferite to the Rescue," *Arkansas Churchman,* Sept. 1932, 5–6.

70. A snippet on p. 9 of the November *Arkansas Churchman* enclosed these remarks regarding the Synod of the Southwest Province, recently concluded in St. Louis: "It is hoped that no one will observe the absence of any [*sic*] one from his accustomed place in the chancel at the opening service of the Synod." Wood was attacking Capers, who led in the opening service at the synod. The allusion, of course, is to Bishop Demby's experience the previous May.

71. T. E. Wood to V. E. Russum, 5 Sept. 1932, Executive Council Papers.

72. H. A. Stowell to T. E. Wood, 4 Nov. 1932, Executive Council Papers.

73. I take my interpretation of Walker's running critique of Rainey from Rainey's daughter, Carolyn (Carolyn Rainey Harris, interview by author, 1 Mar. 1991, Fayetteville, Ark., transcript).

74. "Replies to Holt," *Fayetteville Democrat,* n.d. [Aug. 1932], clipping, Executive Council Papers.

75. Sue Walker to T. E. Wood, 18 Aug. 1932, Executive Council Papers; Sue Walker to T. E. Wood, 18 Sept. 1918, ibid.

76. T. E. Wood to J. P. Brower, 9 Sept. 1932, Executive Council Papers.

77. T. E. Wood to V. E. Russum, 9 Sept. 1932, Executive Council Papers.

78. H. A. Stowell to T. E. Wood, 20 Sept. 1932, Executive Council Papers.

79. Carolyn R. Harris, interview by author, Fayetteville, Ark., 1 Mar. 1991.

80. W. P. Witsell to W. T. Capers, 17 Sept. 1932, Witsell Papers.

81. "Minutes of the Called Meeting of the Executive Council," 16 Sept. 1932, Executive Council Papers; Charles F. Collins to T. E. Wood, 17 Sept. 1932, ibid.; T. E. Wood to C. F. Collins, 19 Sept. 1932, ibid.; Elnathan Tartt to T. E. Wood, 27 Sept. 1932, ibid.

82. H. A. Stowell to T. E. Wood, 4 Nov. 1932, Executive Council Papers.

83. "Minutes of the Adjourned Called Meeting of the Arkansas Executive Council," 22 Nov. 1932, Executive Council Papers.

84. St. Paul's Episcopal Church, Newport, Arkansas, vestry resolution in support of the confirmation of Dean Williamson's election, n.d., Executive Council Papers.

85. J. D. Perry to H. A. Stowell, 19 Nov. 1932, Executive Council Papers.

86. Marguerite Gamble, interview by author, 14 May 1991, Little Rock, Ark., transcript.

87. William M. Green to W. P. Witsell, 29 Sept. 1932, Witsell Papers; W. P. Witsell to W. M. Green, 8 Oct. 1932, ibid.; W. M. Green to W. P. Witsell, 13 Oct. 1932, ibid.; Robert N. Spencer to F. B. T. Hollenberg, 11 May 1932, ibid.; Harry T. Moore to bishops, 29 Aug. 1932, Executive Council Papers.

88. J. B. Cheshire to W. T. Capers, 25 Aug. 1932, Witsell Papers, emphasis in the original.

89. Elmer N. Schmuck to W. P. Witsell, 13 Sept. 1932, Witsell Papers.

90. *Pittsburgh Courier,* 27 Aug. 1932; *Washington Afro-American,* 17 Dec. 1932; "The Very Reverend," *Crisis,* Feb. 1933, 40.

91. W. P. Witsell to the congregation of Christ Church, 25 Nov. 1932, Witsell Papers.

92. Here follows a tally of the bishops compiled primarily from correspondence in the Witsell Papers. While some bishops told how they voted, most did not. Nevertheless, quite a few votes can be deduced by way of the bishops' relationship to Witsell as revealed in the letters. Voting is indicated as "Y" (yes to confirmation), "N" (no to confirmation), "PY" (probably yes), "PN" (probably no), and "NI" (no indication). Some bishops gave reasons for their judgment and these are recorded after their respective votes as follows: "2A" (protest of 2 Aug.), "S" (strife or schism in Arkansas), "IA" (an internal affair), "W" (influenced by Witsell's judgment), "$" (the salary/bishop issue), and "IE" (insufficient evidence to deny confirmation). I also take the liberty of designating "[R]" for those bishops whose votes and/or opinions on the race question are not recorded but whose reputation for black advocacy and/or sympathy for Demby are a matter of record.

M. S. Barnwell, Idaho, PN; W
F. D. Bartlett, North Dakota, PN; W
G. A. Beecher, Western Nebraska, N; 2A
T. D. Bratton, Mississippi, N; $; [R]
B. Brewster, Maine, Y
H. Wyatt-Brown, Central Pennsylvania, PN
H. Burleson, Secretary to the Presiding Bishop, PN
W. T. Capers, West Texas, N; W; $; 2A; S
T. Casady, Oklahoma, N; 2A
J. B. Cheshire, North Carolina, N; S
C. D. Colmore, Puerto Rico, N; [R]
P. Cooke, Delaware, N; W
T. C. Darst, East Carolina, Y; IE
C. J. Davis, Western New York, PN
K. G. Finlay, Upper South Carolina, NI
C. Fiske, Central New York, NI

H. H. Fox, Montana, PN; W

J. M. Francis, Indianapolis, N; 2A

J. F. Freeman, Washington, N; 2A

F. Gailor, Tennessee, PN; S; [R]

F. D. Goodwin, Virginia (Coadjutor), NI

C. Gray, Northern Indiana, NI

W. M. Green, Mississippi (Coadjutor), Y; IA

E. J. Helfeinen, Maryland, Y; IE

F. B. Howden, New Mexico, N; 2A; S

S. A. Huston, Olympia, NI

F. Ingley, Colorado (Coadjutor), N; [R]

T. Jenkins, Nevada, PN; S

R. C. Jett, Southwest Virginia, N; 2A

F. F. Johnson, Missouri, N; 2A

I. P. Johnson, Colorado Y; IE; [R]

F. A. Juhan, Florida, N

B. T. Kemerer, Duluth (Coadjutor), N; W

A. W. Knight, New Jersey, PN

W. T. Manning, New York, PN; [R]

J. M. Maxon, Tennessee (Coadjutor), NI

W. G. McDowell, Alabama, N; 2A; W

H. J. Mikell, Atlanta, Y (possible reversal); W; [R]

W. Mitchell, Arizona, N; S; W

J. C. Morris, Louisiana, NI

G. F. Mosher, Philippines, PN; W

A. W. Moulton, Utah, PN; W

G. A. Oldham, Albany, N; $

E. L. Parsons, California, N; S; W

E. A. Penick, North Carolina (Coadjutor), Y (possible reversal); S; W

J. D. Perry, Rhode Island/Presiding Bishop, N; 2A; W; S

C. S. Quin, Texas, NI

F. F. Reese, Georgia, N; 2A; W; S

W. P. Remington, Eastern Oregon, N; 2A; S

W. L. Rogers, Ohio, NI

L. C. Sanford, San Joaquin, PN

W. Scarlett, Missouri (Coadjutor), NI

E. N. Schmuck, Wyoming, PN; S; W

E. C. Seaman, Northwest Texas, NI

H. K. Sherrill, Massachusetts, N; S; W

R. N. Spencer, West Missouri, PY; IE

G. C. Stewart, Chicago, N; W

E. M. Stires, Long Island, NI; [R]

W. B. Stevens, Los Angeles, NI
F. M. Taitt, Pennsylvania, N; $
A. S. Thomas, South Carolina, NI
H. St. George Tucker, Virginia, NI
J. C. Ward, Erie, NI
B. M. Washburn, New Jersey, NI
R. H. Weller, Fon Du Lac, NI
J. C. White, Springfield, NI
J. R. Winchester, Arkansas (Retired), Y; IE

7

Something Has Gone Out of Us

I was requested at one convention to take the Negro clergy and delegates
in the basement of the church for their communion while the Caucasians
would make theirs in the upper part of the church. I was to be the celebrant assisted by the rector of the parish, and the acting bishop would
be the celebrant in the main body of the church assisted by some of the
Caucasian clergy. I refused to have anything to do with such doings, and
then my hell on earth began, and to say I did not get scorched would be
prevarication.

—Demby, "Off of the Record"

Delegates to the 1933 Arkansas Episcopal convention descended on St. John's,
Fort Smith, like particles of the Oklahoma dust bowl—borne by an ill wind.
Most, if not all, of them knew that this convention could not pass without some
sort of confrontation arising from the events of the previous year. Would round
two be a greater cataclysm than round one? This could explain the absence of
about a third to a half of the lay delegates. No doubt the depressed economy
contributed to poor attendance, but it would be safe to assume that a good
many disillusioned laymen decided to save money, stay home, and let the
priests fight it out.

Of those who did go, there were three groups. The united supporters of Dean
John Williamson of Trinity Cathedral and acting Bishop Edwin Saphore composed the most visible and vocal contingent, whom we will call the "Cathedralites." They wanted to minimize the influence of the Reverend William P.
Witsell of Christ Church, Little Rock, and thereby assume control of the convention; they wanted to persuade any uncommitted delegates of the rightness
of their cause; and they wanted to reelect Dean John Williamson as bishop of
Arkansas. If only they could avoid the race issue, they reasoned, and elect
Williamson a second time, the House of Bishops would have to consent to his
election. Thus, Williamson and the Diocese of Arkansas would be vindicated;
a fitting riposte to Witsell and the House of Bishops. This was no covert plan,
its sponsors having declared their intentions as far back as the October 1932
Synod of the Southwest Province, held in St. Louis. Circulating among the
synod delegates, the Reverend William T. Holt, Williamson's nominator at the

1932 Arkansas convention, let it be known that he and his allies intended to reelect Williamson if the bishops should reject him. When the ax fell in November, the self-styled avengers of Dean Williamson and the Diocese of Arkansas immediately rallied to his reelection.[1] Opposing them was an equally powerful group identified with Witsell, which implicitly included Bishop Edward T. Demby and the black clergy of Arkansas. They were just as determined to prevent the election of Williamson. In the middle were those delegates not privy to the political schism in the Diocese of Arkansas and merely awaiting further developments.

Saphore identified with Williamson in much the same way he did at the 1932 convention; Williamson was a safeguard against Witsell. An alliance with Williamson was not only appropriate in light of the fact that both men were linked together through the cathedral, it also kept the electoral hopes of both men alive and precluded Witsell's election. Outwardly, Saphore was the peacemaker. Since his circular of September 1932, he had made a feeble attempt at reconciling the diocese, calling the Diocese of Arkansas to make peace with itself by way of his pastoral letter of 16 December 1932. At the direction of the Reverend Hanson A. Stowell, Saphore and the Executive Council invited the Reverends W. S. Simpson-Atmore and Samuel H. Rainey to appear and state their grievances before the council at its February 1933 meeting. Rainey and Atmore declined, presumably because they saw the council as more of a tribunal than an agency of reconciliation.

Meanwhile, Witsell laid plans to remake the diocese. Noting the ambivalent position of Stowell with regard to Dean Williamson's election and his evident desire to see the diocese put on a right footing—all political considerations aside—Witsell called on the Pine Bluff rector on 7 December 1932. Together they planted the seed of a new Diocese of Arkansas in the rectory of Trinity Church. Both men expressed their keen desire for a reconciliation within the Diocese of Arkansas and the election of a bishop from outside the diocese. Witsell declared that he had already given up all aspirations to be bishop of Arkansas and would in no wise allow himself to be nominated at any future convention. This was much to Stowell's liking. Both of them acknowledged the folly of any attempt to elect a bishop from among the Arkansas clergy; that is, Williamson and Saphore were totally unacceptable. Furthermore, any attempt to elect a bishop for the next one or two years would be unwise in light of political and economic considerations and should be thwarted, if at all possible. Saphore must be given more time to retire and anger must be allowed to subside in order that cooler heads might prevail in the election of Arkansas's next diocesan. In short, Witsell and Stowell agreed to forestall the elec-

tion of a new bishop until approximately 1934, when they would unite behind
a non-Arkansas candidate with a preliminary consensus in the Arkansas convention. Interestingly enough, Witsell suggested an alternative and more forceful plan, which is reminiscent of the charges laid against him before the 1932
convention. His idea was this: "to go ahead and secure a good strong man from
the outside, if we could get Saphore to agree to agree to retire upon the consecration of the man."[2] Both Witsell and Stowell thought it would be hard, if
not impossible, to obtain Saphore's resignation and this idea was tabled. However, Witsell, speaking to his friends in the episcopate, said that he was prepared to cut Saphore's salary to half the rate of his pension in order to force
the latter's retirement.[3]

Stowell and Witsell immediately got to work recruiting other Arkansas clergy
to what we will call the "Decembrist" cause. In January, they won a valuable,
if temporary, alliance with the Reverend Charles F. Collins of St. Luke's, Hot
Springs. Collins, the erstwhile center of the Saphore "phalanx," as Witsell described it,[4] arrived at the April 1933 convention solidly in agreement with Witsell and Stowell; no election at this time and absolutely no more public wran-
gling over the events of 1932.[5]

In early March, Witsell carried the cause to the opposition. Having heard
from Williamson's allies that Saphore planned to resign in order to remove the
fiscal impediment to Dean Williamson's election, Witsell wrote the bishop an
urgent letter asking if this were true. If so, said Witsell, everyone had a right to
know beforehand, since "there are those of us who are more convinced now
than ever that Williamson is not that man." He then dropped the most unlikely
hook of all: "In my opinion in view of the financial and other conditions in
this diocese it will be better for you to hold on for a while longer. I think that
the election ought to be deferred for at least a year and perhaps longer, but if
we must go into an election, which of course your retirement would force, then
I think that we must go outside of the diocese to secure a man."[6] He then announced his renunciation of all aspirations to be bishop of Arkansas. Saphore
wrote back that he had no intention of resigning. In late March, Witsell wrote
Williamson in what may have been their first contact since the confrontation
of September 1932. In a letter that was perhaps a little too condescending to
draw Williamson into a "brotherly conference," Witsell opened by explaining
to the dean that the 1932 election was "null and void." He then added that he
had decided not to be a candidate for bishop of Arkansas and, being free from
political considerations, had entered into a "perfect personal disinterestedness"
with regard to "the good of the diocese and the church at large." "I am won-
dering," he asked, "if you would be willing in the spirit of perfect forgetful-

ness of self and of renunciation of all personal ambitions to join with me in the united purpose and effort to promote the peace and highest welfare of the diocese?"[7] Williamson replied, "I see no need for such a conference as suggested by you and therefore must respectfully decline your invitation."[8]

Witsell's letter to Williamson had one serious flaw apart from its opening remarks, namely, Witsell wrote it. As with all of his suggestions, Witsell went right to the root of the problem with an appropriate call to action. Yet, as with many of his suggestions, he did not give due consideration to the condition of the recipient. Williamson, by all accounts, was a man heavily influenced by those who supported him, a group exemplified by Tom Wood and William T. Holt. Their indignation was still very much alive in the spring of 1933 and, judging by events, probably compounded the feelings of their former candidate. The dean apparently regarded himself as the offended party in the 1932 election and looked upon Witsell as the perpetrator of this injustice. Naturally, the suggestion of a public reconciliation was ludicrous in Williamson's eyes—insult added to injury. An apology would have been more appropriate. From Williamson's perspective, if anyone were to suggest a public reconciliation for the good of the diocese, it should be either himself or perhaps Bishop Saphore—anyone but Witsell. That being the case, the letter only added to Witsell's megalomaniac image and further alienated the Williamson/Saphore party by suggesting what would appear, for all practical purposes, to be the only wise course of action.

Thus, on the eve of the 1933 convention the Cathedralites came prepared to elect Williamson again and the Decembrists came prepared to stop them. Everyone else came prepared for fireworks and a good many of the laity just stayed home. It was a situation in need of a peacemaker, possibly an arbitrator assigned by the national church. So, at Witsell's suggestion, the presiding bishop, James DeWolf Perry, recruited one: the bishop of Mississippi, Theodore D. Bratton. Or, to be more specific, Perry obtained Bratton's consent and made the suggestion to Saphore, avoiding, of course, any mention of Witsell. Saphore agreed with Perry's suggestion and invited Bratton to preach at the opening service of the 1933 convention.

Bratton was an obvious choice. A bishop renowned regionally for his handling of a recent internal dispute in the Diocese of Louisiana and a man regarded as a sage on both sides of the color line, his coming to Fort Smith was good news to Arkansas's black clergy.[9] As noted in chapter 4, he was an unusually aggressive white bishop when it came to the development of black ministries. Bratton enjoyed the praise of Bishop Demby and that most outspoken of all black Episcopalians, the Reverend George F. Bragg, who lauded him from the pages of his *History of the Afro-American Group of the Protestant Episcopal Church.* If the color line were raised at the 1933 convention, as it well might be, the bishop of Mississippi represented the voice of moderation. Likewise, should there be an election, he might inspire the convention to a less violently partisan approach by virtue of his presence. He was, so to speak, the eyes of the church.

Once the convention assembled, the delegates went through the perfunctory motions of a diocesan convention, all the while waiting for the Cathedralites to make their move. Early in the proceedings, Collins moved "that any and all visiting clergymen be admitted to the courtesies of the floor."[10] The motion was adopted, thereby paving the way for Bratton's intervention, should the need arise. But the first day passed without a motion to elect a bishop, the Cathedralites seemingly inhibited by their lack of numbers and the absence of Tom Wood, their chief layman and secretary of the convention. Noticeably present, however, was the Reverend Smythe H. Lindsay, designated as an assistant to Trinity Cathedral. Lindsay, who had been living abroad for educational purposes, was technically disqualified from voting by reason of his nonresidency in Arkansas. Nonetheless, he came as a clergy delegate, presumably in the van of the Williamson party. When questioned by Witsell about this abridgement of church law, Saphore replied that he had passed on Lindsay's credentials in order to "avoid a row."[11]

As for Bishop Demby, it appears he came to this convention with uncharacteristic boldness. In his memoirs, he recalls three altercations with Arkansas conventions: the 1927 convention discussed in chapter 4, the 1932 convention discussed in chapter 5, and a third convention which someone, presumably representing the diocese and convention, advised him not to attend—but he did anyway.[12] I will venture that this third, unspecified convention was the 1933 assembly held at St. John's, Fort Smith. There are several reasons to justify this conclusion. Demby was manifestly persona non grata with the diocesan authorities as a result of the 1932 controversy and the people most offended by his protest were the people most intent on Dean Williamson's reelection, the same people responsible for organizing the 1933 convention. Rev. Charles D. Lathrop of St. John's and his congregation were avowedly pro-Williamson and welcomed the opportunity to reelect him at their home church. However, the black electoral presence, consisting of Demby and the Reverends James H. King, George G. Walker, and Robert J. Johnson, represented an obstacle. Furthermore, had Demby been warned to stay away, it would explain why Witsell alerted a few of the bishops prior to the convention: "Some of [Williamson's supporters] have been very active on the racial question."[13]

By the second day, the Cathedralites were frustrated. They found themselves clearly in the minority with no hope of initiating an election, let alone electing their candidate. But they took no action until the afternoon, when the convention had dwindled to perhaps twenty delegates and Witsell was safely on the bus en route to Little Rock. Stowell brought them to life when he moved that the salary of the secretary of the convention be reduced from $200 to $100 per annum. The motion passed and the fight was on. The friends of the secretary, Tom Wood, and Dean Williamson moved that the convention adopt a "Resolution of Regret" as follows:

> BE IT RESOLVED, that this convention go on record as deeply regretting the action of the House of Bishops, and be it further
>
> RESOLVED. that this convention restate its admiration, love and confidence in the life, virtue, and learning of the Very Rev. John Williamson and its belief in the strength of his spirituality, his executive ability, and the depth of his consecration as one particularly fitted to receive the Holy Orders of Bishop.[14]

The resolution was adopted, but not without a battle on the floor of the convention. Stowell and Collins, ever determined to put 1932 behind the diocese, protested vehemently, but to no avail. The Reverend E. W. Mellichampe, Witsell's 1932 nemesis on the race question, raised the color line on Williamson's behalf. In a brazen attempt to legislate the black clergy out of the Arkansas convention, Mellichampe argued that the laity of the Diocese of Arkansas were overwhelmingly opposed to black participation in the Arkansas convention. His hearers, however, were at least half clergy and most of them of a less reactionary persuasion regarding black participation. Ultimately, Mellichampe could not elicit a legislative response. Hearing later of Mellichampe's discourse, Witsell figuratively breathed a sigh of relief, telling Stowell, "It is well it did not go further."[15] After the convention, Witsell, Bratton, and Saphore made it a point to try to educate Mellichampe to a more liberal position before the 1934 convention. Mellichampe's behavior, said Witsell, ran counter to the prevailing trend in the Episcopal Church.[16] The black clergy, as was their usual practice, were not present on the second day of the convention.

Once again, the diocese had spoken—once again to its detriment. The official rendering of the 27 April confrontation is a model of editorial prerogative. According to the *Journal of the Sixty-First Annual Convention of the Protestant Episcopal Diocese of Arkansas,* "A resolution of regret introduced by Mr. R. W. Newell was adopted by a vote of more than two-thirds majority and a copy of said resolution ordered sent to each bishop in the church."[17] Meanwhile, Witsell disseminated copies of his March correspondence with Williamson to selected bishops, accompanied by a description of the circumstances surrounding the passage of the resolution of regret.[18] The friends of Dean Williamson were slow to realize an unwritten but unshakable truth of ecclesiastical polity. "Controversy," says J. Carleton Hayden, a prominent historian of black Episcopalians, "is generally regarded as bad form in the Episcopal Church."[19]

The pattern of the 1933 convention held true for the next five years and three episcopal elections. The delegates polarized around Williamson/Saphore and Witsell—the first trying to obtain an election, and the second trying to avoid an in-house candidate and elect a bishop from outside Arkansas. The problem for Witsell and Stowell was to select a candidate and promote his election while making it appear that any intended candidate was not Witsell's "man." This was done in the knowledge that open affiliation with Witsell could handicap their candidate or, worse still, make the election a race issue. Demby, Walker, Johnson, King, and, later on, the Reverend Thaddeus Martin, were generally regarded as supportive of Witsell's candidates, which was almost certainly the case. Even though they were disenfranchised from the legislative process, they found it necessary to attend every convention in the 1930s just in case the convention should proceed to an election unexpectedly. They never spoke of this publicly, of course, but the election of a capable bishop sympathetic to Arkansas's black ministries was high on their agenda.[20]

From 1932 to 1935, Demby struggled to remain afloat, ecclesiastically and emotionally, as national and local problems converged to undermine his ministry. For the second time in nine years, the General Convention challenged the credibility of his office, but this time the critique was more personal in nature. After the 1928 convention failed to act on the findings of the evaluation committee, as discussed in chapter 4, the proponents of the missionary district plan urged the 1931 General Convention to reconsider. The 1931 convention responded by appointing a committee to conduct a more general investigation into the status of African Americans in the Episcopal Church. The committee, which recommended against the plan, reported to the 1934 General Convention that there was no consensus among black Episcopalians regarding the missionary district plan and seriously questioned the advisability of electing black bishops at all. More specifically, the investigators, relying heavily upon their scrutiny of the nation's only black bishop, speculated that there was "some limitation in the Negro which makes him ineffective in the episcopate."[21]

The overtly racist and politically naive nature of this statement made cruel folly of Demby's situation. He was beset by money problems inherent to the national fiscal disaster, compounded by a petty and vicious political climate within the Diocese of Arkansas—whence came his support from the National Council. The income of the Colored Convocation withered with the Great Depression. The appropriations from the National Council for black ministries in Arkansas fell from a high of $9,807 for 1930 to $3,811 for 1936. Simultaneously, Demby's stipend fell from $3,000 to $1,838. The most precipitous drop occurred in 1933, a loss of $1,767, taking with it Bishop Demby's discretionary fund, which he had been using to help his two seminarians at Bishop Payne Divinity School.[22] To make matters worse, St. Philip's in Little Rock burned and had to be rebuilt in 1932, creating a substantial debt on that property. Nevertheless, Demby was able to reduce the original debt of $4,000 to $2,400 over the next year, leaving a total debt of $3,000 for black missions. There was also a nagging problem with money owed on the Dembys' home. A debt of $5,000 remained in 1933, representing the balance owed on the original purchase of the property in 1920. No agency of the Episcopal Church would assume the responsibility for paying it off. The diocese had purchased the house on behalf of the province, but if Demby's reports are any indication, the various sponsors of his ministry—diocese, province, and national council—could not or would not pay it off. Demby once suggested that the house be employed in part as a seminary for black priests in the Southwest, possibly a measure intended to deal with the debt as well. Nothing came of it. After 1932, the apostle of self-sufficiency was compelled to radically "thin out the soup." Simultaneously, the ramifications of the 1932 protest exacerbated the economic decline of the convocation. Bishop Frederick F. Bartlett, chairman of the National Council's Bi-Racial Sub-Committee on Negro Work, conducted another study in 1935 and took exception to the previous committee's estimate of Bishop Demby:

> He has been hampered in his work by circumstances beyond his control. At present he is not even consulted by Bishop Saphore on matters pertaining to Negro work. I found that he [Demby] did not even know what appropriations had been made by the National Council for Negro work in Arkansas. He may be lacking in initiative, but there has been little opportunity for him to demonstrate initiative in Arkansas. What chance has a suffragan anyway? . . . The treatment of Bishop Demby has been nothing less than shameful. . . . We certainly cannot expect results when the church hampers one of its principal leaders in this manner.[23]

To further illustrate the situation, just prior to the General Convention of 1934, Demby was mortified to find that his report for 1933 had never reached the National Council. He was responsible for filing a report every year by way of the secretary of the Arkansas convention, who would in turn forward it to the National Council along with all of the other mission information from Arkansas. Every triennium, the collective report would be published in the *Journal of the General Convention*. Demby insisted that he had faithfully submitted the 1933 report, but the diocese had failed to forward it. It was a particularly embarrassing and grievous matter in light of the remarks of the aforementioned committee and the fiscal disposition of the National Council. Slackness in one's presentation was an invitation to yet another budget cut.[24]

Demby entered the most difficult period of his life. Lewis A. Powell, a young man from St. Simon's, Topeka, whom Demby encouraged to join the ministry, stayed overnight with the Dembys while en route to Voorhees College in South Carolina. Powell was preoccupied with the long, dirty, and miserable trip in Jim Crow cars, but he could not help noticing that all was not well with his host. "Bishop Demby was very kind to me. . . . [Yet] I sensed that there was something amiss—that he was sort of like a man without a country. But he said nothing to me about it, of course. It was just there."[25] Just before Christmas 1933, Demby wrote a letter to retired Arkansas bishop James R. Winchester, describing the vexations of his ministry:

> I am now passing through deep waters and the waves are rough; at times they almost cover me—with the "cut," "re-cuts," and still cutting by the National Council with my same expenses, cost of living, it is most trying and difficult. So much so, I am only existing, not living, but I take my lot patiently, saying all the while, it is as our Lord would have it. The mission of the church to my people especially in the Southwest is not being supported. I know what you would do were you financially able, but your prayers to God raise up friends to help [so] this work will not be in vain. . . . at times, I think there is little chance for the church to make encouraging progress in Arkansas and there is not, unless we get a true man of God [for our bishop] with deep convictions and determination and strong personality, accompanied by the desire to practice the principles of the fatherhood of God and the brotherhood of man, such as you ever manifested while our diocesan bishop. Your leaving the diocese placed it in a most awkward condition. We are praying for the recovery from our present ecclesiastical dilemma.[26]

Meanwhile, the discord continued across the diocese, contributing to the demise, for instance, of the Winchester School for Mountain Boys on Huckleberry Mountain. After a fire destroyed the school in the summer of 1932, Bishop Saphore applied to the National Council for assistance in rebuilding it. In early 1933, a representative of the council wrote Witsell, asking for data on the school and an estimation of its value as a missionary enterprise. Witsell, in turn, wrote the Reverend Gustave Orth, the school's headmaster, asking Orth for the desired information, but not fully explaining why he needed it. Orth, it should be remembered, was a protégé of Saphore. In responding to Witsell, he was evasive and unwilling to divulge information until the Little Rock priest should declare his intent. When Witsell explained in a second letter that he needed the information for a possible benefactor of the school, Orth tarried to respond, he said, by reason of the flu, but indicated that he would continue to withhold the desired information until he could talk to Witsell face-to-face. However, Witsell, unwilling to indulge Orth's suspicions any further, had already recommended against the National Council's contributing to the school by reason of Orth's lack of credentials and his hesitancy to divulge information. Ultimately, the school on Huckleberry mountain closed, the victim of fire, economic depression, and, perhaps, schism.[27]

The stimulus driving all of this discontent was the election of Winchester's successor. The 1934 Arkansas convention balked at electing a bishop, when, according to Witsell, they sensed that there was too much political manipulation going on at the convention.[28] Later that same year, Witsell and Christ Church proposed "an informal conference of the clergy and lay representatives . . . of the diocese to be held for a family discussion of the welfare of the diocese," which Saphore declined. Numerically, Episcopal Arkansas was in a steep decline, showing 1,899 fewer baptized persons in 1935 than in 1934 and contributions falling by $24,500 during the same period. The total of $59,756 for 1935 constituted a drop of $65,000 since 1930.[29] Saphore's salary and Winchester's honorarium were both in arrears. In January 1935, Saphore threatened to withhold the sacrament of confirmation from Christ Church, Little Rock, if Christ Church refused to heed his ultimatum and pay its 1934 diocesan assessment in full by 6 February. However, when the day came, he recanted, persuaded by the counsel of Bishop Clinton S. Quinn of Texas.[30]

In April 1935, the Arkansas convention elected Saphore bishop of Arkansas. Witsell and company made an impassioned—and perhaps too impassioned— attempt to elect the Reverend Charles Clingman, a future bishop of Kentucky, and to prevent Saphore's election. Orth nominated Saphore, seconded by Collins. Stowell nominated Clingman, seconded by a layman, John D. Barlow, and Witsell. But Witsell's second went far beyond an enthusiastic endorsement of Clingman; it entailed a long speech deprecating Saphore for his unmitigated ambition to be bishop of Arkansas. Saphore, he said, looked upon the bishopric merely as a reward for a long and faithful ministry—not the higher call to service that it ought to be. He pled face-to-face, with the eighty-year-old suffragan, begging him to withdraw: "I believe that such is the truly Christian way, indeed the only Christian way out of our present situation, and in the name of our dear Lord, and for the sake of the church that he purchased with His own blood, I beg you with all humility and deep sincerity and earnestness to consider it seriously. If you think that the $1,500 that you would receive from the Church Pension Fund would not be sufficient to maintain you, I for one, would be willing to readjust our budget to add something to it." "[Saphore's] only response," said Witsell, "was [to say] that it was the first time that he had ever been accused in the name of the Lord."[31] Saphore won on the first ballot. Witsell was appalled. He contemplated circularizing against the election, and went so far as to recapitulate the confrontation on the floor of the convention for the benefit of some of his friends in the bishopric. Yet, in all his correspondence, he never took into account that Saphore may have capitalized on a wave of sympathy inspired by the confrontation itself. Had Saphore withdrawn, it would have been an admission that he was the selfish, miserly old man that Witsell had implied that he was. Surely, the bishop's supporters and those whose votes were undecided must have sensed this. The aforementioned fracas over Christ Church's diocesan assessment may have also mitigated against Witsell's cause. At any rate, the bishops counseled the rector of Christ Church to let the majority rule and to bear the difficulties incumbent to Saphore's election patiently.[32]

The situation became more malleable in 1936–37 due to several unexpected developments. First of all, Saphore suffered a heat stroke in July 1936, which seriously debilitated him. He apparently intended to remain in office long enough to promote Williamson's election, but Witsell and Stowell were determined to postpone any election until after the bishop's retirement. Burdened with his physical infirmity, Saphore retired at the 1937 General Convention. Second, Mellichampe left the diocese in 1936, substantially reducing the influence of the color line with regard to the election of Saphore's successor. Perhaps that would better explain why Holt, Mellichampe's former ally and Demby's former enemy, joined the Reverend Harley Bullock of Good Shepherd, Forrest City, in making an unprecedented egalitarian gesture at the 1937 Arkansas convention. They offered a constitutional amendment in favor of placing a black clergyman on the Arkansas Executive Council in order that the interests of the Colored Convocation be given due consideration. However, the Committee on Constitution and Canons of the 1938 convention recommended against the amendment because "any member of the clergy or laity had the privilege of appearing before the Executive Council at any time."[33] Holt and Bullock failed, but it was a significant gesture and a sign of things to come. The Reverend William T. Holt II recalls that his father enjoyed a "cordial" relationship with Demby.[34]

Despite Holt's proposal and the cessation of open racial hostilities after 1933, the banter passing among the white delegates indicates that the prejudice against black membership in the convention continued unabated, though understated. For instance, some Arkansas Episcopalians speculated that Saphore's lack of executive ability could be attributed to his having been "touched with the tar brush," which is to say, he had African American blood.[35]

Demby's ministry was not without its positive aspects during the Depression years. The Reverend Robert J. Johnson renovated St. Mary's, Hot Springs, which was doing a brisk business as an employment agency, and Johnson's daughter, Elnora, established a kindergarten at St. Mary's after her graduation from the University of Kansas. Christ Church Parochial and Industrial School continued to thrive in spite of the general economic decline, and enrollment at St. Philip's Junior College in San Antonio mushroomed as a result of its change from a girls' parochial school to a coeducational junior college in 1927. Always planning for growth, Demby purchased two lots in the Pankey Addition of West Little Rock in the early 1930s with the intent of raising a community/retreat center in this upscale black suburban development. He was not able to build the center, but the purchase demonstrates that the he was still thinking aggressively. Likewise, he made one last nationwide canvass in 1938 in hopes of making some valuable additions to work in the Southwest. Most notably, he tried to establish a badly needed black clinic in Forrest City under the auspices of the Episcopal Church. Drs. William Cason and C. S. Banks, and a nurse, Mrs. C. S. Banks, were already in place and had been treating the students of Christ Church Parochial and Industrial School for some time. Unfortunately, this, too, failed to materialize. Demby faithfully promoted the evangelical Forward Movement throughout Mississippi, Tennessee, and the entire Southwest Province, with particular emphasis on high schools and colleges. However, judging by his remarks, we would guess that the most cherished of his innumerable speaking engagements during these years was the fiftieth anniversary celebration of the Conference of Church Work Workers among the Colored People, convened at St. James's, Baltimore, in 1934. Demby had the pleasure of visiting with his erstwhile critic and longtime friend, the Reverend George F. Bragg, and the honor of preaching the opening sermon.[36]

Demby's ambition to raise up a "native ministry" to the region finally met with some success during the Great Depression. The Reverends Joelzie Thompson, James Temple, Thaddeus Martin, and William H. Bright-Davies, representing the dioceses of Oklahoma, Kansas, Arkansas, and Texas respectively, were ordained into the Episcopal ministry. Initially, Demby supported Temple, a product of St. Simon's, Topeka, and Thompson, a native of Memphis, at Bishop Payne Divinity School by way of his discretionary fund. However, it appears that they had to make some necessary adjustments when the National Council suspended the fund in 1932. Temple transferred and ultimately graduated from the Episcopal Seminary of the Southwest, Austin, Texas. Thompson graduated from Bishop Payne, but only after transferring from the Diocese of Arkansas to the Missionary District of Oklahoma.[37] Bright-Davies and Martin also followed the prescribed route for black seminarians, graduating from Bishop Payne in 1930 and 1936, respectively. Bishop Quinn of Texas sponsored Bright-Davies and Demby sponsored Martin, the only black seminary graduate produced by Arkansas during Demby's tenure. Like Temple and Lewis Powell, Demby's aforementioned houseguest, Martin was the progeny of St. Simon's, Topeka.[38] Bright-Davies, Temple, and Thompson were ordained to the ministry by their diocesan bishops, but Demby ordained Martin, who, interestingly enough, matriculated through the Board of Examining Chaplains of the Diocese of Arkansas. Everything else being parallel, one would think that some kind of similar committee attached to the Colored Convocation would have scrutinized Martin, but it was not so.[39]

The nation's only black bishop was certainly the wiser for his troubles. His annual reports, formerly a model of attention to detail with a determined air of progress about them, became more reflective and more generalized after 1933, and in two cases were only a half of a page in length versus the usual two to four pages. They became more like exhortations or sermons addressed to the "one, holy, catholic, and apostolic church" and less like statistical evidence of progress. By contrast, the "official acts" or "essential acts" sections swelled with entries, describing his emissarial relationship to the Episcopal Church. His agenda became one of preaching rather than proving. Demby realized that a lack of knowledge about black ministries was not the impediment to white involvement that he had thought it was in 1918. The true impediment was something deeper, a prejudice seated in the heart and not in the intellect.

Demby's personal situation improved dramatically in the fall of 1935 when Bishop James M. Maxon of Tennessee requested that he broaden his jurisdiction to include the Diocese of Tennessee. Maxon asked Demby to supervise all "Negro work" in Tennessee, giving special attention to the improvements underway at Hoffman-St. Mary's Industrial Institute, renamed the Gailor Institute in honor of the late bishop. Working hand-in-hand with Maxon and Dr. Robert Patton, field secretary for American Church Institute for Negroes, Demby supervised a substantial renovation of the old campus. The Dembys moved from Little Rock to Memphis, delighted to be back in their southern city of choice.

Outside of his jurisdiction, Demby's most rewarding experience was his work on behalf of the Joint Commission on Negro Work, from 1937 to 1940. As a member of the commission, Demby had the opportunity to contribute the wisdom of his years as he and his colleagues tried to formulate a national agenda for black ministries. The commission's efforts led directly to the establishment of the office of secretary for "Negro work" at the 1940 General Convention. The creation of the new office, says Harold Lewis, indicated a "shift in the Church's strategies regarding race relations."[40] Before the advent of the position, the Conference of Church Workers among the Colored People spoke to the church on behalf of black ministries. With the appointment of the the first secretary to that position in 1943, the conference had "a friend at court, an advocate, someone who could represent their interests at the highest echelons of the church." Not only did the secretary speak to the church on behalf of black ministries, he also spoke to black ministries on behalf of the church.[41]

Demby's retirement was part and parcel of the reconciliation of the Diocese of Arkansas, a three-part drama taking place in 1938–39. With Saphore out of the way, the Decembrists settled on the Reverend Arthur R. McKinstry of Texas, a future bishop of Delaware, as their candidate. Witsell and Stowell walked a fine line in lobbying on behalf of McKinstry, trying to amass support without publicly identifying with him. In fact, they had become so discreet in choosing their candidates that they eschewed naming McKinstry even in their private correspondence.[42] They were so successful in cloaking their intentions that one supporter of Dean Williamson even wrote Witsell a letter, warning him, confidentially, that McKinstry was a heavy-handed, ultra-high churchman who would try to remake Episcopal Arkansas in his own image.[43] Williamson was the opposition's candidate. He retained the loyal support of several important clergy in Arkansas, most notably the Reverend C. F. Collins, famous with regard to Saphore's election in 1935, and the Reverend C. C. Burke of St. Andrew's, Marianna. Tom Wood was still the secretary of the convention and still in the vanguard of Williamson's reelection hopes. Noticeably absent from the Cathedralites, however, were two of Williamson's chief allies, Reverend C. D. Lathrop of St. John's, Fort Smith, who was very pro-McKinstry, and Holt, who had left the Diocese of Arkansas for a Navy chaplaincy.

The 1938 Arkansas convention took place at St. John's, Helena, which had as its rector the Reverend Frank Walters, a newcomer to Arkansas and an enemy of its partisan squabbles. Richard Allin, the perennial "Our Town" columnist for the *Arkansas Gazette* and the *Arkansas Democrat Gazette,* was a young communicant of St. John's at the time. He remembers that there were complaints on the part of some members of St. John's about the presence of the black clergy at the opening service of the convention. However, it seems that Walters was able to quell the discontented and their complaint died peaceably.[44] Richard's brother, John M. Allin, a future presiding bishop of the Episcopal Church, was a page at the 1938 convention. Bishop Robert N. Spencer of West Missouri, one of the few bishops to consent to Williamson's 1932 election, played much the same role as Bishop Bratton had in 1933, a moderating presence representing the church at large. Demby had participated in his consecration.

The convention did not begin the election process until late on the first day, 27 April. The result was a deadlock. McKinstry began with a slight edge in clergy, Williamson with a slight edge in laity. On the second ballot, McKinstry technically won the election by two lay votes and one clerical vote. However, Witsell, having learned many hard lessons about close and divisive elections, was not content with this and he, along with the rest of the convention, insisted that the balloting continue until there was a substantial consensus. The third ballot deadlocked the clergy, 9-9. Presumably, five of McKinstry's nine votes were black clergy. The convention adjourned for the evening and resumed the election the next morning. The fourth ballot merely reaffirmed the previous day's deadlock, McKinstry leading the clergy by three and Williamson leading the laity by three. The convention recessed and the two orders convened separately in hopes of resolving the stalemate. At this time, Witsell called McKinstry and asked him to withdraw on the condition that Williamson do the same.[45] Both candidates concurred. When the convention reassembled, Stowell nominated the Reverend Edward H. Eckel of Oklahoma and Williamson nominated the Very Reverend Claude W. Sprouse, dean of Bishop Spencer's cathedral in Kansas City. Then, to everyone's surprise, Witsell, who had worked with Sprouse in Texas, rose and emphatically seconded his nomination. Another delegate motioned that the convention give Williamson a rising vote of thanks for withdrawing in the name of "Diocesan harmony."[46] On the fifth ballot, Sprouse was elected unanimously. The convention rose spontaneously and sang the Doxology.[47]

Their joy, however, was tempered by Sprouse's response, as he declined the election. His reasons, although he did not specify them publicly, were primarily fiscal. For Sprouse, the Arkansas episcopate represented a substantial loss in income and, especially, benefits. Yet it was here that the Diocese of Arkansas made a long-overdue discovery. As previously noted, the in-house election of 1932 had been motivated by the fear of just this kind of declination. Now, they found out how little it mattered.[48]

Initially, there was dismay, turning in some cases to despair. The Standing Committee of the diocese contemplated asking the House of Bishops to reduce Arkansas from a diocese to a missionary district in order to ease the financial burden of supporting Arkansas's next bishop. Aghast at the possibility, Demby wrote Witsell, "It will be an everlasting shame to all of us: it would be a disgrace, greater, than if it elected me as the diocesan. (Now laugh, for that is what I am doing.) It would be a huge joke." The suggestion perished in committee.[49]

A Special Convention was slated for June 1938 at Christ Church, Little Rock. The Decembrists, including a clear majority of the clergy, made thorough preparations for the election of their candidate, the Reverend Richard B. Mitchell of Alabama. Demby was confident enough of the outcome to circularize Walker, Johnson, Martin, and King in a letter, asking them to join him in voting for Mitchell. He urged them to vote with the white majority in the upcoming election, saying, "if not, we will be held responsible for destroying the present good-will, purpose, and action of the clergy and laity of our diocese, which we cannot afford to do."[50] He extrapolated generously on Mitchell's virtues but, true to the times, avoided naming him. Finally, he requested that his four Arkansas subordinates declare themselves beforehand, confidentially. It appears that he polled them and passed on the results to Witsell.[51]

As the special convention drew near, there was some anxiety among the Decembrists that Williamson might allow himself to be nominated again. As Demby wrote: "I do hope he will not disturb the present peace, harmony, and unity in the diocese and thus make our last condition more serious and damaging than any time during the past several years."[52] Witsell linked his concern over Williamson's plans to a more general concern about the influence of women in the convention. He wrote Stowell, "I am glad to note that you favor an Executive Session of the Convention for our election. There is another point to be considered in that connection and that is that it will be far better that we have no gallery as you know the women did a lot of electioneering at Newport on the floor of the church, and I am told that the same thing happened in Helena, in behalf of Williamson. One person [described] the thing this way, 'the women in the back of the church were simply tearing their hair over the matter.'"[53]

Ultimately, Williamson refused to be nominated and Walters nominated Mitchell, seconded by Burke and W. Henry Rector, a layman from Christ Church. Mitchell won a resounding victory over the runner-up on the first ballot.

The bishop-elect, who had nearly been elected the bishop of Alabama the previous year, came to Arkansas in the summer of 1938 in order to look over the diocese, ascertain its needs, and explain the scope and nature of his ministry. He was greatly troubled at the disheveled state of many of the black mission properties and at the semi-pariah status of the Colored Convocation. He told his hosts unequivocally that he would be bishop of all Arkansas Episcopalians or none of them.[54] He met no objections. This, of course, meant that it was time for Bishop Demby to retire. Relieved to have a diocesan bishop committed to turning Arkansas's five black missions into independent congregations, Demby gladly agreed to step aside.

Mitchell was consecrated in October 1938 at Trinity Cathedral. According to diocesan lore, Demby participated in one of the more poignant consecrations of any bishop, anywhere. Originally, he was not scheduled to lead in the service. The program of the service does not indicate his participation, nor does Margaret Sims McDonald's *White Already to Harvest.* However, the "Roll of the House of Bishops" and the *Living Church Annual* show that Mitchell did, in fact, make a last-minute change to include Demby—and Saphore. The story goes that Mitchell gathered all the participants in a room and briefed them on their respective parts in the service. Turning to Bishop Demby, he said, "And you, Bishop Demby, will read the epistle." Demby, they say, wept. He had not led in the worship of the Arkansas convention since October 1931. Mitchell added, "Bishop Demby, we are all brothers in Christ."[55]

Demby's retirement became effective as of the Arkansas convention of February 1939. He submitted a report to the convention, but did not deliver it in person. In it, he indulged in one relatively brief reflection on his twenty years in the episcopate: "[Although they] were years of personal sacrifices, handicaps, discouragements, and misunderstandings accompanied with doubts and fears, within and without, I never took my eyes off of the Cross of Christ, nor lost faith in Him who promised to be [with] the bishops and priests of the church until the end of the world; when problems became perspicacious I was encouraged by the Reverend Clergy and the faithful lay workers, men and women, and I was able to press on in the work."[56] By contrast, his final address to the Colored Convocation was a voluminous exposition on the world outside the church unrivalled since his *United States and the Negro* speech of Key West in 1907. Speaking to his flock gathered at St. Andrew's, Pine Bluff, Demby stated: "The truth is that no bishop has been forced to have the experiences that I have, and my prayer is that none ever will." Once again, he avowed that the encouragement of clergy and laity of the convocation had sustained him through hard times. He exhorted his hearers to remain faithful to the "Episcopal Church, our Zion, a true part of the Holy Catholic and Apostolic Church of the Ages," to reject Communism, to be fiscally responsible with appropriations and generous in giving, to "keep . . . educationally and intelligently fit," to be "more concerned in the saving of [their] young people" as they strove to improve their lives, and to give Bishop Mitchell their wholehearted support.[57]

Bishop Demby retired at the age of seventy. He and Mrs. Demby lived in Cleveland for most of the remainder of their lives. Yet he was not finished with Arkansas and Bishop Mitchell. They had an appointment with the 1940 General Convention.

In keeping with the liberal nomenclature of the day, Mitchell reconstituted the Colored Convocation of Arkansas into the Negro Convocation of Arkansas and placed it under his direct supervision. He exemplifies what I will call the "new realism" with regard to black ministries. It was a trend that began to emerge in the late 1930s, as evidenced by Demby's reports to the Arkansas convention. Mitchell carried it forward with bracing clarity. In 1940, he offered this synopsis of the black suffragan experiment in the Southwest Province.

> When I took over supervision of [Negro] work, I found the property in bad repair, some of it under mortgage, and the clergy receiving salaries lower than a Christian agency should be willing to offer. . . . We should remember that some 20 years ago Arkansas embarked on the experiment of the racial episcopate and elected a suffragan for Negro work. The logic of that experiment was to set our Negro work off as a separate entity, turn it over to the suffragan, and wish him well with it, and let the national church foot the bills. . . . Bishop Demby was an able and godly man; he did as well as any member of his race could have done under the handicaps he encountered. The logic of the experiment ran its undeviating course—and the result is what I have tried to summarize briefly above. The experiment is over and our diocese is an administrative unity again—and our Negro work is one of my greatest problems, thanks to the experiment. It were better if the experiment had not been tried; and that is no reflection on Bishop Demby.[58]

Having admonished the Arkansas convention for its error, Mitchell proclaimed an end to all plans to segregate the church. In this he did not speak only for himself; rather, he spoke for the bishops and black Episcopalians of both North Carolina and Arkansas, the two dioceses that had elected black suffragan bishops. The black clergy of both dioceses had already voiced their opposition to any renewal of the suffragan bishop plan.[59] Furthermore, Mitchell, Bishop Edwin A. Penick of North Carolina, and all of Arkansas's black Episcopalians were opposed to the passage of the missionary district plan at the 1940 General Convention. "Perhaps the strongest voices raised in opposition to [the missionary district plan]," said Mitchell, "are those of the Bishops of North Carolina and Arkansas. . . . [Should the plan be approved], it would spell disaster for the church's work among the colored race in the South."[60]

All southern bishops, it seems, were ready to acknowledge the failure of ecclesiastical segregation, thus far, but they were sharply divided when it came to choosing a course of remedial action. Their universal theme was what we will call the "new realism." Weary of the deceptive language used to justify the segregation of black Episcopalians, they aspired to, at the very least, a more honest solution to the problem of race, and, in so doing, came perilously close to making the confession of moral inadequacy that W. E. B. Du Bois had urged upon them in 1907. Take, for instance, Bishop James M. Maxon of Tennessee. Maxon was an exponent of segregation because he regarded an integrated church as an impossibility. Therefore, he reasoned, let us stop pretending that our various forms of diocesan segregation are working to the benefit of black ministries—which they are not—and go ahead and constitute the black missionary districts for which they keep asking.[61] Bishop Middleton B. Barnwell of Georgia emphatically agreed with Maxon and wrote Demby a letter on behalf of the pro-missionary bishops. Barnwell explained that he was in favor of the missionary district plan out of "only one desire, and that is to widen the door of service and opportunity to the Negro in the South."[62] In contravention to Barnwell and a majority of the southern bishops were Mitchell, his close friend, C. C. J. Carpenter of Alabama, Edwin A. Penick of North Carolina, and Demby, all of whom opposed the missionary plan because they believed the suffragan plan had demonstrated the fallacies underlying racial segregation. Thus the missionary district campaign was once again in full swing going into the 1940 General Convention, but the impetus, not to mention the opposition, had changed somewhat. The Province of Sewanee drew up the appropriate canon and submitted it to the convention with the blessing of the Conference of Church Workers.

The greatest irony of Bishop Demby's life was that he, more than anyone else, ended the long campaign for the missionary district plan. He did it with a speech to the General Convention of 1940. Many Episcopalians assumed that he spoke against the plan because of his experiences in the Southwest Province, but he turned against the plan that he had cherished so long because he believed that the office of suffragan bishop, as distinct from the suffragan bishop plan, offered the greater hope for a more catholic church. Black suffragan bishops, he saw, need not be elected to separate all-black jurisdictions. Rather, they could be elected as all suffragans are elected—by diocesan conventions—and serve the diocesan bishop in whatever capacity the diocesan should designate. Of course, this would probably mean oversight of black ministries within the diocese, but this "conventional" black suffragan would be representing the diocese and its bishop as part of the diocese's comprehensive design for ministries. His salary would be the responsibility of the diocese, as would the expenses entailed by his ministry. Thus, the ecclesiastical color line that rendered Demby's ministry so anomalous would be withdrawn and the integrity of episcopal government restored.

In opposing the Sewanee legislation, Demby represented not only himself but a countervailing trend embodied in the Joint Commission on Negro Work. The 1937 General Convention had directed the joint commission to conduct yet another investigation into the desirability of the missionary district plan and report back to the 1940 General Convention. The stimulus for this new study was the group of southeastern bishops as described above, acting in concert with the Conference of Church Workers. The bishops, representing the Province of Sewanee, lobbied intensely for a constitutional amendment at the 1940 General Convention. The proposed legislation (article 6, section 6) was designed to allow black churches that wanted to form missionary districts to secede from their dioceses. Simultaneously, the General Convention would be empowered to create a missionary district from the seceded churches. The new district would, in turn, elect a black bishop. The proponents of section 6 maintained that they embraced this method as the most feasible means of stimulating the growth of black Episcopal churches in the South. However, the Joint Commission, including, of course, Bishop Demby, judged section 6 to be a violation of the true faith. They contended "that the ideal of the church is not a policy of segregation, but a living principle of integration."[63]

Bishop Demby had had a change of heart about the missionary district plan. When asked his reasons for the turnabout, he said he was influenced by the following: the report of the Evaluation Committee of the National Council, 1927; the report of the Joint Commission on the Status of the Negro in the Church, 1937; chapter 6 of Bishop Creighton's *Our Heritage*; Bishop Theodore D. Bratton's *Wanted: Leaders!*; a collage of erroneous articles written on "Negro work" in the church; and the example of the newly constituted United Methodist Church, which he considered the most decisive argument of all.

In May 1939, the Methodist Episcopal Church (North) and the Methodist Episcopal Church, South, and the Methodist Protestant Church merged to form the United Methodist Church. Prior to 1939, the greatest impediment to unification had been the status of over three hundred thousand black members of the M.E. Church (North) and their two black bishops. The M.E. Church, South, wanted the black Methodists to form a separate denomination as the price of unification. The northern Methodists and the black Methodists would not relinquish the point. Finally, the two denominations effected a compromise whereby the black Methodists were consolidated into a "Central Jurisdiction." The Central Jurisdiction was the political equivalent of the other five white jurisdictions of the United Methodist Church, but, unlike them, it was constituted along racial lines instead of regional boundaries.

Black Methodists felt compelled to accept the arrangement, whether they approved of it or not—and a majority of them did not. Heretofore they had found limited satisfaction in a government very much like the Episcopalians' missionary district plan. Their all-black conferences were represented by black delegates and black bishops at the national level in a segregated government that had a certain elasticity to it. In 1928, for instance, Bishop Robert E. Jones, Demby's counterpart in the M.E. Church, presided over the M.E. General Conference. However, after two decades of the "Methodist missionary district plan," black Methodists had experienced a change of heart. According to David Reimers, "By the 1930s . . . most Negroes were asking more of their church, and a majority of them opposed the scheme of unification, calling it a step backward in race relations and labeling it racial segregation."[64] Greater black participation, however, ran contrary to the will of the white Methodist majority, who, being intent on unification, were more inclined to segregate than they had ever been. Despite the fact that the Central Jurisdiction retained national representation for black Methodists, the demarcation between black and white Methodists was made more rigid in order to appease southern white Methodists. Thus, for Jones and his colleagues, things were getting worse instead of better. Jones, who had been party to unification proceedings for over two decades and had agreed to the 1939 compromise, reconsidered when he found himself in the minority among his people. At the 1939 unification convention, he angrily declared the Central Jurisdiction to be a "Jim Crow body."[65] David D. Jones, educator and brother of Bishop Jones, was equally angry, "Everyone knows this plan is segregation, and segregation in the ugliest way, because it is couched in such pious terms. . . . This plan turns its back on the historic attitude of the Methodist Episcopal Church."[66] Ultimately, the majority of the church's black Methodists decided, in the words of Bishop Jones, to make "the best of a bad bargain."[67] They continued to do so until 1964, the year of the Civil Rights Act, when the General Conference voted to abolish the Central Jurisdiction by 1968.

The reaction of the black Methodists aroused Demby's fears of a resurgence of interest in George A. McGuire's African Orthodox Church, should the missionary district plan be enacted. The AOC, which numbered approximately twenty thousand souls at its height, fragmented and lost members after McGuire's death in 1934, because of quarrels between its leaders and perhaps a greater black advocacy on the part of the white Episcopal bishops. The actions of Bishop Mann of Florida and Bishop William T. Manning of New York helped curb the appeal of the AOC where it was most successful, among the disaffected West Indian Anglicans in the New York and Miami areas. Demby wrote Barnwell, leader of the Sewanee bishops, forecasting a new exodus of black Episcopalians into the AOC, should section 6 prevail.[68]

On the eve of the 1940 gathering of the House of Bishops, Demby's perception of black Episcopal interests could be summarized this way: one does not segregate to integrate. The ultimate outcome of all legislation on black participation in the church must be integration, the only acceptable theological solution. Voluntary segregation merely begets more segregation. When blacks agree to segregation, any doubts that white people entertain about this unchristian policy are largely dispelled. Segregation, therefore, changes from "necessary and temporarily acceptable" to "good." Thus, voluntary black participation in segregation, even with the intent of restoring unity at some future date, makes segregation stronger; it removes the moral "sting" of racial discrimination. So, the only right and Christian course is to integrate as far as is socially acceptable and "keep the bow pointed into the wind," so to speak— gentle, but unrelenting. One does not sacrifice orthodoxy for the expedient.

Therefore, at the 1940 General Convention held in Kansas City, Demby admonished a rapt House of Bishops: "For twenty-two years I have been sitting in this House of Bishops, and this is the first time I have spoken; the problems brought before you have not been concerned, for the most part, with Negroes, but this matter does. If the request of the Fourth Province for a missionary district for Negroes is passed, it will be the greatest setback to our Negro work it has ever had. . . . We want Negro bishops, but as suffragans working as assistants of the diocesans, helpers of the diocesans."[69]

The bishops of Arkansas, Alabama, and North Carolina gave Demby their enthusiastic support from the podium and, in one of the more impassioned sessions of the House of Bishops, the missionary district legislation was voted down, 54-37. The consensus of those present was that the black suffragan's speech ensured its defeat. Demby was lauded by many black Episcopalians and criticized by others who thought he should have supported it. The missionary district plan was never submitted to the House of Bishops after 1940.

The 1940 General Convention was the death knell of ecclesiastical segregation in the Episcopal Church. Indeed, the convention established a national precedent by calling for an end to all forms of racial discrimination at future General Conventions. Challenged by the Reverend Shelton H. Bishop of New York, the General Convention passed a resolution to this effect.

With the tone thus set by the General Convention, southern dioceses gradually began to desegregate their respective conventions. None is more representative of the trend than the Diocese of Arkansas. In 1941, Bishop Mitchell began dismantling the suffragan experiment by an intermediate step. He appointed the Reverend James H. King as dean of the Negro Convocation and piloted an amendment through the Arkansas convention guaranteeing the convocation representation in the same body. From 1941 to 1947, the Negro Convocation elected one clergy and three lay representatives to represent it at each Arkansas convention.

Mitchell was an enthusiastic and skillful advocate for the convocation. He adjured Arkansas's white Episcopalians to make good on their alleged commitment to black ministries and help make the missions viable and independent parishes. He began by putting new roofs on practically every one of them and found benefactors to help with specific projects. In 1944, for instance, the Reverend Bravid W. Harris, the first secretary for "Negro work," toured Arkansas and helped with repairs and improvements on the black missions. He also helped in the redeployment of Arkansas's black clergy.

Mitchell sorely needed black priests. By 1941, Robert J. Johnson had transferred to North Carolina, Martin had transferred to San Francisco, and Walker had gone into semi-retirement for health reasons. Mitchell responded by ordaining the Reverend Francis G. Johnson, son of Robert Johnson, and recruiting black clergy from outside the diocese—namely, the Reverend Augustus C. Roker, already mentioned in chapters 2 and 4, the Reverend Joelzie Thompson of Oklahoma, and the Reverend James C. Jackson of St. Philip's, Dallas. All the while, he kept the interests of the Negro Convocation before the Arkansas convention with the idea of getting the white delegates used to the idea of desegregation.

By 1946, he felt the diocese was ready to pass the necessary amendments and incorporate Arkansas's black Episcopalians into the diocesan convention. He prepared the delegates to the 1946 convention with a brief history of Episcopal segregation in Arkansas, describing how things had been and how he felt they ought to be:

> Bishop [William M.] Brown, being a Northern man, felt that he brought a freshness to the [question of black inclusion] which made him competent to know all the answers to race relations. He developed a pessimism as to the capacities and future of the Negro and believed that the only solution was to wall off each race

from the other completely—evidently not realizing that our only hope of getting along together is in a common understanding, each race's sharing its best with the other, and a mutual respect for the genius of each race, working out our common destiny through cooperation on the high plane of the Christian religion. . . . We have just won a war for the preservation of human rights and the sanctity of the human personality. There were white regiments and Negro regiments and Japanese-American regiments; but they all belonged to the same army. We have white congregations and Negro congregations, but we all belong to the same church. In all Christian brotherliness, let's face it and make our basic law conform to it.[70]

Mitchell, however, was somewhat of an anomaly. Despite all of his activities on behalf of the black missions, many clergymen, white and black, remember him as "old school." This is best understood by his response to charges that he advocated "social equality" in the Arkansas convention. Again and again, Mitchell found it necessary to make the distinction between ecclesiastical equality in the convention and "social equality." He was not, he said, an advocate of social equality. "It is quite clear to me that if the Lord wanted the distinctions between the races rubbed out on a 'social equality' basis . . . He would never have created the different races in the first place."[71] Likewise, Mitchell had to correct the *Arkansas Gazette* in 1946 for propagating the myth that he intended to consolidate all the black missions into nearby white churches. Just before the 1947 convention passed the amendments into law, he reminded the assembled delegates that he had been promised desegregation as a precondition to his coming to Arkansas and reassured them one last time: "There seems to be some undercover work going on to defeat these amendments by confusing the issue . . . and dragging the red herring of 'social equality' across the trail. . . . You are voting on but one issue: Christian justice concerning representation in our legislative body, the diocesan convention. Vote as Christian men, guided by Christian principles."[72]

Meanwhile, King, who served as Mitchell's emblem of progress on the desegregation issue, made the same distinction on that most delicate of "social equality" issues—the common meal. Asked about the separate eating arrangements incumbent to diocesan conventions, he joked that the black delegates could eat more and better by going to a nearby black restaurant.[73] On a more serious note, however, one lifelong member of Trinity Cathedral remembers a certain clergy conference held in Little Rock. When the white clergy adjourned to the bishop's house for lunch, King stayed behind and sat on the steps of the church, awaiting their return.

However "old school" Mitchell may have been, he and King were ever mindful of the cataclysm of 1932, unwilling to jeopardize the progress of the 1940s in the name of "social equality." Speaking to the 1946 convention, Mitchell recalled: "Three or four years ago I asked one of you who lived through that era, 'What is to prevent my waking up some morning to find the diocese in the same kind of mess it was before I became bishop?' The reply was, 'There is no danger of that; something has gone out of us.'"[74]

The ecclesiastical changes in the Diocese of Arkansas paralleled developments in the state at large. In the mid-1940s, Dr. J. M. Robinson, George G. Walker, and their colleagues in the Arkansas Negro Democratic Association acted in concert with other black civic and political groups to desegregate the Arkansas Democratic primary system. In the aftermath of the Supreme Court's *Smith* v. *Allwright* decision, the Democratic Party had erected a dual primary system all across the South, only to discover that the segregated primary system was too unwieldy to maintain. According to John Kirk, the Arkansas system "proved to be an administrative nightmare and had been grinding to a halt ever since its installment in 1945."[75] As a result, Arkansas's primaries desegregated randomly until only Little Rock was left. In 1947, the year that the Episcopal Diocese of Arkansas voted to desegregate, the Arkansas General Assembly repealed the law which established separate primaries in Little Rock.

Although the Second World War and the subsequent deparochialization of the South contributed heavily to the improved racial climate in the region, at least part of the change in the southern Episcopal frame of mind was directly attributable to the actions of Bishop Demby and his white allies at the 1940 General Convention. According to David Reimers, who wrote extensively on the struggles of black Episcopalians: "Undoubtedly the decision of the church in 1940 against the establishment of racial missionary districts reinforced the movement for Negro equality in the Southern dioceses."[76] Concurrent with the desegregation of Episcopal Arkansas, other southern dioceses desegregated their conventions and institutions. In 1953, for instance, the Diocese of South Carolina, the "last bastion" of the segregated convention, "invited the Negro churches to participate in the diocesan convention on the same basis as the white churches."[77] That same year, St. Luke's Seminary, University of the South, officially opened its doors to black seminarians, the last Episcopal seminary to do so. Bishop Mitchell of Arkansas was chancellor to the University of the South at that time and Reverend William T. Holt II was one of several faculty members who resigned from the seminary in protest of its racist position. In 1954, the struggle over desegregation took on a more churchwide emphasis when the Conference of Church Workers protested against the segregated living accommodations slated for the 1955 General Convention. Citing the 1940 resolution against segregated facilities, the conference was able to persuade the convention planners to change the site of the convention from Houston to Honolulu in order to ensure compliance. Demby was especially keen on the dispute over the 1955 convention and kept up with developments via his correspondence with Charles Shaw, president of the Watchtower Life Insurance Company and a black representative on the General Convention Committee.

Demby rejoiced at these developments while living out his retirement in Topeka, Cleveland, Pittsburgh, and Miami. Immediately following his retirement, the Dembys moved to Topeka, where the bishop served St. Simon's. In 1942, he transferred to the Church of the Holy Cross, Pittsburgh. From 1943 onward, the Dembys lived in Cleveland, where the bishop served St. Andrew's on a part-time basis. During the war years, Mrs. Demby was very active as a Red Cross worker. Demby found the 1940s a gratifying decade as he toured the country speaking to church and civic groups on race relations. Widely regarded as a sage and a sort of grizzled veteran of the race wars, he was sought out as a featured speaker on appropriate occasions, such as the 1945–46 merger of two Philadelphia churches—Calvary Church, a predominantly white church, and the Church of St. Michael and All the Angels, a predominantly black church, under the ministry of a black priest, the Reverend Thomas S. Logan Sr.[78] In 1945, Demby confirmed a large class at the Church of the Ascension, a white Episcopal church in the Cleveland suburb of Lakewood. He found the service a powerful affirmation of his ministry of racial reconciliation. His powers were broadened in 1946 when suffragan bishops were given the right to vote in the House of Bishops. The Dembys spent most of their remaining years summering in Cleveland and wintering in Florida. During this time, Demby was mentor and hero to his great-nephew, Edward Thomas Payne, who is now an Episcopal priest.

Perhaps the most illuminating documents from his retirement years are a collection of letters that passed between the Dembys and a Sister Myrtle Catherine of the Convent of the Transfiguration, Glendale, Ohio. From 1944 to 1949 they corresponded with Sister Myrtle, whose relationship to the Dembys dated back to Demby's tenure at "dear old St. Peter's," Key West. At that time, Sister Myrtle was a child whose parents attended St. Peter's. In the early 1940s she aspired to a religious vocation with the Sisters of the Transfiguration and, having endured a very difficult novitiate, entered the order. She was their first African American sister. The convent operated a black parochial school in Glendale and Sister Myrtle taught kindergarten. Although she enjoyed the devotional life and teaching school, from time to time she struggled with the issue of race. In December 1944, she wrote her "very Dear Bishop and Mother," "There is a white helper here who has said to me more than once, 'Sister Myrtle, you don't belong here. You have had more training than a-lot of the sisters here. I'd love to see you do something in the way of training other women of your race.'"[79] She and the Dembys took this as a well-intended suggestion that betrayed the underlying race prejudice of the speaker. "HYPOCRISY!" wrote Mrs. Demby, "You should not, you must not leave Glendale."[80] Nevertheless, by November 1945, something had so exacerbated Sister Myrtle's situation that she talked of leaving the order. A council was held and Mother Olivia Mary rendered an unspecified decision on the matter, which Demby reviewed. Meanwhile, Sister Myrtle withdrew from the convent to St. John's Home, Painesville, Ohio, in order to distance herself from those she regarded as her antagonists, namely, several other sisters in the convent. There is no intimation of what the trouble was, but Bishop Demby had a great deal to say about Sister Myrtle's desire to quit the order: "I know you well enough, your treatment was far from what it should have been for you to declare your purpose to give up your relationship with the convent. Even so, you must forego any such idea. You must remain and continue to do your full duties in relation to your work as a religious and your great love for humanity. . . . You are, I think, the only real active religious among us in the American church, and you must hold on at any cost."[81] He counseled her to deepen her relationship to God and be strengthened by the same. This, he said, had been his experience in difficult times. Sister Myrtle did not quit and, by 1949, had a flourishing ministry in connection with the convent. All the while, she was becoming more outspoken and more aware of the opportunities for ministry among the country's black population. She yearned to educate African Americans and train them in the religious life. Sister Myrtle, Bishop Demby, and Sister Ruth, a black sister affiliated with the Convent of St. John the Divine in Toronto, were wholeheartedly in favor of an African American teaching sisterhood in the United States. Such a sisterhood, said Demby, would be racial in origin, but not exclusionary. Being a ministry primarily by and for black people, it could not fail to attract black women to religious vocations. Thus, we see in the problems faced by Sister Myrtle a microcosm of Demby's ministry: the desire to be treated on one's merits instead of one's color; the deep-rooted determination not to quit but to stay in the field and provide an example; and, paradoxically, the willingness or need to draw apart as a group from the white majority in order to grow.

In 1953, Demby consolidated his thoughts into "Off of the Record since

1939—" and deposited them, in the form of five notebooks, in the James Weldon Johnson Collection at Yale University. Here he spoke his mind in a rambling topical style and vented his grievances against the evil that men do to one another in the name of race. To summarize some of his remarks: black people are not inherently stupid; black people do not smell; black men are not sexually superior to white men; black men are accused of being lecherous toward white women, but a cursory glance at the various shades of African-Americans indicates that historically it has been white men who have lacked self-control toward black women; the racial duplicity that lighter-skinned African Americans practice against those with darker skin is just plain stupid; people should be free to marry whom they please regardless of race; and the best Americans and the best Episcopalians are black people because they remain faithful to both institutions in spite of the way they are treated. Surprisingly, Demby had very little to say about his altercations with the Arkansas convention. His recollections of the worst incident are quoted in full at the beginning of this chapter, save for this remark: "The only gratification I got out of them was that they were in keeping with my experience, that the people who believe and force race prejudices are Christians for the most part."[82] His anger, moreover, was directed at the ideas that bind men's souls, rather than the men themselves. His hope, welling up implacably from every page, was in the church and, more specifically, in its young people. He believed that racism could be eradicated in one generation if that generation was properly educated in its youth. He embodied his vision in a hymn, "Rise up, O Youth of God," a lyrical variation on the traditional "Rise up, O Men of God." And last but not least, Demby found reason to hope in current events and personalities, most notably, Jackie Robinson and Martin Luther King. Although he did not know Robinson personally, he empathized with "my friend, Jackie."[83]

After Mrs. Demby died in early 1957, he refused to acknowledge her death and would ask occasionally, "When is she coming back?" Finally, just prior to his own death, he said that he was going to meet her. He died on 14 October 1957, at the time of the Little Rock desegregation crisis. The *Living Church* eulogized him as someone who could defeat racism by sheer good example, if that were possible. He was buried as he stipulated: the service was very high and "nothing of a biographical nature" was said. The postscript to his funeral directions indicates that he left this life in his habitual positive outlook. In case his instructions were not followed, he absolved those in charge of the service, "consider it a DEAD issue."[84]

NOTES

1. "Confirmation of Bishop Withheld," *Arkansas Gazette,* 21 Nov. 1932; "Election of Dean Williamson Invalidated," *Newport (Arkansas) Daily Independent,* 21 Nov. 1932, 1.

2. William P. Witsell to James DeWolf Perry, 8 Dec. 1932, Collected Papers of the Reverend William P. Witsell, Archives of the Diocese of Arkansas, Trinity Cathedral, Little Rock, Ark., hereafter cited as the Witsell Papers.

3. Ibid.; W. P. Witsell to J. D. Perry, 12 Dec. 1932, ibid.

4. W. P. Witsell, *A History of Christ Episcopal Church, Little Rock, Arkansas, 1839–1947* (Little Rock, Ark.: Christ Church Vestry, n.d.), 143.

5. W. P. Witsell to William T. Capers, 1 Jan. 1933, Witsell Papers.

6. W. P. Witsell to E. W. Saphore, 8 Mar. 1933, Witsell Papers.

7. W. P. Witsell to John Williamson, 27 Mar. 1933, Witsell Papers.

8. John Williamson to W. P. Witsell, 28 Mar. 1933, Witsell Papers.

9. J. D. Perry to W. P. Witsell, 23 Jan. 1933, Witsell Papers.

10. "Proceedings," *Journal of the Annual Convention of the Protestant Episcopal Diocese of Arkansas* (1933): 13, hereafter cited as *Arkansas Journal.*

11. W. P. Witsell to H. A. Stowell, 28 Apr. 1933, Witsell Papers.

12. Edward T. Demby, "Off of the Record since 1939," MS, James Weldon Johnson Collection, Yale Collection of American Literature, Beinecke Rare Book and Manuscript Library, Yale University, New Haven, Conn., 68, hereafter cited as Demby, "Off of the Record."

13. W. P. Witsell to William T. Manning, 12 Apr. 1933, Witsell Papers.

14. "Resolution of Regret," *Arkansas Journal* (1933): 43.

15. W. P. Witsell to H. A. Stowell, 28 Apr. 1933, Witsell Papers. The exact timing of Mellichampe's speech is an educated guess. Like Holt's tirade of the year before, it was not recorded in the diocesan journals. At first, it would seem that an anti-Negro/pro-laity speech would have taken place on the first day of the convention when there were far more lay delegates present. But the greater likelihood is that the Cathedralites, being determined not to broach the race issue and to elect Williamson, would not have sanctioned Mellichampe's actions. Therefore, the logical place to put Mellichampe's speech is in with the angry debate over the "Resolution of Regret," when there was no longer any hope of electing Williamson. W. P. Witsell to W. T. Capers, 6 July 1933, ibid.

16. In June, Mellichampe sought out Witsell in order to strike an alliance and elect a bishop from outside of Arkansas, but he continued to insist that the black clergy be disenfranchised as a precondition. W. P. Witsell to Theodore Du Bose Bratton, 15 June 1933, Witsell Papers; T. D. Bratton to W. P. Witsell, 20 June 1933, ibid.; W. P. Witsell to T. D. Bratton, 27 June 1933, ibid.

17. "Proceedings," *Arkansas Journal* (1933): 16.

18. To cite three examples of Witsell's circularizing after the 1933 convention: W. P. Witsell to Francis M. Taitt, bishop of Pennsylvania, 22 Aug. 1933, Witsell Papers; W. P.

Witsell to William Scarlett, bishop coadjutor of Missouri, 22 Aug. 1933, ibid.; W. P. Witsell to Eugene E. Seaman, bishop of North Texas, 21 Aug. 1933, ibid.

19. J. Carleton Hayden, telephone interview by author, 13 Feb. 1991, Sewanee, Tenn., transcript. Hayden says this is particularly true of the white establishment when confronted with racial problems within the church.

20. E. T. Demby to James R. Winchester, 23 Dec. 1933, Bishop Edward T. Demby File, box 13, RG 282, Bishop James R. Winchester Papers, Archives of the Episcopal Church, U.S.A., Austin, Tex., hereafter cited as Winchester Papers; E. T. Demby to W. P. Witsell, 20 May 1938, Witsell Papers; E. T. Demby to [black clergy of Arkansas], 14 June 1938, ibid. To further illustrate, Demby wrote Witsell in 1938 recommending two candidates for the Arkansas bishopric, but added: "I would not desire to have my name mentioned in connection with either of these men, because of the spirit of some in the diocese as to me and the Negro work" (E. T. Demby to W. P. Witsell, n.d. [1938], ibid.).

21. *Journal of the General Convention of the Protestant Episcopal Church* (1934): 475–78, quoted in David M. Reimers, *White Protestantism and the Negro* (New York: Oxford University Press, 1965), 123–24.

22. *Annual Report of the National Council* (1930): 286; ibid. (1931): 285; ibid. (1932): 279; ibid. (1933): 295; ibid. (1934): 269; ibid. (1935): 288; ibid. (1936): 298; ibid. (1937): 285; *Arkansas Journal* (1933): 23–37; James W. Temple, telephone interview by author, 1 Dec. 1991, Los Angeles, Calif., transcript.

23. Bishop Bartlett, "Report on Survey of Negro Work for the National Council," 15 Aug. 1935, 5 (in the files of the Bi-Racial Committee of the Protestant Episcopal Church), quoted in Reimers, *White Protestantism*, 124.

24. W. P. Witsell to E. T. Demby, 2 Oct. 1934, Witsell Papers. According to this letter, there was a second report, regarding "Negro work" in the the Diocese of Missouri, which also mysteriously disappeared.

25. After a hard year at Voorhees, where he was one of only four students in the dorm, Powell decided against going into the ministry and followed his father's footsteps by working with the railroad. He was a Pullman porter for most of his adult life (Lewis A. Powell, interview by author, 2 Mar. 1997, Kansas City, Mo.).

26. E. T. Demby to J. R. Winchester, 23 Dec. 1933, Winchester Papers. "Waters" appears to be an allusion to 2 Corinthians 11:26–28, as discussed in chapter 3. We might call this the keynote biblical citation of Demby's ministry.

27. Frank W. Creighton to William P. Witsell, 20 Jan. 1933, Witsell Papers; William P. Witsell to Frank W. Creighton, 24 Jan. 1933, ibid.; William P. Witsell to Gustave Orth, 24 Jan. 1933, ibid.; Gustave Orth to William P. Witsell, 25 Jan. 1933, ibid.; William P. Witsell to Gustave Orth, 26 Jan. 1933, ibid.; William P. Witsell to Frank W. Creighton, 6 Feb. 1933, ibid.; Gustave Orth to William P. Witsell, 10 Feb. 1933, ibid.; William P. Witsell to Frank W. Creighton, 11 Feb. 1933, ibid.; Frank W. Creighton to William P. Witsell, 11 Feb. 1933, ibid.

28. W. P. Witsell to Thomas F. Gailor, 3 May 1934, Witsell Papers.

29. T. F. Gailor to W. P. Witsell, 31 Jan. 1935, Witsell Papers.

30. W. P. Witsell to W. T. Capers, 18 Feb. 1935, Witsell Papers; C. S. Quinn to W. P. Witsell, 6 Feb. 1935, ibid.; E. W. Saphore to the Rector, Vestry, and Wardens of Christ Church, Little Rock, Ark., 5 Feb. 1935, ibid.

31. W. P. Witsell to T. F. Gailor, 6 May 1935, Witsell Papers.

32. T. F. Gailor to W. P. Witsell, 10 May 1935, Witsell Papers.

33. "Proceedings," *Arkansas Journal* (1938): 17. In looking for some common denominator that would draw Holt and Bullock together on behalf of black ministries, we note that they were both former military chaplains. They probably had the already legendary Reverend James H. King in mind as the convocation representative to the executive council.

34. W. T. Holt II to Michael Beary, 28 Dec. 1999, author's private correspondence.

35. Joseph B. Tucker, interview by author, 26 July 1994, Pine Bluff, Ark., transcript. When white delegates to Arkansas's diocesan conventions of the 1930s and 1940s talked among themselves about black delegates, derogatory racial epithets were commonplace. Marguerite Gamble, interview by author, 14 May 1991, Little Rock, Ark., transcript.

36. Robert J. Johnson to W. P. Witsell, 21 June 1938, Witsell Papers; *The Mission of the Protestant Episcopal Church in the Province of the Southwest and Especially the Diocese of Arkansas among the Colored People,* a fund-raising pamphlet commemorating Demby's twentieth anniversary in the episcopate, (n.p., 1938), Demby Family Papers, Manuscripts, Archives and Rare Books Division, Schomburg Center for Research in Black Culture, New York Public Library Astor, Lenox, and Tilden Foundations, New York, hereafter cited as Demby Family Papers; Edward T. Demby, "Report of the Suffragan Bishop," *Arkansas Journal* (1935): 23–24.

37. Thompson's transfer undoubtedly fell in with the plans of Bishop Thomas C. Casady of Oklahoma, who, as noted in chapter 4, needed black clergy. It may also have divested Demby of a clergyman that Arkansas could not support. It is safe to assume that Oklahoma assisted Thompson with his last year at Bishop Payne.

38. St. Simon's, Topeka, a small mission that has operated without a priest of its own for much of its existence, has been phenomenal in its production of clergy. The Reverends Thaddeus Martin, James Temple, Fred Glass, and Joe Thompson are all sons of St. Simon's. The first two knew Demby at the time they entered the ministry. The last two knew him as children, when Demby was vicar to St. Simon's immediately after his retirement (Joe Thompson, telephone interview by author, 16 Oct. 1998, Topeka, Kan., transcript; James W. Temple, interview by author, 1 Dec. 1991, Los Angeles, Calif., transcript).

39. Stowell and Witsell figured prominently in the ordination process and Stowell was especially fond of the energetic Martin, whom he regarded as the best of Arkansas's black clergy. He tutored Martin in sacred languages on behalf of the Board of Examining Chaplains. Martin breathed new life into St. Andrew's, Pine Bluff, establishing a community center adjunct to the church. After three years at St. Andrew's, Martin and his wife, the former Elnora Johnson, left for a better position. Stowell said that had it not been for Demby and the material assistance of Martin's father, he would

not have survived at St. Andrew's (H. A. Stowell to W. P. Witsell, 8 May 1938, Witsell Papers; H. A. Stowell to W. P. Witsell, 23 May 1938, ibid.; H. A. Stowell to W. P. Witsell, 26 May 1938, ibid.; H. A. Stowell to W. P. Witsell, 6 Aug. 1938, ibid; H. A. Stowell to W. P. Witsell, 13 Aug. 1938, ibid.). One should not take Stowell's estimation of Martin, relative to Arkansas's other black clergy, too seriously. It is doubtful that he was well acquainted with any of them other than Martin. All existing correspondence suggests that Arkansas's parallel black church had succeeded in concealing the work, if not the identity, of the black clergy from their white counterparts. All, save the Reverend James King of Forrest City, were and have remained anomalous figures into the 1990s.

40. Harold T. Lewis, *Yet with a Steady Beat: The African-American Struggle for Recognition in the Episcopal Church* (Valley Forge, Pa.: Trinity Press International, 1996), 135.

41. Ibid., 140.

42. H. A. Stowell to W. P. Witsell, 1 Nov. 1937, Witsell Papers.

43. Brandner J. Moore to W. P. Witsell, 7 Apr. 1938, Witsell Papers.

44. Richard Allin, interview by author, 10 July 1994, Little Rock, Ark., transcript.

45. H. A. Stowell to W. P. Witsell, 8 May 1938, Witsell Papers; B. J. Moore to W. P. Witsell, 5 May 1938, ibid.

46. "Proceedings," *Arkansas Journal* (1938): 20.

47. Margaret Sims McDonald, *White Already to Harvest: The Episcopal Church in Arkansas, 1838–1971* (Sewanee, Tenn.: University Press for the Episcopal Diocese of Arkansas, 1975), 224.

48. William T. Capers to Richard B. Mitchell, 1 June 1938, Witsell Papers; W. T. Capers to W. P. Witsell, 1 June 1938, ibid. Note that a shortage of money was also a primary consideration behind Arkansas's 1897 debacle. Witsell, to his credit, understood that some candidates for bishop are simply ready for a challenge, money problems notwithstanding. In fact, the shortcomings of the electing diocese sometimes serve to amplify the "Macedonian cry."

49. E. T. Demby to W. P. Witsell, 20 May 1938, Witsell Papers.

50. E. T. Demby to [Arkansas' black clergy], 14 June 1938, Witsell Papers.

51. E. T. Demby to W. P. Witsell, 20 May 1938, Witsell Papers; W. P. Witsell to Mrs. E. T. Demby, 21 June 1938, ibid.

52. E. T. Demby to W. P. Witsell, 20 May 1938, Witsell Papers.

53. W. P. Witsell to H. A. Stowell, 16 May 1938, Witsell Papers.

54. William B. Mitchell, "Bishop's Address," *Arkansas Journal* (1946): 25–26.

55. Herbert A. Donovan, interview by author, 1 June 1990, Little Rock, Ark., transcript. See also "Roll of the House of Bishops," Episcopal Church Center, New York, 759. The "Roll" is a handwritten record of the consecration of all the Episcopal bishops ever consecrated. *Living Church Annual* (Chicago: Living Church Co., 1939), 62. The Reverend Cotesworth P. Lewis, dean of Trinity Cathedral for almost the entire tenure of Bishop Mitchell, was present at the consecration of Mitchell. He has no knowledge of Bishop Demby having wept (Cotesworth P. Lewis to Michael J. Beary care of Herbert A. Donovan, 10 Mar. 1992, author's private correspondence). I attempted to confirm

the incident by way of various historiographers in the various dioceses of bishops who were present at Mitchell's consecration, but was unable to do so.

56. Edward T. Demby, "Report of the Suffragan," *Arkansas Journal* (1939): 53–54.

57. E. T. Demby, "Address to the Nineteenth Annual Meeting of the Colored Churchmen of the Diocese of Arkansas," "Off of the Record."

58. William B. Mitchell, "Bishop's Address," *Arkansas Journal* (1940): 32–33.

59. Catherine Weston is the daughter of the Reverend M. Moran Weston Sr. of North Carolina, and sister of the Reverend M. Moran Weston Jr., one of the foremost spokesmen for black Episcopalians during the Civil Rights Era. Ms. Weston, like Inez Middleton of chapter 4, is a retired social worker and a graduate of the Bishop Tuttle School for Social Work affiliated with St. Augustine's College, Raleigh, North Carolina. She says that the North Carolina clergy were not pleased with the suffragan experiment in North Carolina and were unequivocally opposed to a second attempt (Catherine Weston, interview by author, 26 Mar. 1995, St. Louis, Mo., transcript). Likewise, Dora Strong Dennis, a founding member of Christ Church Mission, Forrest City, Arkansas, recalls a comment to the same effect by the Reverend James H. King at the time of Demby's retirement and Mitchell's consecration. All would be well, said King, as long as our "next bishop is not a black one" (Dora Strong Dennis, interview by author, 9 Aug. 1991, Forrest City, Ark., transcript). It should be pointed out that King spoke specifically to the suffragan bishop plan. He unabashedly loved and admired Demby, and Demby reciprocated those feelings.

60. Mitchell, "Address," *Arkansas Journal* (1940): 33.

61. James M. Maxon to Robert W. Patton, 6 Jan. 1938, Hoffman-St. Mary's Files, RG 61-6-23, Records of the American Church Institute for Negroes, Archives of the Episcopal Church, Austin, Tex.; R. W. Patton to J. M. Maxon, 10 Jan. 1938, ibid.; J. M. Maxon to R. W. Patton, 3 Jan. 1939, ibid.; J. M. Maxon to R. W. Patton, 18 May 1942, ibid.

62. Middleton Barnwell to E. T. Demby, n.d. [1940], "Off of the Record," 431–32. For an opposing viewpoint on the 1940 debate, see Gardiner H. Shattuck Jr., *Episcopalians and Race: Civil War to Civil Rights* (Lexington: University Press of Kentucky, 2000), 26–29.

63. *Journal of the General Convention* (1937): 33, 333–34, quoted in Reimers, *White Protestantism*, 124.

64. Reimers, *White Protestantism*, 149.

65. E. T. Demby, "Off of the Record," 160.

66. Reimers, *White Protestantism*, 150.

67. Demby, "Off of the Record," 160.

68. Gavin White, "Patriarch McGuire and the Episcopal Church," *Historical Magazine of the Episcopal Church* 38 (June 1969): 133–34; E. T. Demby to M. S. Barnwell, 13 Aug. 1940, "Off of the Record," 433–35.

69. Demby, "Off of the Record," 161–62.

70. William B. Mitchell, "Bishop's Address," *Arkansas Journal* (1946): 24–26.

71. Ibid. (1947): 28.

72. Ibid., 28–29.

73. Marguerite Gamble, interview by author, 14 May 1991, Little Rock, Ark., transcript.

74. Mitchell, "Address," *Arkansas Journal* (1947): 29.

75. John Kirk, "Dr. J. M. Robinson, the Arkansas Negro Democratic Association and Black Politics in Little Rock, Arkansas, 1928–1952," *Pulaski County Historical Review* 41 (Spring 1993): 6; ibid. 42 (Summer 1993): 39–40.

76. David Reimers, "Negro Bishops and Diocesan Segregation in the Protestant Episcopal Church, 1870–1940," *Historical Magazine of the Protestant Episcopal Church* 31 (Sept. 1962): 240.

77. Reimers, *White Protestantism*, 126.

78. *Philadelphia Tribune*, 17 Sept. 1946, E. T. Demby scrapbook, private collection of the Reverend Canon Thomas S. Logan Sr., Logan residence, Yeadon, Pa.; Thomas S. Logan Sr., interview by author, 19 Oct. 1995, Yeadon, Pa. Ironically, it was the bishop of Pennsylvania, Oliver J. Hart, who championed Philadelphia's experiment in integration. As noted in chapter 6, Hart was Edwin Mellichampe's candidate for bishop of Arkansas in 1932. Demby drew encouragement from the Philadelphia merger (Demby, "Off of the Record," 104).

79. Sister Myrtle Catherine to Antoinette M. R. Demby, 15 Dec. 1944, box 1, folder 5, Demby Family Papers.

80. Antoinette M. R. Demby to Sister Myrtle Catherine, 8 Jan. 1945, Demby Family Papers.

81. Edward T. Demby to Sister Myrtle Catherine, 9 Nov. 1945, Demby Family Papers.

82. Demby, "Off of the Record," 68.

83. Dorothy Demby and Elizabeth Demby Payne, interview by author, 14 Oct. 1995, New York, transcript.

84. "Very Important Matter to Be Looked after in the Event of Death of Me or My Wife: By Her or Me," box 1, folder 1, Demby Family Papers.

CONCLUSION
All Things to All People

The Episcopal Church needed an Antioch and Demby provided one. Racial incidents, be they spontaneous or designed, have an inherent value for moral suasion that fine words and sound ecclesiastical policy do not possess. Incidents have power. It is one thing to lobby for change; it is another to suffer for it. It is one thing to learn that the only black Episcopal bishop in the United States has been assigned a largely titular role in a numerically insignificant venture; it is another to see his name emblazoned in the church press, defying the racist conduct of a church convention. In Demby's day, the white moderate, as defined by Martin Luther King at the beginning of this study, was the key to change in the Episcopal Church. Bishop after bishop, priest after priest espoused an "enlightened" approach to the "Negro question"; that is, they exhibited a "catholic" sympathy with their black co-religionists but habitually eschewed behavior that was egalitarian in nature. In contrast to their more liberal clergy stood the vast majority of the white laity, who remained anywhere from conservative to reactionary in their views on race, thereby inhibiting the "enlightenment" of their priests. Thus, the white moderate, in the person of the white cleric, came to represent order. Unless presented with a situation so morally compelling that inaction became a sin in itself, he would not act in defiance of the status quo. It is one thing to see the justice of *Brown* v. *Board of Education;* it is another to see a column of nonviolent protesters assaulted by police, attack dogs, and fire hoses in Selma, Alabama. Give the white moderate an incident and a means of redress and he or she may act, may vote for the Civil Rights Bill, may refuse to pass on the election of a bishop, may dispense with ecclesiastical segregation altogether. But first there must be an Antioch.

Bishop Demby's ministry is painted against the backdrop of a battle over segregation in the Episcopal Church. In fact, if the ministry of one black clergyman could be said to embody that battle, that clergyman is Demby. Let us review the premise behind segregation and its two schools of thought. The premise, that black participation in an integrated Episcopal government is unacceptable, bespeaks the spirit of the age—an endorsement of or, at the very least an acquiescence to, racism. The white proponents of racism argued segregation's supposed efficacy for black churches and white churches alike, namely, order and growth. The black proponents did the same, provided that a certain vestige of political equality be gained for black Episcopalians in the transaction. What Demby discovered, and what Martin Luther King discovered for that matter, is that pragmatic thinking undermines the moral issue. King decries the predilection for order, which has, as its base, the all-important issue of time. Given enough time, says the white moderate, change can come about in an orderly fashion. What King and Demby realized is that formal black acceptance of the time and order formula removes the moral stigma associated with segregation, or so deadens it as to render it useless. We are speaking, of course, of the missionary district plan. Was this wise? According to Harold Lewis, the Conference of Church Workers thought it better to obtain admission to the first-class carriage via the second-class carriage, rather than attempt a leap from the side of the tracks—and according to Lewis, they were "right, historically speaking," in so doing. If by "right" Lewis means merely "it was worth it," then I plead no contest, that being a more subjective judgment, best made by those who inherited the legacy of the Conference of Church Workers—the Union of Black Episcopalians.

However, if "right" in this case means "correct" in the more objective sense, that is debatable. Demby, after his many years as the prototypical black bishop, decided that they were wrong. Voluntary segregation, he decided, merely reinforces segregation. To return to an earlier premise, it makes segregation "good" in the eyes of white people.

And where do we see this happening? Excluding the Methodist example cited by Demby in chapter 7, four instances stand out above the rest. The first is that of infamous Bishop William M. Brown. Remember that Brown and his Arkansas Plan were morally vanquished in the fall of 1903. Blandishments from white and black clergy and white and black newspapers had so filled him with shame that he could scarcely "look a Christian in the eye." Then followed the most unexpected turn of events imaginable. The Conference of Church Workers effectually set aside their old challenge to "define the status of Colored Churchmen" in favor of a new one, namely, voluntary segregation at the price of black bishops and national representation. With this new agenda in place, a contrite Brown met with representatives of the conference in Washington and enlisted their tangible support for the Arkansas Plan. The Washington conference elicited a dramatic change in Brown. Heretofore the acquiescent segregationist, he became a bona fide authority on the "Negro problem," the insufferable bigot of the House of Bishops. Likewise, we see this hardening of the color line in the canons that brought Arkansas's Afro-American Convocation (1903–20) and Colored Convocation (1920–39) into being. The Afro-American Convocation had a modicum of influence with the Arkansas convention, being empowered to vote for bishops, members of the standing committee, and delegates to the General Convention. Furthermore, all references to segregation by color were removed from the canons. With the advent of the Colored Convocation, however, the language of the canons became brazenly exclusionary and the convocation was stripped of its political influence—with two caveats: Demby became the designated representative of the convocation before the Arkansas convention and Arkansas's black clergy were entitled to vote in the election of Arkansas's bishops. To cite a third example, Demby's election tragically illustrates the deadening powers of voluntary segregation upon the white conscience. The authors of Demby's election, the bishops of the Southwest Province, espoused high hopes for the suffragan bishop plan. In their attempt to implement the missionary district plan, ad hoc, they envisioned an opportunity for black Episcopalians to prove their mettle, an opportunity for them to systematically evangelize the Southwest under the guidance of their new leader. The air, of course, immediately went out of the southwestern balloon— if, indeed, it was ever inflated in the first place. Demby's jurisdiction was heavily compromised, he had no salary, and he had no home. The bishops simply failed to underwrite the project. "Segregation works better" translated to "out of sight, out of mind." Only Demby's dogged optimism kept it from folding. The fourth and last illustration of this principle, which follows from the previous illustration, can be seen in the unrealized hope generated by the success of Christ Church Parochial and Industrial School. In 1919, Demby called upon the church to be more openhanded in its support of African American institutional work, primarily in the form of parochial schools. This, he said, would yield a burgeoning ministry to blacks in the Southwest. The "hand," of course, was not that open, but with a very small investment Demby and the Reverend James H. King were able to build and operate Christ Church, an institution renowned for its positive influence upon its students, the community, and the diocese. Having proved their point, they called upon diocese, province, and national church to "ante up" and help Demby establish similar institutions around the province. But there were no more "Christ Churches."

In summary, while some white people rallied to support experiments in segregation and gave tangible assistance to black ministries, the great majority of white people merely took comfort in the establishment of all-white conventions. They were basically indifferent to black ministries unless threatened by them in some way. Thus, the campaign for the missionary district plan, for all its aspirations to the contrary, came to represent the status quo. Moreover, all attempts at voluntary segregation acted as moral safety valves for the white establishment. They gave the white authorities an option short of defending the brazen exclusion of African Americans from their conventions. Returning to Lewis's metaphor, entering the second-class car voluntarily gives sanction to the second-class car; it might have been better to have been dragged bodily from the first-class.

One might argue that all of this is white hindsight, and that I as author, being chronologically and racially distant from the situation, ought not to judge. Remember the times; remember that black Episcopalians needed bishops who could really pastor their priests; remember how the word "equality," or even an outspoken aspiration to ecclesiastical equality, could, in certain quarters, elicit the worst sort of reaction from the white majority; remember that the missionary district plan was only a temporary measure to ensure a vestige of ecclesiastical and political power, to be followed by the eventual reemergence of the church's black constituents into the life of the church—an Episcopal counterpart to Booker T. Washington's industrial education. However, I would point out that it is equally true that voluntary segregation only reinforced the prejudice of the white majority in the sacred and the secular, hardening the color line by deadening the moral issue of segregation itself. This is not to say that black Episcopalians were ignorant of the ramifications of the stand taken by the Conference of Church Workers. One of the recurring factors mitigating against the missionary district plan at each joust with the General Convention was black Episcopal opposition, exhibited most notably by Bishop Demby in 1940. It was indeed a calculated risk and a risk a good many black Episcopalians were unwilling to take.[1]

Yet it would be a gross misstatement to say that the missionary district campaign was counterproductive. Just as Bragg maintained that the slave chapel prepared blacks to exercise leadership when outward circumstances finally allowed them to do so, it could also be said that the years between 1904 and 1940 exhibited the development of a strong lobby on behalf of black ministries, ready to capitalize on a change in outward circumstances. The Conference of Church Workers, having secured a resolution on nonsegregated facilities at the 1940 General Convention and a secretary for "Negro work" in 1943, pressed their suit with unprecedented success in the postwar years, their influence most evident at the time of *Brown* v. *Board of Education*.

And there is another sense in which the campaign for the missionary district plan would have to be called an unequivocal success. It led to the election of black bishops. The missionary campaign made possible the compromise of 1907, which, in turn, resulted in the black suffragan plan. Of course, the black suffragan plan fell into disrepute after two beleaguered experiments, but it dragged the whole idea of ecclesiastical segregation down with it. Meanwhile, the 1907 amendment, which provided for the election of suffragan bishops and made no racial distinctions, remained in place. Enter the black suffragan divested of his "plan." Enter the Right Reverend John M. Burgess, suffragan bishop of the Diocese of Massachusetts. Elected in 1962, Burgess was the first African American Episcopal bishop to exercise jurisdiction in the continental United States since Demby. More importantly, he was suffragan bishop to all of Massachusetts, black and white—the realization of Demby's counsel to the House of Bishops in 1940, and more. In 1969, Burgess was elected bishop coadjutor of Massachusetts and succeeded his diocesan the following year. The missionary district campaign was the impetus behind the events that eventually led to desegregation and the election of black bishops.

Ultimately, arguments about the "rightness" or "wrongness" of the missionary district plan are ahistorical, because a statement declaring the rightness or wrongness of the plan is a statement underwritten by a belief in what would have happened had it passed into law; the very temptation I feel with regard to the suffragan bishop plan. What would have happened if the church had generously supported Demby's episcopate? After all, he did so well with so little. The ice cracks under our historical feet even as we contemplate it.

The campaign for voluntary segregation was a trade-off, an exchange of the ongoing challenge to "define the status of Colored Churchmen" for the election of black missionary bishops, a de-emphasis of the prophetic for the sake of the pastoral—albeit with a vestige of political equality, an exchange that inadvertently sanctioned and thereby hardened the color line while simultaneously mobilizing the church's black minority to action. The all-important question, it seems, is not the rightness or wrongness of voluntary segregation but the discernment and actions of its practitioners at each individual bend in the road. There were times when the greater wisdom was to cooperate voluntarily with segregation—which would make outright resistance "wrong"—and there were times when the greater wisdom was to blatantly resist segregation—which would make voluntary cooperation "wrong." Demby was the embodiment of this dilemma. One may look at his habit of forbearance and say that he carried accommodation too far, that he brought down racial indignities on his own head and those of his subordinates by not speaking up when he should have. On the other hand, one can see that his dignity in acquiescence imparted a gravity to his words that ultimately paid off. He rarely complained, but when he did, people listened.

Racial integration means trouble, but churches are bent on order. Therefore they require a stimulus to integrate, a stimulus to risk order so that order may be reestablished—but in a more orthodox design. Usually this stimulus comes from without. This is why the Episcopal Church follows the national pattern of racial enlightenment so closely. One can see the influence of the secular time and again as Demby's experiences within the Episcopal Church mimicked the struggles of African Americans in general. The convocation system, the suffragan plan, and the missionary district plan were compromises intended to cope with Jim Crow as it emerged within the church. Each measure was underwritten by the same ethos that guided the Atlanta Compromise; that is, in order for a black person to participate in a racist society one must, to some degree, become an agent of order. Here lies the unique contribution of Edward T. Demby. The inimitable agent of order, he ultimately ran afoul of the status quo and used that experience to help elicit a change from within the church, a change that was ahead of its time by comparison with some other Christian bodies and that presaged the direction of the country.

No conclusion to this book would be complete without giving due consideration to the value of Anglicanism in Demby's experience, because Anglicanism and, especially, Anglo-Catholicism, carried with them a greater recognition of things catholic than the Episcopal Church generally acknowledged. Take, for instance, the white clergy who put themselves at risk by playing the white advocate in the heyday of Jim Crow. The Reverend W. S. Simpson-Atmore and the Reverend Rollin Dodd were Englishmen. The Very Reverend P. S. Irwin was an Irishman. The Reverend Samuel H. Rainey was the son of very Anglican Irish immigrants. Likewise, Demby was one among the thousands of West Indian Anglicans who "quickened" the catholic resolve of the church's black contingent between 1900 and 1940, and, in so doing, the rest of the church. Last, but by no means least, was Arkansas's dogmatically Anglo-Catholic Bishop, Henry Niles Pierce. Pierce made "high church" Trinity Cathedral a center of black advocacy during the St. Philip's controversy of 1889–98.

The one glaring exception to the "Anglican pattern" would have to be Demby's friend and ally, the Reverend William P. Witsell, and his parish, Christ Church, Little Rock. Christ Church was the quintessential low church congregation of Arkansas—and proud of it. With the St. Philip's controversy, it acquired a well-deserved reputation as an extremely conservative, if not reactionary, church on the "Negro question." Yet it entered into the 1932 fracas solidly behind its rector. We cannot be sure whether Christ Church acted in support of or in spite of Witsell's advocacy of Demby, but it is testimony to the power of Witsell's personality that it followed him. Besides being a rigorous moralist on more socially acceptable issues, Witsell, as the title of *Our Church: One through the Ages* suggests, was an extremely catholic Episcopalian—with a little "c." He was an enemy of segregation, just as Pierce had been. Or, to put it another way, Christ Church under Witsell was not the Christ Church that excluded Archdeacon George Alexander McGuire in 1907, and Trinity Cathedral under Pierce bore little resemblance to Demby's adversary of 1932. Apart from the influence of Pierce and Witsell, Arkansas's white Episcopalians were an atypical slice of southern culture trying to lead the way for the rest of the church with two experiments in ecclesiastical segregation. "Bad" Bishop Brown, despite all rumors to the contrary, did not launch Arkansas's Afro-American Convocation arbitrarily. Brown created the convocation on the advice of the many Arkansans whom he consulted. Notice, too, that the tumultuous racial controversies that stigmatized the ministries of Pierce and Witsell followed an easily discernible pattern: racist feelings aroused by a black electoral presence in the Arkansas convention exacerbated preexisting conflicts. As it was with 1890s low church Christ Church, so it was with 1930s high church Trinity Cathedral. The most important variable, then, would seem to be a controlling personality mated to catholic convictions, like Pierce, or Witsell, or even Bishop William T. Manning of New York.

And what of the overwhelming majority of white clergy who did not put themselves at risk but supported the status quo on matters of race? Is it realistic to expect them to have done otherwise? Take, for instance, the Reverend William T. Holt of St. Paul's, Newport. Theologically opposed to excluding Demby from the Eucharist at Newport, he found himself pitted against the true seat of power in the Episcopal Church, the local vestry. Should he have challenged them? If he had done so, could he have found another pastorate as the economy ebbed in 1932–33? Would his radical stand have followed him and kept him out of a job? Backed into a corner, Holt compromised. This, however, is not an attempt to make a case for situation ethics; rather, it is an acknowledgment of the way people ordinarily behave when their livelihood and family are threatened, regardless of color. Perhaps the problem, to paraphrase C. S. Lewis, is not that the desire to do evil is so strong in us, but the desire to do good is so damnably weak.

So what shall we say of Demby? Some of those familiar with the details of his ministry, including at least one family member, think that he "stayed too long" in the Southwest Province.[2] The wise thing, they say, would have been to leave when the insolvency of the office became evident. Perhaps this is true. Perhaps not. In any event, we can readily understand why he stayed if we will look at the experience from his point of view. Demby's acceptance of his election was an exercise in faith: faith in God, faith in Winchester and his colleagues, and faith that his successes could elicit a change of heart in the white Episcopal majority. He, too, would be faithful. He would not leave his new charge without giving the enterprise his absolute best effort. This resolve was especially important until 1922–23, when his financial burdens were finally eased and the churches in his jurisdiction began to strive toward self-sufficiency. At that time, Demby began to reap encouragement from their progress, which gave him a new reason to stay. The "care of all the churches," to quote 2 Corinthians 11:28 again, was upon him. To leave them now was to abandon them in their infancy. The tumultuous 1930s compounded this new resolve when it became apparent that leaving Arkansas's black missions would mean abandoning them to an administration only nominally interested in their development. Had Demby left, would the National Council have cut even more deeply into their funding? Possibly. And given Bishop Edwin Saphore's manifest lack of enterprise and the ongoing ramifications of the Newport incident, could Demby, in good conscience, have entrusted the black churches to Saphore's care? Definitely not. In fact, Demby had promised, implicitly, that he would stay in "the field" if the bishops heeded his protest against the Arkansas Episcopal election of 1932, which they did. And, on a more personal note, he had said that his overriding consideration in promulgating the protest was to keep two of his priests from transferring out of Arkansas. When the dust settled and one of them was still there, how then could his bishop leave? Demby's moral imperative, then, was to hang on until the Diocese of Arkansas was placed in more capable hands. Yet beyond his desire to remain faithful to his vision and his desire to care for his charges, Demby was sustained by a transcendent truth, namely, he was, indeed, a "marked man." All that he did, or failed to do, reflected upon the black clergy of the Episcopal Church—with repercussions upon their aspirations for the future. Apart from his 1932 ultimatum, Demby was of the opinion that resignation due to adversity would be tantamount to a public confession of despair in the eyes of many white Episcopalians, an admission of weakness or incompetence on the part of African Americans. As it turned out, his long and difficult tenure became a moral catalyst to the 1940 General Convention, helping to move the church toward a more equitable treatment of its black membership.

Demby's life is a chronicle of African Americans, the church, and the coun-

try. He was, in turn, the assimilationist, the accommodationist, the segregationist, and the integrationist. He, too, moved to the spirit of the times as he
encountered the deteriorating status of black people. He coped. His destiny
was to make the proverbial silk purse out of the sow's ear, and in many ways
he accomplished it. He suffered, as the Reverend George F. Bragg had predicted he would, but he suffered in the interests of reconciliation. He was the
embodiment of W. E. B. Du Bois's challenge: "Do not entice [black Episcopa-
lians] to ask for a separation which your unchristian conduct forces them to
prefer; do not pretend that the distinctions which you make toward them are
distinctions which are made for the larger good of men, but simply confess in
humility and self-abasement that you cannot treat these men as brothers and
therefore you are going to set them aside and let them go their half-tended
way."[3] Demby helped bring the church to terms with its black minority and,
in doing so, he even helped bring the Diocese of Arkansas to terms with itself.

Demby was all things to all people. He represented the zenith and demise
of accommodation in the Episcopal Church. He represented the zenith and
demise of segregation in the Episcopal Church. He was the herald of assimilation, the herald of integration, the herald of the "high" Church Triumphant,
the champion of racial uplift, the champion of self-reliance, the champion of
liberal education, the champion of industrial education, the accomplished
practitioner of the convocation movement, the Jackie Robinson of the Episcopal Church.

The most memorable event for Newport, Arkansas, in 1930 was the completion of a new bridge over the White River, establishing the first direct highway link between Newport and the state capitol at Little Rock. A souvenir program published to commemorate the bridge opening featured a poem by
Mildred Dorsey, Bishop Demby's companion at the Jim Crow table in 1932.
She penned these thoughts.

BRIDGES

Today there is given to us a Bridge complete.
Crossing a river wide and deep;
Linking the noisy, bustling town,
With its traffic and crowds, its smoke and grime,
To the green shore and quiet woods
That lie on the other side;
Where the willows wave their graceful wands
And the Cypress lift their stately heads
In plumed majesty.

. . . .
Does it make us think of Bridges built
Of splendid thought and noble deeds,
Over the chasms that divide
Nations and Races, Classes and Creeds?
Linking the low dull levels of Earth
To the sunlit heights on the other side?
Built upon the arches of Faith and Love,
On the Bottom Rock of Eternal Truth—
For these men have counted their lives well lost
And with priceless treasure have paid the cost.[4]

NOTES

1. At the Washington conference of 1904, the Reverend George F. Bragg Jr. asserted that two-thirds of all black Episcopalians were in favor of some kind of autonomous black government in the church. See *Journal of the Annual Convention of the Protestant Episcopal Diocese of Arkansas* (1904): 81.

2. Edward Thomas Payne, interview by author, 20 Sept. 1993, New York, transcript.

3. Booker T. Washington, and W. E. B. Du Bois, *The Negro in the South: His Economic Progress in Relation to His Moral and Religous Development,* in *Writings by W. E. B. Du Bois in Non-Periodical Literature Edited by Others,* ed. Herbert Aptheker (Millwood, N.Y.: Kraus-Thomson, 1982), 94.

4. Mildred Dorsey, "Bridges," *Stream of History* 26 (Fall 1989): 4–5.

BIBLIOGRAPHY

MANUSCRIPT COLLECTIONS AND ARCHIVAL MATERIALS

Anglo-Saxon Churchman (Little Rock). 1890. Arkansas History Commission. Little Rock, Ark.

"Annual Report of the County Examiner" (1921–55, irregular). Records of the St. Francis County Board of Education. St. Francis County Courthouse. Forrest City, Ark.

Battle, Reverend Wallace. Correspondence. Julius Rosenwald Fund Archives. Amistad Research Center, Tulane University. New Orleans, La.

Brown, Bishop William Montgomery. *Five Years of Missionary Work in the Diocese of Arkansas.* Domestic and Foreign Missionary Society of the Protestant Episcopal Church, 1906. Bishop William M. Brown Papers, Archives of the Episcopal Diocese of Arkansas, Trinity Cathedral, Little Rock, Ark.

———. Papers. Archives of the Episcopal Diocese of Arkansas. Trinity Cathedral. Little Rock, Ark.

———. Publications and Miscellaneous Records. Brown Family Home. Galion, Ohio.

———. Papers. MSS 780. Ohio Historical Society. Columbus, Ohio.

———. "To the Bishops and Standing Committees of the American Church." 15 Feb. 1898. Archives of the Episcopal Diocese of Maryland, Baltimore, Md.

Carvill, H. C. "Episcopal Family Heritage." MS. Family History Files. Arkansas History Commission. Little Rock, Ark.

Casady, Bishop Thomas C. Collected Papers. Bishop Edward T. Demby File. Archives of the Episcopal Diocese of Oklahoma. Oklahoma City, Okla.

Colmore, Bishop C. B. Papers. Puerto Rico Papers. Archives of the Episcopal Church, U.S.A. Austin, Tex.

Colored Churchman (Little Rock). Bishop Edward T. Demby File. Box 13, RG 282. Bishop James R. Winchester Papers. Archives of the Episcopal Church, U.S.A. Austin, Tex.

"County Examiner's and County Superintendent's Register of Black Teachers' Licences" (1919–42, irregular). Records of the St. Francis County Board of Education. St. Francis County Courthouse. Forrest City, Ark.

Demby, Antoinette M. R., comp. *Facts Associated with the Ordination and Consecration of Edward Thomas Demby.* Little Rock, Ark.: Episcopal Diocese of Arkansas, 1927. Bishop Edward T. Demby File. Box 13, RG 282. Bishop James R. Winchester Papers, Archives of the Episcopal Church, U.S.A. Austin, Tex.

———— [?]. *The Mission of the Church among Colored People in the Diocese of Arkansas and the Southwest Province.* N.p., 1927. Bishop Edward Thomas Demby Papers, St. Matthew's Episcopal Church, Wilmington, Del.

Demby, Bishop Edward T. "A Biographical Epitome of Antoinette Martina Ricks Demby." MS. James Weldon Johnson Collection. Yale Collection of American Literature. Beinecke Rare Book and Manuscript Library, Yale University. New Haven, Conn.

————. Biographical File. Archives of the Episcopal Church, U.S.A. Austin, Tex.

————. *A Bird's Eye View of Exegetical Studies: The Writings of St. Paul and St. James.* Waco, Tex.: Paul Quinn College, 1895. Demby Family Papers, Manuscripts, Archives and Rare Books Division, Schomburg Center for Research in Black Culture, New York Public Library Astor, Lenox, and Tilden Foundations. New York.

————, comp. *Devotions of the Cross.* Key West, privately published, n.d. Demby Family Papers, Manuscripts, Archives and Rare Books Division, Schomburg Center for Research in Black Culture, New York Public Library Astor, Lenox, and Tilden Foundations. New York.

————. Diary. PP#64. Archives of the Episcopal Church, U.S.A. Austin, Tex.

————, comp., ed. *The Mission of the Episcopal Church among the Negroes of the Diocese of Arkansas.* (Fund-raising pamphlet) Privately published, 1921. Demby Family Papers, Manuscripts, Archives and Rare Books Division, Schomburg Center for Research in Black Culture, New York Public Library Astor, Lenox, and Tilden Foundations. New York.

————. "Off of the Record since 1939——." MS. James Weldon Johnson Collection. Yale Collection of American Literature. Beinecke Rare Book and Manuscript Library, Yale University. New Haven, Conn.

————. Papers. Howard Chandler Robbins Collection of Bishops' Papers, R088.92 G268. St. Mark's Library, General Theological Seminary. New York.

————. Papers. St. Matthew's Episcopal Church. Wilmington, Del.

————. Scrapbook. Private collection of the the the Reverend Canon Thomas S. Logan Sr. Logan Residence. Yeadon, Pa.

————. *The United States and the Negro* (Emancipation Day speech). Privately printed, 1907. Demby Family Papers, Manuscripts, Archives and Rare Books Division, Schomburg Center for Research in Black Culture, New York Public Library Astor, Lenox, and Tilden Foundations. New York.

Demby Family Papers. Manuscripts, Archives, and Rare Books Division. Schomburg Center for Research in Black Culture. New York Public Library Astor, Lenox, and Tilden Foundations. New York.

Diocese of Arkansas (Hot Springs). 1890. Arkansas Historical Commission. Little Rock, Ark.

Executive Council Papers. Archives of the Diocese of Arkansas. Trinity Cathedral. Little Rock, Ark.

Gailor, Bishop Thomas F. Collected Papers. University of the South Archives. Du Pont Library, University of the South. Sewanee, Tenn.

Gilchrist, Milford. "The Black Man in Delaware during the Reconstruction Period." MS, 1970. Typescript File. Historical Society of Delaware. Wilmington, Del.

Hoffman-St. Mary's Files. Records of the American Church Institute for Negroes. RG 61, RG 94. Archives of the Episcopal Church, U.S.A. Austin, Tex.

Leonard, Bishop William A. Papers. Archives of the Episcopal Diocese of Ohio. Trinity Cathedral. Cleveland, Ohio.

Manning, Bishop William T. Papers. Boxes 13–15. St. Mark's Library, General Theological Seminary. New York.

The Mission of the Protestant Episcopal Church in the Province of the Southwest and the Diocese of Arkansas among the Colored [Negro] People. N.p., 1938. Box 2, Demby Family Papers, Manuscripts, Archives and Rare Books Division, Schomburg Center for Research in Black Culture, New York Public Library Astor, Lenox, and Tilden Foundations. New York.

Monitor (Omaha). Bishop Edward T. Demby File. Box 13, RG 282. Bishop James R. Winchester Papers. Archives of the Episcopal Church, U.S.A. Austin, Tex.

Nelson, Alice Dunbar. "Big Quarterly in Wilmington." *Every Evening,* 27 Aug. 1932, n.p. Historical Society of Delaware, Wilmington, Del.

Norman, Edward. "History of Christ Episcopal Church and Christ Church Parochial and Industrial School, 1921–1982." MS. Records of Christ Episcopal Church. Christ Episcopal Church. Forrest City, Ark.

Phillips, Henry Laird. *Autobiography.* Philadelphia, Pennsylvania: Privately printed, 1943. Private collection of Rev. Canon Thomas S. Logan Sr. Logan Residence. Yeadon, Pa.

Pierce, Bishop Henry Niles. Diaries. Archives of the Episcopal Diocese of Arkansas. Trinity Cathedral. Little Rock, Ark.

Pressley, Gina. "The Black History of Delaware." MS, 1976. Typescript File. Historical Society of Delaware. Wilmington, Del.

"Protest against the Approval of the Election of the Consecration of Archdeacon William Montgomery Brown as Bishop Coadjutor of Arkansas." February 1898. Circular letter in the private collection of the Reverend Joseph B. Tucker. Tucker Residence. Pine Bluff, Ark.

"Record of the Standing Committee, 1932." Archives of the Episcopal Diocese of Arkansas. Little Rock, Ark.

Records of St. Andrew's Episcopal Church. Episcopal Church Records of Arkansas. Arkansas History Commission. Little Rock, Ark. Microfilm.

"Register of William Montgomery Brown [and Bishop James R. Winchester], 1898–1916." Item No. 7. Episcopal Church Records of Arkansas. Arkansas History Commission. Little Rock, Ark. Microfilm.

"Roll of the House of Bishops." Episcopal Church Center. New York.

Spielmann, Richard M. *Bexley Hall: 150 Years—A Brief History.* N.p., n.d. Special Collections, Olin Library, Kenyon College, Gambier, Ohio.

Winchester, Bishop James R. Papers. Bishop Edward T. Demby File. Box 13, RG 282. Archives of the Episcopal Church, U.S.A. Austin, Tex.

Witsell, Reverend William P. Collected Papers. Archives of the Episcopal Diocese of Arkansas. Trinity Cathedral. Little Rock, Ark.

———. "My Contact with Some High Points of the History of the Diocese of Arkansas, 1927–1957." MS. Archives of the Episcopal Diocese of Arkansas. Trinity Cathedral. Little Rock, Ark.

Yancy, J. W. *Meet the Most Illustrious Dean of Paul Quinn College.* Waco, Tex.: n.p., n.d. Bishop Edward T. Demby Biographical File, Archives of the Episcopal Church, U.S.A. Austin, Tex.

CORRESPONDENCE AND MISCELLANEOUS UNPUBLISHED MATERIALS

Allin, John M., Kennebunkport, Maine, to Michael J. Beary, Batesville, Arkansas. 1 Sept. 1993. Author's private correspondence.

———, Jackson, Miss., to Michael J. Beary, Batesville, Ark. 17 Apr. 1996. Author's private correspondence.

Beary, Michael J. "Birds of Passage: A History of the Separate Black Episcopal Church in Arkansas, 1902–1939." M.A. thesis, University of Arkansas, 1993.

Carden, Ron, Levelland, Tex., to Michael J. Beary, Batesville, Ark. 14 Dec. 1998. Author's private correspondence.

———, Levelland, Tex., to Michael J. Beary, Batesville, Ark. 4 Jan. 1999. Author's private correspondence.

———, Levelland, Tex., to Michael J. Beary, Batesville, Ark. 19 Jan. 1999. Author's private correspondence.

Donovan, Herbert A., Little Rock, Ark., to Michael J. Beary, Batesville, Ark. (with enclosures). 27 Aug. 1991. Author's private correspondence.

Holt, W. T., II, Santa Rosa, Calif., to Michael Beary, 28 Dec. 1999. Author's private correspondence.

Leinecke, Betty H., Springfield, Ill., to Michael J. Beary, Batesville, Ark. 19 May 1998. Author's private correspondence.

Lewis, Cotesworth P., Williamsburg, Va., to Michael Beary in care of Herbert A. Donovan, Little Rock, Ark. 10 Mar. 1992. Author's private correspondence.

Logan, Thomas S., Yeadon, Pa., to Michael J. Beary, Batesville, Ark. N.d. Author's private correspondence.

Luker, Lady Elizabeth, Newport, Ark., to Michael J. Beary, Batesville, Ark. 30 Aug. 1994. Author's private correspondence.

Matthews, Beth. List of Arkansas clergy, by parish and tenure, 1920–1985. Episcopal Diocese of Arkansas.

Rahming, Harry E., Denver, Colo., to Thomas S. Logan Sr., Yeadon, Pa. 10 May 1978. Private collection of the Reverend Canon Thomas S. Logan Sr. Logan Residence, Yeadon, Pa.

Tucker, Joseph B., Pine Bluff, Ark., to Michael J. Beary, Batesville, Ark. 29 Mar. 1993. Author's private correspondence.

OFFICIAL PUBLICATIONS

A Brief Sketch of St. Philip's Normal and Industrial School, San Antonio, Texas. Published privately, n.d. (Fund-raising pamphlet published 1918–27). Archives of the Episcopal Church, U.S.A. Austin, Tex.

Demby, Edward Thomas. *Address by the Reverend Venerable E. Thomas Demby to the Ninth Convocation of Colored Churchmen in the Diocese of Tennessee, April 1915.* N.p. Collected Papers of Bishop Thomas F. Gailor. University of the South Archives. Du Pont Library, University of the South. Sewanee, Tenn.

Domestic and Foreign Missionary Society of the Protestant Episcopal Church in the United States of America. *Annual Report of the Board of Missions (National Council) of the Protestant Episcopal Church.* Fenalong, N.Y.: Domestic and Foreign Missionary Society, 1918, 1921–38.

Episcopal Church Annual, 1998: General Convention Issue. Harrisburg, Pa.: Morehouse Publishing, 1998.

Episcopal Diocese of Alabama. *Journal of the Annual Convention of the Diocese of Alabama.* 1884, 1941.

Episcopal Diocese of Arkansas. *Journal.* 1883–1955.

Episcopal Diocese of Colorado. *Journal.* 1895–97.

Episcopal Diocese of Florida. *Journal.* 1884, 1941.

Episcopal Diocese of Georgia. *Journal.* 1884, 1941.

Episcopal Diocese of Kansas. *Journal.* 1918.

Episcopal Diocese of Kentucky. *Journal.* 1884, 1941.

Episcopal Diocese of Mississippi. *Journal.* 1884, 1941.

Episcopal Diocese of Missouri. *Journal.* 1884, 1918, 1941.

Episcopal Diocese of Oklahoma. *Journal.* 1918, 1932, 1933.

Episcopal Diocese of North Carolina. *Journal.* 1884, 1941.

Episcopal Diocese of South Carolina. *Journal.* 1884, 1941.

Episcopal Diocese of South Florida. *Journal.* 1904–7.

Episcopal Diocese of Springfield (Ill.). *Journal.* 1902, 1903, 1904.

Episcopal Diocese of Texas. *Journal.* 1884, 1918, 1941.

Episcopal Diocese of Tennessee. *Journal.* 1898–1918.

Episcopal Diocese of Virginia. *Journal.* 1884, 1941.

Episcopal Diocese of West Missouri. *Journal.* 1901, 1902, 1918.

Episcopal Diocese of West Texas. *Journal.* 1884, 1918, 1941.

Episcopal Diocese of West Virginia. *Journal.* 1884, 1941.

Episcopal Missionary District of Eastern Oklahoma. *Journal.* 1918.
Journals of the General Convention of the Episcopal Church.
Living Church Annual. Chicago: Living Church Co., 1939.
Stowe's Clerical Directory. New York: Church Hymnal Corporation, 1932, 1935, 1941, 1956.

NEWSPAPERS

Arkansas Churchman (Little Rock). 1925–55.
Arkansas Democrat (Little Rock). 1932.
Arkansas Gazette (Little Rock). 1897–1932.
Church Advocate (Baltimore). Vols. 16–31 (1907–24), incomplete. St. Mark's Library, General Theological Seminary. New York. I note that the Reverend Kirtley Yearwood has recently discovered of a complete set of *Church Advocates* at St. Paul's College, Lawrenceville, Va.
New York Churchman. 1883–1932.
Cleveland Herald. 1945.
Diocese of Springfield (Ill.). 1902–4.
Forrest City Times Herald (Ark.). 1923–27.
Living Church (Milwaukee). 1921–89.
Newport Daily Independent (Ark.). 1932.
New York Times. 1932.
Oklahoma Churchman. 1932.
Pittsburgh Courier. 1932.
Southern Churchman. 1932.
Sentinel Record (Hot Springs, Ark.). 1932.
Washington Afro-American. 1932.

INTERVIEWS

Allin, Richard. Interview by author, 10 July 1994, Little Rock, Ark. Transcript.
Arrington, Phoebe. Interview by author, 18 Oct. 1995, Brooklyn, N.Y. Transcript.
Beckwith, Peter H., bishop of the Diocese of Springfield. Telephone interview by author, 12 May 1998, Springfield, Ill. Transcript.
Black, Carl. Interview by author, 14 Sept. 1993, New York. Transcript.
Breck, Alan D. Telephone interview by author, 24 June 1998, Denver, Colo. Transcript.
Church, Roberta. Interview by author, 17 Aug. 1994, Memphis, Tenn. Transcript.
Cochran, Priscilla. Interview by author, 27 Sept. 1998, Mason, Tenn. Transcript.
Cracraft, George K. Interview by author, 10 Aug. 1991, Little Rock, Ark. Transcript.
Demby, Dorothy. Interview by author, 16 May 1992, Cleveland, Ohio. Transcript.
Demby, Dorothy, and Elizabeth Demby Payne. Interview by author, 14 Oct. 1995, New York. Transcript.

Dennis, (Aunt) Dora Strong. Interview by author, 9 Aug. 1991, Forrest City, Ark. Transcript.

———. Interview by author, 14 May 1995, Forrest City, Ark. Transcript.

———. Telephone interview by author, 22 May 1995, Forrest City, Ark. Transcript.

———. Telephone interview by author, 4 July 1995, Forrest City, Ark. Transcript.

Donovan, Herbert A., bishop of Arkansas. Interview by author, 1 June 1990, Little Rock, Ark. Transcript.

Driver, Ethel Broadnax. Interview by author, 14 May 1995, Forrest City, Ark. Transcript.

———. Telephone interview by author, 21 May 1995, Forrest City, Ark. Transcript.

Fennell, Beverly (Granny). Interview by author, 24 Mar. 1997, Little Rock, Ark. Transcript.

Gamble, Marguerite. Interview by author, 14 May 1991. Little Rock, Ark. Transcript.

Hall, Charlie. Telephone interview by author, 22 May 1995, Cleveland, Ohio. Transcript.

Harris, Thomas E. Interview by author, 14 May 1995, Forrest City, Ark. Transcript.

Harris, Carolyn R. Interview by author, 1 Mar. 1991, Fayetteville, Ark. Transcript.

Hayden, J. Carleton. Telephone interview by author, 13 Feb. 1991, Sewanee, Tenn. Transcript.

———. Interview by author, 29 June 1991, New Orleans, La. Transcript.

Jones, Jim. Interview by author, 21 May 1995, Forrest City, Ark. Transcript.

Jones, Mrs. O. E., Sr. Interview by author, 13 Aug. 1992, Batesville, Ark. Transcript.

Lancaster, Clarence M. Telephone interview by author, 22 May 1995, Memphis, Tenn. Transcript.

Lewis, Cotesworth P. Interview by author, 3 Mar. 1992, Williamsburg, Va. Transcript.

Lewis, Harold T. Interview by author, 29 June 1991, New Orleans, La. Transcript.

———. Interview by author, 17 Sept. 1992, New York. Transcript.

———. Telephone interview by author, 20 Oct. 1992. New York. Transcript.

Logan, Thomas S., Sr. Interview by author, 19 Oct. 1995, Yeadon, Pa. Transcript.

McNeely, Michael. Interview by author, 30 Jan. 1995. Little Rock, Ark. Transcript.

Middleton, Inez. Interview by Joyce Howard, Dec. 1981, Raleigh, N.C. Transcript.

Morgan, James. Interview by author, 11 May 1991, Newport, Ark. Transcript.

Neal, Charlene Shaw. Interview by author, 21 May 1995, Forrest City, Ark. Transcript.

Nimocks, Al. Telephone interview by author, 19 May 1995, Forrest City, Ark. Transcript.

Norman, Edward. Interview by author, 14 May 1995, Forrest City, Ark. Transcript.

Page, Mildred W. Interview by author, 11 May 1991, Newport, Ark. Transcript.

Parks, Lemuel. Interview by author, 16 May 1995, Batesville, Ark. Transcript.

Payne, Edward Thomas. Interview by author, 20 Sept. 1993, New York. Transcript.

Payne, Elizabeth Demby. Interview by author, 14 May 1992, New York. Transcript.

Powell, Lewis A. Interview by author, 2 Mar. 1997, Kansas City, Mo. Transcript.

Temple, James W. Telephone interview by author, 1 Dec. 1991, Los Angeles, Calif. Transcript.

Thompson, Joseph. Telephone interview by author, 16 Oct. 1998. Topeka, Kan. Transcript.

Tucker, Joseph B. Interview by author, 1 Oct. 1991, Pine Bluff, Ark. Transcript.
———. Interview by author, 26 July 1994, Pine Bluff, Ark. Transcript.
———. Interview by author, 13 Nov. 1994, Pine Bluff, Ark. Transcript.
Valdez, Joseph T. Telephone interview by author, 17 Jan. 1999, Key West, Fla. Transcript.
Walker, Orris J., Episcopal bishop of Long Island. Interview by author, 15 Sept. 1993, New York. Transcript.
Warren, Minnie Shaw. Interview by author, 21 May 1995, Forrest City, Ark. Transcript.
———. Telephone interview by author, 22 May 1995, Forrest City, Ark. Transcript.
Washington, Emery. Interview by author, 1 June 1991, St. Louis, Mo. Transcript.
———. Interview by author, 25 Mar. 1995, St. Louis, Mo. Transcript.
———. Telephone interview by author, 8 May 1995, St. Louis, Mo. Transcript.
———. Telephone interview by author, 19 May 1995, St. Louis, Mo. Transcript.
———. Telephone interview by author, 30 May 1995, St. Louis, Mo. Transcript.
———. Interview by author, 29 Sept. 1998, Little Rock, Ark. Transcript.
Watkins, Bobbye. Interview by author, 27 Sept. 1998, Mason, Tenn. Transcript.
Weston, Catherine. Interview by author, 26 Mar. 1995, St. Louis, Mo. Transcript.
White, Rosemary Walker, and Charles White. Interview by author, 26 Mar. 1997, Little Rock, Ark. Transcript.
Whitley, Wooley. Interview by author, 21 May 1995, Forrest City, Ark. Transcript.
Wilson, Donald. Telephone interview by author, 11 June 1991, Palm Coast, Fla. Transcript.
———. Telephone interview by author, 2 July 1991, Palm Coast, Fla. Transcript.
Wood, Clark. Interview by author, 10 Aug. 1991. Transcript.
Yearwood, Kirtley. Interview by author, 29 Sept. 1998, Little Rock, Ark. Transcript.
Young, R. K. Interview by author, Aug. 1994, Little Rock, Ark. Transcript.

BOOKS AND ARTICLES AND OTHER SOURCES

Addison, James Thayer. *The Episcopal Church in the United States, 1789–1931.* New York: Charles Scribner's and Sons, 1951.
Ahlstrom, Sydney E. *A Religous History of the American People.* Garden City, N.Y.: Image Books, 1975.
Albright, R. W. *A History of the Protestant Episcopal Church.* New York: Macmillan, 1964.
Arnold, Roberta. *A Man and His Work: The Life Story of James Solomon Russell, Founder of St. Paul's Normal and Industrial School, Lawrenceville, Virginia.* Lawrenceville, Va.: St. Paul's Normal and Industrial School, 1938.
Barnes, Kenneth C. "Who Killed John M. Clayton? Political Violence in Conway County, Arkansas, in the 1880s." *Arkansas Historical Quarterly* 52 (Winter 1993): 371–402.
Bennet, Robert A. "Black Episcopalians: A History from the Colonial Period to the Present." *Historical Magazine of the Protestant Episcopal Church* 43 (Sept. 1974): 231–45.

Besancon-Alford, Julia G. "Bartlett: A Model Manufacturing Town," *Pulaski County Historical Review* 42 (Summer 1994): 46–51.

Botkin, Samuel L. *The Episcopal Church in Oklahoma.* Oklahoma City, Okla.: American Bond Printing Co., 1958.

Bragg, George F. *The Episcopal Church and the Black Man.* Baltimore: Church Advocate Press, 1918.

———. "The Episcopal Church and the Negro Race." *Historical Magazine of the Protestant Episcopal Church* 4 (Mar. 1935): 47–52.

———. *History of the Afro-American Group of the Protestant Episcopal Church.* Baltimore: Church Advocate Press, 1922.

Bratton, Theodore D. *Wanted—Leaders! A Study of Negro Development.* New York: Presiding Bishop and Council, Department of Missions and Church Extension, 1922.

Breck, Allen D. *The Episcopal Church in Colorado, 1860–1963.* Denver: Big Mountain Press, 1963.

Britton, Nancy, and Dora Lee Baker Ferguson. *Worthy of Much Praise: A History of St. Paul's, Batesville, Arkansas from Its Earliest Beginnings to 1952.* Newport, Ark.: Craig Printing Company, 1989.

Brown, William M. *The Church for Americans.* New York: Thomas Whitaker, 1909.

———. *The Crucial Race Question.* Little Rock, Ark.: Arkansas Churchman's Publishing Co., 1907.

———. *Heresy: "Bad Bishop Brown's" Quarterly Lectures, No. 1, The American Race Problem.* Galion, Ohio: Bradford-Brown Educational Co., 1930. Publications of Bishop William Montgomery Brown and miscellaneous documents, Brown family home, Galion, Ohio.

———. *The Level Plan for Church Union.* New York: Whitaker, 1910.

———. *My Heresy: The Autobiography of William Montgomery Brown.* Galion, Ohio: Bradford-Brown Educational Co., 1931.

Burkett, Randall K. *Garveyism as a Religious Movement: The Institutionalization of Black Civil Religion.* Metuchen, N.J.: Scarecrow Press, 1978.

Cantrell, Ellen M. H., comp. *Annals of Christ Church Parish of Little Rock, Arkansas, from A.D. 1839 to A.D. 1899.* Little Rock, Ark.: Arkansas Democrat Co., 1900.

Carnahan, Wallace. *Odd Happenings.* Jackson, Miss.: Tucker Printing House, 1915.

Caution, Tollie L. "The Protestant Episcopal Church: Policies and Rationale upon Which Support of Its Negro Colleges Is Predicated." *Journal of Negro Education* (Summer 1960): 274–83.

Chowning, Robert W. *History of St. Francis County, Arkansas [through] 1954.* Forrest City, Ark.: Times Herald Publishing Co., 1954.

Church, Annette E., and Roberta Church. *The Robert R. Churches of Memphis: A Father and Son Who Achieved in Spite of Race.* Ann Arbor, Mich.: Edwards Brothers for Annette E. Church and Roberta Church, 1974.

Church, Roberta, and Ronald Walter. *Nineteenth Century Memphis Families of Color.*

Edited by Charles W. Crawford. Memphis, Tenn.: Murdock Printing for Roberta Church and Ronald Walter, 1987.

Cortner, Richard C. *A Mob Intent on Death: The NAACP and the Arkansas Riot Cases.* Middletown, Conn.: Wesleyan University Press, 1988.

Crawford, Nelson A. "We Elect a Bishop." *American Mercury,* 17 Aug. 1929, 420–29.

Delany, Sarah, and A. Elizabeth Delany. *Having Our Say: The Delany Sisters' First One Hundred Years.* Edited by Amy Hill Hearth. New York: Kodansha International, 1993.

De Man, George E. N., ed. *Helena, the River, the Ridge, the Romance.* Little Rock, Ark.: Phillips County Historical Society, 1978.

Dollard, John. *Caste and Class in a Southern Town.* 1937. Reprint, Garden City, N.Y.: Doubleday and Co., 1957.

Donovan, Mary S. *A Separate Call: Women's Ministries in the Episcopal Church, 1850–1920.* Wilton, Conn.: Morehouse-Barlow, 1986.

Donovan, Timothy P., and Willard B. Gatewood Jr. *Governors of Arkansas: Essays in Political Biography.* Fayetteville: University of Arkansas Press, 1981.

Dorsey, Mildred A. "Bridges." *Stream of History* 26 (Fall 1989): 4–5.

———. "Jackson County as It Used to Be." *Stream of History* 26 (Fall 1989): 6–9.

Du Bois, W. E. B. "My Character." In *W. E. B. Du Bois: Writings.* New York: Literary Classics of the United States, 1986.

———. *The Negro Church.* Atlanta: Atlanta University Press, 1903.

Egerton, John. *Speak Now against the Day: The Generation before the Civil Rights Movement in the South.* New York: Alfred A. Knopf, 1994.

Eison, James R. "Dead, but She Was in a Good Place, a Church." *Pulaski County Historical Review* 30 (Summer 1982): 30–42.

Emmanuel Episcopal Church. *Centennial Celebration: Emmanuel Episcopal Church.* Memphis, Tenn.: Emmanuel Episcopal Church, 1975.

Farmer, Marjorie Nichols. "Different Voices: African American Women in the Episcopal Church." In *Episcopal Women, Gender, Spirituality, and Commitment in an American Mainline Denomination,* ed. Catherine M. Prelinger, 222–38. New York: Oxford University Press, 1992.

Federal Writers' Project of the Works Progress Administration, comp. *The W.P.A. Guide to 1930s Arkansas.* Introduction by Elliot West. Lawrence: University Press of Kansas, 1997.

Finch, David E. "Little Rock's Red Bishop Brown and His Separate Black Church." *Pulaski County Historical Review* 20 (Sept. 1972): 27–34.

Finley, Randy. *From Slavery to Uncertain Freedom: The Freedmen's Bureau in Arkansas, 1865–1869.* Fayetteville: University of Arkansas Press, 1996.

Fletcher, Mary P. "A Reminiscence of Little Rock Churches." *Arkansas Historical Quarterly* 13 (Autumn 1954): 257–63.

Furnas, J. C. *The Americans: A Social History of the United States, 1587–1914.* New York: G. P. Putnam's Sons, 1969.

Gaillard, E. C. "A Negro Suffragan—A Puppet Bishop." *Church Advocate,* Jan. 1912, 3.

Gatewood, Willard B., Jr. *Aristocrats of Color: The Black Elite, 1880–1920.* Bloomington: Indiana University Press, 1990.

———. *Theodore Roosevelt and the Art of Controversy: Episodes of the White House Years.* Baton Rouge: Louisiana State University Press, 1970.

Gayle, Addison. *Richard Wright: Ordeal of a Native Son.* Garden City, N.Y.: Anchor Press, Doubleday, 1980.

Gordon, Fon Louise. *Caste and Class: The Black Experience in Arkansas, 1880–1920.* Athens: University of Georgia Press, 1995.

Graves, John W. *Town and Country: Race Relations in an Urban-Rural Context, Arkansas 1865–1905.* Fayetteville: University of Arkansas Press, 1990.

Harris, Odell Greenleaf. *A History of the Seminary to Prepare Black Men for the Ministry of the Protestant Episcopal Church.* Alexandria: Virginia Theological Seminary, 1980.

Hayden, J. Carleton. "After the War: The Mission and Growth of the Episcopal Church among Blacks in the South, 1865–1877." *Historical Magazine of the Protestant Episcopal Church* 42 (Dec. 1973): 403–27.

———. "Conversion and Control: Dilemma of Episcopalians in Providing for the Religious Instructions of Slaves, Charleston, South Carolina, 1845–1860." *Historical Magazine of the Protestant Episcopal Church* 40 (June 1971): 143–71.

Hempstead, Fay. *History of Arkansas.* Chicago: Lewis Publishing Co., 1911.

Hewitt, John H. "The Sacking of St. Philip's Church, New York." *Historical Magazine of the Protestant Episcopal Church* 49 (Mar. 1980): 7–20.

Holly, Donald. "The Second Great Emancipation: The Rust Cotton Picker and How It Changed Arkansas." *Arkansas Historical Quarterly* 52 (Spring 1993): 44–77.

Howell, John A. "The Church and Black Folk." *Crisis,* Feb. 1933, 32.

Kirk, John. "Dr. J. M. Robinson, the Arkansas Negro Democratic Association and Black Politics in Little Rock, Arkansas, 1928–1952." *Pulaski County Historical Review* 41 (Spring 1993): 2–16; ibid. (Summer 1993): 39–47.

Lewis, Harold T. "Archon Edward Thomas Demby, Pioneer of Social Justice." *Boulé Journal* (Fall 1992): 8–9.

———. *Yet with a Steady Beat: The African-American Struggle for Recognition in the Episcopal Church.* Valley Forge, Pa.: Trinity Press International, 1996.

Lewis, Todd E. "Booker T. Washington and His Visits to Little Rock." *Pulaski County Historical Review* 42 (Fall 1994): 54–65.

———. "Mob Justice in the 'American Congo': 'Judge Lynch' in Arkansas during the Decade after World War I." *Arkansas Historical Quarterly* 52 (Summer 1993): 156–84.

Lindsley, James E. *This Planted Vine: A Narrative History of the Episcopal Diocese of New York.* New York: Harper Collins, 1984.

Lyman, Elizabeth P. *Historical Memories of Trinity Cathedral, Little Rock, Arkansas and a Short Biography of Its Founder, Rt. Rev. Henry Niles Pierce, D.D., L.L.D., Third*

Missionary Bishop of Arkansas and First Diocesan Bishop of Arkansas. Little Rock, Ark.: Pattee Printing Company, 1934.

Martin, Clyde. "A Dream Realized—Arkansas Society for Crippled Children." *Arkansas Historical Quarterly* 5 (Winter 1946): 359–72.

McDonald, Margaret Sims. *White Already to Harvest: The Episcopal Church in Arkansas, 1838–1971.* Sewanee, Tenn.: University Press for the Episcopal Diocese of Arkansas, 1975.

McKee, Daniel D. *Laborers in the Vineyard: A History of St. Paul's Episcopal Church, Newport Arkansas.* Newport, Ark.: Craig Printing Co., 1993.

Miller, Nathan. *Theodore Roosevelt: A Life.* New York: Morrow, 1992.

Moneyhan, Carl H. *Arkansas and the New South, 1874–1929.* Fayetteville: University of Arkansas Press, 1997.

Morton, Floyd W. "Eight Downtown Little Rock Churches: An Architectural History." *Pulaski County Historical Review* 34 (Winter 1986): 74–89.

"The 1905 'New Handy Map of Little Rock.'" *Pulaski County Historical Review* 34 (Winter 1986): 90–92.

Northern Ohio Chapter of the Union of Black Episcopalians, comp. *He Is as He Ever Was.* (Pamphlet commemorating the dedication of Bishop Demby's gravestone). Cleveland, Ohio: Northern Ohio Chapter of the Union of Black Episcopalians, 1992.

Page, Mildred W. "Mildred Ann Wilmans Dorsey." *Stream of History* 26 (Fall 1989): 3.

Prichard, Robert W. *A History of the Episcopal Church.* Harrisburg, Pa.: Moorehouse Publishing, 1991.

Rahming, Harry E. "Church Work among Negroes: A Plea for Recognition of Negro Leadership." *Living Church,* 4 Aug. 1928, 463–64.

Rector, Charles J. "Lily-White Republicanism: The Pulaksi County Experience, 1888–1930." *Pulaski County Historical Review* 42 (Spring 1994): 2–18.

Reimers, David M. "Negro Bishops and Diocesan Segregation in the Protestant Episcopal Church, 1870–1954." *Historical Magazine of the Protestant Episcopal Church* 31 (Sept. 1962): 231–40.

———. *White Protestantism and the Negro.* New York: Oxford University Press, 1965.

Schroeder, Theodore. *The Bishop of Bolsheviks and Atheists.* Detroit, Mich.: By the author, 1922.

Shattuck, Gardiner H., Jr. *Episcopalians and Race: Civil War to Civil Rights.* Lexington: University Press of Kentucky, 2000.

Vernon, Walter N. *Methodism in Arkansas, 1816–1976.* Little Rock, Ark.: Joint Committee for the History of Arkansas Methodism, 1976.

Washington, Booker T., and W. E. B. Du Bois. *The Negro in the South: His Economic Progress in Relation to His Moral and Religious Development.* In *Writings by W. E. B. Du Bois in Non-Periodical Literature Edited by Others,* edited by Herbert Aptheker. Millwood, N.Y.: Kraus-Thomson, 1982.

Washington, James M., ed. *A Testament of Hope: The Essential Writings of and Speeches of Dr. Martin Luther King, Jr.* San Francisco: Harper, 1986.

Weatherford, W. D. *American Churches and the Negro.* Boston: Christopher Publishing House, 1957.

White, Gavin. "Patriarch McGuire and the Episcopal Church." *Historical Magazine of the Protestant Episcopal Church* 38 (June 1969): 109–41.

Williams, Lee E., and Lee E. Williams II. *Anatomy of Four Race Riots: Racial Conflict in Knoxville, Elaine (Arkansas), Tulsa, and Chicago, 1919–1921.* [Hattiesburg]: University and College Press of Mississippi, 1972.

Wise, Dorothy B. "St. Mary's Episcopal Church, 1905–1966." *Garland County Record* 26 (1985): 17–23.

Witsell, William P. *A History of Christ Episcopal Church, Little Rock, Arkansas, 1839–1947.* Little Rock, Ark.: Christ Church Vestry, n.d.

Woodward, Earl F. "The Brooks and Baxter War in Arkansas, 1872–1874." *Arkansas Historical Quarterly* 30 (Winter 1971): 315–36.

Woodward, Joseph H. *The Negro Bishop Movement in the Protestant Episcopal Diocese of South Carolina.* McPhersonville, S.C.: By the author, n.d.[c. 1916].

Work, Monroe V., ed. *Negro Yearbook: An Annual Encyclopedia of the Negro, 1931–1932.* Tuskegee, Ala.: Negro Yearbook Publishing Co., 1932.

Yenser, Thomas, ed., *Who's Who in Colored America, 1930–1932.* Brooklyn, N.Y.: By the author, 1933.

INDEX

Michael J. Beary is an independent scholar with a keen interest in the history of ecclesiastical conflict, especially as it bears on the struggle for orthodoxy in the Christian church. A graduate of Lyon College and the University of Arkansas, he describes *Black Bishop* as a sort of ten-year "calling." When he is not writing or researching, he enjoys small-town life with his wife, Camille, and his two sons, Joe and Sam, in Batesville, Arkansas.

STUDIES IN ANGLICAN HISTORY

Typeset in 10.5/13 Minion
with Minion display
Designed by Dennis Roberts
Composed by Celia Shapland
for the University of Illinois Press
Manufactured by Thomson-Shore, Inc.

University of Illinois Press
1325 South Oak Street
Champaign, IL 61820-6903
www.press.uillinois.edu